FORMS OF LATE MODERNIST LYRIC

Forms
of
Late Modernist Lyric

EDITED BY

Edward Allen

LIVERPOOL UNIVERSITY PRESS

First published 2021 by
Liverpool University Press
4 Cambridge Street
Liverpool
L69 7ZU

Copyright © 2021 Liverpool University Press

Edward Allen has asserted the right to be identified as
the editor of this book in accordance with the Copyright, Designs
and Patents Act 1988.

British Library Cataloguing-in-Publication data
A British Library CIP record is available

ISBN 978-1-78962-242-3 cased

Typeset by Carnegie Book Production, Lancaster
Printed and bound by CPI Group (UK) Ltd, Croydon CR0 4YY

Contents

Acknowledgements

The idea for this book came about in the wake of my discovering that someone had already penned its first chapter. Fiona Green's approach to the aubade sets the scene for this volume, and I am indebted to her for encouraging me to write the proposal that gave rise to it. She was probably right to persuade me that *Lyricish Allsorts* was the wrong name for it. Studious eyes and shows of support, however fleeting, have been gratefully received since then, particularly those of John Kerrigan, Peter Nicholls, Chris Townsend, and Marta Werner.

The book has benefited significantly from the attentions of Anthony Cond, who was my first point of contact at Liverpool University Press. Many thanks, too, to the readers who responded so wisely to the initial proposal and final manuscript – their advice was invaluable – and to those who subsequently helped to make the book what it is, particularly Sarah Warren and Alwyn Harrison, Jenny Howard and Christabel Scaife. The latter has been patient and encouraging in equal measure.

Our thanks also go to the National Gallery, London, for permission to reproduce artwork, and to Andrea Jensen for the same reason: her painting is exactly what I wanted for the book's cover. J. H. Prynne was kind, as always, to grant his permission to quote extensively from his work.

Several things happened to disrupt the passage of this book between its materialising as an idea and its appearance in the print you're reading now. One of these made a hard term much harder, and I will always be grateful to those who helped me through it: Alyson and Barry Allen, Semele Assinder, David Elliot, Bob Evans, Harriet Lyon, Livvy Marshall, Sophie Read, and Natasha Tanna.

Notes on Contributors

Ruth Abbott is a Lecturer in English at the University of Cambridge, and a Fellow of St John's College. Her research focuses on textual scholarship and eighteenth- and nineteenth-century manuscripts, chiefly writers' notebooks.

Edward Allen is a Lecturer in English at the University of Cambridge, and a Fellow of Christ's College. His first monograph, *Modernist Invention: Media Technology and American Poetry*, has just come out with Cambridge University Press.

Gareth Farmer is a Senior Lecturer in English at the University of Bedfordshire, UK. He has published widely on modern and contemporary poetry and poetics. His book *Veronica Forrest-Thomson: Poet on the Periphery* was published by Palgrave in 2017.

Fiona Green is a Senior Lecturer in American literature at the University of Cambridge, and a Fellow of Jesus College.

Drew Milne is the Judith E. Wilson Reader in Drama and Poetry at the University of Cambridge, and a Fellow of Corpus Christi College. He is the editor of *Marxist Literary Theory*, with Terry Eagleton, and the anthology *Modern Critical Thought*. His collected poems, *In Darkest Capital*, came out in 2017.

Jeremy Noel-Tod is a Senior Lecturer in the School of Literature, Drama and Creative Writing at the University of East Anglia. His publications as an editor include *The Oxford Companion to Modern Poetry* (revised edition, 2013), R. F. Langley's *Complete Poems* (2015), and *The Penguin Book of the Prose Poem* (2018).

Esther Osorio Whewell is a Career Development Fellow at Corpus Christi College, University of Oxford. She has recently published articles on the 'Arguments' in *The Faerie Queene* and the interdisciplinary Spenserian stanzas of seventeenth-century amateur poet-lawyer-ecclesiastic Robert Aylett, and is writing a book provisionally titled *Modernist Renaissance*, with chapters pairing Lancelot Andrewes with Gertrude Stein, Thomas Nashe with early radio, printed devotional handbooks with diagrams of *Finnegans Wake*, and *Faerie Queene* paratexts with blurbing.

Sophie Read is a Senior Lecturer in English at the University of Cambridge, and a Fellow of Christ's College. She works primarily on seventeenth-century literature, with some excursions forward into contemporary poetry. Her first book was *Eucharist and the Poetic Imagination in Early Modern England* (Cambridge, 2013); she has also published on the work of Peter Manson, Veronica Forrest-Thomson, Andrea Brady, and Ian Patterson.

Matthew Sperling is a Lecturer in Literature in English from 1900 to the Present at University College London, and previously worked at the Universities of Oxford and Reading. He is the author of a monograph, *Visionary Philology: Geoffrey Hill and the Study of Words* (Oxford, 2014), and of two novels published by riverrun books, *Astroturf* (2018) and *Viral* (2020).

John Wilkinson is Professor and Director of Creative Writing in the Department of English at the University of Chicago. His recent collections of poetry are *Reckitt's Blue* (Seagull, 2012), *Ghost Nets* (Omnidawn, 2016), and *My Reef My Manifest Array* (Carcanet, 2019). His most recent critical book is *Lyric in Its Times* (Bloomsbury, 2019).

Reference Notes

All quotations from Shakespeare are taken from *The Oxford Shakespeare: The Complete Works*, ed. John Jowett, William Montgomery, Gary Taylor, and Stanley Wells, second edition (Oxford: Oxford University Press, 2005). Act, scene, and line numbers are provided in the notes, where appropriate.

Frequent reference is made to the *Oxford English Dictionary* (*OED*). Definitions are taken from its online version.

Introduction

Too Late for Lyric Studies?

Edward Allen

It's not every day you see a poet in the news. Further unrest in the Middle East, the latest twist in the MMR vaccine saga, a leaked Pentagon report on the security risks of climate change – there were so many reasons on 22 February 2004 not to think of lyric poems. But someone had other ideas, and that someone was Jeremy Halvard Prynne. His was not a planned intervention that day, it must be said, nor a solo revolution, though you'd have been hard-pressed to draw any other conclusion from the injured parties at *The Sunday Times*. Trusting to alliteration, one called him a 'baffling bard', replete with 'basket' and 'bicycle'; the fact of his being 'an engineer's son originally from Kent' – if only he'd been born in Bedfordshire! – was just a small part of the mystery.[1] Another thought it best to put 'the little-known Cambridge don' in his place by inferring a connection – not incorrectly, as it happens – between his little ways and those of a fearsome practice once espoused by Ezra Pound and his 'semi-articulate disciple', Basil Bunting.[2] Seventy years after the fact, the former might have smiled to see his almost-headline come almost true: '"Literature is news that STAYS news"'.[3]

And so the story did – or Prynne's part in it – for some weeks to come, touching nerves, spawning interviews and reaction pieces, and driving the editors of the BBC's *Today Programme* back to first principles:

[1] Maurice Chittenden, 'Oxbridge Split by the Baffling Bard', *The Sunday Times* (22 February 2004).

[2] John Carey, 'Cover Book: *The Oxford English Literary History* by Randall Stevenson' [review], *The Sunday Times* (22 February 2004). All subsequent quotations are taken from the online version: https://www.thetimes.co.uk/article/cover-book-the-oxford-english-literary-history-by-randall-stevenson-rf92lmfd7lh [accessed 3 October 2019].

[3] Ezra Pound, *ABC of Reading* (New York: New Directions, 1960 [1934]), p. 29.

'Who Is the Poet J. H. Prynne?'[4] The reasons for his becoming the story in February 2004 remain instructive, whatever you wish to call the splash, a 'flurry of media interest' or a good old 'kafuffle'.[5] But they should not obscure the cause of the furore. For the issue at stake had to do less with the kind of poems readers were now being goaded to read, or to dismiss, and more with the way these poems had appeared suddenly to galvanise an alternative mode of literary historiography. 'This is not a method for bringing out a writer's subtler qualities', John Carey argued, not of Prynne's writing but of Randall Stevenson's, the real troublemaker in all this, whose volume for *The Oxford English Literary History, 1960–2000: The Last of England?*, had made Prynne such an easy target. The 'method' Carey couldn't abide had apparently involved Stevenson in a weird sort of post-nuclear derby – 'weighing the postmodern content' in each of his chosen authors – and this, Carey implied, an eccentric and highly 'scattered' means of selection, was as much as one could expect from a critic so beholden to the lessons of that awkward noun: *postmodernism*. Where Stevenson had done what he could to call time on 'time', and to suggest that post-war writers had woken to find that dimension 'shattered' – '[o]bviously this fact has not filtered through to the population at large', Carey remarked – he himself considered it the job of a reviewer, or his duty, to put back the clocks. Larkin in particular (Philip, not Peter) had suffered something appalling in this survey of postmodernist verse: Stevenson had not only questioned his time-honoured place on school curricula, but had lopped a quotation at just the moment Larkin would appear in one poem to have glimpsed real happiness. 'This omission', Carey observed, happy in his own way to supply the rest of 'Born Yesterday', 'does not suggest a careful reading'.

To which one might offer just three words in reply: stones and glasshouses. For Carey's reading of Stevenson's survey hardly indicates a scholar's care; nor does it indicate a nature any less 'religious' than Stevenson's if its concluding bow to Dr Johnson is anything to go by. Scepticism, incertitude, problems of legitimation, the irresistible rise of *petits récits* – these all rank significantly in Stevenson's effort to

---

[4] The segment, first broadcast on 27 February 2004, is still available to listen to on the *Today: Listen Again* website: http://www.bbc.co.uk/radio4/today/listenagain/listenagain_20040227.shtml [accessed 3 October 2019].
[5] Robert Potts, 'Through the Oval Window', *Guardian* (10 April 2004); John Wilkinson, 'Tenter Ground', in *The Lyric Touch: Essays on the Poetry of Excess* (Cambridge: Salt, 2007), pp. 21–32 (p. 21).

characterise postmodernism, and it's clear that his grounds for doing so are commensurate with a healthy respect for, in Carey's phrase, 'the usual bunch of foreign theorists'. But it's simply not true to say that 'postmodernist' in Stevenson's book amounts to the 'highest accolade', or that he believes that writing in such a vein necessarily meant bidding adieu in this period to 'social justice', 'scientific discovery', or pleasure. Stevenson is no fool: he is alive in *The Last of England?* to the affect of 'a postmodernist manner', to obscurities that may seem 'gratuitous, or self-indulgent', and to the most crucial detail of all, which is that literary practice, whilst bound to theory in a complicated sort of chore-ography, is not reducible to 'postmodern thinking'.[6] If it were, literature in England and far beyond would look very different to us now: Derek Walcott might have declined to do what he does with 'towering babble' in *Omeros* (1990) – a 'metanarrative', in Lyotard's well-worn idiom, and a 'voyage' too, whose debts to Homer and Dante are complex but not 'incredulous';[7] and no one would be drawing on the influence of Wallace Stevens in this day and age – much less building his 'various and vagrant' ways into new writing, as Susan Howe continues to – because they'd have taken Fredric Jameson's word for it that Stevens's high modernism is a 'spent and exhausted' thing.[8] One could go on, and the point would sharpen with every case: the 'postmodern age' is a construction like any other, an aid to reading rather than a rationale, and one that's best followed with a question mark – as Stevenson suggests – if for no other reason that its prefix sounds so final.[9]

It is in that searching spirit, of lingering doubt and exploration, that I introduce to you the present volume. Though more inclined to Stevenson's way of thinking than to Carey's – the contents page will reveal certain leanings, persuasions, and emphases – *Forms of Late Modernist Lyric* is a collective effort to imagine a third way. We mean to do so with a view to recognising a rich and oddly destabi-lising seam of formal praxis that has been allowed once too often to

[6]   Stevenson, *The Oxford English Literary History, vol. 12: 1960–2000: The Last of England?* (Oxford: Oxford University Press, 2004), pp. 236, 81.

[7]   Derek Walcott, *Omeros* (New York: Farrar, Straus and Giroux, 1990), p. 6; Jean-François Lyotard, *The Postmodern Condition: A Report on Knowledge*, trans. Geoff Bennington and Brian Massumi (Manchester: Manchester University Press, 1984), p. xxiv.

[8]   Susan Howe, *The Quarry* (New York: New Directions, 2015), p. 3; Fredric Jameson, *Postmodernism; or, The Cultural Logic of Late Capitalism* (Durham, NC: Duke University Press, 1991), p. 1.

[9]   Stevenson, *The Last of England?*, p. 87.

recede or melt away entirely in the course of critical debate.[10] Joseph Brooker would seem to sound a familiar refrain when he characterises this 'alternative tradition' as 'metrically irregular, rarely beholden to conventional metre or rhyme, often indifferent to traditional poetic forms'; yet he goes one step further than most when he recognises that these forms '(like the sonnet)' have in some cases been 'retained as the site of subversion'.[11] In drawing out the implication embedded in that parenthesis – that we're not dealing with poetries drafted and crafted without design – the contributors here propose something of a move sideways in order to catch at the kinds of form that have proved more than usually resistant to textbook description. These are forms that materialise as so many modes of articulation, polymorphic shapes of thought, styles of vocal habit which exhibit even as they ruffle up the stitch and colouring of earlier technique. To live a little with Jorie Graham's aubades, as we'll see, is to reckon her debts to Hopkins and Stevens; to trace R. F. Langley's character sketches is to contemplate a long and contested lineage, guided by the shades of Browning, Pound, and Shakespeare. One of the aims of *Forms*, then, is to show that the sometime deconstructive agenda is only a small part of the picture, and that these 'conductors of chaos' have more in common with earlier practitioners than we've supposed.[12] Where some have attempted to separate so-called mainstream verse from its opposite number,[13] *Forms* makes the case for rubbing down distinctions, or for reconceiving them at any rate, by drawing into conversation voices apparently dead or long-lost to a live tradition of making the old new.

What to call such a tradition? Where to start? And what to make of Aaron Jaffe's reply – an answer to his own innocently

---

[10]   The present collection of essays speaks in this regard to a couple of volumes in Palgrave Macmillan's Modern and Contemporary Poetry and Poetics series: *Modernist Legacies: Trends and Faultlines in British Poetry Today*, ed. Abigail Lang and David Nowell Smith (New York: Palgrave Macmillan, 2015); Robert Sheppard, *The Meaning of Form in Contemporary Innovative Poetry* (New York: Palgrave Macmillan, 2016).

[11]   Joseph Brooker, *Literature of the 1980s: After the Watershed* (Edinburgh: Edinburgh University Press, 2010), p. 132.

[12]   I borrow the phrase from a book that belongs on every shelf: *Conductors of Chaos: A Poetry Anthology*, ed. Iain Sinclair (London: Picador, 1996).

[13]   Compare, for example, the following very different accounts of post-war British poetry: *Complicities: British Poetry, 1945–2007*, ed. Robin Purves and Sam Ladkin (Prague: Litteraria Pragensia, 2007) and *The Movement Reconsidered*, ed. Zachary Leader (Oxford: Oxford University Press, 2009).

revealing question, '[w]hat comes after postmodernism?' – that 'a retro-revenant thing continues to stalk the present'?[14] Stevenson for his part acknowledges the ghostly shape of 'modernist legacies' even as he would appear to privilege the 'radical challenges to established forms and foundations of thinking' that might be thought to have characterised a post-war avant-garde.[15] Jameson, too, had his suspicions back in the day, sensing as he could the need to 'make some place' in the depths of *postmodernism* for the likes of Samuel Beckett and Charles Olson.[16] These, he claimed – warming a little to the idea of a 'late modernism' – had 'had the misfortune to span two eras and the luck to find a time capsule of isolation or exile in which to spin out unseasonable forms'.[17] Luck, we may feel, had little to do with it, but Jameson was right to suspect that anyone wanting to anatomise this latest *-ism* – late but somehow timely – should attend as a matter of priority to the 'forms' of its presentation. In gladly taking up that thought, the present volume does however resist the urge to call such forms 'unseasonable', or to suggest that the act of spinning them out was in some sense a final act of prolongation and an expression therefore of recalcitrance or dreamy anachronism. Unseasonable is so last century. The forms at issue here may be taken rather as the indices of a late modernism that is still perceptible today in anglophone verse culture, a late modernism whose fidelity to the forms of avant-gardes past – for all forms, however old, were new once upon a time – renders it a crucial countermeasure to the activity of periodisation. If nothing else, talking about late modernism seems nothing less than good form if it does something to expose the politics of thinking in too linear a fashion about high modernism and the results of its post-mortem.

Several critics since Jameson have looked to expand the possibilities of the category in relation to its more appealing relative. These, Tyrus Miller states, with an eye trained on the architectures of late and postmodernism, should not be construed as 'successive stages but rather alternative responses to the legacy of modernism and its possible continuation'.[18] Nor should the works at issue be 'viewed

---

[14] Aaron Jaffe, *The Way Things Go: An Essay on the Matter of Second Modernism* (Minneapolis: University of Minnesota Press, 2014), p. 20.

[15] Stevenson, *The Last of England?*, pp. 231, 69.

[16] Jameson, *Postmodernism*, p. 305.

[17] Ibid.

[18] Tyrus Miller, *Late Modernism: Politics, Fiction, and the Arts Between the World Wars* (Berkeley and Los Angeles: University of California Press, 1999), p. 9.

simply as cultural curiosities salvaged from time, aesthetic souvenirs that exert their unsettling fascination by reviving an already moribund modernism'.[19] Miller's anti-narrative – which is also an antidote to Jameson's time capsule thesis – has proved influential, though other readers have come to doubt what they consider to be its own rather limited timeframe. Anthony Mellors, for one, will not be swayed by the idea that late modernism erupted in 1926, or that its kindling *entre deux guerres* should now command our attention if (as Mellors feels) such a directive threatens to foreclose the category's possible application to later styles of innovative writing.[20]

Mellors worries about a way of thinking that seems to him 'negative in character', and he's right to worry about the rhetoric critics use when they rise to contemplate modernism the morning after.[21] Bob Perelman's book of that name begins by flinching at the 'unsubtle whisper of violence' which hangs still around formations of poetic taste and value; 'canons, named or assumed, fixed or trending, are as loaded an issue as ever', he writes, '(dull pun intended)', before doing what he can – though not enough, perhaps – to defuse the issue by fingering the 'shrapnel pointed fuzzily but accurately enough at the heart of what we do'.[22] Because this shrapnel sticks, embeds itself, works its way – so the logic goes – into the very body of subject-oriented discourse. The metaphor is as alive today, in a dead sort of way, as it was in Perelman's San Francisco days. Looking back, you can detect its crackle through L=A=N=G=U=A=G=E writing – its 'wild schizzed-out eruptions', the 'explosion / of nonabsorptive forms' – whose outbursts had served in the 1970s to estrange and distinguish small-press outfits from their mainstream rivals.[23] Self-descriptions of this sort *have* stuck, and have only deepened the alleged fault lines of contemporary poetry and poetics. Readers of lyric since the early 1990s have been asked time and again to assent to the notion that 'ours is indeed a schizophrenic poetry scene', a

[19] Ibid., pp. 12–13.

[20] Anthony Mellors, *Late Modernist Poetics from Pound to Prynne* (Manchester: Manchester University Press, 2005), pp. 20–23.

[21] Ibid., p. 22.

[22] Bob Perelman, *Modernism the Morning After* (Tuscaloosa: University of Alabama Press, 2017), pp. 5, 2.

[23] Bruce Andrews, 'Writing Social Work & Political Practice' (1979), in *The L=A=N=G=U=A=G=E Book*, ed. Bruce Andrews and Charles Bernstein (Carbondale: Southern Illinois University Press, 1984), p. 135; Charles Bernstein, *A Poetics* (Cambridge, MA: Harvard University Press, 1992), p. 54.

veritable pathology of 'chaotic systems, mathematical singularities, and noise'.[24] When she decided to 'reclassify' the scene a year or so ago, Fiona Sampson had to admit that one branch of 'continually reactive practice' was still, in 2012, the stuff of fear and loathing, and a sure-fire way to anger 'poetry commentators'. This she simply called 'the exploded lyric'.[25]

That Sampson came, in doing so, to appreciate a writing 'dense with purposive pleasure' – the writings of Denise Riley, Barry MacSweeney, and Jeremy Prynne – must have shocked all those delicate commentators.[26] Her attempt in *Beyond Lyric* to reconnoitre a field so often assumed to be off-limits to the many, or just off-putting, was not the first of its kind to make the point that a 'radical poetics' is no less conditioned or shaped by 'formal care', or responsive to it, than verse produced in the name of a new formalism.[27] There are several ways one could express such equations – that 'form does not depend only on rhyming the line-ends', that the appropriation of a specific subgenre (for they 'must be claimed') need not imply 'a dangerous nostalgia'[28] – and each time we'd get closer to knowing a little more of the ways certain sorts of contemporary poetry have been mistaken or misconstrued. We've known this, and known that we might, for some time. Back in 1967 – a year before the *événements* that did so much to shake up academy politics – René Wellek was rebellious enough to suggest that '[g]enres can be observed even in the apparently anarchic welter of twentieth-century literary activity'.[29] He went on:

---

[24] Marjorie Perloff, *Poetic License: Essays on Modernist and Postmodernist Lyric* (Evanston: Northwestern University Press (1990), p. 60; Susan Vanderborg, *Paratextual Communities: American Avant-Garde Poetry since 1950* (Carbondale: Southern Illinois University Press, 2001), p. 64.

[25] Fiona Sampson, *Beyond the Lyric: A Map of Contemporary British Poetry* (London: Chatto & Windus, 2012), p. 259.

[26] Ibid., p. 276.

[27] Ibid., p. 272.

[28] Ruth Padel, *The Poem and the Journey: And Sixty Poems to Read Along the Way* (London: Vintage, 2008 [2007]), p. 22; David Caplan, *Questions of Possibility: Contemporary Poetry and Poetic Form* (Oxford: Oxford University Press, 2005), p. 6. Caplan refers to a once typical admonishment in Ira Sadoff, 'Neo-Formalism: A Dangerous Nostalgia', *American Poetry Review*, 19.1 (January–February 1990), 7–13.

[29] René Wellek, 'Genre Theory, the Lyric, and *Erlebnis*', first publ. in *Festschrift für Richard Alewyn* (1967), repr. in *Discriminations: Further Concepts of Criticism* (New Haven: Yale University Press, 1970), pp. 225–52 (p. 225).

> One must abandon attempts to define the general nature of
> the lyric or the lyrical. Nothing beyond generalities of the
> tritest kind can result from it. It seems much more profitable
> to turn to a study of the variety of poetry and to the history
> and thus the description of genres which can be grasped in
> their concrete conventions and traditions.[30]

You could quibble with the 'concrete'; plenty of critics have, indirectly,
by assenting instead to a model which allows more obviously for the
fact that genres, as 'orders of discourse', are wont to 'change, shift,
travel, lose force, come and go over time and cultures'.[31] Most, too,
would hesitate to abandon 'the lyric' and 'the lyrical' entirely: that
subtle distinction alone can be a handy tool. And yet, and yet – 50
years on and so many lyrics later – Wellek's remains a perfectly
cogent counterproposal, and a tantalising one at that.

Those who've come closest to realising its possibilities in recent
years have moved lyric studies on. Chief among them, Virginia
Jackson has done more than most, starting with *Dickinson's Misery*
(2005), to apprehend the effects of 'lyricization'. This is the process
which continues to this day to idealise poetry, she claims – to
imagine its evacuation from history, 'independent of social contin-
gency' – to privilege the thing we've got used to calling 'lyric'
precisely because it would seem to 'require as its context only the
occasion of its reading'.[32] Jackson doesn't mean to deny the existence
of lyric as such at different times for different people, but 'simply to
propose that the riddles',

> papyrae, epigrams, songs, sonnets, *blasons, Lieder,* elegies,
> dialogues, conceits, ballads, hymns and odes considered lyrical
> in the Western tradition before the early nineteenth century
> were lyric in a very different sense than was or will be the
> poetry that the mediating hands of editors, reviewers, critics,
> teachers, and poets have rendered as lyric in the last century
> and a half.[33]

---

[30]   Ibid., p. 252.

[31]   Stephen Heath, 'The Politics of Genre', first publ. in *Issues in World Literature*
(1994), repr. in *Debating World Literature*, ed. Christopher Prendergast (London:
Verso, 2004), pp. 163–74 (p. 169).

[32]   Virginia Jackson, *Dickinson's Misery: A Theory of Lyric Reading* (Princeton:
Princeton University Press, 2005), p. 7.

[33]   Ibid.

Why should this matter to us? Isn't it a classic case of semantic drift? It matters, Jackson argues, because 'when the stipulative functions of particular genres are collapsed into one big idea of poems as lyrics' – specifically, 'into the single abstraction of the post-Romantic lyric' – 'then the only function poems can perform in our culture is to become individual or communal ideals':

> Such ideals might bind particular groups or sub-cultures (in slams, for example, or avant-garde blogs, or poetry cafés, or salons, or university, library, and museum reading series), but the more ideally lyric poems and poetry culture have become, the fewer actual poetic genres address readers in specific ways.[34]

And those 'ways' themselves sound increasingly slight, as a recent textbook reveals. 'Short poems like the ones in [your anthology] are often called lyric poems', observes the editor, having advised students already that there's no criterion more important for judging such things than their 'overall emotional impact'.[35] Never mind the fact that Thomas Hardy's 'The Ruined Maid' is a satire, knowingly voiced in couplets; or that 'Cold Knap Lake' by Gillian Clarke – rippled with *cynghanedd* – sounds the depths of elegy.[36]

These forms were formative, and could be again, but Jackson's wish to see the 'idealized scene of reading' entangled or repopulated with them has given other critics pause for thought.[37] The urge to disaggregate lyric into so many kinds of form 'limits the scope of the problem', Jahan Ramazani cautions, but it would be foolish to suppose that an eye for specificity doesn't risk oversights of a different but no less glaring nature.[38] 'What about poetry's transnational bearings and transhistorical memory?' His point is not that we should cease and desist, but that we must go into such work with our eyes open, attentive – in the case of his book's terrain – to the ways poetry 'feasts on, digests, and metabolizes linguistic forms of other kinds'.[39] Jonathan Culler harbours a different appetite altogether. Indeed, he

---

[34] Virginia Jackson, 'Who Reads Poetry?', in 'The New Lyric Studies', *PMLA*, 123.1 (2008), 181–87 (p. 183).

[35] *Moon on the Tides: The AQA GCSE Poetry Anthology – A Guide for Students*, ed. David Wheeler (Morrisville: Dog's Tail Books, 2011), pp. 9, 3.

[36] Ibid., pp. 73–77, 104–08.

[37] Jackson, *Dickinson's Misery*, p. 7.

[38] Jahan Ramazani, *Poetry and Its Others: News, Prayer, Song, and the Dialogue of Genres* (Chicago and London: University of Chicago Press, 2014), p. 3.

[39] Ibid., p. 7.

puts it more forcefully than Ramazani when he remarks that 'even the more popular and persistent categories' to which we might turn, Wellek-style, are far from 'stable':

> The complaint about the term *lyric* – that it means different things in different times and places – can be lodged against *elegy, ballad,* and even *ode,* which is rather different in the hands of Pindar, Horace, Ronsard, Collins, Keats, Neruda, and Robert Lowell. The historical disparities that appear to motivate the desire to abandon the category *lyric* reappear in the case of more narrowly defined genres, and do so more insidiously, one might imagine, since while it is blatantly obvious that the lyric changes, it is less obvious that *ode* might be a slippery, even dubious category.[40]

This smacks of conspiracy theory, and does rather provide a false impression of the kind of work to which Jackson and others are committed. That work has always, to my mind, appeared invigorating, heuristic – in a slightly geeky, historicist way – never once swindled by the illusion that a 'comprehensive set of subcategories' is there for the taking, or that any one category is 'stable'.[41] Given that important caveat, what harm could our thinking more resourcefully about 'the ode, elegy, and song' actually do? More than you'd think, apparently. It isn't a 'very promising strategy for nineteenth- and twentieth-century poetry', Culler affirms, 'where many of the most interesting lyrics do not seem to belong to those particular genres or subgenres'.[42] It sounds an open-and-shut case.

The purpose of the present volume is to show that it's not. The ode, elegy, and song sit at the heart of this study, for some (if not many) of the most interesting late modernist lyrics have been written with precisely those forms in mind, and should be read accordingly. They sit here in relation to a constellation of other forms that have come down to us no less compromised and full of promise. Some of these, such as the aubade and souvenir, would seem to make a virtue of knowing they're belated, to pose, as Susan Stewart once remarked, as 'objects both in and out of time'; to think of Graham's morning song and Brock-Broido's taste for kitsch as 'distressed' might be to

---

[40] Jonathan Culler, *Theory of Lyric* (Cambridge, MA: Harvard University Press, 2015), p. 87.

[41] Ibid., pp. 87–88.

[42] Ibid., p. 87.

assume a different attitude to their relish for found objects, particularly the kinds we used to call intertexts.[43] If 'the distressing of forms', according to Stewart, 'involves a process of separation and manipulation serving certain ideological functions', we may feel persuaded to think of late modernism itself as renovation work, or the practice of revival.[44] The very structure of nostalgia, or 'the desire for desire', is certainly part of it.[45] Yet many of the forms at stake here – the hymn, the nocturne, even the costume dramas of dramatic monologue – do not have the look so much of hand-me-downs or New Age antiques as of reclaimed apparatus, forms in which and for which 'a context of function' has been restored just when we thought those forms had given up the ghost.[46]

In this sense exactly we might wish to contemplate the 'affordances' such forms embody. The word itself is a borrowing, and it comes to stand in Caroline Levine's recent work for 'the potential uses or actions' to which 'materials and designs' are put, some of them planned, others 'generated by imaginative users'.[47] By extending it to literary forms – doorknobs to sonnets, forks to couplets – Levine expects the principle of 'affordances' to help us grasp the ways in which 'forms can be at once containing, plural, overlapping, portable, and situated'.[48] There's no getting away from it, *affordances* is an unwieldy term, yet it might just do the job Levine suggests. What would it mean in this light to think of that evergreen form, pastoral, not as a setting or set of conventions, but as a mode that enables shocking growths of thought? How might it sit with you right now to feel exposed or called out by a form that has its doubts about address, and which trusts instead to a more oblique process of interpellation? What did these forms once afford, and is there more to come?

These are some of the sorts of question posed in and by the chapters of this book. Taken together, they may be said to build on the detailed and often provocative work of those who have made the study of lyric genres what it is today: Jackson and Culler, Prins and Jeffreys, Cohen

---

[43]   Susan Stewart, *Crimes of Writing: Problems in the Containment of Representation* (Durham, NC and London: Duke University Press, 1994), p. 67.

[44]   Ibid., p. 68.

[45]   Ibid., p. 74.

[46]   Ibid.

[47]   Caroline Levine, *Forms: Whole, Rhythm, Hierarchy, Network* (Princeton and Oxford: Princeton University Press, 2015), p. 6.

[48]   Ibid., p. 11.

and Fowler.[49] Our hope, of course, is that *Forms of Late Modernist Lyric* will determine to some degree what that study looks like tomorrow. That the greatest threats to our understanding of 'lyric' as a pluralistic category have come historically from within *and* without – from the desire to conflate poetry's internal differences, and from the persistent impositions of narrative, the narrativising instinct, and questions of a narratological cast – seems to us a double view which has just about hardened into orthodoxy.[50] The next step is to move ever more deliberately towards a thick description of lyric forms, but to do so – as we try to here – without replicating the assumptions that underpin tellings of literary history as though it were a straight linear narrative, parcelled up into discrete chapters. Although the pressures of historical circumstance play their part in much of the work that follows, the reason for making *late modernism* the focus of this collective intervention in lyric studies is precisely because it is *not* a period that is susceptible to dating, clean demarcation, or the rage to order. It is a means, rather, of describing a dimension of poetic practice in which the dynamics of formal design and an otherwise reactive sensibility are imbricated to a remarkable degree, and in ways that should confound chronological survey. Among other things, late modernism teaches us that it's never too late to capture the shape-shifting nature of lyric.

---

[49] See, for instance, 'Genre Theory', in *The Lyric Theory Reader: A Critical Anthology*, ed. Virginia Jackson and Yopie Prins (Baltimore: Johns Hopkins University Press, 2014), pp. 11–16; Culler, *Theory of Lyric*, pp. 39–90, 244–95; Mark Jeffreys, 'Ideologies of Lyric: A Problem of Genre in Contemporary Anglophone Poetics', *PMLA*, 110.2 (1995), 196–205; Ralph Cohen, *Genre Theory and Historical Change*, ed. John L. Rowlett (Charlottesville: University of Virginia Press, 2017); Alastair Fowler, *Kinds of Literature: An Introduction to the Theory of Genre and Modes* (Cambridge, MA: Harvard University Press, 1982).

[50] For a snapshot, compare the answers provided to the questions posed by Jackson, 'Who Reads Poetry?', and Culler, 'Why Lyric?', in 'The New Lyric Studies', *PMLA*, 123.1 (2008), 201–06.

CHAPTER ONE

Aubade

Jorie Graham
and 'the pitch of the dawn'

Fiona Green

At the beginning of *Great Expectations*, Dickens's Pip remembers trying to make sense of things before he could read:

> As I never saw my father or my mother, and never saw any likeness of either of them (for their days were long before the days of photographs), my first fancies regarding what they were like, were unreasonably derived from their tombstones. The shape of the letters on my father's, gave me an odd idea that he was a square, stout, dark man, with curly black hair. From the character and turn of the inscription '*Also Georgiana, Wife of the Above*,' I drew a childish conclusion that my mother was freckled and sickly.[1]

Infant Pip was not mistaken in fancying that he might resurrect a living presence from written text; reading a novel, after all, involves deriving human character from inscribed characters. His unreason lay rather in his childish assumption that letters are iconic: Pip had yet to discover that the shapes of words bear no resemblance to what they represent. Learning to read means recognising that the 'character and turn of the inscription' is a distraction from sense-making, and in that respect Pip's memory of the graveyard has something more general to say about our relation to language. The acquisition of language, like

I am grateful to Luke Carson and Heather White for their judicious comments on earlier drafts of this chapter, which first appeared in their guest-edited issue of *Genre*, 45.1 (Spring 2012), 121–42.

[1] Charles Dickens, *Great Expectations* (Oxford: World's Classics, 2008 [1860–61]), p. 3.

learning to read, entails setting aside its material constituents. We learn to tune out or turn down the sounds, durations, and rhythms of words, their surface likenesses and patterns of coincidence, so that the conventional or 'arbitrary' workings of the linguistic code can come through. Except, that is, when it comes to poetry: the power of verse resides precisely in its bringing back into range and putting into arrangement those material aspects of language that may lie at cross purposes to discursive sense.

This chapter takes as its ground the thought that lyric poetry reminds us how to read unreasonably. Mutlu Konuk Blasing has offered the most persuasive recent formulation of this story: in tempting us to get caught up again with those aspects of language we learned in infancy to forget, Blasing argues, lyric returns us to the very threshold of that forgetting.[2] If the bliss of infancy prior to language 'exists only as a memory trace marking its loss', and if such traces are preserved in the fabric of lyric language, then the aubade – the dawn song – provides a special case of that threshold condition.[3] Lovers woken at dawn by the cry of the watchman or the calling of birds lie in the aftermath of a wordless oneness to which we were not privy and to which they cannot return. Edward Hirsch puts it this way in some brief but brilliant pages of his essay 'The Work of Lyric: Night and Day': the aubade, says Hirsch, 'remembers the ecstasy of union. But it also describes a leave-taking at dawn, and with that parting comes the dawning of individual consciousness; the

---

[2] 'Poetry formally returns us', Blasing writes, 'to that crux, to the emotionally charged history of the disciplining and seduction into language' (*Lyric Poetry: The Pain and the Pleasure of Words* (Princeton: Princeton University Press, 2007), p. 13). Although my chapter does not share the psychoanalytic framework of Blasing's book, it does draw, like that book, on Roman Jakobson's foundational thinking about poetics. In 'Linguistics and Poetics', for example, Jakobson argues that the poetic function, 'by promoting the palpability of signs, deepens the fundamental dichotomy of signs and objects' ('Linguistics and Poetics' (1960), in *Language in Literature*, ed. Krystyna Pomorska and Stephen Rudy (Cambridge, MA: Harvard University Press, 1987), p. 70). My term 'unreasonable', borrowed from Dickens, corresponds to Blasing's 'non-rational'. These are distinct from 'irrationality' as most commonly understood. Blasing puts it this way: 'the non-rational order that the formality of poetic language keeps audible is distinct from any cultivated, induced, pathological, or "deviant" irrationality, or the irrationality of dreams [..] Nor is it to be understood as some "primal" irrationality' (*Lyric Poetry*, p. 2).

[3] Blasing, *Lyric Poetry*, p. 78.

separated, or daylit, mind bears the grief or burden of longing for
what has been lost'.[4] The seven aubades collected in Jorie Graham's
1997 book *The Errancy* dilate these slender moments between waking
and leave-taking, and in doing so draw us closely into the workings
of lyric. This chapter begins by showing how Graham's aubades
instantiate and figure the interference of linguistic materiality with
discursive logic. I go on to argue that Graham's fostering these
cross purposes – the poems' formal patterns getting in the way of
the things they say – serves both as a stay against time, prolonging
the interlude between darkness and the broad daylight of transparent
sense, and, paradoxically, as a conduit between the private sphere of
waking consciousness and the busied world that lies traditionally
beyond the scope of lyric.

Graham's has always been a profoundly intertextual poetics.
Whereas others of her books before and since *The Errancy* have
shown off her wide readings in European philosophy, and tempted
some readers to translate the verse back into the theoretical modes
from which it borrows, it is in keeping with this chapter's attention
to the substance of Graham's medium that in *The Errancy* you can
hear her listening hardest to other poets.[5] My particular focus is on
her bringing the shades of Shakespeare, Stevens, and Hopkins into
the sphere of her dawn songs, their presence felt by way of quotation
or veiled allusion (for the most part unacknowledged in Graham's
appended notes), but also, and perhaps more significantly, in those
formal borrowings and reflections whereby Graham cultivates the
art of reading unreasonably. Finally, reading between these precursor
lyrics and Graham's aubades brings new light to the condition of
aftermath or late time in and against which Graham's turn-of-the-
millennium dawn songs speak.

'My first and most vivid and broad impression of the identity
of things', remembers Pip, 'seems to me to have been gained on a
memorable raw afternoon towards evening'. He goes on:

> At such a time I found out for certain [..] that the dark flat
> wilderness beyond the churchyard, intersected with dykes and
> mounds and gates, with scattered cattle feeding on it, was

---

[4] Edward Hirsch, 'The Work of Lyric: Night and Day', *Georgia Review*, 57.2
(2003), 368–80 (p. 371).

[5] Bonnie Costello rightly calls *The Errancy* 'Graham's most allusive and echoic
volume' and notes, among other echoes, those of Eliot and Stevens. See 'Jorie
Graham, *The Errancy*', *Boston Review* (October–November 1997), 49–50 (p. 49).

the marshes; and that the low leaden line beyond, was the river; and that the distant savage lair from which the wind was rushing, was the sea; and that the small bundle of shivers growing afraid of it all, and beginning to cry, was Pip.[6]

The sequence of this narrative unfolds in time with the coming to consciousness it recalls. Featureless space ('the dark flat wilderness') is partitioned and measured before each thing can be brought out by name. The 'low leaden line' is both the river and the means of distinguishing one thing from another, with the suggestion of pencil or movable type in 'leaden' reminding us that Pip's deciphering runs parallel to our experience of reading. At the end of it all, as though ejected from a state of primal oneness with his environment, Pip finds himself alone in the landscape he has just learned to read, his small solitude now scaled and felt in relation to the bleak marsh country among whose objects he is distinguished and named. In much the same way that establishing 'the identity of things' means finding their edges and making distinctions, acquiring language involves bringing sense units out from the wilderness of noise, or, when we learn to read, from the mass of marks on paper. It is in these matters of edge and identity that lyric poetry is most at odds with itself. W. K. Wimsatt makes this point specifically in relation to metrical pattern:

> It is possible to point out examples, in balladry and in other primitive types of poetry, where the equalities of verse coincide with the parallels of meaning [...] But on the whole the tendency of verse, or certainly that of English verse, has been the opposite: the smallest equalities, the feet, so many syllables, or so many time units, are superimposed upon the linear succession of ideas most often without any regard for the equalities of logic. Two successive iambs may be on two words, or one word, or parts of two words, and so on.[7]

Wimsatt's acute description here of 'the sensory resistance of verse nonparallel to logic' can be enlarged from the specific case of metrical units to the thought that the work of lyric language lies exactly in the noncoincidence of visual or acoustic arrangements with the means by which propositions are organised: as Blasing also observes, the sonic

---

[6] Dickens, *Great Expectations*, pp. 3–4.

[7] W. K. Wimsatt, Jr., 'One Relation of Rhyme to Reason' (1944), in *The Verbal Icon: Studies in the Meaning of Poetry* (London: Methuen, 1970 [1953]), p. 154.

and visual patterns that make up the formal textures of verse operate regardless of lexical, grammatical, and sense units.[8]

The aubade offers Graham a place and time in which to stage and observe this mismatch that generates the power of lyric. At sunrise things come to light, and the discovery of their identity coincides with the dawning of individual consciousness; yet at precisely the same time, the waking mind, befuddled from sleep, may find itself more than usually drawn to those material features that cut across and so distract from units of sense: on waking, as in infancy, you register the sound patterns and shapes of words before you make out what they say. Edges proliferate in all of Graham's aubades, and 'Sea-Blue Aubade' in particular thinks through the formal hindrances that verse puts in the way of sense. It does so in relation to poems by Shakespeare and Stevens, whose words Graham borrows and whose rhetorical schemes she by turn adopts and resists.

The outcome of every dawn song is solitary selfhood. In its reluctant movement towards that end, 'Sea-Blue Aubade' carries a moment of hesitation. Suspended in parenthesis is the closing line of Shakespeare's Sonnet 66: '– (save that to die I leave my love alone.) –'.[9] The sonnet begins:

> Tir'd with all these, for restful death I cry:
> As to behold desert a beggar born,
> And needy nothing trimmed in jollity,
> And purest faith unhappily forsworn,
> And gilded honour shamefully misplaced.

The rhetorical force of anaphora is to project equivalence between the things it lines up, and in this case to stabilise the antithetical structure of the lines it organises. Shakespeare's sonnet piles up its teetering stack until the closing couplet gathers in all the items on the list – 'Tir'd with all these, from these would I be gone' – only for

---

[8] Blasing takes up this thought in general, and in the particular case of metre, though she does not refer to Wimsatt: 'bodily produced acoustic phenomena and signifying sounds converge and diverge in their separate, overlapping patternings. The phonemes are organized in two different systems: the formal patterns or recurring sounds in such schemes as rhyme, alliteration, assonance and conso-nance, and the linear phoneme sequences that organize sounds for sense [...] metrical order and syntactic order, with their different patterns of accent and stress, exist alongside, and interfere with, each other' (*Lyric Poetry*, p. 28).

[9] Jorie Graham, 'Sea-Blue Aubade', in *The Errancy* (Hopewell: Ecco, 1997), p. 43.

the last line to preserve itself on the brink of departure: 'Save that to die, I leave my love alone'. Graham summons Shakespeare not only by quoting that last line, but also in the rhetorical framework of her 'Sea-Blue Aubade'. It begins:

> Dawn – or is it sea-blue – fills the square.
> Two in a room asleep with that window.
> And dark thinning inside the view.
> And human breathing.
> And freedom in the room like a thin gray floating.
> And doctrine.
> And other kinds of shine rising off the edges of things –
> as if the daylight were a doctor arriving,
> each thing needing to be seen.[10]

You peer into the half-light of this opening, through the Bishop-like self-revision, to 'the square', glimpsed first as a breezy piazza until the second line turns inward to recast 'square' as a window filling with light. The Shakespearean anaphora supplies for the eye a frame along the left margin, its vertical order promising to sort a cluttered pile of stuff into an itemised list of things. And yet alongside that sharp edge something else is going on with the acoustic and visual material – something that arises from an accretion of 'ing's. Graham's addiction to this morpheme shows symptoms in titles such as 'The Scanning', 'Thinking', 'The Turning', as well as in the gerunds and present participles of passages like this one. The special thing about 'ing' in 'Sea-Blue Aubade' is that it's also there in 'thing', the word you can track along various routes through 'thinning', which is voiced softly at the end of 'breathing', and draped across the space between words in 'thin gray floating'. The morpheme 'ing' whereby gerunds and participles are formed and the 'ing' of 'thing' have different roots – their surface sameness is an accident of the language – but their patterning along these lines persuades us to imagine some motivated connection, as though 'th-ing' were a gerund, the precipitate of something you could do, or as though 'breathing' were heavier for the noun it carries. This is Graham dwelling on the distracted condition of the aubade, filling out its pause in a thickening of the medium that encourages us to read against the grain of sense. Because what these lines say is that things are getting clearer: the edges that would help us decipher 'the

---

[10] Graham, *The Errancy*, p. 42.

identity of things' should be coming more sharply into view. And yet it is precisely edge and identity that this play with 'things' and 'ing's obscures, because of its disregard for lexical units ('thin gray'), and its muddling the parts of speech ('th-ing').

Daylight should give things their edge and so make sense of them: as Graham puts it in 'Easter Morning Aubade', 'light pour⌈s⌉ down the difference'.[11] In 'Sea-Blue Aubade' daylight arrives in an inherited figure:

> as if the daylight were a doctor arriving,
> each thing needing to be seen ...

If the neediness of 'each thing' reminds us of the 'needy nothing' at the start of Shakespeare's sonnet, perhaps Graham's 'doctor' draws also on that source. A derivation from Shakespeare's line, 'And folly, doctor-like, controlling skill' would cast this sun – like Donne's 'busie old foole' – as meddling intruder.[12] At the same time another aubade, this one by Wallace Stevens, filters in to 'Sea-Blue Aubade' and makes its presence more strongly felt as the poem goes on. 'Sea-Blue Aubade' is awash with Stevensian colour from its title; more specifically, 'The Latest Freed Man', and 'On the Road Home', both from Stevens's 1938 *Canonica* sequence, lend words and phrases to this first section.[13] Despite sharing its idiom, however, Graham's aubade differs markedly from Stevens's in mood, and as regards the relations between linguistic pattern and propositional logic. Where Sonnet 66 began, 'Tired with all these ...', Stevens's dawn song opens like this:

---

[11] Ibid., p. 101.

[12] John Donne, 'The Sunne Rising', in *The Complete English Poems*, ed. C. A. Patrides (London: Everyman, 1994), pp. 7–8.

[13] Wallace Stevens, *Collected Poetry and Prose* (New York: Library of America, 1997), pp. 187, 186. Stevens's *Canonica* poems were first printed as a sequence in *The Southern Review* in 1938. They subsequently became the first 12 poems in *Parts of a World* (1942). Graham's 'Sea-Blue Aubade' shares its 'doctrine', 'doctor', 'freedom', and 'an ox', as well as its early morning setting, with 'The Latest Freed Man', and the lines '⌈o⌉utside, slowly, the grapes seem fatter', 'wherever an eye falls', and 'smokes through the blues', are close to the words of 'On the Road Home'. Bonnie Costello remarks that '"Sea-Blue Aubade" recalls several poems from *Parts of a World*, where meaning-generating mind (the "doctor" of "doctrine" in Stevens) confronts the unformed morning' ('Jorie Graham', p. 49). I am grateful to Luke Carson for pointing out and encouraging me to pursue the connection with 'The Latest Freed Man'.

> Tired of the old descriptions of the world,
> The latest freed man rose at six and sat
> On the edge of his bed [..][14]

In Stevens, the sun supplants 'the doctrine of the landscape' and 'ris[es] upon the doctors in their beds'. On waking into its light, the freed man leaves behind 'the old descriptions' and steps out into the strength and fullness of pure being. Stevens holds the self-generating energy of sunlight in the following symmetrical scheme: 'The light he gives – / It is how he gives his light', and the antimetabole that reverses 'light he gives' into 'gives his light' goes on to govern the local organisation of the poem, especially where it touches on edges:

> It was how the sun came shining into his room:
> To be without a description of to be,
> For a moment on rising, at the edge of the bed, to be,
> To have the ant of the self changed to an ox
> With its organic boomings, to be changed
> From a doctor into an ox, before standing up [..][15]

The third line quoted here stabilises the moment of rising around a delicate symmetry, the crux of which is 'bed'. Bed is a kind of visual palindrome: whereas 'Pip', for instance, sounds identical to itself in reverse, 'bed' looks inward from its edges – and in fact the tricky business, for those learning to read, of distinguishing 'b' from 'd', is settled in the happy accident of that little word's showing bedposts at its outer limits.[16] The reverse ordering of 'edge of the bed, to be' pivots on 'bed', with the 'ed' of 'edge' mirrored in 'be' at the end of the line. This small balancing act tropes the discourse of centrality and self-generation that is this poem's theme, so putting its rhetorical energy towards the fullness and plenitude imagined for the freed man towards its end:

> It was everything being more real, himself
> At the centre of reality, seeing it.
> It was everything bulging and blazing and big in itself [..].[17]

Whereas we saw Graham's aubade exploiting and dwelling on lyric interference, in having the punning surface of its language at odds

---

[14] Stevens, *Collected Poetry and Prose*, p. 187.
[15] Ibid.
[16] An exact visual palindrome would not be 'bed', but 'bid'.
[17] Stevens, *Collected Poetry and Prose*, p. 187.

with sense, Stevens's centralising schemes (antimetabole, chiasmus) cooperate with what 'The Latest Freed Man' proclaims. And Stevens's poem *is* more transparently discursive than Graham's, straightening out towards its end into anaphoric self-summary:

> It was how he was free. It was how his freedom came.
> It was being without description, being an ox.[18]

For Stevens 'the edge of the bed' marks an instant in time and a hinge in space from which the heroic 'freed man' strides forth, bathed by the sun in a moment of conversion from imprisoning doctrine to 'being without description', in a poetics revived from tiredness to 'bulging and blazing' plenitude. 'On the Road Home', the other *Canonica* poem from which Graham borrows, also ends in superlatives of sphericity and fullness, having marked the moments at which things were transformed:

> It was when I said
> 'There is no such thing as the truth,'
> That the grapes seemed fatter.[19]

In Graham the dawn is more gradual: her line, 'Outside, slowly, the grapes seem fatter' ('Sea-Blue Aubade') is reminiscent of Stevens, but differently paced. '[S]lowly', and the commas that keep the sentence in check, illustrate a holding back that is characteristic of Graham and especially of her dawn songs. Whereas these two poems of Stevens satisfy themselves in the freedom and fullness beyond the transformative instants on which they hinge, the body of 'Sea-Blue Aubade' is detained for longer in its transitional state by the fabric of its verbal materials: in this aubade, being 'caught up in the weavings of freedom' is an entangled and protracted business. In its second half, 'Sea-Blue Aubade' puts to sea, and in this phase its densely punning idiom weighs against the 'freedom' the lines ostensibly speak:

> all of the freedom swirling and slapping round the keel, the here,
> foaming round, as feelings – and still the pitch of the dawn
> grasping at transparence [..].[20]

'Pitch' pulls back towards the blackness before dawn, while also throwing (pitching) forward, and that very motion is replicated in the

---

[18]   Ibid.
[19]   Ibid.
[20]   Graham, *The Errancy*, p. 43.

pitch of a boat, a bilious see-saw both settled and prolonged by 'still'. All this 'grasps at transparence' while simultaneously doing precisely the opposite, because transparent sense and linguistic density are pitched here in direct competition.

In 'Sea-Blue Aubade', then, the surface frictions of language, its accidental coincidences and clottings, catch in the ear and anchor the verse against discursive progress. Graham has herself spoken of the way her poetry pits the unit of the poetic line against what she calls 'the swift scary suction of the sentence', a tension borne out by the noncoincidence of verse and sense units that I have identified in 'Sea-Blue Aubade', and more generally in an aversion to linear trajectories and end-directed narratives that is well known to Graham's critics.[21] In the same 1987 interview, Graham drew a connection between 'the way the sentence operates [...] and notions like ending-dependence and eschatological thinking. With ideas like manifest destiny, westward expansion. Imperialisms of all kinds'.[22] Whatever you think of this sweeping conflation of linguistic structure, historical narrative, and ideology, Graham's preference for stays against time, for 'forms of delay, digression, side-motions', is legible in part as a symptom *of* its time. 'It's *late* in history, after all', Graham claims, and the delaying tactics familiar in her poetry bespeak that *fin-de-siècle* mood others have identified as peculiar to the end of the twentieth century.[23]

The Errancy, published at the eve of the millennium, shows symptoms of belatedness and fatigue. 'The Guardian Angel of the

---

[21]   Thomas Gardner, 'An Interview with Jorie Graham' (1987), in *Regions of Unlikeness: Explaining Contemporary Poetry* (Lincoln: University of Nebraska Press, 1999), p. 219. Of the many Graham poems that think about and play with delay, see especially 'Orpheus and Eurydice', 'Self-Portrait as Apollo and Daphne', and 'Self-Portrait as Hurry and Delay' in Jorie Graham, *The Dream of the Unified Field: Selected Poems 1974–1994* (Manchester: Carcanet, 1996), pp. 58, 70, 80.

[22]   Gardner, 'Interview', p. 218.

[23]   Ibid., p. 217. For Graham as a *fin-de-siècle* poet, see Helen Vendler, '*Fin-de-siècle* Lyric: W. B. Yeats and Jorie Graham', in *Fins de Siècle: English Poetry in 1590, 1690, 1790, 1890, 1990*, ed. Elaine Scarry (Baltimore: Johns Hopkins University Press, 1995). Forrest Gander describes Graham's turn-of-the-century exhaustion in his review of *The Errancy*: see 'Listening for a Divine Word: Review of *The Errancy*', in *Jorie Graham: Essays on the Poetry*, ed. Thomas Gardner (Madison: University of Wisconsin Press, 2005), pp. 75–81. For an account of what he calls 'the cultural psychopathology of lateness' and its particular symptoms at the turn of the millennium, see Martin L. Davies, 'The Lateness of the World, or How to Leave the Twentieth Century', in *Romancing Decay: Ideas of Decadence in European Culture*, ed. Michael St. John (Aldershot: Ashgate, 1999), pp. 247, 253–55.

Little Utopia', for example, inhabits a lofty sphere, 'the tireless altitudes of the created place', but her fussy rearrangements ('and I have arranged the flowers for you / again') make that removed space feel stuffy with memories of Eliot.[24] Like 'Portrait of a Lady' ('You have the scene arrange itself – as it will seem to do – / With "I have saved this afternoon for you"'), this poem puts on stage a hostess with bohemian airs, her tiresome fussing with the décor signalling an aesthetic project too consciously 'arranged' to come to life.[25] The title poem of Graham's book is self-thwarting in a different way. 'The Errancy' looks down from a vantage point 'upon the hill' as though having arrived at Winthrop's prophesied city, as it were looking back over the visionary errand that had brought it to that utopian place.[26] The poem's retrospective survey eventually comes full circle to quote towards its end some lines from its beginning:

> towards the little town on the hill – the *crystal-formation?* –
> how long ago was it we said that? do you remember? –
> and now that you've remembered – and the distance we've
> traveled – and where we were, then – and
> how little we've found – aren't we tired?[27]

In this rearward glance 'The Errancy' gets the measure of the time and space it has so far taken up in being 'put down', and it is in this reworking of its own stuff that we find both the cause and symptom of a particular kind of exhaustion. In these and other instances Graham's poems wear themselves out and hold themselves in check by perpetual commentary on their own meanings, so that you might even catch yourself nodding with these lines later in the 1997 book: 'The reader is tired. / I am so very tired'.[28]

Given this lassitude, and the lateness of the times, it makes sense that Graham should resort to a quintessentially early subgenre: the aubade not only belongs to the first part of the day, but also lays claim to first place in chronologies of European literary history.[29]

---

[24] Graham, *The Errancy*, p. 1.

[25] T. S. Eliot, *The Poems*, ed. Christopher Ricks and Jim McCue, 2 vols (London: Faber, 2015), I, p. 10.

[26] Graham, *The Errancy*, p. 4.

[27] Ibid., p. 6.

[28] Graham, 'That Greater Than Which Nothing', in *The Errancy*, p. 50.

[29] Ezra Pound, for example, tells us that '[r]omance literature begins with a Provencal "Alba", supposedly of the Tenth Century', in *The Spirit of Romance* (New York: New Directions, 1968 [1910]), p. 11. For a worldwide history of

But whereas in Stevens morning supplies refreshment in the form of a new way of being, my contention is that the risings in Graham's aubades derive their energy from those very mechanisms that delay their forward progress, and from a state of inattention that is *akin* to the weariness of their time. 'The Errancy' ends like this: 'dread fatigue, and drowsiness like leavening', so prompting the thought that tiredness itself might supply the enlivening ingredient – the raising agent – for a worn-out poetic practice, while the closing passage of the gridlocked poem 'So Sure of Nowhere ...' observes the mid-air motion of a plastic grocery bag – an instance of 'utter particularity' – as it 'ris[es] on the widening circles of accumulating exhaust'.[30] Late modern exhaustion, then, is not a dead end, nor merely a waste product in Graham. In her aubades the half-conscious state of the waking mind, caught up with the sounds, shapes, and schemes that accumulate in its own and its predecessors' language, jams up the traffic in sense; yet it is in and on this mood of distraction, and by means of these stallings, that unintended by-products can arise.

Graham's thinking through the vexed relationship between time and lyric comes out in a different way in 'Spelled from the Shadows Aubade', and especially in its whispered conversation with two crepuscular poems – Stevens's 'Martial Cadenza' and Hopkins's 'Spelt from Sybil's Leaves' – poems which are themselves transfixed by temporality, and in Hopkins's case, with endings.[31] Wallace Stevens's 'Martial Cadenza' is a poem of evening poised on the brink of great change. Stevens wrote it in the autumn of 1939, shortly after the invasion of Poland, and as Alan Filreis has elegantly shown, it captures the isolationist mood of the years preceding Pearl Harbor. This was a mood that lasted no longer in Stevens than it did in the wider American sphere, but for its brief time it produced what Filreis calls 'an American paradox: intensely focused indecision' of which 'Martial Cadenza' shows symptoms.[32] This pressing historical circumstance having been loudly announced and immediately distanced in the conscious archaism of its title, 'Martial Cadenza' begins in and about repetition:

---

dawn poetry, see *Eos: An Enquiry into the Theme of Lovers' Meetings and Partings at Dawn*, ed. Arthur T. Hatto (The Hague: Mouton, 1965). This magisterial volume offers an outline of the Alba tradition (pp. 75–82).

[30]   Graham, *The Errancy*, p. 13.

[31]   Ibid., p. 34.

[32]   Alan Filreis, *Wallace Stevens and the Actual World* (Princeton: Princeton University Press, 1991), p. 12.

Only this evening I saw again low in the sky
The evening star, at the beginning of winter, the star
That in spring will crown every western horizon,
Again ... as if it came back, as if life came back,
Not in a later son, a different daughter, another place,
But as if evening found us young, still young,
Still walking in a present of our own.[33]

'Again' refers to the daily cycle (the star comes back each evening) and to the larger turn of the year: it promises a rising in the West, a spring beyond the dark time that lies immediately ahead. Yet in these periodic returns no time will pass; these repetitions 'shall maintain' a perpetual present. What Stevens later in the poem calls 'the present close, the present realised' is not the winter of 1939; rather, he finds in this lyric a form of refreshment that keeps things circulating without moving them on, sealing off speaker and nation so that on reading 'Martial Cadenza' we find them 'still walking in a present of [their] own'. Graham's 'Spelled from the Shadows Aubade' takes up the words and the formal repetitions of 'Martial Cadenza' and brings them into a different circumstance and an altered mood more than half a century later. The poem begins in a similar-sounding place to Stevens's:

Trying to whisper *life came back*, the light came back.
It harshed-up the edges of the window-shade, curling its rims,
the room still grainy, dimpling,
and shinglings of shadows, layerings.[34]

'Life came back', the phrase picked up from 'Martial Cadenza', is italicised but unacknowledged in Graham's notes, as when, on the point of waking, a half-remembered saying muddles its way through from sleep, its tone weighty but unplaceable, its origin lost.[35] Such bits of language sink Eurydice-like into oblivion the moment the waking mind turns to meet them. In this instance 'life came back' stammers into 'light came back', losing in that translation the Stevensian mode of repetition whose power was in keeping things as they are. Stevens comes back again, and again in a kind of translation, later in 'Spelled from the Shadows Aubade':

---

[33] Stevens, *Collected Poetry and Prose*, p. 217.
[34] Graham, *The Errancy*, p. 34.
[35] Graham's notes to *The Errancy* do acknowledge Stevens as the source of some lines in 'Oblivion Aubade'. They are from 'The Auroras of Autumn'.

Oh not as if evening had found me.
Or even the winter   rushing.
Get up, get up. You are to walk and talk again, and breathe,
    and move.
And breathe.
Any manner of *want*, any world will do – any tint of mind –
lift up the shade.[36]

This breaks up and reassembles some lines from 'Martial Cadenza', and changes their mood by changing their tone. Stevens's isolationist poem ended with the return of its beginning:

Only this evening I saw it again,
At the beginning of winter, and I walked and talked
Again, and lived and was again, and breathed again
And moved again and flashed again, time flashed again.[37]

The lyrical work of Stevens's Cadenza has been to transform hesitation into incantation, fixing its stargazer in an ageless space that is dense with, and calmed by, repetition. In Graham's aubade Stevens's words come through instead as imperatives ('You are to walk and talk again, and breathe, and move'). 'Harshed-up', as it were, from their quieting sense at the close of 'Martial Cadenza', these lines in Graham break in on the privacy of the aubade as though in rude retort to the isolationist mood of their predecessor. 'Lift up the shade', demands this urgent voice, let in the light, break the lyric spell.[38]

As though deaf to the watchman's wake-up call, rather than raising the shade, Graham's speaker tries instead to decipher what's out there from the shapes cast on it:

it is nice in here, in the blur,
in the year, and then the year, in the sleep where nothing's won,
or lost, the shade leaking its ancient storyline,

---

[36]   Graham, *The Errancy*, p. 34.
[37]   Stevens, *Collected Poetry and Prose*, p. 217.
[38]   Thomas J. Otten argues that the latex shade in this poem offers a material instance of Graham's 'blanks', a form of 'mediation [..] thickened into matter'. Noting further instances of latex elsewhere in *The Errancy*, he goes on, '[h]ence, latex substantiates a link between inner and outer, between a "tint of mind" and the objects the mind takes in' ('Jorie Graham's ____s', in *Jorie Graham: Essays on the Poetry*, ed. Thomas Gardner (Madison: University of Wisconsin Press, 2005), pp. 193, 194).

shadows of flags – or are they birds – flapping across it now
    and then,
or maybe banners where the strong go by,
or clouds, or shrivelings of place, late leaves just now torn free,
or calculations tossed by a profounder logic – green? –
    I couldn't
tell from here.[39]

Like a willing prisoner of Plato's cave, this drowsy thinker hazards
some readings of the shadows that pass before her. The relaxed tone
of this spelling out ('or are they [..] / or maybe [..] / or [..]')
contrasts markedly with that of the poem most obviously summoned
in Graham's title. 'Spelled from the Shadows Aubade' works in the
aftermath of 'Spelt from Sibyl's Leaves', Hopkins's crepuscular poem
of death and judgement which he called 'the longest sonnet ever
made'.[40] Graham's 'Spelled from the Shadows Aubade' wonders idly
how to read the shades of early morning, whereas Hopkins's tortured
telling spells death and judgement from the signs of evening's fall.
In 'Spelt from Sybil's Leaves', evening is 'over us', poised above and
finished, 'her dapple is at end'. The fading light foreshadows our
inevitable end:

> Lét life, wáned, ah lét life wínd
> Off hér once skéined stained véined varíety | upon, áll on twó
>   spools; párt, pen, páck
> Now her áll in twó flocks, twó folds – bláck, white; | ríght,
>   wrong; réckon but, réck but, mínd
> But thése two; wáre of a wórld where bút these | twó tell, éach
>   off the óther; of a ráck
> Where, selfwrung, selfstrung, sheathe- and shelterless, |
>   thoúghts agáinst thoughts ín groans grínd.[41]

To 'pen' is to separate sheep from goats and to spell things out in
black and white; thus in our endings variety spools off into twoness,
and difference abolishes shade. And yet, as always with lyric, and
especially in Hopkins, the language plays for both sides, so that we
hear, as Eric Griffiths sharply puts it, 'th[e] strain between texture

---

[39] Graham, *The Errancy*, p. 35.
[40] Gerard Manley Hopkins, *The Major Works*, ed. Catherine Phillips (Oxford: Oxford University Press, 2002), p. 380.
[41] Hopkins, 'Spelt from Sibyl's Leaves', in *The Major Works*, p. 175.

and drift in the sonnet', the punning texture of the writing preserving indecision against the drift of its argument, which is towards black and white.[42] The tortured self in Hopkins's last line is born of such a 'rack', strung out between the two things the language can do. Such a self is both compacted ('selfwrung') and stretched to breaking point ('selfstrung'), yet not able to say, as Larkin later would, that 'One side will have to go'.[43]

Given Graham's resistance to teleological and especially escha-tological thinking, it is no surprise to find her rewinding Hopkins's sonnet, from his penning of black and white back into the penumbral state of shady transition. Against Hopkins's self-torturing 'these | twó tell, éach off the óther', Graham's speaker gives up on the business of exegesis: 'I could not tell', she says, and sounds happy to leave it at that. Yet if in her relish of half-light, that careful particu-larity over indistinction ('the room still grainy, dimpling, / and shinglings of shadows, layerings'), Graham shows herself still the student of Hopkins, his sonnet also teaches a harsher lesson: 'Spelled from the Shadows Aubade' knows that there is something a bit too comfortable in 'the sleep where nothing's won, or lost'. Its speaker may say 'it is nice in here, in the blur', but in letting us hear the complacency of that voice, the poem acknowledges that a late modern distaste for binaries can seem an excuse for fuzzy thinking. Graham's aubades, then, may keep themselves 'braced against morning', and so trope lyric's capacity to delay time along the same lines that their close-textured language impedes discursive sense. But to my hearing, the tone of 'Spelled from the Shadows Aubade' suggests that verse cannot supply a permanent retreat from the discourses that matter in the outside world, nor the transactions made and the conflicts aired in them. What I want to show now is that the punning textures of Graham's aubades, even as they hold back from transparency, also, paradoxically, facilitate crossings between the lovers' chamber and the wider world.

According to the tradition of the aubade, morning brings 'sweet division' to lovers, and discord on a larger scale. What lies outside the comfort of the lovers' lofty room is most often war. Louis MacNeice's brusque 1934 'Aubade' sums this up:

[42]   Eric Griffiths, *The Printed Voice of Victorian Poetry* (Oxford: Oxford University Press, 1989), p. 319.

[43]   Philip Larkin, 'Aubade', in *The Complete Poems*, ed. Archie Burnett (London: Faber, 2012), p. 116.

What have we after that to look forward to?

Not the twilight of the gods but a precise dawn
Of sallow and grey bricks, and newsboys crying war.[44]

William Empson's cryptic 1937 'Aubade' is likewise set against the background of approaching war, this time in a bedroom in Japan, with earthquakes registering inside and out.[45] Shadows of flags or banners play across the shade in Graham's 'Spelled from the Shadows Aubade', and although, to borrow Griffiths's terms, the drift of that aubade is to savour the comfort of staying inside, its texture says something else. This comes through in a small stirring of 'arms':

Across the shade now hands without arms – a picnic of bits –
    generations of
seeds – or are they wings – or instruments – a business deal, an
    alphabet?[46]

Are 'hands without arms' amputated, or peaceable? Do they lack limbs or weapons? This equivocation exploits a coincidence that is easily mistaken for a motivated connection. You might idly think that weapons are called arms because of the way they are carried; but arms in the sense of limbs has an Old English root, whereas defensive armaments derive from the Latin *arma*. In the lovers' room, arms keep twoness wrapped into one, until the watchman's warning to rise and go sounds a call to arms of the other, less comforting kind. Whereas Stevens's 'Martial Cadenza' harks back to 'the silence before the armies', its effort to keep still inside the returning patterns of poetic artifice matching the isolationists' bid to 'stay out' of the war, the verse of Graham's *The Errancy* cannot help but tune into the outside world because its shade, the density of its lyric medium, is exactly where crossing points in the language proliferate, and so where there is traffic – in this case in 'arms' – from the timeless lovers' sphere to the historical noise of weaponry.

The most heavily armed poem in *The Errancy* is not an aubade, but it does end in a rising. 'The Scanning' begins on a busy highway with travellers searching for radio stations:

---

[44] Louis MacNeice, 'Aubade', in *Collected Poems*, ed. Peter McDonald (London: Faber, 2007), p. 28.

[45] William Empson, 'Aubade', in *Collected Poems* (London: Chatto & Windus, 1955), pp. 48–49.

[46] Graham, *The Errancy*, p. 35.

> After the rain there was traffic behind us like a long kiss.
> [..]
> Meanwhile the stations the scanner glides over, not selecting,
>   hiss –
> islands the heat-seekers missed
> in the large sea of ... And after lunch
> the long-distance starts up pianissimo [..].[47]

This crosses commuter comforts with military manoeuvres, the 'piloting minds' of highway drivers also those of an air force scanning the ground below. 'Islands' in 'the large sea' are just recognisable as something you might dream of while stuck in traffic on a rainy day, even as the suggestion of vacationing 'heat-seekers' is overwritten, because of 'missed', by a stronger implication of missiles. 'After lunch' tries to keep things homely, while 'the long distance' encourages a wider perspective; and, given this context, 'carpet bombing' later in the poem is estranged into a merging of home furnishings with brutal attack from the air – as when, during the first Gulf War, pilot's-eye views relayed in news footage offered an armchair experience of 'precision' bombing. In section 3 of 'The Scanning' the hiss of the radio comes back in the form of a 'mess of geese':

> Maybe two hundred geese – now beginning to stir,
> purring and cooing at my walking among them.
> Groping their armless way, their underneaths greening.
> A slow roiling. As of redundancy.[48]

'Armless' perfectly captures the massing of birds on the ground – 'all shoulder and waddle' – while their hiss recalls the 'piloting mind' that scans the ground prior to arming. At the end of 'The Scanning' this roiling flock takes triumphant wing, the birds' 'unperfectable mess' on the ground lifted on the perfect cadence of wing beats into a legible sign and clear direction: the flying geese become 'a diagram appearing on the air, at arctic heights, / an armoring'. This aeronautic display ('the sky lustrous with the skeleton of the dream / of reason') is unmistakably a national project, emerging as it does from a version of the Great Seal: 'out of the manyness – / a molting of the singular'.

If 'The Scanning' asks us at its end to 'look up' to this bellicose sign of national progress whose teleological drive parallels, according

---

[47]   Ibid., p. 7.
[48]   Ibid., p. 8.

to Graham's alignments, 'the swift scary suction of the sentence', it is
the moment just before that terrifying rise which corresponds to *The
Errancy*'s aubades. Notice, in this earlier passage from 'The Scanning',
the arms:

> what the whole madness led to – the curiosity – viral – here,
> like a sign – thick but clear – here at the bottom of the sedge,
> the city still glimmering over there in the distance,
> but us here, for no reason, where the mass of geese are rousing,
> necessity and circumstance quivering in each other's arms,
> us in each other's arms, or, no, not really.[49]

The utopian project of nationhood ('the city still glimmering') is
glimpsed as yet at the edge of this frame. At its centre is the muddle
of circumstance, held back from reason's abstraction. This is the
unreasonable place where signs are still caught up with their own
substance, and where, as in the lovers' room, 'quivering in each other's
arms' is a peaceable thing to do. What the tradition of the aubade tells
Graham is that this kind of refuge cannot supply a permanent alternative to historical time; and she might have learned that lovers' arms
are always the prelude to more worldly arming from Shakespeare. In
the brief aubade scene in Act 4 of *Antony and Cleopatra*, Antony wakes
and calls his servant:

> ANTONY (*calling*):   Eros! mine armour, Eros!
> CLEOPATRA: Sleep a little.
> ANTONY: No, my chuck. Eros, come, mine armour, Eros![50]

The presence of 'Eros' tempts a slippage of armour and amour, and as
Cleopatra playfully helps to arm her lover, her fiddling with buckles
and grasping the wrong piece of equipment teases him to rise and stay
rather than rise and go. '[T]hou art / The armourer of my heart',
pleads Antony, and tears himself away. It has been noticed before that
in this scene 'the insignia of state affairs [...] infiltrate the language
of love', and the reverse is also true: primed by this amorous leave-
taking, Antony says, 'To business that we love we rise betime, / And
go to't with delight', taking the steel aroused in the bedroom with
him into battle.[51]

---

[49] Ibid., p. 9.
[50] William Shakespeare, *Antony and Cleopatra*, IV.iv.1–3.
[51] Theodore B. Leinwand, '*Coniugium Interruptum* in Shakespeare and Webster',
ELH, 72.1 (2005), 239–97 (p. 245); *Antony and Cleopatra*, IV.iv.20–21.

This foray into arms and armour was occasioned by my trying
to construe the 'hands without arms' that pass across the shade in
Graham's 'Spelled from the Shadows Aubade'. Were the arms in
question limbs or weapons? The answer is not a drowsy 'I couldn't /
tell from here' but crucially that they must be both, because the lyric
medium is where one becomes the other, where a fortuitous resemblance – a pun – makes us attend to language as a conduit between
inner and outer spheres, in the case of 'arms', between private and
public, lovers and warriors, lyric and history. It must follow that
the unreasonable readings cultivated in the poetic sphere will carry
over and infiltrate the discursive modes outside. This, then, is how
Graham's turn-of-the-millennium poetics learns to speak outward as
well as inward, not – or not, to my ear, most persuasively – in direct
references to world events, but by setting off small disturbances of
sense in the sphere of lyric that will resonate beyond it.

When he leaves his love alone, Donne's 'busied man' – whether
he is, like Antony, a lover whose 'business' is soldiering or, like
Stevens, a poet whose day job is as an insurance executive – will
be caught up with worldly transactions and pulled into the sweep
of history.[52] Going out into the day means stepping into time and
narrative, and it means leaving the lover who stays behind to the
solitary contemplation that is the proper domain of lyric. Whereas
the unrecoverable past of the dawn song is blissful unity, then, its
aftermath lies along these divergent paths. But for as long as it
can be made to last, the threshold of the aubade has room for two
subjects, heard dramatically as two voices (as in Chaucer's *Troilus
and Criseyde*, and Shakespeare's *Romeo and Juliet* and *Antony and
Cleopatra*), or, when only one voice is heard, in the inference of
a second person close by in the room (as in Donne's 'The Sunne
Rising' or 'Breake of Day'). Twoness comes through formally in
Empson's 'Aubade' because his is a villanelle that puts the quarrel
over staying and going into its alternating refrain lines ('It seemed
the best thing to be up and go', against 'The heart of standing is
you cannot fly').[53] Even in the most solitary of such songs, Philip
Larkin's 'Aubade', in which death and wardrobes loom the more

---

[52] Donne, 'Breake of Day', in *Complete English Poems*, p. 20. For a compelling
account of 'the daily exchange of darkness for light in Stevens's verse', especially
as it intersected with the rhythms of Stevens's working life, see Stuart M. Sperry,
'Wallace Stevens and Poetic Transformation', *Raritan*, 17.3 (1998), 25–46 (p. 35).

[53] Empson, *Complete Poems*, p. 48.

starkly because its speaker is so steadfastly alone, there is a remnant of coupledom in the dark acknowledgement of mortality:

> what we know,
> Have always known, know that we can't escape,
> Yet can't accept. One side will have to go.[54]

So Larkin's dawn song, like every aubade, anticipates a future more solitary still, in which the lonely self who 'stays' must address a more distant and disembodied 'you', or fall back on talking to himself. I want finally to turn to these matters of twoness and solitude, and to show that the belated condition of lyric utterance in Graham is properly figured not in speech or dialogue, but in listening.

The paradigmatic aubade is surely Act III scene 5 of *Romeo and Juliet*. The following exchange comes from the end of that scene:

> JULIET: Some say the lark and loathèd toad changed eyes.
> O, now I would they had changed voices, too
> Since arm from arm that voice doth us affray,
> Hunting thee hence with hunt's-up to the day.
> O, now be gone! More light and light it growes.
> ROMEO: More light and light, more dark and dark our woes.
> *Enter the Nurse.*[55]

Throughout the scene it is verbal exchange that has held off Romeo and Juliet's separation: '[l]et's talk. It is not day', Romeo says, as though talk were the thing that would keep daylight from them. And yet talk is the very thing that heralds the dawn, because it is the first symptom of twoness. Much though these two may try to hold the dawn at bay with their words, and with their playful wishes that things were other than they are (that larks were nightingales or toads, that daylight were not daylight but a meteor), it is dialogue that foretells the uncoupling of 'arm from arm' and makes plain a less playful exchange:

> JULIET: O, now be gone! More light and light it growes.
> ROMEO: More light and light, more dark and dark our woes.[56]

It was sound rather than light that first woke Romeo: the birdsong that Juliet says 'pierced the fear-full hollow of thine ear' is the conventional inheritor of the watchman's cry. In having the calling of birds

---

[54] Larkin, *Collected Poems*, p. 116.
[55] Shakespeare, *Romeo and Juliet*, III.v.31–37.
[56] Ibid.

as its governing trope, Graham's 'Red Umbrella Aubade' comes down
in the end to a matter of listening. This aubade begins in the wrong
place, at the wrong time, and with the wrong number of people:

> On my way home I hear, somewhere near dawn,
> forged and stamped onto the high air,
>   one bloodshot
> cardinal-call – bejangled clarity gripping firm –.[57]

A single 'I' spoken outdoors sounds as though it has already left the
usual parameters of the aubade, whose conventional starting point
Graham put so squarely in 'Sea-Blue Aubade' ('Dawn [...] / Two in a
room asleep'). It is not this human voice, then, that presides over the
poem; rather the 'cardinal call' sets the note whereby the rest of the
verse unravels. The cardinal bird sends threads of redness through this
aubade to replicate the 'envious streakes' of Romeo and Juliet's dawn,
and its name offers material for anagrammatic play, meeting blood-
redness by another route through 'carnadine' to 'incarnate' and so back
to the carnal encounter of which this dawn song is the aftermath.

The cardinal is not just an early bird but a marker of origin or
firstness: it shares its red plumage with the garb of ecclesiastical
cardinals and so descends from the original sense of cardinal, which
is the principle on which other things hinge. In this way Graham
cross-breeds her aubade with those Romantic lyrics in which the
songs of larks and nightingales serve as figures for wordless oneness
rather than, as the lark does in *Romeo and Juliet*, as intrusions on
it. In Shelley and in Keats, birdsong pours down the music from
which all human song descends but whose transparency no earthly
poet can match. According to this figuration, the lyric's densely
diverting wordiness is a mark of its fallen condition. Yet if the name
of Graham's cardinal bird conjures these pure origins, we must also
remember that the speaker of 'Red Umbrella Aubade' hears a 'cardinal
call' rather than a song; indeed it would be hard to hear the strange
'bejangled' upward inflections of the cardinal bird as music.[58] Perhaps
the cardinal call in this aubade, then, carries something of that
subgenre's prelude and its aftermath, the wordless and timeless song
that precedes all human utterance, and the harsher, less tuneful sound

---

[57] Graham, *The Errancy*, p. 59.
[58] I am grateful to Amy Morris for pointing this out. Sound files of cardinal
calls can be heard at www.soundboard.com/sb/Cardinal_bird_sounds.aspx
[accessed 3 October 2019].

of historical exigency. This sense of before and after takes spatial form in the closing parabola of Graham's 'Red Umbrella Aubade', where two cardinal calls knit into a hemisphere:

> and then the answering call again, the back-and-forth
>   syringed, perfectly
> designate, abyss all around the arc – above, below –
> and the arc not suffering time – unwrinkling everything –
> no dialogue,
> no errancy,
> just the red currency of back and forth. [..]⁵⁹

A larger version of Romeo's 'lark whose notes do beat / The vaulty heaven so high above our heads', this arc abstracts and enlarges the constituents of the dawn song, as though turning the suspended twoness that belongs in the lovers' chamber inside out.⁶⁰ But 'Red Umbrella Aubade' does not end with this atemporal hemisphere, because vaulty heaven is not where written language or human voices belong. The poem ends with a listener confined to mortal ground:

> me in the wide romance of aftermath,
> [..]
> and then an aftertaste, as of ashes, in my mouth,
> from listening –.⁶¹

The aubade is the genre of earliness, and also, insofar as its morning always follows a night before, of aftermath too. To feed on ashes is to taste the lateness of all human language, and so to place Graham's speaker in a line of descent from other Romantic listeners, from Shelley and Keats to Stevens's 'listener, who listens in the snow'.⁶² Having woken and left her lover's room, Graham's speaker is doubly belated, and from that position 'an aftertaste, as of ashes' cannot help but

---

⁵⁹ Graham, *The Errancy*, p. 60.

⁶⁰ Shakespeare, *Romeo and Juliet*, III.v.21–22.

⁶¹ Graham, *The Errancy*, p. 60.

⁶² Stevens, 'The Snow Man', in *Collected Poetry and Prose*, p. 8. Willard Spiegelman surveys references to listening, hearing, and sound across Graham's oeuvre, culminating in her 2002 book *Never*, in his 'Jorie Graham Listening' (in *Jorie Graham: Essays on the Poetry*, ed. Thomas Gardner (Madison: University of Wisconsin Press, 2005), pp. 219–37). Birdsong and the Romantic listeners in whose aftermath Graham writes have an important place in Spiegelman's discussion, though he does not make the distinction I have emphasised, between the sounds of words and what they say.

savour of regret and longing. And yet with the bitter taste of '*ashes in my mouth*' comes texture: if you listen to the sounds of that saying as well as to its symbolic resonance you can hear in it the remnants of '*aftermath*', one more small instance of acoustic materials regenerated in the mouth-ear circuit through which all lyric language must pass. Ashes in the mouth, then, like the granular greyness of all Graham's dawn songs, taste of lateness, but the textured materiality of their sounding offers a medium in which new things can rise.

Jorie Graham's poems have a habit of going repeatedly over the same ground. In *The Errancy* we come again and again across arms, birds, ladders, traffic jams, and shades, and see the same structures and trajectories – from congestion and muddle to triumphant lift-off – built up and dismantled numerous times. Across Graham's larger oeuvre, too, there are obsessive returns to particular myths and mechanisms – to Orpheus's turn and Eurydice's vanishing, or to the vectoring geese in 'The Scanning' whose former incarnation was in an early poem 'The Geese'.[63] This persistence bears witness to the special effort of attention and inattention that seems to have been involved in the making of Graham's verse, and which corresponds to the concentrated way in which her aubades foster distraction. In an interview of 1996, Graham was asked how teaching affected her work as a poet. She answered first by registering the breadth of experience her students had brought through the door, but then added a less positive note to the effect that the 'talking out' involved in pedagogy can prove disabling to poetic practice: 'I need certain things to remain secret from my own conceptual intellect for a poem to actually "happen"', she said.[64] What I have tried to show in this chapter is that it is Graham's listening to what lyric language can do in the voices and hands of other poets – Shakespeare, Stevens, Hopkins – that serves to tune out, or at least hold at bay, the things that conceptual intellect might say. This capacity for listening is the means whereby Graham primes her own language so that unforeseen things might happen in it. If the poems in *The Errancy* 'happened' in this sense by accident, that does not mean that they were put together carelessly or without serious purpose. Rather, it is by asking us, in turn, to listen with and also against the grain of their conceptual sense that Graham's poems pass on their learning.

[63] Graham, *The Dream of the Unified Field*, p. 12.
[64] Jorie Graham, 'The Glorious Thing: Jorie Graham and Mark Wunderlich in Conversation', *American Poet* (1996): http://www.poets.org/viewmedia.php/prmMID/15774 [accessed 3 October 2019].

CHAPTER TWO

Hymnody

From Lowell to Riley
in Common Measure

Matthew Sperling

I.

For most literary readers in the twentieth century, the poetry of the English hymn was difficult to admire. Hymns seem to go against many of our most cherished ideas about what it is for poems to be good: they can be conventional in form and phrase, unoriginal in thought and expression, dogmatic in theme, and almost hypnotically monotonous in metre. 'Hymns are usually a second-rate type of poetry', Lord David Cecil wrote in the introduction to his *New Oxford Book of Christian Verse* in 1940, encapsulating the typical post-Romantic view of the matter: '[c]omposed as they are for the practical purposes of congregational singing, they do not provide a free vehicle for the expression of the poet's imagination, his intimate soul'.[1]

In 'Waking Early Sunday Morning' (1965), Robert Lowell versifies several of the major objections to hymns as a literary form, writing not in hymn form but in the eight-line tetrameter couplet stanza perfected by Andrew Marvell. As the speaker of the poem lies in bed in a state of existential crisis, he wonders whether his 'spirit' would be better off somewhere else, and travels in his mind to join the congregation at the local church:

> Better dressed and stacking birch,
> or lost with the Faithful at Church –
> anywhere, but somewhere else!
> And now the new electric bells,

---

[1] Cited in Donald Davie, *The Eighteenth-Century Hymn in England* (Cambridge: Cambridge University Press, 1993), p. 155.

clearly chiming, 'Faith of our fathers,'
and now the congregation gathers.[2]

In the phrase 'lost with the Faithful' and the tawdriness of the 'electric bells', the grounds for Lowell's major theme – the degradation of civic life in mid-century America – are steadily being laid in this stanza. 'Faith of Our Fathers' is an 1849 hymn by Frederick William Faber written in memory of the Catholic martyrs of the English Reformation. Composed in quatrains followed by a two-line couplet refrain repeated at the end of each of its five stanzas, the hymn is, in the words of the great modern scholar of English hymnody, J. R. Watson, 'as tightly bound to generations of Roman Catholics as Wesley's hymns were to the Methodists':[3]

> Faith of our Fathers! living still
>   In spite of dungeon, fire, and sword:
> Oh how our hearts beat high with joy
>   Whene'er we hear that glorious word:
> Faith of our Fathers! Holy Faith!
> We will be true to thee till death.[4]

For Watson, the language of 'Faith of Our Fathers' is 'grandly enthusiastic, but also obviously rhetorical', and in that sense, the hymn is 'fatally undermined by the temper of an age in which [...] there was little scope for such dramatic response'.[5] This seems a fair judgement.

Watson is talking about the 'temper' of the middle of the nineteenth century; by the middle of the twentieth century, the scope for such ardency had diminished even further. By the time Lowell was writing,

[2] Robert Lowell, *Collected Poems*, ed. Frank Bidart and David Gewanter (London: Faber, 2003), pp. 383–86 (p. 384). I take the text as it was printed in *Near the Ocean* (London: Faber, 1967).

[3] J. R. Watson, *The English Hymn: A Critical and Historical Study* (Oxford: Oxford University Press, 1997), p. 366. Watson's book is the best starting point for study of the hymn as literary form; other valuable books not cited elsewhere in this chapter include *An Annotated Anthology of Hymns*, ed. J. R. Watson (Oxford: Oxford University Press, 2002); *Dissenting Praise: Religious Dissent and the Hymn in England and Wales*, ed. Isabel Rivers and David L. Wykes (Oxford: Oxford University Press, 2011); and Kirstie Blair, *Form and Faith in Victorian Poetry and Religion* (Oxford: Oxford University Press, 2012).

[4] Frederick W. Faber, *Jesus and Mary: Or Catholic Hymns* (London: James Burns, 1849), pp. 133–34 (p. 133).

[5] Watson, *The English Hymn*, pp. 366–67.

the strident repetition of Faber's first-person plural ('our' and 'we' occur five times in those six lines) must have seemed a bogus attempt to shore up a vanished commonality; the Faithful are all 'lost' in Lowell's congregation. In the next stanza, 'Faith of Our Fathers' gives rise to a consideration of all that can be poetically bad about hymns:

> O Bible chopped and crucified
> in hymns we hear but do not read,
> none of the milder subtleties
> of grace or art will sweeten these
> stiff quatrains shovelled out four-square –
> they sing of peace, and preach despair.[6]

Here the major charges against the hymn are all in place: it is a form which is both parasitic upon and inadequate in regard to scripture; it doesn't stand up to reading as a literary text; it is lacking in subtlety and artfulness; it is metrically and formally indifferent and uninspiring; it is depressing, in spite of its supposedly uplifting message.

The couplet at the end of Lowell's stanza, however, shifting from the present to the past tense, gives us a turn. Notwithstanding their lack of subtlety and artfulness, it seems to say, hymns still have a peculiar force:

> yet they gave darkness some control,
> and left a loophole for the soul.[7]

The hymn, then, has (or at least had) some quality or capacity about it; it was a useful and specifically *useable* form of words, a spiritual tool. A 'loophole' is a weakness in a legal system that can be exploited by somebody wanting to circumvent the intention of the system, but etymologically it was the arrow slit in the castle wall out of which the defending soldier could shoot at assailants who could not shoot back at him. Lowell's image combines weakness and strength in a way that captures well the mixed qualities and defects of the hymn.

If religious hymns were for Lowell lacking in 'the milder subtleties' of art, Ralph Waldo Emerson's 'Hymn: Sung at the Completion of the Concord Monument, April 19, 1836', thereafter generally known as 'The Concord Hymn', a poem looking back to the beginnings of the American Revolution, was conversely one of his favourite poems, a lifelong touchstone:

---

[6] Lowell, *Collected Poems*, p. 384.
[7] Ibid.

By the rude bridge that arched the flood,
  Their flag to April's breeze unfurled,
Here once the embattled farmers stood,
  And fired the shot heard round the world.

The foe long since in silence slept;
  Alike the conqueror silent sleeps;
And Time the ruined bridge has swept
  Down the dark stream which seaward creeps.[8]

For Lowell, the 'conscious, urbane exaggeration' of the line 'the shot heard round the world' shows how Emerson 'always maintains an ironic and urbane distance from the Concord farmers who themselves simply thought they were out-shooting the English tax collectors'. The poem 'becomes more internal as it goes on', and this, for Lowell, is where its 'freshness, gentleness and calmness' come from.[9] Taken like this, Emerson becomes the precursor to Emily Dickinson, the poet who would pre-eminently turn adapted hymn forms into the vehicle for the most searching, ironic, highly sophisticated experiments in tone of the nineteenth century.[10] Lowell also makes Emerson sound rather like a modernist poet: ironic, self-conscious, and impersonally distanced from his subject matter.

In the contrasting ways he talks about 'The Concord Hymn' and 'Faith of Our Fathers', Lowell sets out the terms for an opposition between hymn and true poem very clearly: whereas the hymn is graceless, artless, unsubtle, bound to false ideas of commonality, and rigid with received ideas, the achieved literary poem that adopts the form of the hymn is self-conscious, ironic, removed from its community, inward-looking, and original. The option of updating hymn form for a modern lyric poem, however, does not seem to have been possible for Lowell himself, as it was for Emerson. Lowell composed his own poem, 'Concord', published first in *Land of Unlikeness* (1944) and then lightly revised in *Lord Weary's Castle*

---

[8] R. W. Emerson, *Poems* (Boston: James Munroe and Company, 1847), pp. 250–51. ('1836', in the poem's first printing, was a slip of Emerson's memory; the dedication of the monument took place in 1837.)

[9] John McCormick, 'Falling Asleep over Grillparzer: An Interview with Robert Lowell' (1953), in *Robert Lowell: Interviews and Memoirs*, ed. Jeffrey Meyers (Ann Arbor: University of Michigan Press, 1988), pp. 23–32 (p. 28).

[10] See Victoria N. Morgan, *Emily Dickinson and Hymn Culture: Tradition and Experience* (Farnham: Ashgate, 2010).

(1946), in response to 'The Concord Hymn': in that poem, Emerson's 'shot heard round the world' is transformed, by a memory irrupting from the violent early history of the United States, into 'The death-dance of King Philip and his scream / Whose echoes girdled this imperfect globe' – but Lowell cast his poem as a sonnet, the most urbane and self-conscious of literary forms.[11]

Just as for Lowell the hymn was a form 'we hear but do not read', so for D. H. Lawrence, the hymn was a preliterary form; yet, as Lawrence wrote in his 1928 essay 'Hymns in a Man's Life', it nonetheless had a personal and cultural power which could be even greater than that of more sophisticated poetry. '[T]he hymns which I learned as a child, and never forget', Lawrence writes, looking back to his religious upbringing in the Nonconformist Congregational Chapel in Eastwood,

> mean to me almost more than the finest poetry, and they have for me a more permanent value, somehow or other. It is almost shameful to confess that the poems which have meant the most to me, [...] which after all give the ultimate shape to one's life; all these lovely poems, woven deep into a man's consciousness, are still not woven so deep in me as the rather banal nonconformist hymns that penetrated through and through my childhood [...] They love and glisten in the depth of the man's consciousness in undimmed wonder, because they have not been subjected to any criticism or analysis.[12]

In this retrospective account, Lawrence claims that he had rejected all articles of religious faith by the age of 16, yet considers the power of these hymns to be a thing apart from these orthodoxies, the 'wonder' of which survives rational questioning.

In his earlier poem 'Piano', Lawrence tried to recapture this sense of wonder mingled with half-understood nostalgia. As the speaker listens to a woman singing, he is transported back to a childhood memory of sitting under the piano as his mother played and sang:

---

[11] Lowell, *Collected Poems*, p. 30. In the two earlier versions of the poem published in *Partisan Review* (1943) and *Land of Unlikeness* (1944), Emerson is mentioned by name: see Lowell, *Collected Poems*, pp. 874, 1152.

[12] D. H. Lawrence, 'Hymns in a Man's Life' (1928), in *The Cambridge Edition of the Works of D. H. Lawrence: Late Essays and Articles*, ed. James T. Boulton (Cambridge: Cambridge University Press, 2004), II, pp. 128–34 (pp. 130, 132).

> In spite of myself, the insidious mastery of song
> Betrays me back, till the heart of me weeps to belong
> To the old Sunday evenings at home, with winter outside
> And hymns in the cosy parlour, the tinkling piano our guide.[13]

In the final lines of the poem, nostalgia and sadness at being cut off from the past and the culture of his childhood overtake the speaker completely, and syntactical composure gives way to a banal comma splice: 'my manhood is cast / Down in the flood of remembrance, I weep like a child for the past'.[14] The poem itself is no hymn (try singing 'the insidious mastery of song' to a hymn tune), yet the rough-and-ready, anapaest-heavy, tripping rhythm provides an approximate counterpart to the speaker's homely memory of amateur hymn-singing to the accompaniment of a beaten-up old piano.[15] Hymns stand for a lost sense of belonging – to the family, to the chapel community, to the domain of the preliterary – which can only be recaptured by giving up maturity and formal sophistication.

II.

And yet one of the most important modern English poet-critics, Donald Davie, took deep interest in eighteenth-century English hymnody, giving it full credit as a sophisticated art. Davie's critical writing on the hymn began with the chapter entitled 'The Classicism of Charles Wesley' in his landmark book *Purity of Diction in English Verse* (1952), and continued for four decades, culminating in his monograph *The Eighteenth-Century Hymn in England* (1993).[16] Already,

---

[13] D. H. Lawrence, 'Piano' (1918), in *The Cambridge Edition of the Works of D. H. Lawrence: The Poems*, ed. Christopher Pollnitz (Cambridge: Cambridge University Press, 2013), I, p. 108.

[14] Ibid.

[15] For more on Lawrence's nonconformist upbringing, see Andrew Harrison, 'Hymns in a Man's Life: The Congregational Chapel and D. H. Lawrence's Early Poetry', in *Ecstasy and Understanding: Religious Awareness in English Poetry from the Late Victorian to the Modern Period*, ed. Adrian Grafe (London: Bloomsbury, 2008), pp. 46–57.

[16] Donald Davie, *Purity of Diction in English Verse and Articulate Energy*, second edition (Manchester: Carcanet, 2006), pp. 61–70; Davie, *The Eighteenth-Century Hymn*. For more on hymns, see Davie's trio of scholarly works published between 1978 and 1982: *A Gathered Church: The Literature of the English Dissenting Interest, 1700–1930* (London: Routledge, 1978), *The New Oxford Book of Christian Verse* (Oxford: Oxford University Press, 1981), and *Dissentient Voice: Enlightenment*

in *Purity of Diction*, many of the essentials of Davie's thinking on the importance of the hymn were in place. There he seeks to rescue the hymns of William Cowper, Charles Wesley, and Isaac Watts from the poetical disrepute into which they have fallen because of the combined effects of the perceived opposition between 'lyrical' and 'didactic' poetry, and 'the long period when religious experience was considered almost exclusively a matter of fervent feeling', which resulted in the belief that religious poetry should not be didactic.[17] Between these two preconceptions, Davie argues, the work of the great hymnodists, which is at once religious, lyrical, and didactic, goes unregarded, even though its qualities of 'prosaic strength, exactness and urbanity' are equal to those of the greatest late Augustan verse.[18]

Davie admits the difficulties for a reader in taking the hymn as a literary genre. First, the reader needs to 'disentangle [...] the appeal which is literary from others which derive from our own religious persuasions, our memory of musical melodies, or even less tangible attractions as childhood associations' (which rules out the Lawrencian view of the 'permanent value' of hymns); second, he or she needs to overcome the 'sense of an unfair advantage enjoyed by the hymn-writer over other poets', in that the urgency of theme and message in the hymn may compensate for a certain 'poverty of expression'.[19] Davie does not deny that a great many hymns, including many by Charles Wesley, are merely competent in their expression. He rather seeks to demonstrate that Wesley's work at its strongest was 'a sophisticated art', and that this sophistication was sponsored by an advantage that he enjoyed over modern-day poets: that he had access to an 'extra poetic dimension' in being able to appeal to a communally held vocabulary of scriptural and ritual conventions.[20] Whereas T. S. Eliot, writing *The Waste Land* (1922), had to synthesise this dimension by supplying his own endnotes each time he wished an allusion to Dante, Baudelaire, or Webster to be detected, Wesley could rely on a deep knowledge of scripture in his readers and congregations, equivalent

---

and Christian Dissent (Notre Dame: University of Notre Dame Press, 1982). The essays from *A Gathered Church* and *Dissentient Voice* were republished together, with some others, in *Essays in Dissent: Church, Chapel, and the Unitarian Conspiracy* (Manchester: Carcanet, 1995).

[17] Davie, *Purity of Diction*, p. 61.
[18] Ibid.
[19] Ibid., p. 62.
[20] Ibid., pp. 63–64.

to the knowledge of Virgil and Horace that Pope or Johnson could expect from their readers – 'the "field of force" lying behind the most apparently guileless of eighteenth-century poems'.[21] These are the grounds for Wesley's very exact, understated verbal effects and what Davie calls his 'urbane tone'.[22]

In describing Wesley's hymns as 'urbane', Davie prefigures the terms in which Robert Lowell would praise Emerson's 'Concord Hymn', while disparaging the 'stiff quatrains' and chopped-up scripture of less subtle hymnodists. Yet Davie's argument is more counterintuitive than Lowell's position: for him, 'Wesley's verse exhibits these virtues *because* it is throughout doctrinal, that is, didactic'.[23] It is not by holding an ironic, self-conscious distance from doctrine that the hymnodist achieves his urbanity, but by addressing doctrine head-on in common language with self-conscious intelligence, so that the 'common word takes on unusual clarity and force':

> In the Methodist chapel, as in the drawing-room, the poet used the language spoken by his hearers. He did not try to heighten, or even, in the first place, to enrich the language, but to sharpen it, to make it more exact and pure, and thereby (paradoxically) more flexible. He seldom used shock tactics. His concern was not to create a distinctive style, but to contribute to a common stock, to safeguard a heritage and to keep it bright as new.[24]

Both the Poundian injunction to 'make it new' and the Eliotic ambition to 'purify the dialect of the tribe' are hovering around Davie's formulations in this beautiful portrait of the hymnodist's happy situation.[25] Pound is quoted in Davie's very next sentence on the classicism of Anatole France, and Eliot's words had been alluded to earlier in the chapter. If Pound's phrase was associated with the first burst of iconoclastic, manifesto-writing modernist vigour, and Eliot's with his later

---

[21] Ibid., p. 64.

[22] Ibid.

[23] Ibid., p. 69 (my italics).

[24] Ibid., p. 70.

[25] Michael North's account of the literary career of the phrase 'make it new' shows that it had only recently been brought into prominence as a slogan by Hugh Kenner in the years when Davie was writing *Purity of Diction* (see *Novelty: A History of the New* (Chicago: University of Chicago Press, 2013), pp. 162–74); T. S. Eliot, 'Little Gidding', in *The Poems of T. S. Eliot*, ed. Christopher Ricks and Jim McCue, 2 vols (London: Faber, 2015), I, p. 205.

turn towards a poetics of community and order, by foreswearing 'shock tactics' and translating 'make it new' into 'keep it bright as new', Davie is clearly siding with late-Eliotic purification over Poundian novelty, as he obliquely expresses much about his own ambitions for English poetry in the early 1950s.

It is no coincidence that Davie conceptualises the virtues of eighteenth-century poetry in terms drawn from the then-recent history of modernism. In a retrospective foreword written for the 1992 reissue of *Purity of Diction* (along with his second book, *Articulate Energy: An Inquiry into the Syntax of English Poetry* (1955)), Davie reflects on the influence that the mid-twentieth-century outlook, and his own ambitions for poetry in the present time, had on his critical writing: for literature in the post-war period, he writes, it was 'a matter of "picking up the pieces"', after the Second World War had 'invalidated even those radically diminished principles and sentiments that had survived the war of 1914–18'.[26] Davie and his contemporaries had to go 'back to basics', offering poetry in an 'austerity package' which later came to seem 'prescriptive and constricting', but which was necessary in a time when the assumptions of the 1920s and 1930s seemed to have collapsed.[27] For poets in Davie's time and after, the confidence in a common stock of language and reference that a Methodist hymn writer could have in 1750, was, and is, impossible. The sense of a coherent linguistic community, to whom the poet could speak in their own language, had to be reconstructed, even if it had more reality in the poet's mind than in the world.

The poetry of the great eighteenth-century hymnodists suits Davie's presentist polemical purposes, since he is a poet who could refer to himself with considerable urbane irony in 'Homage to William Cowper' as a 'pasticheur of late-Augustan styles'.[28] *Purity of Diction* is often taken to be the manifesto or poetics manual for what would become known as 'the Movement'. There is some truth in this, although Davie's speculative reach and his engagement with Russian poetry by Pasternak and Mandelstam and with American experimental work by Ezra Pound and Edward Dorn clearly set him apart from the narrower stringencies of Philip Larkin or Kingsley Amis. The idea that the poet should use 'the language spoken by his hearers', not trying to 'heighten'

---

[26] Davie, *Purity of Diction*, p. x.

[27] Ibid., pp. x–xi.

[28] Donald Davie, *Collected Poems*, ed. Neil Powell (Manchester: Carcanet, 2002), p. 8.

or 'enrich' it, not using 'shock tactics', but trying to 'contribute to a common stock': this is the starting point for Davie's own poetry, on which the influence of his absorption in the English hymn is palpable.

Although he writes in hymn-like tetrameter quatrains in a number of poems, the true influence of hymns on Davie's earlier poetry is felt more at the level of diction and dispersed throughout his work. Long before Davie published critical books entitled *A Gathered Church* (1978) and *Dissentient Voice* (1982), for instance, he published the poetic sequence 'Dissentient Voice' (1957), of which 'A Gathered Church' is the fourth section; and in this sequence he exhibits the full range of his urbane command upon the range of precise yet plain-spoken English, finding occasion to address the same religious histories he was engaged with as a critic:

> Watts thought his church, though scant of privilege,
> Walled in its own communion. In its walks
> Some may have doubted if so sparse a hedge
> Tempered the blast to blooms still on their stalks.[29]

Pertinent here is Davie's remark, in a note written in 1957, that his poems were mostly 'not natural poems' because 'the thought in them could have been expressed – at whatever cost in terseness and point – in a non-poetic way'.[30] These lines from 'A Gathered Church' are versified non-fiction about the history of English Dissent, labouring its way into poetic embodiment by sensuous images. The whole of 'Dissentient Voice' – a poem which is very much 'about' something, and full of information and argument, in the way that a hymn is full of doctrine – shows well how this inclination can be converted into strength as much as limitation.

In the late poem 'After Watts' from the posthumously published *Poems and Melodramas* (1996), Davie returns much more directly to the eighteenth-century hymn as poetic inspiration, effectively composing a perfect neo-Augustan hymn in short metre (6-6-8-6):

> Behold! what wondrous grace
>   The Father has bestow'd
> On sinners of a mortal race –
>   To call them sons of God![31]

[29]   Ibid., pp. 50–54 (p. 53).
[30]   Ibid., p. 608.
[31]   Ibid., pp. 598–99.

In the 1950s, Davie's task had been to reconstruct a coherent linguistic community in the present day, to which the poet might address himself in a common language, as the eighteenth-century hymnodist did, only for Davie to find by the end of the 1960s that the actually existing literary community of his country had little use for his addresses, precipitating his departure to Stanford in 1968. Two decades later, in 'After Watts' we find him skipping the troublesome task of imagining a present-day community of readers and travelling in time to address himself directly to the 'common stock' of eighteenth-century nonconformists. In the conclusion to his critical book *The Eighteenth-Century Hymn in England*, published just a few years before *Poems and Melodramas*, Davie had written, in a pose of wry regret, that 'the clock is not to be put back' on literary history: 'the Romantic Movement has irreversibly happened', so that even readers who 'may subscribe themselves "modernist" or "post-modernist", proceed on Romantic suppositions' which inevitably 'obstruct the entrance to Watts' hymns'.[32] Davie the critic may not be able to put back the clock; in 'After Watts', however, Davie the poet achieves it at the very end of his writing life by a wilful act of straight-faced historical pastiche, turning out the finest eighteenth-century hymn of the twentieth century.

III.

When a modern lyric poem mimics, alludes to, or describes itself as a hymn, presenting itself as adhering to conventions established within a known linguistic community, its true work takes place in the gap between the fiction of community and the actual, fractured relations between the language of the poet and of his or her society.

If Davie's *Purity of Diction* was the manifesto of the Movement, the hymn-like poems written by the greatest poet of the Movement, Philip Larkin, seem to take on board the point that the poet should use 'the language spoken by his hearers', but to subject the idea that he should 'contribute to a common stock' or 'safeguard a heritage' to wilful and joyous vandalism. Foremost is 'This Be the Verse' (1971):

> They fuck you up, your mum and dad.
> They may not mean to, but they do.

---

[32] Davie, *The Eighteenth-Century Hymn*, pp. 155–56.

> They fill you with the faults they had
> And add some extra, just for you.[33]

The immediate source of the title is in Robert Louis Stevenson's 'Requiem': '[t]his be the verse you grave for me'.[34] But as John Osborne suggests in *Radical Larkin*, the expression also 'designates the church and chapel practice of citing on wall or pulpit the biblical chapter and verse to be explicated in that day's sermon', where 'hymn numbers were also displayed'.[35] The poem itself is written in perfect long metre (quatrains of iambic tetrameter rhyming ABAB), composed entirely of monosyllables save for one word, with thumpingly emphatic end rhymes. In hymn metres, one song may be sung to the tune of another – 'This Be the Verse' has been set to music many times – and here Larkin plays the conventions of hymnody for laughs by adhering to them metrically while transgressing them thematically and tonally. In Osborne's words, 'religious rhetoric is being marshalled to rewrite Christian metaphysics', taking the concept of original sin transmitted by procreation but stripping it of 'both its Edenic prelapsarianism and its paradisal redemption'.[36]

Larkin's other hymn-like poem – the only one he explicitly named as a hymn – was circulated privately in letters, but now takes its place in the canon of his work in the extensive selection of 'Poems not published in the poet's lifetime' included in Archie Burnett's 2012 edition of *The Complete Poems*. In a letter to Robert Conquest dated 26 May 1976, Larkin wrote: '[t]he latest campaign is for "the right to work", i.e. the right to get £70 a week for doing bugger all. It's led me to begin a hymn'. Almost three years later, he quoted the first four lines of the same poem in a letter to Kingsley Amis on 10 February 1979, describing it as a 'dreary little hymn', and did so once again in a letter to Colin Gunner on 30 July 1980.[37] This is the first stanza of the untitled 'dreary little hymn' now known after its first line as 'I want to see them starving':

---

[33]   Philip Larkin, *The Complete Poems*, ed. Archie Burnett (London: Faber, 2012), p. 88.

[34]   See the editorial matter in Larkin, *The Complete Poems*, p. 463.

[35]   John Osborne, *Radical Larkin: Seven Types of Technical Mastery* (London: Palgrave Macmillan, 2014), p. 174.

[36]   Ibid.

[37]   Larkin, *The Complete Poems*, p. 652; and Larkin, *Selected Letters: 1940–1985*, ed. Anthony Thwaite (London: Faber, 1999), pp. 541–42 and 595.

> I want to see them starving,
> The so-called working class,
> Their weekly wages halving,
> Their women stewing grass.[38]

These were lines intended only for private eyes, but the fact that Larkin thought them worth repeating three times, spread across more than four years, suggests the prominence they had in his mind. Larkin engages hymn form, the traditional site for poetic voicings of community and shared belief, at the moment of his greatest contempt for the common; the formal tension between the melodious tune and the reactionary message gives the poem its force.

Like Donald Davie, Geoffrey Hill has taken the poetic claims of eighteenth-century hymnody very seriously. In the essay 'The Weight of the Word' (1991), he numbers 'the great hymns of Watts and Charles Wesley' among those works in which 'we may receive, at any instant, a sense of things inaccessible suddenly made accessible, where grammar and desire are miraculously at one', in a 'sustained moment of communion between the two kinds of eloquence and appre-hension' – the studied and the spontaneous.[39] In Charles Wesley's work, he writes, 'the "peculiar edge" of the writing is the line which reason draws between enthusiasm and grace [...] which separates the "delicious relish" of spiritual self-regard from the experiential relish of the awakened heart discovering, or recovering, its true temper' and gives his greatest hymns their 'effect of perfect balance'.[40] But Hill also shows how the hymnodist can lose his verbal balance and slip off the edge, when he quotes two 'wretched' lines from John Wesley's 'Rock of Israel, Cleft for Me' ('Now, even now, we all plunge in, / And drink the purple wave'), and remarks:

> I think it entirely possible for a hymn to be, at one and the same time, joyful and 'unhappy'; that kind of oxymoron is inherent in the creative matter, the ganglion of language and circumstance from which the piece of divine poetry is created.[41]

---

[38] Larkin, *The Complete Poems*, p. 317.

[39] Geoffrey Hill, 'Weight of the Word', in *Collected Critical Writings*, ed. Kenneth Haynes (Oxford: Oxford University Press, 2008), pp. 349–65 (p. 349). Hill's essay is a review of Isabel Rivers, *Reason, Grace and Sentiment: A Study of the Language of Religion and Ethics in England 1660–1780*, volume 1 ('Whichcote to Wesley') (Cambridge: Cambridge University Press, 1991).

[40] Hill, *Collected Critical Writings*, p. 361.

[41] Ibid.

Each of these observations shows how much is at stake, for Hill, in taking the English hymn as a literary form; in identifying their instances of verbal felicity and infelicity, he credits the best English hymns with being capable of gathering the same poetic power as the great religious poems of Donne or Herbert.

Hill's critical interest in the hymn has shown itself in his poetry too, but perhaps not in the expected way. Although he has named two of his major poetic sequences 'hymns' – *Mercian Hymns* (1971) and 'Hymns to Our Lady of Chartres' (1982/2012) – neither has very much formally or linguistically in common with the English hymn.[42] There are, of course, many kinds of poem or song which we might call a 'hymn', most of which this chapter has not touched on (Homeric hymns, Hebrew psalms, Sanskrit Vedas), as well as poems called 'hymns' which have little or no connection to congregational singing, such as Donne's 'Hymne to God my God, in my sicknesse' (1623) or Shelley's 'Hymn to Intellectual Beauty' (1816), which is really an ode. Hill's two great sequences of 'hymns' fall into this class; they are works whose titles propose what Hugh Haughton calls a 'fraught structural analogy between poems and musical compositions', and which then immediately complicate the analogy further.[43] The numbering and sequencing of *Mercian Hymns* recall a hymn book; the roll call of names for King Offa at the beginning of the sequence ('King of the perennial holly-groves, the riven sandstone: overlord of the M5 [..]') recalls the naming function of hymns, by which the *I-Thou* relationship between singer and God is established.[44] The presentation of *'the Argument'* in prose on the title page of the revised 'Hymns to Our Lady of Chartres' ('that the doctrine of the Immaculate Conception of the Blessed Virgin in the womb of Anna [..] is a sentimental late intrusion that infantilizes faith') parodically recalls the traditional relationship between the words of a hymn and the doctrines and scriptural sources which precede and exist outside of it.[45] But both sequences immediately range far beyond the idea of hymn form defined in the golden age of English hymnody – as we would expect from a poet with a deep sense of the

[42] Geoffrey Hill, *Broken Hierarchies: Poems 1952–2012*, ed. Kenneth Haynes (Oxford: Oxford University Press, 2013), pp. 81–112, 155–68.

[43] Hugh Haughton, '"Music's Invocation": Music and History in Geoffrey Hill', in *Geoffrey Hill and His Contexts*, ed. Piers Pennington and Matthew Sperling (Oxford: Peter Lang, 2011), pp. 187–211 (p. 187).

[44] Hill, *Broken Hierarchies*, p. 83.

[45] Ibid., p. 155.

fractured nature of the English and European religious inheritance, who nonetheless has an abiding interest in the common.

The short poems of Hill's which do reflect the formal influence of the English hymn also tend to take as much from neo-Latin hymnody. The foremost example is the pair of poems called 'Two Chorale-Preludes: On Melodies by Paul Celan' from *Tenebrae* (1978). A chorale prelude is the organ composition that preceded a hymn in the Protestant liturgy – an art that reached its greatest heights in Germany in the Baroque period. The first poem of the pair, 'Ave Regina Coelorum', takes its title from the Marian hymn beginning with that line ('Hail, O Queen of Heaven'), and is composed in trimeter. The second, 'Te Lucis Ante Terminum', takes its title from the Compline hymn in the Roman breviary ('To Thee before the close of day, / Creator of the world, we pray'), and is, allowing for a few metrical substitutions, composed in what a hymnodist would call long metre (iambic tetrameter quatrains rhyming ABAB):

> immortal transience, a 'kind
> of otherness', self-understood,
> BE FAITHFUL grows upon the mind
> as lichen glimmers on the wood.[46]

These two poems have a sort of lost companion piece in the unpublished poem 'Fauxbordon on a C15th Carol' from 1966, which takes inspiration from the plainchant hymn 'Ave Maris Stella' ('Hail, Star of the Sea'), set to music many times since the ninth century.[47] All of them stand in a dialectical relationship to the commonplace: rhythmical simplicity and clarity rebound upon the self-conscious, intellectual distancing of placing the words 'a kind / of otherness' in inverted commas; the piety of the line 'BE FAITHFUL grows upon the mind' is revoked by presence in the poems of prior texts by Paul Celan, the twentieth-century poet most testing of the ability to keep faith in language. For Hill, the idea of the modern hymn as a poem which can 'contribute to a common stock' and 'safeguard a heritage', in Davie's terms, would be absurdly optimistic; the cultural heritage has almost been destroyed, and the poet is harshly alienated from the unhappy circumstances of civic life. Andrew Duncan acidly

---

[46] Ibid., p. 132.
[47] For the text of this poem and its background, see Matthew Sperling, *Visionary Philology: Geoffrey Hill and the Study of Words* (Oxford: Oxford University Press, 2014), pp. 168–69.

remarks in *The Failure of Conservatism in Modern British Poetry* that Hill is a 'conservative, Christian, stalwart representative of the millions of working-class Tories' who 'has the problem that ordinary conservative readers can't understand him'.[48] The first half of this now looks quite wrong – you would struggle to find Hill's red-Tory attacks on 'plutocratic anarchy' reflected anywhere within the mainstream range of British conservative political opinion – yet the second half contains some truth, and Duncan's next sentence is on the money: 'The Anglican Church is commissioning new hymns, but not from Hill'.[49]

The most recent contemporary poet to draw upon the formal resources of the English hymn, and perhaps the most unexpected, is Denise Riley. Having made an extraordinary return to poetry with the long elegiac poem 'A Part Song' in 2012, after publishing no new work since her *Selected Poems* in 2000, Riley published two poems in 2013 that adapt hymn form to their own purposes with great intelligence and formal awareness.[50] Both are in common measure (8-6-8-6), rhyming ABAB. First came 'Death makes dead metaphor revive', of which this is the last stanza:

> Over its pools of greeny melt
> The rearing ice will tilt.
> To make *rhyme* chime again with *time*
> I sound a curious lilt.[51]

And then came 'You men who go in living flesh', of which this is the first stanza:

> You men who go in living flesh
> Scour clean then drape your souls
> In plumy dress that they may rise
> Clear of those thrashing shoals.[52]

---

[48]   Andrew Duncan, *The Failure of Conservatism in Modern British Poetry* (Cambridge: Salt Publishing, 2003), p. 2.

[49]   Ibid., pp. 2–3.

[50]   Denise Riley, 'A Part Song', *London Review of Books*, 34.3 (9 February 2012), 14.

[51]   Denise Riley, 'Death makes dead metaphor revive', *Shearsman*, 97–98 (Winter 2013–14), 4.

[52]   Denise Riley, 'You men who go in living flesh', *Intercapillary Space* (May 2013): www.intercapillaryspace.blogspot.de/2013/05/a-poem-by-denise-riley.html [accessed 3 October 2019].

In an interview with Kelvin Corcoran in 2014, Riley made comments on these hymnic poems that are worth quoting at length:

> 'Death makes dead metaphor revive' [...] is a curious piece in that it's so consciously thought-saturated, its thought was willed and imposed by its writer, and it sets down these thoughts quite baldly [...] The speculation is, as you can see, about rhyme's own relation to temporality, and how this links to that feeling of 'time stopped' that you might inhabit after someone's unexpected death. Whereas rhyme, both anticipated and recurring, acts as a guarantor of continuing and perceived time, and of human listening, attuned to that faithfulness of sounding language.
>
> Also, I wrote it (and its less didactic companion piece 'You men who go in living flesh') with an eye to the kind of affect that rises up from Isaac Watts' boxy hymn quatrains. I was wondering about the 'automated' nature of the feeling that can shine through rhyme. I'm struck by rhyme's capacity to lend its mechanical aspects to feeling. For it to exist as feeling. There's an impersonality in rhyme that's, in the same breath, deeply personal. Like a marriage of the material and the ideal.[53]

Lurking behind these remarks are Tennyson's lines, from *In Memoriam*, on the 'sad mechanic exercise' of composing 'measured language' to console 'the unquiet heart and brain'[54] – Tennyson, who elsewhere remarked that '[a] good hymn is the most difficult thing in the world to write', since you need to be both 'commonplace and poetical'.[55] At several points in her remarks, Riley shows how deeply enmeshed her poems are with the tradition of English hymnody: in conceiving the relationship of her verses to pre-existing thoughts and arguments, as hymns relate to pre-existing doctrines and scriptural sources; in engaging with the forms of the English hymn not just in an imitative way but with a searching regard for the phenomenological meaning of rhyme; and in attempting to enter, through adapting Watts's 'boxy' form, into a serious encounter with the 'impersonal' nature of

---

[53] Kelvin Corcoran, 'Interview with Denise Riley', *Shearsman* (April 2014), archived online at www.shearsman.com/ws-blog/post/365-an-interview-with-denise-riley [accessed 3 October 2019].

[54] Alfred Tennyson, *Tennyson: A Selected Edition*, ed. Christopher Ricks, revised edition (London: Longman, 2007), p. 349.

[55] Cited in Watson, *The English Hymn*, p. 1.

language into which centuries of personal thoughts and feelings have been fed.

I began this chapter by citing Lord David Cecil's view, from 1940, that hymns are 'a second-rate type of poetry' because they 'do not provide a free vehicle for the expression of the poet's imagination, his intimate soul'. By the time of Denise Riley's hymnic poems of the twenty-first century, Cecil's post-Romantic insistence on the free expression of the poet's soul, and likewise Donald Davie's arguments for the hymn as a form which 'contribute[s] to a common stock' of conventions within a known linguistic community, have given way to a more developed awareness of how the personal and impersonal may be subsumed into the experience of entering into prosody as a historical domain, where hymn form seems to be speaking the possibility of poetic language itself.

CHAPTER THREE

Pastoral

'Language-Landscape Linkage' in Michael Haslam's Verse

Sophie Read

Give us a break, ye scholars schooling us
syllabic feet, caesural intervals, some solemn
syllabus without the holy silliness. We should be
taking syllabubs off buffet trestles, making accolades
of ale for Easter Day, or plucking milkmaids
from the ditch [..]
on a day like today.[1]

Michael Haslam, according to a biographical note at the back of one of his volumes of verse, 'makes his life an arcade of continual song': for at least the last 40 years, he has been at work on a lyric sequence that is personal – almost at times pathological; that is profoundly influenced by some of the most difficult and innovative poetry of the post-war period, but impatient, too, of its premises and procedures; that is grounded in a forensically precise sense of the poet's local environment, but capable of dizzyingly abstract figurative flights.[2] As is evident from the lines quoted at the head of this chapter, Haslam presents himself as something of an iconoclast, a naïf, a holy fool, out of step with the intellectual economies of poetic reception and response on which his contemporaries depend, but with which he nonetheless has the scholar's familiarity. The rejection of academic discourse ('caesural intervals') in favour of a wholesome if slightly ribald pastoral of ale-drinking and milkmaid-rescuing is

---

[1] Michael Haslam, 'Old Hall Down in the Hollow; Spring up Sunny Bank', in *A Cure For Woodness* (Todmorden: Arc, 2010), p. 35.

[2] Haslam, *A Sinner Saved by Grace* (Todmorden: Arc, 2005), p. 79.

marked by the utterly characteristic progression from 'syllabic' and 'syllabus' through 'silliness' to 'syllabubs', words whose connection is the merest phonetic chance, and whose collocation here is indecorous to the point of deliberate absurdity. This acoustic parlour game is counterpointed by a much subtler patterning of assonance and rhyme ('br**eak**', '**tak**ing', '**mak**ing', accolades', 'ale', '**Day**', 'd**ay**', 'tod**ay**') which holds the lines deftly and delicately together. Here, in miniature, is much of what fascinates and frustrates across the whole of Haslam's 'continual song': the playful, hyperdeveloped musical sense; the work of writing as subject; the writer himself jigging through in cap and bells; an unpretentious folkloric impulse in the grip of what in some moods he clearly sees as the long, dead hand of the Cambridge School. Elsewhere in the poem we find other fixed characteristics: topographical dialect words that suggest a self-conscious local groundedness ('The sike is feathery with spate') and natural-historical field notes rich with botanic detail ('greens that moss on stone to sheen a lane / with marigold and pink purslane'). In what follows, I want to suggest that a lifetime's complicated engagement with the pastoral trope might account for some of Haslam's most distinctive poetic practices, and offer a framework within which to read his work. Pastoral, the poetics of nature and experience paradoxically dependent on a highly theorised and formalised literary construct, is not just the only lyric mode capable of negotiating between intuition and education: it also provides a difficult but compelling model for compositional practice.

Pastoral is an ancient kind of poetry. In some ways, it is the pre-eminent lyric mode. The tradition begins with the *Idylls* of Theocritus, which rehearse scenes from the poet's native Sicily for the urban audience of the Alexandrian court. From Theocritus, aside from the useful word 'idyllic', we get pastoral's strong sense of retreat and return, the artificiality of its occasion, and its association with figures who work on the land (typically shepherds or herdsmen). Music saturates a stylised landscape and fosters a heightened diction; it stands also as restitution and compensation for the pains of love and loss that impel the shepherds' songs. Virgil's *Eclogues*, two centuries later, introduce Arcadia as an idealised rural location and a nostalgic evocation of a Golden Age; they bring, too, a political edge, both in the contrast with an unstable present, and in an explicit concern for questions of land ownership, dispossession, and alienation. As William Empson recognised, pastoral treats complex matters under the cloak of simplicity: it figures the real in the fictive, the urban in the rural, labour in ease.[3] As the pastoral tradition is inherited and developed in the Renaissance and long eighteenth century, further conventions emerge: the landscape itself in aesthetic or affective guise starts to become the focus of poetic attention; the political element found in Virgil is sharpened by debates over the enclosure of common land and growing awareness of the working conditions of rural labourers into something approaching anti-pastoral.[4] 'No other lyric mode depends on – indeed, requires – such complex webs of irony to complete it', David Baker explains; '[t]his is in itself ironic, since the presiding tone and stance of the pastoral is typically extremely sincere, its aspiration pure, its promise ideal'.[5] Pastoral derives much of its interest and force, in other words, from the attention it draws to what it pretends so strenuously to exclude; the vanishing fragility of its warm beauty depends on a proximity to something cold and dark. For Raymond Williams, pastoral is the song of the grasshopper fully aware of the summer's imminent end: '[w]ithin the beautiful development of the pastoral songs this sense of a simple community, living on narrow margins and experiencing the delights of summer and fertility the more intensely because they also know winter and barrenness and accident, is intensely present'.[6]

A mode of writing so socially and culturally alert, and so topographically dependent, cannot possibly have made it through the centuries unchanged, and there is an influential school of thought – articulated most stridently by John Barrell and John Bull in their collection *English Pastoral Verse*, published in 1974 – that we no longer inhabit a world in which it is possible to write authentic pastoral: the tradition is defunct. 'Today, more than ever before, the pastoral simply will not do', they write; '[i]t is difficult to pretend that the English countryside is now anything more than an extension of the town'.[7] As with most such announcements, while there may be an element of

[3] William Empson, *Some Versions of Pastoral* (London: Chatto & Windus, 1966 [1935]).

[4] For a useful discussion of anti-pastoral, see Terry Gifford, *Pastoral* (London: Routledge, 1999), pp. 116–45.

[5] David Baker, 'The Pastoral: First and Last Things', in *Radiant Lyre: Essays on Lyric Poetry*, ed. David Baker and Ann Townsend (Minnesota: Greywolf Press, 2007), pp. 133–41 (p. 139).

[6] Raymond Williams, *The Country and the City* (London: Penguin, 2016 [1973]), p. 21.

[7] *English Pastoral Verse*, ed. John Barrell and John Bull (Harmondsworth: Penguin, 1974), p. 432.

truth here, death notices seem premature; generic forms have a habit of adapting and evolving, sometimes radically, in order to escape the threat of extinction, and twentieth- and twenty-first-century pastoral exists – though in a different form. Harriet Tarlo, again in an introduction to a verse anthology, recognises this; for her, too, an added problem with an 'unproblematic' pastoral is the intensifying ecological threat facing much of the natural world, and she thinks of a 'radical landscape poetry' as in some way an evolution from, a successor to, the pastoral mode: '[u]ltimately, this contemporary poetry contemplates a world that has moved so far away from the landscapes out of which pastoral was born, that it can no longer be seen to be within the pastoral in an unproblematic way'.[8] The upshot of this position is that 'pastoral' comes to be regarded as a pejorative term: it loses the intelligent assimilation of its opposing urban forces, and becomes either the anodyne versifying of an always-sunlit pasteboard past, or just another way of exploiting a plundered and vulnerable landscape.[9] This puts a poet like Haslam, whose interactions with the genre are – as I've suggested – profound and serious, on yet another cultural margin: he begins a lifelong commitment to some version of pastoral just as the tradition starts to come under serious critical scrutiny in the 1960s and '70s.

Haslam is of course not the only poet of that time to explore the possibilities of an experimental pastoral mode (though he may be one of the most determined): Andrew Lawson identifies a variant strain of what he calls 'philosophical pastoral' which 'flourished in the small windy city of Cambridge during the late 1960s and 1970s'.[10] One inhabitant of that city was J. H. Prynne, whose early collections at least were so intensely important for Haslam and his contemporaries (he was taught by Prynne in the 1960s, and thanks him for encouragement through despondency in the first printing of *Continual Song*).[11] *The White Stones* (1969), in particular, offers among the luminous complexity of its verbal bricolage what will become a familiar vision

---

[8]   Harriet Tarlo, 'Introduction' in *The Ground Aslant: An Anthology of Radical Landscape Poetry*, ed. Harriet Tarlo (Exeter: Shearsman, 2011), p. 12.

[9]   'That the pastoral has become not only a "contested term", but a deeply suspect one, is the cultural position in which we find ourselves' (Gifford, *Pastoral* (p. 147)).

[10]   Andrew Lawson, 'On Modern Pastoral', *Fragmente*, 3 (1991), 35–41 (p. 38).

[11]   Michael Haslam, *Continual Song* (Hebden Bridge: Open Township, 1986), p. [iv].

of constricted and crossed desire for the simple, illusory beauties of pastoral.[12] When the term itself features, it is ordinarily with a suspicious distance – an ironic, even comic, undercutting, as in 'Chemins de Fer': Prynne complains that 'The plants stare at my ankles in / Stiffness', and thinks perhaps that the figure he has conjured of Adam among the branches is the result of 'an invert logic brought in with too vivid a pastoral sense'.[13] It is the social dangers of pastoral that seem most to concern the poet in 'Moon Poem', the sense that its fictions may work to preserve a feudal relation, or – a concern shared by Barrell and Bull – that an exodus to the country in search of 'the compact modern home' might displace the native population; but

> The consequence of this
> pastoral desire is prolonged
> as our condition.[14]

I will return to the idea of a 'pastoral desire', as compromised as it is; for now, though, I want to draw attention to another influential aspect of Prynne's treatment of pastoral themes. *The White Stones* inaugurates in its momentary images of geologically, politically, and meteorologically inflected landscapes a pastoral of deep ambivalence which starts explicitly to contain its own despoilment: trees 'grow and / grow', bathed in 'sodium street-lights'; the 'green hills, pleasant with / waters running to the sea' mark 'the bones of a chemical plan / for the world's end'; 'the prairie twitching with herbs, / pale' is 'the city run out and retained / for the thousands of miles allowed'.[15] This is an embattled

---

[12] Prynne doesn't abandon pastoral at this point; in fact, Haslam will later describe *High Pink on Chrome* (1975), admiringly, as 'pastoral immersed in agricultural chemicals' (Michael Haslam, 'Prynne's Gold-Mine: *The Fateful Mark – Enjoying Prynne – Falling off the Trail*', in *For the Future: Poems & Essays in Honour of J. H. Prynne on the Occasion of His 80th Birthday*, ed. Ian Brinton (Bristol: Shearsman, 2016), pp. 41–47 (p. 47)). For a consideration of Prynne's language of flowers as technical botanical pastoral, see, in the same volume, Peter Larkin, 'If Flowers of Language Will (Have) Been a Language of Flowers: Trails of Florescence in the Poems of J. H. Prynne', pp. 99–114.

[13] J. H. Prynne, 'Chemins de Fer', in *Poems* (Hexham: Bloodaxe, 2015), p. 123.

[14] Prynne, 'Moon Poem', in *Poems*, p. 53. See Barrell and Bull, *English Pastoral Verse*: 'the last sad remains of the Pastoral are parcelled up and auctioned off in semi-detached lots' (p. 432). For more on 'Moon Poem', see below, Edward Allen, 'Nocturne: J. H. Prynne Among the Stars', pp. 243–78 (pp. 244–49).

[15] Prynne, 'Against Hurt', 'Song in Sight of the World', 'The Corn Burned by Syrius', in *Poems*, pp. 52, 76, 126.

pastoral, its warm consolations only half-remembered in the breath of night ('The white rose trembles by the step it is / uncalled for in the fading daylight').[16] For Prynne, each stage in the land's long history makes itself felt as a tremor or eructation under the feet: successive geographies, centuries overlain, can be sensed, palimpsested, and the sunlit, song-filled Arcadian era is simply one of the world's old incarnations, a neverland seen still in brief glimpses through the fabric of urban sprawl – though it is not, in the end, a habitable place. In 'Thoughts on the Esterházy Court Uniform', Prynne invokes pastoral themes of retreat and return to imagine an environment animated with music as a condition of its existence, almost like a Theocritan hillside, humming with a submerged eroticism:

> I walk up on the hill, in the warm
> sun and we do not return, the place is
> entirely musical. No person can live there
> & what is similar is the deeper resource, the
> now hidden purpose. I refer directly to my
> own need, since to advance in the now fresh &
> sprouting world must take on some musical sense.[17]

He invokes these themes, however, only to invert them, as the pastoral is once again held off by its precise negation: 'we do not return', 'we / do mimic the return', 'we don't return, not really', 'we do *not* do it'. The gentle Virgilian nostalgia for a life of ease and harmony, shepherds in song at one with the land at the innocent birth of the world, is exposed and transfigured into a savage desolation. 'How can we sustain such constant loss': saved from hysteria by the omission of its question mark, this moment nonetheless comes close to an unwriting of pastoral; 'The sun makes it easier & worse'.

What is evident in Prynne, and will be evident in the verse of those to various degrees influenced by him and interested in the pastoral mode (a necessarily selective list would include R. F. Langley, Peter Larkin, Peter Riley, Ian Patterson, Veronica Forrest-Thomson, and Barry MacSweeney, besides Haslam), is both the enduring strength of its appeal and the utter compromise of its modern incarnation. Pastoral in the 1960s and '70s comes to inhabit the second life of an exhausted

---

[16] Prynne, 'Night Song', in *Poems*, p. 119.

[17] Prynne, *Poems*, p. 99. For the connection of pastoral and song, see also 'Aristeas, in Seven Years': '[s]ong / his transport but this divine / insistence the *pastural clan*. / sheep, elk, the wild deer' (*Poems*, p. 90).

form. In *Poetic Artifice* (written in 1972 but published, posthumously, in 1978), Veronica Forrest-Thomson reflects on pastoral poetry in the light of William Empson's influential theories. For her, 'the association of Parody and Pastoral seems inevitable':

> For Pastoral is the genre which asserts connection on the conventional level, which is granted, by convention, the right to put the complex into the simple, to unify the natural with the highly artificial, to bring together the tribe and the poet. Parody is its counterpart, as a technique stressing connection on the thematic level by taking another language as its theme.[18]

Although Forrest-Thomson seems here to be thinking of parody in the neutral sense of imitation without satire, her poetic works – particularly the companion pieces 'Pastoral' (originally for '*il miglior fabbrio*', Prynne) and 'Not Pastoral Enough' (subtitled '*homage to William Empson*') – avail themselves of the term's sharper edges. The first poem is a brilliantly compressed expression of a feeling that is not so much post-pastoral as mock-pastoral: 'they love us / through the long summer meadows' diesel fumes'.[19] The second abandons bucolic trappings entirely, asserting instead its 'right to put the complex into the simple' by borrowing the form of Empson's 'Villanelle' ('It is the pain, it is the pain, endures') to raise some cogent doubts about his theoretical position: 'It is the sense, it is the sense controls'.[20] Parody, here, has swallowed pastoral whole.

Despite this climate of scepticism and his own periodic misgivings ('O Ye Gods / authentic pastoral absurd'), for Haslam pastoral acts as a thematic touchstone.[21] This is particularly true of *Continual Song*, where, though the parodic spirit is never very far away, brief moments of pure lyric grace make self-conscious gestures towards an originary, unspoilt pastoral:

[18] Veronica Forrest-Thomson, *Poetic Artifice: A Theory of Twentieth-Century Poetry*, ed. Gareth Farmer (Bristol: Shearsman, 2016), p. 167.
[19] Veronica Forrest-Thomson, *Collected Poems* (Exeter: Shearsman, 2008), p. 123.
[20] William Empson, *Collected Poems* (London: Chatto & Windus, 1955), p. 22; Forrest-Thomson, *Poems*, p. 124. As Haffenden points out (*Complete Poems*, p. 219), Empson himself borrows the line's structure from *Othello*: 'It is the cause, it is the cause, my soul'.
[21] Haslam, *Continual Song*, 69/16. Future references will be given as poem numbers; the sequence is numbered both backwards and forwards.

> The Sun is this day's shepherd
>   as the wind comes to a whistle
> driving a flock of cumulus to sky-pasture.[22]

This scene of perfect poetic idleness manages to exist in a kind of mystical suspense, troubled only by vague apprehensions of its own compromised cultural memory ('[w]ho is this shepherd metaphor?'). Such moments, however, are rare. Starting with that early collection,[23] and continuing through to *Scaplings* (2017), which ends with the reiterated desire to sing 'folkish songs, pastorals of the common man', Haslam finds it difficult to invoke a pastoral ideal without the roar of diesel, or some other rude interruption, somewhere near at hand.[24] Passages of lyric achievement are frequent, but as in Prynne they are routinely undercut – or at times, even, intensified and sharpened – by the contrasting moments of ugliness or mundanity or just plain modernity that seem their necessary concomitant. Sometimes, the intention is clearly yobbishly iconoclastic: 'I was in the garden delph', the poet informs us, 'and pissed / against a slender willow trunk'.[25] As well as its register, the verse's soundscape is given to sudden shifts, with birdsong in particular constantly vulnerable to mechanical or domestic assault. If we hear 'the single fluting of a moorland curlew', this delicate sound will – with an obvious pastoral irony – be shattered by 'a shepherd chasing sheep along by motorbike'; 'A score of tricky peewits twisting in the dusk' faces cacophonous competition from 'Late-evening back-street engineering works'; '[a] quarry blast' lifts some poor rooks 'off tall trees'; 'flapping nappies' offset 'squeaking peewits, croaky magpie cries, / snipe drumming from a crowded sky'.[26]

The world of work and care, or 'winter and barrenness and accident' in Williams's more dramatic formulation, has always been just beyond the fringes of pastoral, and to draw it within those confines, even so systematically, might not in some lights seem very

---

[22] Haslam, *Continual Song*, 32/53.

[23] This is the earliest work Haslam has preserved and reprinted (in *A Whole Bauble* (Carcanet, 1995) and *Mid Life* (Exeter: Shearsman, 2007)); it is preceded by three pamphlets, *various ragged fringes* (Oxford: Turpin, 1975), *The Fair Set in the Green* (1976) and *Son Son of Mother* (Cambridge: Lobby, 1978), not considered here.

[24] Haslam, *Scaplings* (Calder Valley Poetry, 2017), p. 40.

[25] Haslam, 'Sothfastness', in *Mid Life* (p. 125).

[26] Haslam, *Continual Song*, 51/34; 'The Love of English', in *Woodness*, p. 84; 'Singleton's 10p Recital', in *Mid Life*, p. 199; '15', in *Scaplings*, p. 19.

radical. But this principle of bathetic interruption is capable of more complex modulations than might at first sight appear, particularly when it is worked out over the course of a single poem. *Continual Song* 11/74 opens like this:

> The Swallow dives into the wood
> as if for the last time.
> All the colours of the earth are dying.
> Moths flit over gossamer and purple heather;
> flocks of small bright birds alight on
> tongues of fern jutting abruptly from
> a tumbled limestone rubble dry-wall.

Birds are, again, the symbols of natural wildness: though the image of the swallow is swiftly lost in eschatological foreboding, scores of other birds come in its place to illuminate the dusk; partly because of the restraint of its sound patterning (echoes tend to be confined to two or three instances and kept to individual or successive lines, as 'moths' / 'gossamer', 'bright' / 'alight', 'jutting' / 'abruptly', 'tongues' / 'tumbled' / 'rubble'), the scene has a quiet, even sombre, integrity. A few lines later, the flash and catch of the day's last light has taken us 'over the spires and clumps of trees' to where 'Streetlights burst to bloom / the moment stars appear'. Clearly, we are no longer on the rural uplands of northern England, but though the contrast in this urban image is sharp, the transition this time has been managed without rupture. Prynne's 'sodium street-lights' utterly refuse to be described in any terms other than their own chemical composition; Haslam's mirror the stars' net and mimic the flowers' bloom. The poem itself then resolves to resist the lure of figuration ('from the flash of dawn there follows [...] no metaphor'), and its next movement rewrites its central contrast in starker terms:

> The moment stars or night or daylight fade
> the sun or moon strikes down upon
> the tin roof of the Standard Tyre and Exhaust Centre,
> or moonwind on the wave.

This plays with the lyric convention of descriptive accuracy, however fictional we understand that to be ('[l]yrics very often offer representations of events', as Jonathan Culler reminds us);[27] this moment

---

[27] Jonathan Culler, *Theory of the Lyric* (Cambridge, MA: Harvard University Press, 2015), p. 275.

is a habitual moment, a recurrent moment, something that happens
three, at least, times a day, and everywhere: light in transition catches
reflective surfaces both utterly banal and prosaically specific ('the tin
roof of the Standard Tyre and Exhaust Centre'), and as romantically
vague and expansive as the night sea ('moonwind on the wave'). The
pastoral mood of the opening returns, transfigured, in the poem's final
movement, as the last lines reach chiastically back towards the first:[28]

> My fear is that I have
> no place on earth
>
> and unspeakable flashes zig-zag through the sky.
> The Dark Wood Aboriginal.
> It is the thinning of the veil to take a dive,
> a dip into the depth of time alchemical,
> as rich as colour dye,
> just to be written in inconsequential weather.

The apocalyptic overtones here pick up on the swallow's initial dive
into the wood, now a 'Dark Wood Aboriginal' in the grip both of the
thunderstorm that has been threatening since the start, and some old
magic; 'the thinning of the veil' is a familiar phrase to psychics and
mystics, to whom it means that the barriers between worlds are fragile
and permeable. The spiritual dimension is, though, subordinate to the
historical: it is a 'dip into the depth of time' this rarefaction seems to
offer, to the old world, perhaps, of the wood. Any portentousness is
tempered by the insistence of an image of cloth manufacture flapping
at the edges – the veil dipped into dye – for the earth's 'dying' colours
are now 'colour dye', and the 'purple heather' of the opening lines is
carried all the way over here by finding a rhyme at last in 'inconse-
quential weather'.

From this brief account of an elliptical and involved poem I want
to draw out a feature that informs Haslam's poetic practice at every
level: his almost intuitive trust in organic patterns of resemblance,
whether of sound or image. He can no more resist a striking analogy
than he can a surprising phonetic coincidence, and all the better if
the two can be made to coincide: 'Slowly traffic flows with flowers'.[29]
As with the blooming streetlights, this brings the opposing ideas

---

[28] Haslam describes the entire sequence as an 'almost palindromic whole'
(*Continual Song*, 00/00), and this shape is sometimes evident, too, in individual
poems.
[29] Haslam, *Continual Song*, 72/13.

of natural growth and urban mechanisation so closely together that distinctions between tenor and vehicle (an apposite term here) seem no longer completely stable; it also feels as if the poet, slightly on autopilot, has let the progressive logic of the language (slow – flow – flower) take over the sense, like a game of laddergrams. This image morphing is rather different from the motorbike-through-a-field model of pastoral interruption, though there is certainly a shared sensibility. The closeness of the twinning can, however, have the effect of a dangerous neutrality:

> The crucial
> Figure, of a Shepherd or a Gardener
> who keeps his flock of flowers. Park-keeper who
> minds the cemetery by the ring road, while the
> blue blasts of exhausts perfume the air.[30]

Our senses are sieged: instead of the colour and scent of the flowers, we are offered the 'perfume' of blue car exhausts. Peter Riley feels no disruption in this technique: 'conceptually and phonetically', he writes, with a generous if generalising optimism, 'pastoral and realist elements are harmonized in the gamut of experience'.[31] For Peter Larkin, in contrast, writing an important review of *A Whole Bauble* (1995), such poetry is guilty of 'a strong pastoral *affront*': he sees Haslam as exploiting the poetic resources of an impoverished and discredited form, rather than acknowledging its insufficiency to a traumatised world with any kind of ironic or revitalising distance.[32] Larkin finds 'shocking' what he characterises as 'flights of genuine urban pastoral' like those floriform exhausts, or blossoming street-lights: '[t]his defying of irony is breath-taking, as ecological offence is overlooked by the appetite for lyric: here blessing is to be preferred before nature'.[33] Appetite for lyric: Larkin casts the pleasure in pattern, a purely poetic satisfaction, as the fatal Cleopatra for which Haslam loses the world, and is content to lose it. It is a serious charge.

This reading is in some ways acute, and is right to identify something that has the potential to be troublingly irresponsible in the

---

[30] Haslam, *Continual Song*, 04/81.
[31] Peter Riley, 'A Sounding Dome' [review of *Four Poems* (Equipage, 1993)], *Parataxis*, 6 (1994), 83–85 (p. 84).
[32] Peter Larkin, 'From the Saturated Porch' [review of *A Whole Bauble: Collected Poems, 1977–1994*], in *Parataxis*, 8.9 (1996), 216–20 (p. 216).
[33] Ibid., 218.

very richness of this invention: but its condemnation overlooks both the complexity of Haslam's engagement with pastoral (in which parody is undoubtedly one element), and the various other commitments his writing performs. Haslam is not obviously ecologically minded, but his work is far from being politically inert; the circumstances under which much of it was written ('he has worked as a labourer most of his life, and is currently a machine-operator') would make that difficult, as Andrew Duncan obliquely recognises: 'Haslam, leading an unconventional and unprosperous life in a remote hill region, following an unfashionable philosophy, is certainly justifying his life by his work: it is at stake in every poem he writes'.[34] If he can derive a perverse enjoyment from the post-pastoral state of the land in some moments, in others it is the occasion for sardonic reflection. This, from *Scaplings*, is so careful to avoid the consolations of lyric appetite in its reflection on the desolation of the countryside as to escape the censure even, presumably, of Larkin: 'The ground it seems is owned by some / consortium of infrastructure funds'.[35] Haslam shares Prynne's interest in the successive historical and political identities of particular stretches of the world's surface, but not his wonderingly neutral regard; 'Scar Edge Valley Diction', for example, offers a kind of sharply elegiac biography of a local mining area: 'Scar edge was badly broken by the delvers' arms'.[36] The account is explicitly edged with pastoral fantasy (there are daffodils, and 'I'd sleep / beneath the stars and wake to be / a figure on the greening edge of folded sheep'), but this is not permitted to sugar the realities of the 'shit leach sump' or 'fishless / slagbanked brook' that are the legacies of local industry (cloth manufacture as well as coal), now stilled: 'iron rusts and cotton sogs to mush'. This is land damaged and exhausted by economic depredations, shrugging off its surface in a 'heavy freight of boulder-tumble' that buries rooks' eggs and 'sycamore and oak in leaf / beneath a landslip rockfall'. Prynne's visionary palimpsests are reimagined here, as history moves backwards

[34] From the biographical note to *The Music Laid Her Songs in Language* (Todmorden: Arc, 2001), p. 47; Andrew Duncan, 'Froth and Delphs of the Atlantic Fringe: Michael Haslam', in *Centre and Periphery in Modern British Poetry* (Liverpool: Liverpool University Press, 2005), pp. 155–65 (p. 157).

[35] Haslam, *Scaplings*, p. 16. This concern is not new: *Continual Song* mourned land '[p]rivatized, enclosed, with lawns and car-keys, / door-keys, mortgages and curtains, babies, washing, / angels, crashes and divorces' (78/07) – though this is clearly complicated by the intrusion of some distinctively personal effects at the list's end.

[36] Haslam, *Sinner Saved by Grace*, pp. 64–68.

(dizzyingly, suddenly, to the creation of the universe) and the image of a fossilised town emerges from the ground's grand shudder:

> There were these streets and there there were
> the precinct and a busy thoroughfare,
> and on these streets
> beneath scar edge there had been these
> arcades of stone and glass.
> It's almost infinite, the amount of time in the past.
> But what's fifteen billion years or less
>   between friends, I asked.
> The stone-flagged passage. The stone-shaded shops.

It is true that playful pleasure in phonetic pattern, and in the rhymes of things, is irrepressible; if it is muted in this passage, it is still present, in the deceptively demotic repetitions and in the word 'arcades', which carries strong pastoral resonances in its similarity to 'Arcadian', as well as close connections with the idea of poetic song.[37] Playfulness is not always the same thing as flippancy, however. Etymology can be a kind of archaeology, but there are alternative models of linguistic divination, too, and rhyme is one of them; the 'lyric appetite' careless of culpable incongruity censured by Larkin starts to seem less an unfortunate failure of self-regulation than an aesthetic absolutely central to the 'life's project' Haslam describes elsewhere: 'to let the whole weary band of poetic image settle easily on an equally worn topography'; to find 'arcadia among remains and ruins, textile mills down deep ravines'.[38] 'Scar Edge Valley Diction', with its rusted moorland mills, its proleptically ruined arcades of stone and glass, certainly fulfils the terms of this manifesto with some fidelity: and it is not a poem that goes in wilfully blinkered search of lyric grace. Watching a flower uncurl in a puff of exhaust need not be the moral dereliction of 'cultural alarmlessness',[39] in fact, but a way of recognising that lyric language these days is every bit as worn out and beaten up as the land with which the pastoral mode connects it, in delicate symbiosis, as fantasy and refuge.

---

[37] Particularly in this volume: three of the poems use the word in their titles ('Arcades in Anglish', 'Arcades in Ruins', and 'A Last Arcade'); the biographical note claims that Haslam 'makes his life an arcade of continual song' (*Sinner Saved by Grace*, p. 76).

[38] Haslam, 'Sample Prosaic Note', in *Music Laid Her Songs*, p. 46.

[39] Larkin, 'Saturated Porch', p. 220.

Worn-out language can be difficult to use, or to take, straight, and another of the objections Larkin makes that seems in need of a response is to the effect the persona of the poet has on the gravity, the credibility, of the enterprise. 'The Post-arcadian pastoral', he writes, 'normally thought of as the Wordsworthian moment of childhood, is taken a stage further as the Pastoral of the Fool'.[40] Where Duncan sees a whole life 'at stake in every poem he writes', Larkin sees a facetious refusal to take poetry, or anything else, seriously enough – forgetting, perhaps, the privileged position sometimes occupied by the liminal figure of the Fool. Both views are of course facilitated by Haslam's own motley self-presentation over the decades of his writing. Here, through flurries of alliteration and half-formed image, is the unmistakable stamp of passionate grief, the distancing pronouns in this apostrophe to the self in no danger of fooling anyone as to whose is the heart that suffers:

> Who'll flail you for your frailty?
>> Who can tell your failure from your blatancy of tone?
>>> Ravenous preacher prating from the pulpit
> of a broken heart, whose seed falls like your
> flour of snow on stony ears.[41]

And here, from *Scaplings*, is an older poet in altogether sprightlier mood, though with some of the same things on his mind:

> For her I want to utter eloquence in art,
> but I have butterflies at this, to kiss, to buss the blessed
>> blooming bliss,
> so I just spout what words come out to supplicate, to conquer
>> doubt
> about a poetry that's proud to be composed of flipping flippancy
>> about
> a lass no less half-dressed cantripping spells of frippery, a frilly
>> pair
> of pants for her in her wet underwear.[42]

Both passages preoccupy themselves with their mode of expression, and both encode a self-castigating mockery of the unstoppable garrulity that threatens to collapse all precarious rhetorical flights into mere

---

[40]   Ibid., p. 219.
[41]   Haslam, *Continual Song*, 15/70.
[42]   Haslam, *Scaplings*, p. 34.

sound – or wash them into the gutter. But where the later lines prance and vaunt, flourishing their quick rhymes and phonetic declensions (butter – this – kiss – buss – bless – bloom – bliss) as all the justification that's needed for their existence, 15/70 makes its words' matches and mismatches a matter of difficult utterance, impediment rather than spur. As Ian Patterson astutely recognises, '[h]ow the figure of the poet exists in these poems is a function of their engagement with lyric process: sometimes comic, sometimes serious'; the work is no less than 'a continually unfolding poetic drama of a situated, and sometimes clownish, self'.[43] The poet plays Harlequin, and he plays Pierrot too. His identities matter so much in part because this figure is the only one rendered with any vividness, any emotional distinction; for all its characters of folklore, boggarts, elves, angels, lads and frilly knickered lasses, Haslam's lyric landscape is a lonely place.

If this work represents the struggle for a poetry of place that recognises and assimilates myth and memory without succumbing to the impossible archaisms of a comfortable pastoral, then the poet's own presence – dissonant and disruptive; sprightly and silly – is an important strategy in its achievement. 'Enter Fool, who rings a bell'; 'the polyphonic comic's gone so far'; 'A clown comes stumbling' – rather than 'tumbling' – 'from the wings': his appearances are carefully staged to punctuate and puncture any threatening scene of lyric grace.[44] The poet's self-presentation is rather more diverse and complex than this might suggest, however, partly because his identity is variously and complicatedly bound up with the land his incessant rhyming both mimics and articulates, and hectors into silence (poetic self-portraits often isolate the rhyming habit for disparaging reflection). The self does not avoid scrutiny. Often, in fact, it stands harshly accused:

> At last I am puffed on the edge of this
>   self-celebratory comic foolishness, wired
> on vocal struts across toward
>   what trips me, self-upstaged
> by puritan reaction, who, with quick humiliation
> silencing the universal silliness, returns

---

[43] Ian Patterson, 'No Man Is an I: Recent Developments in the Lyric', in *The Lyric Poem: Formations and Transformations*, ed. Marion Thain (Cambridge: Cambridge University Press, 2013), pp. 217–36 (p. 231).

[44] Haslam, *Continual Song*, 74/11; 'A Fourth', 'A Lancashire Chimaera', in *Mid Life*, pp. 149, 192. See also *Sinner Saved by Grace*: 'I find my figure richly comic' (p. 10).

> upon the clear bliss world and would the pure
> woodland tone maintain, of contemplation
>   self-explained.[45]

This little vignette tells a conflicted story: the irrepressible pleasure
in a poetic technique ('self-celebratory') that in less bullish moods
the poet nonetheless regards – or pretends to regard – as something
rather like doggerel ('comic foolishness', 'universal silliness'); the
corrective desire for a true pastoral ('would the pure / woodland tone
maintain'), unlikely to be fulfilled, and in any case undercut by the
archly highfalutin' grammatical inversion with which it is expressed.
As children everywhere know, however, you can't apologise satis-
factorily for something until you've demonstrably stopped doing it.
Closer to the bone, perhaps because the second person again affords
the distance of ventriloquism, is this, from *A Cure for Woodness*:

> You overplay the clown. Infantile fancy makes you mime
> the peewit's tune. The real green plovers piping
> up and down the bank's green field complain.
>   Real poetry is tough.
> Yours is a frothing at the mouth in rhyme.[46]

As the introduction to that volume informs us, '*Wood* is a dead word
for Mad', and for Haslam poetry can be both disease and therapy
– ordinarily, in fact, the former: '[p]oetry is a *grice*: a hobby, a predicament, an obsession not unlike a medical condition – acute or chronic'.[47]
Incessant rhyming risks unravelling the threads that connect sound
and sense, and approaching the verse not to the elevated condition
of music, but to a noise less tuneful and less comprehensible than
birdsong – the noise of a rabid dog, or a madman ('frothing at the
mouth in rhyme'). This interlude is unanswerable and unanswered,
but it does not seriously deter the poem. Though the relentlessness
of the rhyming eases up a little, it loses none of its audacity: rhyming
'a bluetit' with 'ablute it', for example (or rather hearing the perfect,
and perfectly accidental, phonetic coincidence of otherwise entirely
unrelated words), is surely yet another kind of pastoral affront.[48]

---

[45]   Haslam, 'A Fourth', in *Mid Life*, p. 148.

[46]   Haslam, 'Old Hall Down in the Hollow', in *A Cure for Woodness*, p. 35.

[47]   Haslam, *A Cure for Woodness*, p. 7; Haslam, 'The Subject of Poems', in *Poets
on Writing: Britain, 1970–1991*, ed. Denise Riley (Basingstoke: Macmillan, 1992),
pp. 70–80 (p. 75).

[48]   Haslam, 'Old Hall Down in the Hollow', in *A Cure for Woodness*, p. 36.

Such moments of self-reflection may have an apotropaic function in anticipating hostile critique, but they also betray a genuine anxiety surrounding the triangulated relationship between the poet, his means, and his material (in this case, the natural world rendered or distorted in verse). Rhyme is supposed to make sense of the world: to forge connections, to assay intuited relationships. Madly multiplied, out of conscious control ('I hadn't meant to go so deep into doggerel', the poet confesses, 'but the scribble seemed to have its own intentions'), it does precisely the opposite; the ear simply loses its bearings, and 'the endless rhyming drains':

> Good times are rare as moorcrop greenery.
> Wages low. Clapped machinery. Foolery
> Ghoulery Scenery. Singleton's Creamery.[49]

The landscape that has come so sharply into focus risks being drowned in the cacophonous tumult of rhyme and alliteration and assonance: it is not just the frequency, the indecorousness of these phonetic patternings, but that – concatenated thus – they have the very opposite effect from the mellifluous musicality for which they are usually praised ('this beautiful control of sound'; 'this gorgeous, concentrated music'; '[w]hat holds it all together is an innate musicality').[50] Music is of course a crucial condition of the pastoral aesthetic, animating the Theocritan idyll from its first line with a scene of poet and nature in perfect reciprocal harmony: 'A sweet thing is the whispered music of that pine by the springs, goatherd, and sweet is your piping, too'.[51] The complaints of the piping plovers at the madman's frothing rhymes mark a knowing contrast to this musical ideal, however, and should prevent the too-easy celebration of a triumphant dispersal of self and sense in song.

Rhyme and music, despite their seductive material similarities, are different things, and cannot aspire to one another's state, except in blunt figuration, without loss; '[w]e can never emulate music',

---

[49] Ibid., p. 33; *Cure for Woodness*, p. 14; 'Scar Edge Valley Diction', in *Sinner Saved by Grace*, p. 66.

[50] Robert Potts on *Music Laid* in the *Guardian* (17 November 2001); Simon Coppock, 'Compression Fitting' [review of *The Music Laid her Songs in Language*], *Poetry Review*, 92 (2002), 88–90; Billy Mills, [Review of *Scaplings*], *Elliptical Movements* (May 2017): https://ellipticalmovements.wordpress.com/2017/05/fay-musselwhite/ [accessed 3 October 2019].

[51] Theocritus, *Idyll* 1, in *Theocritus, Moschus, Bion*, trans. and ed. Neil Hopkinson (Loeb, 2015), pp. 15–35 (p. 19).

T. S. Eliot warns, 'because to arrive at the condition of music would be the annihilation of poetry'.[52] Peter Robinson's remarks on Dylan Thomas sharpen further what's at stake here; he characterises an over-reliance on the sound of words, on their 'musical' qualities, as infantile and therefore shameful. 'The revulsion that some readers experience from Dylan Thomas's music', Robinson believes,

> may be explained by the poet's dependence on the sounds of words: Thomas's poetry can be felt to reveal a weak subjection to verbal music, a helplessness that relies on auditory power alone to restore the bliss of a satisfied infant. The more the poem appears to coordinate sounds for their own sake, at the expense or in excess of purposeful conceptual speech, the worse embarrassment may become.[53]

Robinson associates the sensory gratifications of rampant rhyme not with the Fool's bells but with the baby's rattle; sound for sound's sake in this context – verse that tries itself out as music – is not annihilated so much as rendered both repulsive and ridiculous. Don't be *silly*, Michael.

For all that it exhibits a deliberate flirtation with these realms, however, Haslam's lyric is frequently dependent on the contrast in verbal texture that a true musical aspiration would surely preclude. A poem like 31/54 signals the unfolding drama and its shift in registers through its variant densities of rhyme. As it opens, an earnest attempt to render the world right – to tell things as they are – is felt phonetically in the restrained refusal to rhyme words with words other than themselves:

> Clear light, an air of glass
> through which light celebrates itself.
> Clear shadow of the hawkweed on the meadow.
> Dockflower clear and slender as a flame of rust.
> An orange scarlet pimpernel.
> Clear sound of gorse-pods popping.

---

[52] T. S. Eliot, 'Poetry and Drama' (1951), in *On Poetry and Poets* (London: Faber, 1957), pp. 72–88 (p. 87).

[53] Robinson is talking about Thomas here as a way of thinking about W. S. Graham's verse. Peter Robinson, 'Dependence in the Poetry of W. S. Graham', in *W. S. Graham: Speaking Towards You*, ed. Ralph Pite and Hester Jones (Liverpool: Liverpool University Press, 2004), pp. 108–29 (p. 113).

This impersonal depiction of the landscape vanishes with the setting sun, when the poet's shadow looms and 'blends into the dark', 'unclear / and undistinguished'; thus introduced, however, the figure of the poet starts to dominate, and the poem cannot or will not sustain its fragile lyricism. It turns to the subject of its own difficult composition, and the moment of rupture comes simultaneously with – yet again – the sound of a distant car:

> Clarity of light escapes my art
> of writing. Writing of the clarity
> escapes a breakdown.
> I can hear a wagon changing gear
> as starlight saturates my poor ......
>   *(unclear—*
> *poor dear, poor heart, poor home,*
> *poor hearth, poor eyesight or poor ear?)*

It is an obvious joke, really, to change the poem's gear at the same time as the car's, as if broken concentration breaks the poem in the middle of a line; but the blatancy of the effect – the sudden, disappointing dive into bathos – is part of its point. A carefully unrhymed and unmetrical poem is 'fixed' not just with pounding iambics and one ringing rhyme (on, of course, the word 'hear': 'gear / unclear') but with several possible options, of varying degrees of plausibility, both rhymed ('gear / dear / ear'; 'art / heart'; 'starlight / eyesight') and not; the joke is compounded by the realisation that the only fit, metrically, is the first one: 'unclear'.[54] And one thing this poem demonstrably does not have is a 'poor ear'. The proliferation of 'hear' sounds, reaching back to the repeated 'clear' of the vivid first passage, sets off, again, an inner echo chamber; earlier discipline is quite forgotten:

> Pour on, ye Agents of the Pure!
> As rhymes occur, the brain begins to blur.
> *Return to her!*
> The starlight rains down on the fields
>   and on the shore.
> I wish it to effect a cure.

---

[54] 'Eyesight' won't do, because it is stressed on the initial syllable. I make the two lines quite strong iambic pentameter, though the first ('I can hear ...') is missing an unstressed beat from the start.

The characteristic self-evolving sound patterns (pour – pure – shore – cure; occur – blur – her) dizzy and distract in sharp contrast with the realised detail of the first part of the poem. No clarity or restraint here, only the blur of rhyme, both intoxicant and anaesthetic.

The heartbreak in these lines decided not, in the end, to take itself too seriously (*'Return to her!'*), but here and elsewhere the pastoral elements of Haslam's writing exist in response to the strongest and darkest of emotional imperatives. The world's first pastoral song, after all, tells of the oxherd Daphnis's death from unrequited love: '[p]astoral is not an escape from difficulties in the rest of the world', as Forrest-Thomson reminds us; 'it is a transmutation of these difficulties into a landscape'.[55] For Empson, too, the pastoral mode must acknowledge and assimilate what he calls 'the central feeling of tragedy': '[t]he waste even in a fortunate life, the isolation even of a life rich in intimacy, cannot but be felt deeply'.[56] (Another way of putting this, of course, is *Et in Arcadia ego*.) There is sometimes a suspicion that Haslam's prancing poet-fool and his gargling rhymes are a feint to distract from the effects of disappointed desire – erotic desire, of course, but also the much more shameful desire for a really pure pastoral lyricism, every bit as difficult to gratify. The unstoppable copiousness of Haslam's unending world of rhyme tries to act as a defence against loss, against hurt, as an alternative to the modernist aesthetic of lines in half-breathed bits against which it has to play in his verse: '[i]t was already clear we were free to be fragmentary', he remembers of this stylistic evolution; 'I don't like feeling broken'.[57] Often, however, feeling broken becomes the whole subject of the song; these moments lay bare the poor bargain of pastoral consolation, in which the price of the poetry is the sense of loss that engenders it – acute, but never so acute that its grit cannot be enamelled over in rhyme.

Always lurking in such moments is the spectre of silence, bound up with an obscure sense that were the terms of the transaction to be scrutinised, the suffering might after all turn out to be the song's fault: 'My living forms my need to write. / I hurt myself too much'.[58] The connections are made even more explicit in this, from *Sinner Saved*

---

[55]   Theocritus, *Idyll* 1; Veronica Forrest-Thomson, 'Pastoral and Elegy in the Early Poems of Tennyson', *Chicago Review*, 56.2–3 (2011), 48–76 (p. 54).

[56]   Empson, *Some Versions of Pastoral*, p. 12.

[57]   Haslam, 'Prynne's Gold Mine', p. 44.

[58]   Haslam, *Continual Song*, 12/73.

by Grace: 'Arcades in Ruins. This is the depressive pit. / The book is broken up as nonsense'.[59] But the threatened dissolution never happens: the verse contains and exploits its own self-destructive urges, often in its customary comic strain. The last poem in the sequence *Something's Recrudescence through to Its Effulgence* ('A Fourth') exemplifies this dynamic. It is a relatively long and episodic piece, composed, rewritten, and restored over some time; the poet was 'quickly embarrassed' by it, fearing it was 'merely bad and silly poetry', 'unconscionably foolish', 'a joke that I was failing to laugh at'.[60] Nonetheless, it is preserved in *Mid Life*, the story of a love affair brought – disconcertingly – to a successful consummation ('our love has come off / in the same green garden delph'), but structured rather round foreshadowings of failure and the difficulty of its own processes of composition.[61] All the hallmarks of Haslam's desecrated pastoral are here: the poem lovingly assembles its woods, fields and cloughs, its flowers and birdsong, even 'the Midsummer Dream' as a backdrop for its sweethearts, 'the lucky beings looking out to blooming lilac / among rowanflower, mayblossom, broom' through to 'roses and kisses in practice / poetic as wings'. Even the usual dissonant elements are managed with little sense of disruption. 'Reflection cast / an angled new scatter of street-lights / out'; 'ignition of a car / that yet lifts a turbulence of air / that lifts a pigeon': for once, the intimations of modernity belong in the poem's gentle pastoral register, neither incongruously described as if they were natural things nor yet felt as ugly intrusions. Where the poem's tensions do threaten rupture, however, is in the treatment of 'the ghost / Despair, that mournful haunter of the / bathroom door': a self-consciously poetic diction sets up each articulation of pain for a comic fall, for the undercut of bathos. In the passage that follows, the poet goes in search of 'the face of Mater Dolorosa / on a boulder':

> And when I found it there the sense of
>   fallen hope, in a space
> of blown-down trees was like a pastoral
>   and picture-natural of faithlessness,

---

[59] Haslam, 'Arcades in Ruins', in *Sinner*, p. 35.

[60] Haslam, Introduction to *Mid Life*, p. 8; see also the notes on the *Continual Song* website: http://www.continualesong.com/bridgesings.html [accessed 3 October 2019].

[61] Haslam, 'A Fourth', in *Mid Life*, pp. 141–49. Sometimes the two – the love affair and the struggle of writing – are startlingly conflated: '[m]y song when it comes comes / all heartdrums and pips like a linnet / in spattering bits'.

> misery, and the always-legendary knowledge
>   of more youthful folly, and me
> decked with weeds, wildflowers, sorrow,
>   lost.

What he finds is a Spenserian landscape accented by Byron via Hopkins, with Shakespearean touches; he ends the stanza dressed as mad Ophelia. Here, the effects of rhythm, rhyme, alliteration, and assonance form a kind of *entrelacement* rather than a compounding or bombardment: in particular, the phonetic connection between 'knowledge', 'folly', 'sorrow', and the powerfully isolated last word 'lost' (/ɒ/) plays against the /w/ that links 'weeds', 'wildflowers', and 'sorrow', and again against the submerged rhyme of 'trees', 'me', and 'weeds'. The more obvious effects have a controlled exuberance: the reverse portmanteau of 'pastoral' / 'picture-natural' manages not to let its jauntiness upset, quite, the image of the heart's twilit, dripping grove projected onto the world outside: 'a pastoral [..] of faithlessness, misery'.

This mood is precarious, and unsustainable; the poem gradually turns its back on the effort and ends preoccupied with the interesting business of its own composition; any heartbreak is cancelled and written through in this 'performance / wherein shadow sheds itself'. It is in this last phase of the poem that the poet comes to accuse himself of 'self-celebratory comic foolishness', a moment of convulsive reflection considered earlier that is developed and extended into a meditation on writing and endings: 'I was struggling with such lines as / might maintain the rhymes and sense of / an earlier personal draft, but no such luck';

> Three springs I've breathed with *something's*
>   *recrudescence through to its effulgence.* Now I finish off this
> formal immaterial event, just shuddering this
>   side of the acceptance of the fence of full hawthorn
> effulgence and the scent, *Mayblossom on my*
>   *heart,* the woodland cloughs and the adjoining fields'
> luxuriance.

The mock-performative flourish ('Now I finish off this / formal immaterial event', two dozen lines before the end) ushers in a glorious paralipsis of pastoral, offered in the moment it is withheld, as the poet stands 'just shuddering this / side of the acceptance of the fence of full hawthorn'. Just which side? In fact, of course, Haslam is firmly *on* the fence again, casting armfuls of poesies at the reader with instructions not to inhale. The difficulty of writing right has again found its way to the forefront: in an aesthetic of unstoppable verbosity, even the hidden silences behind the scenes, the pages rewritten and unwritten, must be commemorated, given some kind of permanent verbal imprint. This compulsion might have broken the poem apart (as indeed it did, temporarily, in the 'mangled and awkward revisions' of its other life), were it not for the fact that, as Patterson recognises, 'the work of the poem, not its source, creates its lyric power': the real subject of Haslam's writing is writing.[62] That this results in poetry anything but earnest, inward-looking, or sterile is because the contested pastoral at the heart of Haslam's continual song is not just a mode but a model: not just something to write about, but the governing genius of the compositional process.

Ultimately, Haslam's version of pastoral is radical and revivifying not so much for its dystopian outlook or ecological conscience, but because of the strength of its investment in the idea of poetry itself as a form of organic growth: copious, riotous, self-proliferating, comically undirected, and – importantly – unending. This is what happens to the exhausted form of pastoral and worn-out lyric language in Haslam's hands, and it is more than a figurative analogy – though it is that too ('I learned to let great draughts of loose talk run like weeds'; 'the creative element in writing [...] may as well / take flower form and sprout and seed itself itself').[63] It is a precise and profound structural aesthetic, anything but easy. The paradox by which Haslam is caught is that patterns of natural growth are highly unnatural as the determining logic of poetic works, and trusting in the seductions of their resemblance leads one occasionally up the garden path: 'it prints its sprints, / it lodges logs, ecologies and eclogues / like the boggart in its clogs'.[64] The pleasures of this are primarily physiological, felt at the tongue's tip and on the teeth; if there's a way of wringing meaning beyond the momentary startlement of an impossible image from its various phonetic coercions, it is not at first apparent. It should be

---

[62] Haslam, Introduction to *Mid Life*, p. 8; Patterson, 'No Man Is an I', p. 230. And see also Forrest-Thomson's preface to *On the Periphery* (1976), where she formulates one of the chief problems facing a poet as 'the quest for a subject other than the difficulty of writing' (*Collected Poems*, p. 168).

[63] Haslam, 'Loose Talk', in *Sinner Saved by Grace*, p. 13; '[It]', in *Cure for Woodness*, p. 97.

[64] Haslam, 'The Love of English', in *Cure for Woodness*, p. 85.

evident that such writing is neither comfortable nor safe, however:
Peter Larkin wrote of Prynne that 'a prolonged pastoral sensitivity
can bear a mark of defiance, if not quite self-mutilation', and the same
is certainly true of Haslam, though in a very different sense from that
intended; in Riley's words, 'Michael Haslam risks it all'.[65] This is not
news for the poet, whose self-scrutiny in verse (and prose) often anticipates the insights of the 'scholars schooling us'; before the boggart
gets its clogs, the poet stages a mock-epiphany:

> I slipped onto my knees on being told there really is
> no landscape-language linkage: all the rides in pine
> are over-run with quibbles, brambles, puns and rhyme.
> The pit of farmyard scrap is not the hellhole of the soul.
> What pipes and clogs are can't be both
>   a drainage problem and a country dance.
> The tongue of land between the streams is stricken with disease.
> They told me 'arbitrary' isn't choice but chance.[66]

The pastoral aesthetic, language's ability to intuit a leading logic of
its own, is defiantly asserted against the ventriloquised scepticism of
humourless rationalists; pipes and clogs most certainly are both idle
pastoral playthings and the stuff of plumbers' working days: they have
to be. The most important pun here, though, and perhaps anywhere
in Haslam's work, is not so showy: it is the 'tongue of land' that might
look literal were it not for what flows by on either side. Instead, this is
the voice of the natural world that speaks in resistless song, defying
its diagnosis, asserting the 'landscape-language linkage' after all; and
when it reappears at the end of *Scaplings*, it is the poet's, too. And if a
reader sees him stick it out, that's the language's fault, not his:

> I'll stick my ears out on this tongue of land, for babble sprung
> of folkish songs, pastorals of the common man.[67]

It is one of the enduring conceits of these wilful, protean 'pastorals of
the common man', that connects the immanent music of the Theocritan
hillside with the scarred, possessed beauties of England's north: if the
land had a voice, it would sound a lot like Michael Haslam.

---

[65] Larkin, 'Flowers of Language', p. 104; Peter Riley, [review of *Continual
Song*], *Reality Studios*, 9 (1987), 93–95 (p. 94).
[66] Haslam, 'The Love of English', in *Cure for Woodness*, p. 79.
[67] Haslam, *Scaplings*, p. 40.

CHAPTER FOUR

Elegy

Surreptitious and Prospective, from W. S. Graham to Margaret Ross

John Wilkinson

A generic problem of elegy is how to keep faith with the mourned 'you' so that it is *your* fame and continuing life that the poem serves rather than *mine*. Perhaps the foundational poetic elegy of English poetical tradition, John Milton's 'Lycidas', was in part an exhibition piece designed to advertise the young poet's skills. The genre's longest-influential English model, Thomas Gray's 'Elegy in a Country Churchyard', displaces the poet's own fear of eternal obscurity onto the nameless dead; it is Gray's own futurity which is the poem's successful issue. The self-serving nature of elegy cannot be negated, since an elegy unworthy of fame must fail to serve the elegised well. Furthermore, there is frequently a suspicion that the elegist mourns an aspect of himself projected, as Geoffrey Hill's 'September Song' admits with an edge of moral narcissism while mourning the victims of Nazi death camps ('(I have made / an elegy for myself it / is true)').[1] But neither is ambition for the poem necessarily exploitative; nowhere do ambition and mourning unite, both simultaneously restrained and affirmed, to such devastating effect as in Ben Jonson's 'On my First Son', which finishes:

> Rest in soft peace, and, ask'd, say, 'Here doth lie
> Ben Jonson his best piece of poetry.'

I am grateful to Ned Allen, Richard Strier and Angela Leighton for their comments on a draft of this chapter.
[1] Geoffrey Hill, 'September Song', in *Broken Hierarchies: Poems, 1952–2012* (Oxford: Oxford University Press, 2013), p. 44.

>   For whose sake henceforth all his vows be such,
>   As what he loves may never like too much.[2]

The problem of elegy is a special instance of a larger problem of
lyric address when readers have become touchily aware of a lyric's
pronominal identifications, resenting both absorption into a poem's
presumptuous 'we' or location in an interpellating 'you'. Who are
you to speak? Or, to allude to another great English elegy, who are
you to reckon God's purpose as in 'The Wreck of the Deutschland'?
And the poem done, 'who would I show it to?' – according to Diana
Fuss 'the unspoken challenge of our times', but answered unhesitat-
ingly by 'myself!' in thousands of students' elegies for their own
soon-to-be-lost youth, the prevalent selfie elegy.[3] This phenomenon
takes another step beyond David Kennedy's contentions that 'poetry
itself and wider attitudes to experience have become overwhelmingly
elegiac' and that 'national identity has become synonymous with
remembrance', or Jahan Ramazani's claim that 'the genre is central
to the history and development of twentieth-century lyric. Broadly
defined, the elegy permeates a wide range of poems about war, love,
race, gender, meditation, the self, the family, and the poet'.[4]

While this chapter agrees with Fuss in discovering 'in the elegy
not a moribund genre in historical decline but a vital form in aesthetic
transformation', it finds this vitality elsewhere than in those dying
words, reviving corpses, and surviving lovers which provide the titles of
her book chapters, conducive (by her account) to a social role for poetry
as consolation in cultures queasy about facing death. Instead it attends
chiefly to the surreptitious elegy, to instances of what Sam Ladkin calls
'the non-heroic elegiac mode', poems so reluctant to admit their generic

---

[2] Ben Jonson, 'On My First Son', in *Ben Jonson*, ed. Ian Donaldson (Oxford:
Oxford University Press, 1985), pp. 236–37.

[3] Diana Fuss, *Dying Modern: A Meditation on Elegy* (Durham, NC: Duke
University Press, 2013), p. 8.

[4] David Kennedy, *Elegy* (New York: Routledge 2007), p. 7. The remark on
national identity probably derives from Homi Bhaba's influential contention
that 'The nation fills the void left in the uprooting of communities and kin, and
turns that loss into the language of metaphor. Metaphor, as the etymology of the
word suggests, transfers the meaning of home and belonging, across the "middle
passage", or the central European steppes, across those distances, and cultural
differences, that span the imagined community of the nation-people' (Homi
K. Bhaba, *The Location of Culture* (New York: Routledge, 1994), p. 139); Jahan
Ramazani, *Poetry of Mourning. The Modern Elegy from Hardy to Heaney* (Chicago:
University of Chicago Press 1994), p. x.

status as elegy that none dares use the name.[5] Some are non-heroic to the extent that elegiac intent can go undiscerned by a reader until a poignant twist or a breach in the surface, escaping what Fuss recognises as the inveterate banality of grief and pious hope alike, and capable of surprising with grief – indeed, W. S. Graham's 'Dear Bryan Wynter' appears in the anthology *Poems That Make Grown Men Cry*.[6] At the end of this chapter, however, the persistence of elegy in a world of scarcity and loss is found to be thrown into question through a reading of Margaret Ross's book *A Timeshare* as prospective elegy. The chapter's ambition is restricted to identifying these few tendencies in recent elegy; there is no attempt to survey so capacious a genre. For example, no discussion is attempted here of the AIDS crisis as an exemplary intersection of the intimate with the public, or of its exemplary poetic work, Thom Gunn's collection *The Man With Night Sweats*.[7]

One notable strategy of twentieth-century English-language poets in managing the constitutional problems of the lyric genre has been to write out of sociability (including shattered sociability as during the AIDS crisis), at any point along a line from friends' shorthand for shared experience to barroom anecdotage to coterie gossip. Elegy then can become mutually serving, keeping alive a way of talking which is at once intimate and public but not presumptuous or evidently exploitative; and the social gathering can stand for an imaginary readership too. The two paramount poets in this idiom, however greatly their poetic diction differs, are Frank O'Hara and W. S. Graham; each of them felt drawn to elegise not fellow poets but composers and musicians, or painters who were their friends, Jackson Pollock for O'Hara and Peter Lanyon and Bryan Wynter for Graham. It is no coincidence that their greatest elegies allude to bar and pub life. These elegies cannot be reproached as a competitive use of shared language but on the contrary

---

[5] Fuss, *Dying Modern*, p. 3; Sam Ladkin, 'Ornate and Explosive Grief: A Comparative Commentary on Frank O'Hara's "In Memory of My Feelings" and "To Hell with It", Incorporating a Substantial Gloss on the Serpent in the Poetry of Paul Valéry, and a Theoretical Excursus on Ornate Poetics', *Glossator*, 8 (2013), 189–315 (p. 201).

[6] *Poems That Make Grown Men Cry: 100 Men on the Words That Move Them*, ed. Anthony and Ben Holden (London: Simon & Schuster, 2014). The book is proudly marketed as 'deckle edged' – even the paper is affected. Graham's poem is chosen by the poet Nick Laird. Salman Rushdie selects Auden's 'In Memory of W. B. Yeats', raising thereby a question about the ethics of reading as well as of writing elegies.

[7] Thom Gunn, *The Man with Night Sweats* (London: Faber, 1992).

rely on shared language, perception, social milieu, and place; they are situated between poet and painter/musician, or triangulated between poet and painter or musician and audience, between the living and the dead. Frank O'Hara was himself elegised by a more reticent poet, James Schuyler, who had felt intensely competitive with him and in his elegy managed this complication with evasive delicacy.

No post-war elegy in English has been more influential on subsequent poetry than Frank O'Hara's 'The Day Lady Died', generally assigned to a subgenre invented by O'Hara, the 'I do this, I do that' poem of busy distraction.[8] Its influence has been marked more in the 'overwhelmingly elegiac' tone of poems mourning the passage of time than in elegy strictly conceived. O'Hara's poem is certainly an elegy, even if this dawns on a first-time reader only through a gradual unease. Its originality becomes clear by comparison with W. H. Auden's two immediately pre-war elegies, 'In Memory of Sigmund Freud' and 'In Memory of W. B. Yeats', representing a high-water mark of the Anglo-American public elegy – memorialising great men in full-on address to a mourned 'you' embodying a set of contributions to civilised values (at a time when insurgent barbarism would have made irony in that regard sound casuistical). In poems whose dominant tone is instructive, accounts are drawn up of what Freud and Yeats taught humanity, while human failings are acknowledged so 'you' might fitfully be humanised when prosopopoeia starts to sound too sermonising. Writing that Yeats was 'silly, like us', and of Freud that, 'if often he was wrong and, at times, absurd', softens a voice that strives to do justice to achievements in terms that can match them. And match them the poet undoubtedly feels competent to do; the final three stanzas of 'In Memory of W. B. Yeats' clearly assume the earlier poet's mantle, starting with the ambiguous apostrophe:

> Follow, poet, follow right
> To the bottom of the night,
> With your unconstraining voice
> Still persuade us to rejoice. [...][9]

The patriarchal tone of Auden's elegies is apt enough in the elegy to Freud; there are few elegies which more decidedly 'recall Freud's

---

[8] The poem can be read online at the Poetry Foundation website: http://www. poetryfoundation.org/poem/171368 [accessed on 3 November 2020].

[9] W. H. Auden, 'In Memory of W. B. Yeats', in *Collected Shorter Poems: 1927–1957* (London: Faber, 1969), pp. 141–43.

suggestion that the superego is made up of "the illustrious dead," a sort of cultural reservoir, or rather cemetery, in which one may also inter one's renounced love-objects and in which the ruling monument is that internalized figure of the father'.[10] This tone would soon become unsustainable, with the presumption of speaking for 'a people' echoing Fascist and Stalinist authoritarianism, wartime solidarity, or Cold War professions of patriotism. And not long afterwards the question of who exactly 'the people' are would make it problematic to adopt a spokesman's stance. But from the perspective of the 1940s it would surely have been unimaginable that a great elegy would commemorate a great black female artist (Billie Holiday), include the line 'it is 1959 and I go get a shoeshine', and consist largely of a record of an afternoon's scurrying about Manhattan, while shying away from black polish, black poetry, the play *Les Nègres*, and anything that might trigger distress through reminding the poet of a loss he cannot face.[11] 'The Day Lady Died' does not aim to account for Holiday's greatness; rather, it evidences the effect of her greatness. Nor does the poem set out to mourn Holiday, for mourning seeks to hold the departed steadily in memory and enacts a ritual of demonstrative bereavement in oneself if not among others; here his loss haunts the poet, but avoidance fails and loss returns in a surge of grief united with gratitude. Determined to avoid reflecting, the poem tacks away from blackness as a mobile metonym for Holiday, through multiple distractions towards a breach brought about by 'a NEW YORK POST with her face on it'; through the breach floods what Billie Holiday's art had delivered to the heart of the poet, and what in tribute the poem delivers to a reader.

Yet for all its seeming casualness and intimacy in 'the non-heroic elegiac mode' of his earlier elegies to James Dean, O'Hara's poem, like Auden's, is a public elegy. In O'Hara's 'Ode on Causality', linked to 'The Day Lady Died' through its earlier title 'Ode on Causality (in the Five Spot Cafè)', he had written an elegy for a friend, the painter Jackson Pollock. This poem is closer to Fuss's 'reviving corpses' elegiac category, spun out of Pollock's young daughter's insistence at his graveside that 'he isn't under there, he's out in the woods' for a wild version rather than a repudiation of Wordsworth's 'Rolled

---

[10]   Peter M. Sacks, *The English Elegy: Studies in the Genre from Spenser to Yeats* (Baltimore: Johns Hopkins University Press, 1985), p. 15.

[11]   Frank O'Hara, 'The Day Lady Died', in *The Collected Poems of Frank O'Hara*, ed. Donald Allen (Berkeley: University of California Press, 1995), p. 325.

round in earth's diurnal course, / With rocks, and stones, and trees'.[12]
Wordsworth's return to nature is converted by O'Hara into a rampant
phallicism that refuses to allow the dead artist 'to be layed at all!
romanticized, elaborated, fucked, sung, put to "rest"'.[13] 'Lay' unites
'laid to rest' with poetic 'lays' in an abrupt break from the previous
stanza's ending in 'the tender subjects of their future lays'. O'Hara's
distraction here is breached by the word 'lays', for Pollock's cock
becomes a metonym for his living; his death means the end of Pollock's
lays as he is himself laid and liable to be 'fucked'. The poem culmi-
nates in the re-erecting of Pollock's penis followed by its enormous
orgasm; a revived corpse indeed. Although the over-the-top rhetoric
of this poem greatly differs from 'The Day Lady Died', the quality of
distraction in space is shared. The 'Ode on Causality' scampers from
Pollock's memorial at Springs Cemetery through surrounding forest
and through cultures, historical periods, music, painting, theatre,
and religion, before inevitably making its way to the legendary
space of distraction, 'standing still and walking in New York'. Here
the avoidance is of the penis that the poem shies away from seeing
directly – 'everyone's supposed to be veined, like marble', 'then swell
like pythons' – before lays emerge from ballads and the poem accedes
fully to the also-absurd phallicism it has been resisting.

The shortcoming of 'Ode on Causality' as an elegy lies in its
rhetorical abstraction. The poem could be written only by someone
deeply versed in Pollock's art, and at the time of writing this would
likely have been a friend of the painter. But it gives little sense of
personal friendship and loss; rather it offers a general (although
strongly gendered) meditation on death which is as tendentious (and
as magnificent) as Hopkins's 'Wreck of the Deutschland' – and has
the disadvantage of playing into an already well-developed caricature
of Pollock as emblematic of the virile heterosexual artist. Since the
poem does not advertise itself as an elegy, criticism of its short-
comings in these terms may seem unfair; but it is legitimate to ask
to what end Pollock's corpse (his cock) is being revived. And the
answer to that question is broadly, 'in the service of art', affirmed
in the final lines as organism sublimates transcendently into a work
of art: 'love-propelled and tangled glitteringly / has earned himself
the title *Bird in Flight*'.

---

[12]   William Wordsworth 'A Slumber Did My Spirit Seal', in *The Poems*, 2 vols,
ed. John O. Hayden (Harmondsworth: Penguin Books 1977), I, p. 364.
[13]   O'Hara, 'Ode on Causality', in *Collected Poems*, pp. 302–03.

The distractions of 'standing still and walking in New York' correspond to 'meanders' across a more abstract terrain in W. S. Graham's poems, but Graham's meanders follow tracks rather than distractions. It is tempting to hear 'Dear Bryan Wynter' as Sydney Graham (the name by which his friends knew him) talking to his dead and dear friend, the painter Bryan Wynter (1915–75), but the poem's idiom is explicitly that of a letter. A letter to an intimate, but an intimate to whom he wrote few letters when alive because their near proximity meant there was no distance to be bridged. The letters Graham did write to Wynter are mainly dunning letters, resorted to as a distancing device, in embarrassment.[14] A letter to an intimate belongs to a now rare genre, letter writing having become an awkward task, marked by a struggle with the desire or the necessity to express deep feeling, as in a letter of condolence. An intimate letter must strive for a voice truer than words said could sound, in their haltingness or inconsiderateness. So a love letter might be addressed to a person working in the next office booth or met frequently, to deliver what could only be stuttered in encounter. But Graham's poems often show frustration with the gap between the abstraction of the lyric voice and the incarnate poet's voice, and with the separation from a reader whom the poet wishes to join or rejoin through unified movement. That said, the voice of Sydney Graham's published letters is remarkably close to the poems – and several poems emerge out of first formulations in letters, benefiting from the subtle modulations of tone registered in Fiona Green's sensitive survey of Graham's elegiac practice.[15] Notes becomes notes of a different kind, for 'This is only a note' is an ambiguous formulation. Whilst a note is a brief letter, it is also a musical note that sets the tone for a lyric poem whose first stanza follows:

DEAR BRYAN WYNTER

1

This is only a note
To say how sorry I am
You died. You will realise
What a position it puts

---

[14] The prevalence of dunning letters in Graham's epistolary archive is noted by Fiona Green: 'Achieve Further through Elegy', in *W. S. Graham: Speaking Towards You*, ed. Ralph Pite and Hester Jones (Liverpool: Liverpool University Press, 2004), pp. 134–35.

[15] Ibid., esp. pp. 152–54.

Me in. I couldn't really
Have died for you if so
I were inclined. The carn
Foxglove here on the wall
Outside your first house
Leans with me standing
In the Zennor wind.[16]

The musical note leads to the prosody of this work. Although the poem's idiom is epistolary, the need to insist on that testifies to the poem's voice effect. The decisions made in reading can oscillate between the voices of a letter, intimate speech, and a lyric poem. These voices are subtly distinct, since a lyric poem's voice demands attention to its prosodic make-up, whereas a letter's voice rides on semantic stresses. Decisions are required from the very beginning; and how the first line is sounded (the second line if including the poem's run-on title) will influence the way the whole poem is spoken and heard – as indeed does the specifically poetic echo of William Carlos Williams's 'This is Just to Say', another poem whose title runs on into what might be a note.[17] In an elegant and astute paper, Angela Leighton cites the many poems by Graham cast in epistolary form and explains:

> The idea of a letter, as an address to someone who cannot (yet) answer for themselves, involves a knotty contradiction which Graham loves to exploit. Someone is there, yet not there; the poem becomes an obstacle, not a way through. His playful, informal, loving, ragging tone invokes a reader who ought to be the intimate recipient, but who is, like the writer himself, an invented anyone.[18]

But in a poem entitled 'Dear Bryan Wynter', this cannot be 'an invented anyone' even if Graham's poem is anxious lest it be 'greedy to make you up'. The title announces a specific address. The writtenness of talking (as in a letter) and the talking of writtenness (as in a poem) have to be dealt with throughout, from that first line break ('a note / To say'). How can a note say? Well, in sending a letter to an intimate, that's what is presumed, sending a voice as much or more than information.

---

[16]   W. S. Graham, 'Dear Bryan Wynter', in *New Collected Poems*, ed. Matthew Francis (London: Faber, 2004), pp. 258–60.

[17]   I owe this observation to Richard Strier.

[18]   Angela Leighton, '"Only practising how to speak to speak": W. S. Graham's Art of Letter Writing', *PN Review 200*, 37.6 (June–July 2011), 54–58.

And a lyric note might introduce anything, but chiefly alerts the ear so that the mournful and guilty balance across the line break of the simple pronouncement 'I am / You died' can be registered. This is a break that must be healed, and can only be healed prosodically. Reparation begins with proposing other things that might be sent by the same lyric service – 'Rice-wine, meanders' – and this poem will indeed deliver a meander formally, so Wynter can continue to paint in the beyond, having available to him the gestural repertoire, the meanders, of his late canvases. As for rice wine, that may pertain to some fantasy of Wynter as a Zen monk, since the Tinners Arms in Zennor wouldn't have served anything half so exotic. And not knowing allows an assumption, oddly enough, that we know along with Bryan Wynter. Graham's generous offer of provisions knowingly echoes Guillaume Apollinaire's epitaph on Le Douanier Rousseau's tombstone, inscribed by Brâncuşi and including the lines: 'Laisse passer nos bagages en franchise à la porte du ciel / Nous t'apporterons des pinceaux des couleurs des toiles' ('Let our luggage pass duty free through the gates of heaven / We will bring you brushes paints and canvas'). There at modernism's portals, an elegy.

'Dear Bryan Wynter' is a poem which it feels clumsy to interpret pertinaciously, but you'd have to be obtuse to not grasp what the poem is saying and doing. There are, however, a few things that aren't obvious. Before Derek Attridge's revisionist work, English prosody was conventionally understood in terms of feet, and 'Dear Bryan Wynter' like 'The Day Lady Died' is a walking poem, but troubled by the disconcerting unreliability of once-familiar landmarks, and by interruption. Here is the West Penwith Cornish landscape which Sydney Graham and Bryan Wynter walked habitually, to the pub and elsewhere, and one which they could have walked, as the saying goes, with their eyes shut. So many paces in this direction or that. The oddities of the poem cluster around dislocations, and difficulties in setting out:

> You will realise
> What a position it puts
> Me in. I couldn't really
> Have died for you if so
> I were inclined.

The line breaks dislodge 'Me' from its position, so that it stands against the left margin with peculiar assertiveness and then might be inclined. This subtle effect is characteristic of late Graham, and the poem's colloquialism should not induce us to take its performance for granted. As Hannah Brooks-Motl notes, Graham came to eschew the rich vocabulary of his early poetry in favour of language that tends to colourlessness.[19] This puts greater pressure on stresses and internal echoes, especially as there is little in the way of sound patterning asserting itself. In this poem the work of attention must train on line breaks, caesuras, modifications in cadence rather than nests of consonants or stretches of vowels. The poem is almost wilfully self-effacing. But within its unobtrusive sonic world, 'Me' comes to be recognised exactly as *positioned*, while 'I' also standing against the margin might be so 'inclined'. It takes a while to tune in to such delicate dispositions, but when we do we can notice that 'The carn / Foxglove' also stands against the wall of the left margin, and leans. 'If so / I were inclined' shifts spoken word order fractionally to achieve its positioning, its effect. One might pass over the unfamiliar word 'carn', for the enjambment gives the ordinary non-botanist the idea that a 'carn foxglove' may be a particular variety of foxglove. It isn't, and there's a reason for declining to stress the unusual word; which is a Scottish form of 'cairn', a heap of stones. Arriving in Cornwall, Wynter first lived in a house named The Carn, and it belongs to the texture of intimacy that he would recognise the allusion but we wouldn't – but should not be halted in our reading as though this were the kind of poem that demands frequent recourse to the *OED*. Hesitation and resumption become a shared rhythm. True, not much could mitigate the specificity of the place name Zennor, but the peculiar name is made a qualifier so it's the wind that seems significant even as 'Zennor' signals to Wynter that this is their familiar landscape. We might now look back and notice how the word 'died' before a caesura avoids portentousness owing to the repeated address to 'you'. If you're still there, you who are able to realise this or that, death can't be so categorial. 'I am' and 'You died' can therefore be enjambed.

But the 'position / It puts me in' is more complicated yet. In day-to-day usage it means you've put me in a fix, a jam, a place I can't get out of. The dilemma is of standing outside The Carn and being unable to move away because Wynter isn't there to walk beside as he leaves his old home. There is only the 'carn foxglove' which stands in for him (Wynter was tall and skinny too). Writing the note and striking a

---

[19] Hannah Brooks-Motl, 'W. S. Graham: "Dear Bryan Wynter": How a Poem Brings Language to Loss and Speaks to the Dead', *Poetry Foundation Poem Guide*: http://www.poetryfoundation.org/learning/poem/242916#guide [accessed 3 October 2019].

note again puts Graham in the position of being the poet who is alive, and the third part removes to the poet's own house. So 'here on the wall' identifies a shared world which can continue to be shared only through this poem's intimate voice, a poem whose geography is not so much a map as lines of prosody, lines traced in familiar walks that accompany and rhythmically organise two people's way of talking to each other and laughing together, only one of them now surviving and left with his words unanswered, repeatedly broken off, since there is no one with whom to walk in step, except an unknown reader whose pace may fail to fall in. The salient performance of this interrupted walking is the instance of a single iamb followed by a strong caesura and then a two- or three-beat stumble. Thus the inclination to the rhythm of walking is frustrated time and again: 'if so / I were inclined', 'The carn / foxglove here', 'Outside your first house'. The enforcement of a pause after 'Outside' in reading the line, separating the iamb from the following three syllables, is felt powerfully. Along with its multiple interrogatives, this prosodic signature influences the curious sense of always starting out in this poem.

The second stanza of this first part begins with a brisk reference to how things are, but this ordinary phrase is perceived as shifting through rhythmic stress to a question about the status of 'things' in Wynter's distanced world, things which in the second part recede into the vagueness of 'anything' and 'something', overcome by mist. The stanza introduces a problem arising unmistakably from dislocation:

> your long legs
> And twitching smile under
> Your blue hat walking
> Across a place?

Across 'a place'? What place? How does an articulation walk over an abstraction, a 'somewhere'? How can you 'still' be 'somewhere' as against being located? Only if the question is ontological, but 'somewhere' pales against 'Zennor'. As for these things, legs and smile and hat, they belong to an attempt to make you up from which the poem recoils back into inclining – inclining across a distance to a you that isn't so much made up, as subject to attempted reanimation by way of apostrophe and prosody, through shared walking, shared too by us as readers if not so presently and surely. The poem seeks to make Wynter up from the requirements of setting forth – he needs his legs, he must put on his hat, his twitching smile is the sign of his companionship. Fiona Green discerns an allusion to 'Lycidas': 'At last he rose, and twitched his mantle blue'.[20] But the re-creation fails, and the inclining solitary poet can make up Wynter only as solitary and walking across 'a place', somewhere not traversed by paths of shared experience. Abandoning this attempt to make you up, the poem strives to restore 'you' not in a landscape abstracted by your absence, but more compellingly remembered through shared relationships, including Wynter's wife Monica, 'you' becoming so close as to join in an inter-subjectivity resisting collapse into 'things': you live in the memories of those who love you. 'Place' further dissolves into the question 'Are you there at all?', from which Wynter is summoned back, as it were from the caesura after 'place' and the characteristic iamb before the line break, a moment of doubt followed by lines seeking comfort in imagining Wynter separated from his family by distance rather than death and preoccupied with thoughts of them; even if 'all right' might signal the aftermath of a failed work of restoration – and nobody and nothing in this poem is 'all right', but 'inclined' at best.

Is this speech or a letter? Part 2 of the poem restages the question:

> Speaking to you and not
> Knowing if you are there
> Is not too difficult.
> My words are used to that.
> Do you want anything?
> Where shall I send something?
> Rice-wine, meanders, paintings
> By your contemporaries?
> Or shall I send a kind
> Of news of no time
> Leaning against the wall
> Outside your old house.
>
> The house and the whole moor
> Is flying in the mist.

The notoriously disorientating quality of moorland mists unmoors Wynter's old house and every landmark. The dissolution is intol-erable, since the landscape cannot be crossed by Graham and Wynter; but more especially, it cannot be crossed by language as shared, and threatens to become as abstract as 'a place', unspecified. Part 3 reverts decisively to the poet in present solitude, beginning with a striking

---

[20]   Green, 'Achieve Further through Elegy', p. 153.

displacement into a mirror, or so I imagine, for the phrase 'The front of my face' cannot be found by online search except in this poem:

> I am up. I've washed
> The front of my face
> And here I stand looking
> Out over the top
> Half of my bedroom window.

Furthermore, it confronts the collapse of intersubjectivity into a reflective solitude that relinquishes the joshing tone of shared speech and no longer expects to be joined in response. There is a suggestion of putting on a front for the day, making oneself up, which we know from attempts to make up Bryan Wynter is liable to fail. The phrase also catches attention because it's a rare unambiguously two-beat line and oddly assertive. The immediate effect lies in contrast with 'The house and the whole moor / Is flying in the mist'.

The blunt opening 'I am up' clashes with 'flying in the mist'. The embodied grief into which the landscape dissolves, now needs the reaffirmed 'I am' passed over at the start of the poem. Such assertion, such a recovery, is as positional as St Buryan's church tower – that's how directions are given in Cornwall, in relation to churches and pubs, not points of the compass, characteristic of a landscape experienced through paths rather than roads, worn by walking between gathering places. But in bereavement the poem has recourse to a world of mapping, not of prosodic lines. The face is being touched as a kind of trigonometrical point, from which a flying landscape may now be mapped in sure coordinates, not necessarily visible, resituating Wynter in a nameable place, although in the past. The three vertical assertions with which Part 3 continues, a 'dark rise' alongside 'I am up' and a church tower, map a relationship between the living and dead with remarkable subtlety, almost beneath notice:

> There almost as far
> As I can see I see
> St Buryan's church tower.
> An inch to the left, behind
> That dark rise of woods,
> Is where you used to lurk.

The dark rise conjures the burial mounds prolific in Cornwall; since Wynter used to lurk in the woods, and since the verb 'lurk' implies a continuous presence out of sight, possibly he is there still, a persistence of a different order from the abstraction proposed by a church tower as metonymic of eternal life. That, I take it, is why Part 4 refers to Housman's starlit fences, found in an elegiac poem ('Far in a Western Brookland' from *A Shropshire Lad*) tracing the soul's persistence in a well-loved landscape, even if that soul is A. E. Housman's rather than a loved friend's, and its distancing is from his own body asleep in the city.[21]

Housman's poem sounds confident in its ascription of 'here' and 'there', in 'pools I used to know' and 'fields where I was known', although they are drawn together by a wanderer in 'brookland', a place of watery meanderings. Yet this confident prosody is that of a confirmed solitary while Graham is mourning the impossibility of shared walking. We are returned to the poet against the wall, unable to move away but striving to find the prosody he needs – not making it up with the feet and hat of Bryan Wynter, but starting forward and falling back into standstills.

The knowing at the end of Graham's poem is difficult to parse. The apology in 'I know I make a symbol / Of the foxglove on the wall' could refer to the pub debates on aesthetics in which Graham and Wynter jousted; as an abstract artist in his maturity, even if his abstraction derived from the Cornish landscape, Wynter would have disdained symbolism. He probably wouldn't have approved of making things up either, in the sense of a fiction or a lie; Graham's recording of 'Dear Bryan Wynter' lays an insatiable child's quality of stress on 'again' in the first section's 'Or am / I greedy to make you up / Again out of memory?', as though to bring a deceased Bryan Wynter into a poem as a living presence, again, were greedy.[22] But

---

[21]   The Housman poem (from *The Poems of A. E. Housman*, ed. Archie Burnett (Oxford: Oxford University Press, 1997), pp. 55–56) is as follows:

LII. Far in a western brookland

FAR in a western brookland
   That bred me long ago
The poplars stand and tremble
   By pools I used to know.

He hears: no more remembered
   In fields where I was known
Here I lie down in London
   And turn to rest alone.

There, in the windless night-time,
   The wanderer, marvelling why,
Halts on the bridge to hearken
   How soft the poplars sigh.

There, by the starlit fences,
   The wanderer halts and hears
My soul that lingers sighing
   About the glimmering weirs.

[22]   Accessible at the Poetry Archive: http://www.poetryarchive.org/explore/browse-poems?f%5B0%5D=field_poet:192486 [accessed 3 October 2019].

Wynter's presence is formal, too; the poem's meanders around a shared landscape constitute a tribute to Wynter procedurally, a set of meanders or curves where things are very sparingly referenced, and inclining takes the place of representing or making up. The word 'meander', as the *OED* advises, is a transferred use of the name of the river Maeander in Caria (now western Turkey), noted for its winding course. The meanders of Bryan Wynter's paintings are true to this derivation, based on close study of riverine behaviour, both the meanders of river courses, and the meandering and eddies of currents in a river's flow. 'Dear Bryan Wynter' is a poem of obstructed fluency, which must meander, or proceed according to a set of curves, in order to make its way. How then does the foxglove know Bryan Wynter? He must have passed it every day, for it's a perennial. But perhaps there's a shared joke, since Wynter suffered heart problems for some time before his fatal heart attack, possibly treated with digitalis, derived from foxgloves. The second of the 'Two Poems in Zennor Hill' comes closer to making this explicit:

> O foxglove on the wall
> You meet me nicely today
> Leaning your digitalis
> Bells toward the house
> Bryan Wynterless.[23]

All the knowing then becomes quite *knowing*, but, as with the reference to carn, could pass without troubling the companionate reader. This quality of reference in Graham's poetry has been noted by Peter Riley, who qualifies his particular obscurity by noting that 'all items of vocabulary remain Graham's [either] local or not; they derive entirely from his life, the where and when of him'.[24]

It's a commonplace to say that a poem makes us feel more alive. An elegy might, disgracefully, make one feel more alive through contemplating the deadness of the dead. But what does it mean for a poem deliberately to set out to make a dead person live? If a poem makes us more alive, does it mean that deprived of animation by prosody we are dead ourselves or as good as dead? Ceasing to walk is certainly bad for us:

---

[23] Graham, 'Two Poems on Zennor Hill', in *New Collected Poems*, p. 209.
[24] Peter Riley, [review of W. S. Graham, *New Collected Poems*], *Jacket*, 26 (October 2007): http://jacketmagazine.com/26/rile-grah.html [accessed 3 October 2019].

Or shall I send a kind
Of news of no time
Leaning against the wall
Outside your old house.

There is a leaning, an inclining, a distance from the event of the
poem, which is simply not enough for life. If there are no steps, no
feet, there is no time. There is no setting out again in Bryan Wynter's
company – that cannot be denied: 'I am aware / You are not here'.
'I am / You died'. Only the anaclisis persists, Graham's dependence
on Wynter transferred to his house. But in its fifth part the poem
accompanies Wynter walking in his other world, in parallel, where
he can 'scout things out' and still be addressed, wearing his blue
hat. He is in motion again because he is walking proleptically, for
Graham. They will walk these paths together. We, too, proleptically, in our parallel world. The foxglove 'knows you' in the sense
of 'it knows the kind of person you are', the inclining person who
walks again, and the single inclining foxglove resembles the departed
Wynter standing again next to Graham; because of that symbolic
resemblance one might even say the foxglove wants to start out, too,
to follow its *semblable*. Shall we all go unified in time? But foxgloves
are frequently pulled apart in Graham's poetry, for instance in 'His
Companions Buried Him' ('I see Earth's operator within his glade /
Gloved in the fox of his gigantic hour'), and in 'Approaches to How
They Behave' ('Shines the red / Fox in the digitalis grove' and 'If you
can't fit me in / To lying down here among the fox / Glove towers
of the moment').[25] The foxglove in 'Dear Bryan Wynter' might then
also be a linguistic joke about putting the thing back together as a
symbol, having pulled it apart so often.[26]

But the seeming confidence of 'It is because it knows you' disgorges
as it must into the unknowable. This is true of every section of the
poem, each brought up against a break that cannot be gainsaid, except
perhaps the second where a vertiginous 'flying in the mist' erases
both letter writer and addressee, unendurably. 'This is only a note' is
repeated and then echoed in 'Although I am not', hastily negated. This
poet is still alive. Is he? Where? In these lines and their movement.
And why are the final three lines so haunting, apparently careless?
Maybe because that redoubled knowing, echoing Housman, is ours too

---

[25]   Graham, *New Collected Poems*, pp. 37 and 178–82, respectively.
[26]   I owe this observation to Ned Allen.

as readers, out of this note, out of the knowledge that now this poem is not Graham's alone but is the path we have followed and in so doing joined in a walk to bring back a news of no time we are bound to share – for if Graham can no longer walk in time with Wynter, and is reduced to 'news of no time / Leaning against the wall', inclined towards the impossibility of lyric unjoined, any of us can join in reading and make such inclination, across time and place, into lyric prosody and so walk with Graham and Wynter along these paths.

Both 'The Day Lady Died' and 'Ode on Causality' ended in the air and in the restoring of inspiration granted by great art, whether in breath held by the audience at Billie Holiday's Five Spot performance or the cloud that gives birth to an artwork named *Bird in Flight*.[27] Poets are as much inclined to air and airs (and to air their views) as they are to feet, but Graham fights to return the airy and the abstract to earth. Graham has an antipathy to air, and it's personal. His superb elegy 'The Thermal Stair' is dedicated to 'the painter Peter Lanyon killed in a gliding accident 1964', and while it asks Lanyon to

> Find me a thermal to speak and soar to you from
> Over Lanyon Quoit and the circling stones standing
> High on the moor over Gurnard's Head [..][28]

it is the quoit, a stone dolmen linking Lanyon with Cornwall (as the only major St Ives artist of Cornish extraction and birth), the 'circling stones', and the poem's later 'carn to carn' that correspond to the poem's unusually resonant and unfretful declaration of artistic purpose:

> The poet or painter steers his life to maim
>
> Himself somehow for the job. His job is love
> Imagined into words or paint to make
> An object that will stand and will not move.

---

[27] This provides an opportunity to correct a careless error in my paper on O'Hara's odes, where I mistake *Bird in Flight* for Brâncuşi's *Bird in Space*, misnaming Brâncuşi's sculpture. There may be an allusion but not an identity (John Wilkinson, '"Where Air Is Flesh"': The *Odes* of Frank O'Hara', in *Frank O'Hara Now: New Essays on the New York Poet*, ed. Robert Hampson and Will Montgomery (Liverpool: Liverpool University Press, 2010), pp. 103–19 (p. 112)).

[28] Graham, 'The Thermal Stair', in *New Collected Poems*, pp. 163–66.

Air itself becomes a hard support under a buzzard's wings, and the poem honours Lanyon's resistance to the Cornish picturesque, citing the industry of tin miners and beam engines and the 'vesselled men' who were 'maintained' by the sea. Lanyon's flying was a way of getting closer to earth, of surveying its topography and geology, connected categorically to place, not to space – so the poem ridicules a woman who 'turns to mention space' at an exhibition opening, and reverts to the homosocial place of the pub, opening time being signalled by 'the phallic boys' (the Godrevy and Wolf lighthouses). Both Graham and O'Hara insist repeatedly on the social origin and hoped-for destination of lyric even when isolation and loss are most deeply felt; and it is this social discourse that replaces discourse on behalf of a no-longer-available general public. 'Climb here where the hand / Will not grasp on air', the poem enjoins the dead Lanyon; its waymarks as in 'Dear Bryan Wynter' are shared places, and both poems go walking to reinvoke the presence of the lost friend, along tracks familiar to Graham and the friend and quite possibly to them alone. Yet the reader does not demur and feels solid ground underfoot. Tacita Dean in a recent book on Lanyon comments accurately on 'The Thermal Stair' that the 'intimacy of the poem beguiles you into feeling you know the place that Lanyon knew. Both poet and painter understood that to evoke a sense of place is to do so indirectly, and that place is about the local, and about biography, actual or assumed, and that place is felt'.[29] The only inventions of 'The Thermal Stair' are its title, constructed from the thermals on which Lanyon's glider rose and fell, and the attribution of 'Lanyon's stair' after 'Lanyon's Quoit' to further suggest a kind of Jacob's ladder dreamt up to heaven out of 'one of the stones of the place' (Genesis 28:11). But this unusual fancy is superseded immediately by the request: 'Uneasy, lovable man, give me your painting / Hand to steady me taking the word-road home'. W. S. Graham is a great poet of male friendship, taciturn, down to earth. His response to loss, rooted in the particulars of shared life and a friend's gestures, is to put his suffered taciturnity into words, a word-road others may walk.

If Frank O'Hara walks under the pressure of distraction and W. S. Graham walks shared tracks in a summoning of the departed (a euphemism made poignant at the opening of 'The Thermal Stair' in the quiet phrase 'you were away'), James Schuyler's response to grief

[29]   Tacita Dean, 'Then the Wind's Hand Brushed the Picture Away', in Chris Stephens, *Peter Lanyon* (St Ives: Tate St Ives, 2010), p. 120.

in 'Buried at Springs' is simply to sit and stare out of the window on a Maine island, declining 'to go / out the window into the late / August midafternoon sun'.[30] This poem is linked intimately to 'Ode on Causality' since it is Frank O'Hara who now is 'buried at Springs', but it has little in common with O'Hara's poem in its rhetoric of understatement – of which Schuyler is a master. Schuyler was a lover of eighteenth-century diarists and naturalists, and it is the exactitude of his attention to the natural world, the wandering and training of his eye, that govern the poem's fluent but exactly stitched syntax. Pulling back from the distance where 'two lines of wake' are visible, attention arrives at a near point where precise description leads to

> Rocks with rags
> of shadow, washed dust clouds
> that will never bleach.
> It is not like this at all.[31]

The title 'Buried at Springs' has hovered above this poem and tints a phrase like 'two lines of wake' with a funereal wash, but it is recourse to simile that produces a crisis in the poem, however subdued – a crisis comparable to those in the O'Hara poems, precipitated in one by the word 'lays' and in the other by a glimpse of a newspaper photograph. When rocks appear like 'washed dust clouds', the simile alludes to classical Chinese landscape painting; perdurable rocks become transient through this simile and vulnerable to light – and rocks may turn to dust. The simile is tersely rejected, but the breach cannot be caulked; the poem continues:

> The rapid running of the
> lapping water a hollow knock
> of someone shipping oars:
> it's eleven years since
> Frank sat at this desk and
> heard and saw it all
> the incessant water the
> immutable crickets only
> not the same [..].[32]

---

[30]   James Schuyler, 'Buried at Springs', in *Collected Poems* (New York: Farrar, Straus and Giroux, 1993), pp. 42–44 (p. 42).

[31]   Ibid., pp. 42–43.

[32]   Ibid., p. 43.

The immutable now is seasonal, the incessant is changeable, and the meticulously described landscape depends upon a present consciousness. Rocks give way to the muted metaphor of running water for the transience of life, an oarsman's resignation from strife and yielding to the current. The first part of the poem ends with a granite boulder which 'quite / literally is not the same' not only because rocks turn to dust, but because the consciousness in which it is held has been altered by the loss of Frank's coextensive attention. It is this delicate apprehension which brings Schuyler's poem close to Graham's. O'Hara and Schuyler were not striders across rough terrain like Graham and Hilton or Lanyon, but the loss of shared experience of a place alters that place for both poets and recalls the lost sharer. What Peter Riley notes in Graham is as true of Schuyler; the second part of 'Buried at Springs' offers further meticulous description that time and again breaches the even surface to reveal fleetingly the pain of loss, in 'the thin scream / of mosquitoes', and in pine cones with their 'gum, pungent, clear as a tear' leading to a final view of the scene 'like wet silk / stained by one dead branch / the harsh russet of dried blood'. The earliest Chinese painting (and writing) was on silk, using pigment made from pine soot. While strict convention governs Chinese landscape painting, the brushstrokes of the particular artist can be identified; the scene is mediated by the subtlest distinguishing marks of attention. To know how a scene looks through someone else's eyes is to know them exceptionally well; both Frank O'Hara and James Schuyler used their eyes professionally as art critics, and the 'one dead branch' on wet silk would have united them in recognising its calligraphic style even as now it suggests that Schuyler has lost a limb with the loss of his friend.

'Buried at Springs' elegises a poet whom Schuyler envied for his published achievements and his charisma. It is remarkable that the poem makes no allusion to O'Hara's vocation; Frank 'saw and heard' but is not remembered as a poet. As much as a surreptitious elegy, this might be thought a suppressive elegy; grief is admitted through bracketing O'Hara's public persona, allowing love to be expressed for a man unrecognisable as the Frank O'Hara of his poems and of others' memoirs. It is telling that Schuyler translates O'Hara from the Manhattan where he so influentially walked and stood still, to a Maine he visited only briefly. There is something of a levelling of the scales here, for Great Spruce Head Island, where Schuyler lodged for years with the painter Fairfield Porter and his family, was as familiar to him and present to his poems as Manhattan to O'Hara.

In Margaret Ross's remarkable first book, *A Timeshare* (2015), there is no place name other than 'Antarctica', and no person's name besides 'Captain Scott' in the same poem and in another the 'Lewis' of Lewis and Clark fame – both naming walkers in unmapped territory.[33] Not only is this peculiar in contemporary American poetry, which ordinarily comes either anchored by locality and family or studded with commodity names and cultural detritus, but it would seem to disqualify the book from being considered under the sign of elegy, since it is impossible to identify one or several persons elegised except possibly the present self by its future self. *A Timeshare* might, however, be considered a sequence of elegies much as Rilke's *The Duino Elegies* is – that is, a general meditation on loss and mortality.[34] The salient difference is that Ross's book consists of *prospective* elegies. With its intricate syntactical pleating and nested verb tenses, *A Timeshare* constitutes an extended elegy for the present, for 'a timeshare' which from the start discounts any possibility of dwelling and hence of the naming that signifies persistence. The first poem sets the tone; titled 'Of Late', which shifts retrospectively amidst its shades of meaning from 'recently' to 'of end times', the poem ends:

> [..] Before the obviously chemical
>
> blue dark, gold strands like
> shrimp veins thread the human
> skulls of girls. Lawns drenched in iodine.
> All along the river flickering pills,
> if they would just align,
> could be taken to mean *Tear Here*.[35]

The here-ness has already been torn to the point that perspectivally the poem can contemplate 'the human / skulls of girls' as though evidence of a lost species. Such estrangement may, the poem hints, be induced by drugs, but the poem itself is torn across at its ending, and

[33]　Margaret Ross, *A Timeshare* (Oakland: Omnidawn, 2015).

[34]　Whether *The Duino Elegies* are elegies in anything but name is controversial among scholars of poetics. The most recent edition of *The Princeton Encyclopedia of Poetry & Poetics* notes slightly sniffily: '[p]erhaps the most distinguished 20th-c. poems to call themselves elegies are R. M. Rilke's *Duineser Elegien* (written 1912–1922)' ('Elegy', in *The Princeton Encyclopedia of Poetry & Poetics*, ed. Roland Greene et al., fourth edition (Princeton: Princeton University Press, 2012), pp. 397–99 (p. 398)).

[35]　Ross, 'Of Late', in *A Timeshare*, p. 17.

having started with the curt one-word sentence 'Countdown', it turns out that the countdown does not lead to the fully experienced present of an event, but counts the present down into a drifting platform, an effect of alignment such as a poem might, when once torn free, be found to have achieved.

Ross's poems do have a significant affinity with 'Buried at Springs' and with the paintings of Fairfield Porter in that the boundaries between inside and outside shift like curtains or effects of light, and the positioning of the subject lies uncertainly between inside and outside. Like Schuyler's poem in being neither introspective nor tropic to objects, Ross's poems differ in that it is not the veils between past and present that are disturbed, but rather those between a future poetically realised in the present and the present it displaces. The titular poem, which is 76 lines long, opens stealthily:

> Five o'clock again in the rented living
> room. Nothing wrong. Heliotrope continuing
> to fade into upholstery.[36]

The sunlit present is evidently withdrawing (it fades), and sunlight itself is conspiring to efface the heliotrope. The time, five o'clock, is a repeated time of day which oscillates between the present of the poem as written or read, and the historical present – the next phrase is 'Buttons pressing back' which make 'the surface // cave'. The act of attention through attempting to pin down its observed objects pushes them into a cave, obscured from the sun and indeed from continued attention. Before long the tenses of the poem become impossibly tangled and the syntax mournful:

> Q: *What are you*
> *doing down there in the*
>
> *there in the meantime?* X: *All day*
> *I am an orchard at midday when the stunned air*
> *pauses, bronze and stupid, terse with flies.* Don't lie. I'm
> in the living room. Seconds dropping
>
> from the faucet to the metal bed
> of the sink: *this is your one*
> *now this is, now late,* nobody waits for thee
> on the greeny moor where I was

---

[36] Ross, 'A Timeshare', in *A Timeshare*, p. 20.

lain all stuck with yew, or the Q: *Did we*
outgrow our dream of a point repaired to when alone?[37]

While this may bear some resemblance to the selfie elegy of a young
woman mourning her lost youth, it is closer to W. S. Graham's 'news
of no time'; the passage's opening question *'What are you / doing down*
there in the / there in the meantime?' shares Graham's pressure on
deictics and his poems' temporal warping:

> And this place is taking
> Its time from us though these
> Two people or voices
> Are not us nor has
> The time they seem to move in
> To do with what we think
> Our own times are.[38]

And in Ross's poem the 'Two people or voices' are not Q and A, but
Q and X; they are 'in the meantime', *'an orchard at midday'*, 'in the
living room', *'your one / now this is, now late'*, and *'repaired to when*
alone'. The punning 'lying' in the poem introduces a view of a dead
body, reinforced by the pun on 'yew', a tree associated actually and
poetically with graveyards. Such a body will also be viewed by a
lover or God once 'all persons disappear / and he alone looks down
to freeways / embroidering the vacant earth'. This shift is performed
repeatedly in Ross's poems, in 'Caller', 'Dissolution', 'Antarctica', 'A
Day in Space and Another Day', and 'Futures Exchange', and by the
end of the book the trope of dissociative lift-off has come to regard not
only the abandoned and lifeless body (sometimes in post-coital satiety,
all desire spent) but the 'vacant earth' itself, viewed extraterrestrially
and from a future where the freeways cover a post-human planet.
Often the body is viewed on a narrow concrete ledge, as though only
its weight makes any part of the world's furniture actual. In her online
commentary on 'A Timeshare' Margaret Ross writes of her

> feel for intersecting systems and for the multiple, entangled
> nature of a life lived between them. To my mind that meant
> scale shifts. Each poem is set in a single scene from which
> the feeling comes, but truly seeing that scene means seeing
> its ties to other times and places, hearing echoed voices not

---

[37] Ibid.
[38] Graham, 'The Dark Dialogues' (Part 4), in *New Collected Poems*, p. 173.

the speaker's: the past inscribed in the present's gestures, the traces everywhere of other lives. The ambition is visceral plurality via image and music.[39]

But this is only part of the story; the most compelling and novel aspect of the poems is that here the contemporary has become a superseded historical period, and the possibility of living in the present has withdrawn. What is obsessively contemplated is the self as that which is expelled time and again from a world no longer providing the bounty of presentness. As Kate Marshall notes in discussing a *New York Times* article by literary scholar and Iraqi war veteran Roy Scranton titled 'Learning How to Die in the Anthropocene':

> This kind of death, however, or this kind of learning, may be mortal but is anything but humble. For the geological media-tions achieved by death in the Anthropocene constitute a wild counterpunch to the presumed indifference of a material stratum by redefining the geological layer left behind by the departed species as constituted itself by that species and its detritus.[40]

The furniture, the chemicals and the dyes which are the impress and marks of the dissociated self in the abandoned contemporaneity of Ross's poems, are the equivalent of the 'geological mediations' Marshall tracks in recent American fiction; the self of the poems looks down on the freeways girdling the earth and sees a vacancy that is defined by her departure. This may be related to the selfie elegy but is subject to 'scale shifts', a loss that empties the entire world, a devastation. The defence against this catastrophe, however, is an infantile fantasy of omnipotence, preserved through a radical depersonalisation; the self that does not receive and respond to the (originally maternal) response that assures it that it exists, abandons the body to take over the universe. Indifference is met with super powers that defeat all restrictions of time and space.

Depersonalisation was defined in 1939 by Paul Schilder as

---

[39] 'A Timeshare' can be found on the Poetry Society's website, along with the author's commentary: https://www.poetrysociety.org/psa/poetry/crossroads/own_words/Margaret_Ross/ [accessed 3 October 2019].

[40] Kate Marshall, 'What Are the Novels of the Anthropocene? American Fiction in Geological Time', *American Literary History*, 27.3 (2015), 523–38 (p. 529).

a state of the personality in which the individual feels changed in comparison to his former state. This change extends to both the awareness of the self and of the outer world and the individual does not acknowledge himself as a personality. His actions seem automatic to him; he observes his own actions like a spectator. We find, therefore, in this picture changes of the self, or depersonalisation in the narrower sense, and changes in the environment, or feelings of unreality, alienation of the outward world, 'Entfremdung der Wahrnehmungswelt'.[41]

It is hard to resist the thought that depersonalisation accompanied by omnipotence precisely describes a more general human response to the apprehension of lack, of restricted resources, in a universe previously thought to be one of inexhaustible plenitude. The achievement of a constituted true self through a recognition of differentiated places and persons – a singular absence in Ross's poems – might be substituted by a simulacrum, a false and compliant identity, or by a radical denial of any restriction. Ross's poems perform a striking displacement from the inhabitant of the present furniture, for they are full of environmental simulacra, and indeed her book ends with imprisonment in a simulacrum: 'the street / convincingly painted onto glass as if you could go'.[42] This is where the question of the persistence of elegy may meet the radical question: if lack is denied, can mourning take place? The elegies to lost youth characteristic of amateur student poetry start to come into focus as a phenomenon; what is mourned there may be the moment where a true self was starting to be realised within a reassuring familiar matrix, from a depressive position where a false self has been assumed, a compliance that may be transitional before the constitution of a renewed true self becomes possible through chosen attachments.[43] The mourning in such elegies may be itself conventional – American culture is endlessly sentimental about childhood – but the fascination of *A Timeshare* stems in part from an inability to mourn that makes reality dreamlike, an endless shifting of gauze, curtains, and veils in exquisitely pleated syntax, the present of losses dissolving under the gaze of futurity.

[41] Paul Schilder, 'The Treatment of Depersonalization', *Bulletin of the New York Academy of Medicine*, 15.4 (1939), 258–66.

[42] Ross, 'Assisted Living', in *A Timeshare*, p. 93.

[43] This language is derived from D. W. Winnicott. See the exposition in Adam Phillips, *Winnicott*, new edition (London: Penguin 2007), pp. 127–30.

Although Graham's elegies may project creative power through their celebrations of Peter Lanyon, Roger Hilton, and Bryan Wynter, they strive also to incorporate the power of those artists which Graham's poems fully sense as generous and living (as is also true of O'Hara's elegiac poems for artists). Even more importantly, Graham's and O'Hara's are poems of love whose language harkens to the lost other and the self now affected by loss, the talkers it developed between. The joshing tone which Graham introduced into English elegy and the odd mixture of gossipy sociality with the melancholy of loss characteristic of O'Hara are both effective in restoring an interlocution that serves to embody the loved dead lyrically.

The devastation of the world in Margaret Ross's poems thwarts the work of restitution. They can only orbit the site of loss even while loss may not be endured or recognised in its specificity. Yet a Rilkean tone is audible in *A Timeshare* even if Ross's perspective is that of an angel surveying the abandoned earth:

> Did the time change? Did little
>   savings of a day glint on blades
> wind tilted towards the illuminated
>   capital? Starting again, did change
>
> course.[44]

When David Kennedy wrote that 'national identity has become synonymous with remembrance', he was writing in Britain a decade after the death of Princess Diana, an event which left many shocked at how shocked they had been by the death of one who meant so little to them when alive. Although comparable to disturbance at the cancellation of a beloved TV series, albeit on a huge scale, this was also a subjunctive grief, a grief for an extinguished national fantasy of what might have been, as well as another episode in the British mourning for imperial influence, no longer decently expressible. A decade later, the death of David Bowie had a similarly unanticipated impact despite his more advanced age and prior intimations of his mortality; but there, expressions of grief were more characteristically shaped as grief for loss of parts of the self, through recognition of those potent moments of self-construction which Bowie's songs or his own performances of self-construction were felt to have motivated. However, the rapid dissipation of grief in the publicity sphere which

[44] Ross, 'Decay Constant', in *A Timeshare*, p. 58.

now substitutes for a public sphere, bears on a continuing and vital role for poetic elegy; with human memory increasingly offshored from the flesh to electronic devices or fading as swiftly as vapour trails, the poetic elegy can nonetheless capture and make available for a reader's reanimation, a memory of feelings. So it does in the examples discussed, which embrace the confusion of the nominally elegised with a lost part of the elegist, as do the two major English-language elegiac sequences of the 1990s, Thom Gunn's *The Man with Night Sweats* and Barry MacSweeney's *Pearl* (the deaf young girl Pearl elegised by MacSweeney may not even have existed).[45] In that sense, all elegies have become selfie elegies, but they also hold the promise of a restored public and a continually reviving poetic memory, for instance in Gunn's echoes of Jonson and MacSweeney's of Wordsworth's Lucy poems.

But against such promise, the pervasiveness of an elegiac tone in popular culture as well as in poetry may be explained by the back projections of prospective elegy, responsive to the withdrawing expectation of a bountiful future, especially painful in the United States and therefore especially subject to denial. The richness of a remembered or delusory past, also suffused back in the day by that now-attenuated promise, is what modern lyric repeats in all its varieties and subgenres. How can the poet, sending into a world of loss and indifference the language she learnt to love in intercourse with poetry and those people she loves and has been loved by, not feel a grievous sense of prospective loss? As with Ben Jonson, the poet time and again must lay down her pen and pronounce:

> Rest in soft peace, and, ask'd, say, 'Here doth lie
> Ben Jonson his best piece of poetry.'

---

[45] Barry MacSweeney, *Pearl* (Cambridge, Equipage 1995).

CHAPTER FIVE

Interpellation

Addressing Ideology in Claudia Rankine's American Lyric

Drew Milne

The shared subtitle of Claudia Rankine's books *Don't Let Me Be Lonely: An American Lyric* (2004) and *Citizen: An American Lyric* (2014) draws attention to questions of national identity and poetic genre. The adjectival force of *American* can be taken variously to position these books both as continuations of a distinct tradition of form and as fragments of a distinct political geography of experience. The lyric compound suggests a mode of national address implicitly offering as yet unacknowledged legislations and representations for America as a polity, a republic of citizens. Such ambition is somewhat deflected by the indefinite article. As *lyric*, rather than lyrics, the associated senses of short form and experience undermine any suggestion of epic or documentary political representation, but without becoming an album or a collection of lyric leaves. This is structured neither as narrative nor as discrete fragments, but as a book: a book of lyric or a lyric book.

Much of the interest excited by Rankine's work, especially by *Citizen*, reflects this opening up of the book form to become an engaging lyric medium that addresses contemporary society in new ways. Rankine's poetics of lyric as book, a form of textual composition also layered with other media, owes something to earlier conceptual models of long-form poetic prose sequences, such as Lyn Hejinian's *My Life* (1980 onwards). In 'The New Sentence' (1977), Ron Silliman sketches another possible antecedent:

> Alfred Kreymborg's 1930 anthology, *Lyric America*, has four prose poems. One is a long and tedious one by Allura Giovanni, called 'The Walker.' The other three are by the black poet

Fenton Johnson. Johnson uses a device which points in the direction of the new sentence. Each sentence is a complete paragraph; run-on sentences are treated as one paragraph each, but two paragraphs begin with conjunctions. Structured thus, Johnson's is the first American *prose* poem with a clear, if simple, sentence: paragraph relation.[1]

The development of the paragraph as a structural verse unit, paratactically articulated across paragraphs as a lyric book, generates a plurality of forms held within the book form. The lyric book, by extension, is a composition across a play of different forms. Rankine's American lyric also works with prose poems, dramatised situations, and intermedial conjunctions that mediate the experience of other media, such as visual art, photographs, video installations, and television. Indeed, Lauren Berlant offers a synoptic sense of the quality of Rankine's American lyric books by analogy with television: '[e]ach [work] is like a commentary track on the bottom of a collective television screen where the ordinary of racism meets a collective nervous system's desire for events to be profoundly transformative'.[2] There is more than a passing analogy with television in Rankine's work. Poetry's complicity with other social media is constitutive for her work, providing a significant source of found materials, linguistic and visual. This implicates lyric in other media and mediating forms, and there is no attempt to claim autonomy for lyric language or form. In an interview, Rankine herself suggests that: '*Citizen* is about white liberal collusion in white supremacist violence'.[3] Put differently, *Citizen* offers a texture of representations which reproduces apparently discrete micro-aggressions in ways that implicate readers in the ideological structures constitutive of American society, from scenes of everyday life to televised 'sport' and news media.

Rankine's American lyric engages readers, interpellates them, often through an open-ended and indeterminately singular and plural 'you'. In a review, Rankine suggests of Amiri Baraka's poetry that even in a final 'personal moment', 'the language opens out to its

---

[1] Ron Silliman, 'The New Sentence', in *The New Sentence* (New York: Roof Books, 1989), pp. 63–93 (pp. 82–83).

[2] Lauren Berlant, 'Claudia Rankine', *Bomb* (1 October 2014): https://bomb magazine.org/articles/claudia-rankine/ [accessed 3 October 2019].

[3] Aaron Coleman, 'The History Behind the Feeling: A Conversation with Claudia Rankine', *The Spectacle*, 7 (2015): https://thespectacle.wustl.edu/?p=105 [accessed 3 October 2019].

community of readers'.[4] Rather than personal revelation or spoken-word standards of conversational implicature, it is the relation to reading through lyric *writing* that characterises Rankine's poetics. The displacement of conventional lyric structures of address, and the difficulty of specifying her work in relation to the history of lyric forms, has not made Rankine's work inaccessible or 'difficult', quite the contrary. Amid many conflicting attempts to offer formal descriptions of Rankine's work, the argument here is that the forms in play remain indeterminate across a structure of interpellation that addresses both the language and the social experience of ideology. The poetics of spoken forms of address, notably through second-person forms, plays conversation off against writing, without effacing the book's condition as writing as if it were a form of direct dialogue or spoken address: articulated as writing, lyric language is more mediated in its modes of address. As interpellation, then, the lyric book opens up a structure of address to ideology that reflects new modes of intermedial hybridity now widespread across prose and poetry publishing, and across print, performance, and digital platforms. With particular clarity and focus, Rankine exemplifies this emergent formation of the lyric book as interpellation.

This chapter, then, explores the way Claudia Rankine's recon-figuration of lyric address engages the 'you' and 'us' of racism and ideology across the English-speaking world. The 'American' dynamics of her books are mediated, moreover, by collage techniques and 'prose poetry', and by intermedial dialogue with visual materials, not least video and television. In her work, poetic articulations of conversation and conversational implicature are mapped on to implied social experiences of complicity and ideological interpellation.[5] In this chapter, interpellation is understood as the aggregation of processes by which individuals are hailed by ideology – through social interaction and language – and mediated into misrecognising their social being and interests through various subject positions and identities. Mapping experiences of ideological interpellation onto a structure of lyric inter-pellation bears witness to wounds of affect and experience, not so as

[4] Claudia Rankine, 'Amiri Baraka's "SOS"', *New York Times* (11 February 2015): www.nytimes.com/2015/02/15/books/review/amiri-barakas-s-o-s.html [accessed 3 October 2019].

[5] For related reflections on implicature, see Drew Milne, 'Poetry after Hiroshima? Notes on Nuclear Implicature', *Angelaki: Journal of the Theoretical Humanities*, 22.3 (2017), 87–102.

to reproduce such experiences for literary consumption, but rather to trouble readers into recognitions of their perspectives and complicities. Lyric interpellation offers a more oblique structure of address than modes of address which confirm the identity of speaker and audience. This troubling of ideological common sense mirrors and deflects readers into new forms of socialised agency, recognition, and activism. Lyric interpellation works analogously to ideological processes that domesticate and internalise ideology, while also suggesting critical resistances to ideological interpellation. Remaining *grounded* in recognisable situations, experiences, and emotional alienations from contemporary culture and society, Rankine's American lyric offers a structure of address that moves beyond individual and private voicings to challenge the ideological grammar, legal personhood, and environmental complicities of lyric. She offers a *mirror* to existing structures of ideological production and literary reproduction. Lyric interpellation is persistently troubled, *ungrounded*, however, when confronted by ideological structures of racism in everyday life. As Pierre Macherey suggests, '[t]he mirror extends the world: but it also seizes, inflates and tears that world. In the mirror, the object is both completed and broken ...'.[6] Readers, freshly displaced from their consumption of mediated introspection, are drawn into differential conditions of possibility and injustice, and then into the recognition that lyric wounds are not simply private, but are produced by structures of experience that are historical, social, and environmental.[7] This is brought into focus through a performed 'lack' or absence of confident response: a sense of speechlessness, of disturbance, and of being lost for words in the face of ongoing injustices. This lack opens up structures of implication and implicature amid the workings of ideological interpellation. The argument explored here is the extent to which Rankine's work articulates poetic resistances to the understanding of ideological interpellation pioneered by Louis Althusser, and in so doing, necessarily engages with the ecology of contemporary lyric, both its conditions of possibility as a social medium and, more obliquely, with the new environmental politics of Anthropocene intersectionality.

Early on in *Citizen*, the question of American positioning is made explicit: 'A friend argues that Americans battle between the

[6]   Pierre Macherey, *Theory of Literary Production*, trans. Geoffrey Wall (London: Routledge & Kegan Paul, 1978), p. 151.
[7]   For a contemporary analysis of social media politics, see Richard Seymour, *The Twittering Machine* (London: Indigo Press, 2019).

"historical self" and the "self self" [...] sometimes your historical selves, her white self and your black self, or your white self and her black self, arrive with the full force of your American positioning'.[8] Seemingly friendly arguments can also reveal themselves to be racist micro-aggressions. Much ink has been spilt attacking and defending the confessional first-person 'I' as the privatised 'subject' of lyric, but Rankine undermines this 'subject' through a plurality of conflicting subject positions and moments, revealing an ideological terrain of divided and positioned selves. Through prosaic frames, Rankine makes lyric alienations of such materials into objects of reflection, experiences mirrored to reveal their ideological productions. Rankine herself has coedited collections that articulate conflicting traditions, both of American lyric and of writing addressed to the 'racial imaginary'.[9] Such critical and theoretical resources are not external or supplementary to American lyric, however, but constitutive of its conditions of possibility and its environment as a social medium.

Rankine's inclusion of explicit arguments within lyric textures – the citing of friends, colleagues, and contemporary theorists – breaches the 'show, don't tell' taboo constitutive of so much contemporary writing and lyric. This taboo circumscribes the ideological privatisation of 'literary' writing within a structure of feeling that preserves the entitlements of 'common sense': known injustices are only to be glimpsed, savoured even, amid the ironies of literary margins. Indirect scruples and ironies of private 'character' and 'identity' are to be favoured over anything remotely didactic. This privatisation of experience and feeling would delimit lyric as an apolitical representation or entertainment to be enjoyed by individual readers. Ideological misrecognitions can then be represented as mediations of particularised personalities and characters, as the anecdotal but thoroughly mediated and familiar 'subjectivity' of bourgeois common sense as it is embodied in literary prose and poetry. Rankine's American lyric works through and against this powerful taboo on any kind of writing that resembles activism fighting the complacent complicities of common

---

[8]   Claudia Rankine, *Citizen: An American Lyric* (London: Penguin, 2015 [2014]), p. 14.

[9]   *American Women Poets in the Twenty-First Century: Where Lyric Meets Language*, ed. Claudia Rankine and Juliana Spahr (Middletown: Wesleyan University Press, 2013); *The Racial Imaginary: Writers on Race in the Life of the Mind*, ed. Claudia Rankine, Beth Loffreda, and Max King Cap (Albany: Fence Books, 2016).

sense, but does so by remaining within the difficulty of representing the symptomatic aporia of felt injustices. As Rankine herself puts it: 'I don't like telling people what they have to do. I think people should do what they want to do, especially in the realm of creative work. I think you can't really legislate the imagination, and if you do it's something else. It's journalism, it's sociology'.[10]

Part description, part manifesto, then, Rankine's subtitle can nevertheless be understood as a challenge to rethink American lyric and experience, a challenge primarily addressed to Americans but with implications for the wider English-speaking world. The address to Americans becomes more obtrusive and historically alienated where, for example, in *Don't Let Me Be Lonely*, the writing evokes 'the English':

> The Museum of Emotions in London has a game that asks *yes* and *no* questions. As long as you answer 'correctly,' you can continue playing. The third question is: Were you terribly upset and did you find yourself weeping when Princess Diana died? [...] The English were very distraught after her death.[11]

Rankine's endnotes indicate that the Museum of Emotions was a temporary, interactive art showcase funded by The Body Shop, but the main text scarcely hints at the ironic, humorous potential of this game as a project engaged in 'relational aesthetics'.[12] The subversive or satirical potential of the wording – '[w]ere you terribly upset and did you find yourself weeping ...' – is left implicit. Perhaps what prompts inclusion of this material in Rankine's book, however, is the recognition that this aesthetics of public engagement reveals an implicit set of ideological questions about the status of 'national' grief. 'Correct' conformity to 'English' affect is framed ironically by the game, but in ways that leave indeterminate how to engage with British unease with 'the English', as distinguished from American unease. And then, across the difference between the publishing contexts of the American Graywolf Press edition of 2004 and the London Penguin reissue of 2017, who is this 'you', the present tense 'you' of the question as it

---

[10]   Kayo Chingonyi, 'Interview with Claudia Rankine', *The White Review*, 21 (2018): www.thewhitereview.org/feature/interview-claudia-rankine/ [accessed 3 October 2019].

[11]   Claudia Rankine, *Don't Let Me Be Lonely: An American Lyric* (London: Penguin, 2017 [2004]), p. 39.

[12]   Nicholas Bourriaud, *Relational Aesthetics*, trans. Simon Pleasance, Fronza Woods, and Mathieu Copeland (Dijon: Presses du réel, 2002).

reads both then and now, and how might any 'you' relate to invocations of 'the English' or the 'American'?

By inversion, this sense of the indeterminacy of inclusion within what it means to be 'American' runs through Rankine's work, but in ways that are necessarily registered differently by readers who experience 'America' as a structure of ideological exclusion, or, more simply, because they are part of the global audience forced to engage with American culture without identifying as American. 'American lyric' suggests a kind of global theatre of ideological representation addressed primarily to Americans, but through intimations of alienation from what it means to be or feel American, as if it were possible to survey American lyric from some outside. For this framing of perspectives, it is perhaps relevant to note that Rankine was born in Kingston, Jamaica, and is sometimes identified as 'Jamaican-American', though the function of such identifications is often itself part of the culture of ideological interpellation that Rankine's work distrusts. In an interview, Lauren Berlant suggested to Rankine that her work offers a kind of spectatorship on the hinge of an inside/outside opposition: '[y]our form of spectatorship is not from a protected space that gets projected into a public, but from an intimate distance that's both singular and collective, overwhelming and alienated, crowded and lonely'.[13] But even if understood as a theatre of ideological recognition and misrecognition, this work cannot readily be read or understood critically without some identification with American spectators or readers, with the imagined citizens of American letters. Rankine's poetry, especially in *Citizen*, questions the complacent limits of racial inclusivity in America, but there is nevertheless an awkward affinity between readers of her work who identify as American 'citizens' and readers who do not, whether from positions of alienation within American ideology, or from positions of alienation whose realisation as citizens would engage with other states. Rankine herself suggests, in an interview, that her work is not about representing truth to power, but about allowing readers to develop their own forms of projection:

> I worked hard for simplicity in order to allow for projection and open-endedness in the text, for a sort of blankness and transparency that would lose the specificity of 'the truth.' [..]
> I am not interested in narrative, or truth, or truth to power, on a certain level; I am fascinated by affect, by positioning,

[13] Berlant, 'Claudia Rankine'.

and by intimacy [..] The simplicity of the language is never
to suggest truth, but to make transparent the failure.[14]

The making of Americans and the makings of American lyric
have many histories. English-speaking readers cannot mirror the
ideological production of American lyric without addressing conflicts
and complicities, and without taking the risk of reinscribing colonial
privileges and the injustices of historical selves: but these are also
the burdens of lyric citizenship. In an earlier historical formation,
for example, the anthology *America: A Prophecy* (1974)[15] sought
new ways of mapping traditions of indigenous American poetics,
working eclectically and variously out of Mayan, Sioux, and Shaker
writings alongside modernist and neo-modernist reconfigurations
of F. O. Matthiessen's *American Renaissance* (1941).[16] Contemporary
lyric citizenship imagines new republics of letters out of the historical
legacies of indigenous peoples, colonial settlers, slaves, and migrants.
The invoked or interpellated citizens of the world, mediated by
English as a global and imperial language, cannot readily resolve the
intersecting claims of American poetry to constitute themselves as
native or non-native, as American or non-American. The attempt to
do so might even be resisted as some kind of un-American activity.

Critical differences between the United States and America are
often elided, even in academic accounts of the history of American
poetry and poetics. Such critical differences mask uneven powers of
tradition, of inclusion and exclusion, that have been fought out between
American poetics and the English-speaking world. It is nevertheless
heavy-handed to place the full weight of such pressures on the fragile
resources of lyric. In the introduction to *In the American Tree*, Ron
Silliman suggests, rather, that: '[t]he more pertinent questions are
what is the community being addressed in the writing, how does
the writing participate in the constitution of this audience, and is
it effective in doing so'.[17] This framing of these questions helps to
specify 'lyric', not as a knowable set of techniques or technology,

[14] Ibid.
[15] *America, a Prophecy: A New Reading of American Poetry from Pre-Columbian
Times to the Present*, ed. Jerome Rothenberg and George Quasha (New York:
Vintage, 1974).
[16] F. O. Matthiessen, *American Renaissance: Art and Expression in the Age of
Emerson and Whitman* (London and New York: Oxford University Press, 1941).
[17] Ron Silliman, 'Introduction', in *In the American Tree*, ed. Ron Silliman (Orono:
National Poetry Foundation, 1986), p. xxi.

but as an address to community that is represented and constituted through writing and reading, an address that is collective and public. The projection of wounded private experiences across the public media of radio, film, television, and social media is constitutive, too, for the ideological terrain of the performance theatres of American popular song, from blues to rap, and from protest song to negations of lyric. As Lyn Hejinian suggests: '[t]he coercive, epiphanic mode in some contemporary lyric poetry can serve as a negative model, with its smug pretension to universality and its tendency to cast the poet as guardian to Truth'.[18]

Much of the history of lyric and its performance turns on the projection of some kind of lyric 'I' into public song. This lyric 'I', however fictional, is variously mapped on to the persona of the reader, of the singer, of the 'voice' of the author and, by extension, of the community or audience addressed, represented, and constituted. This public song variously implicates the work of poetry as a collective representation, within which the 'we' that mediates and receives this song as writers and performers is mirrored by readers and audiences. Historical modes of poetry have articulated this as a choric condition, recognising poetry as a collectively produced and performed activity that is directly or indirectly related to the congregational 'we' of the psalm, the choric ode, the hymn, or the anthem. Such modes persist, but the ideology of modern lyric, its social production and consumption, has persistently turned on the political fiction that lyric poetry somehow projects the private, alienated first-person 'voice' and epiphanic experience of the poet towards the world of poetry's loving or indifferent, but somehow simultaneously collective and individual or individuated, audience.

Lyric poetry often articulates this burden across the grammatical fiction of an 'I' / 'you' relation, in which the 'I' of the poem is aligned with various personae and masks that stand in for the poet and for privatised bourgeois experience. The 'we' of the poem remains implicit in the possibility of the poem's public and political reception. The 'you' of the poem, whether explicitly represented as friends, family, or lovers, is implicitly aligned with the 'we' of bourgeois society. In its

---

[18] Lyn Hejinian, 'The Rejection of Closure: Essay on Poetic Theory' (1983): https://www.poetryfoundation.org/articles/69401/the-rejection-of-closure [accessed 3 October 2019]. See also Jonathan Dunk, 'A Theory of Negative Lyricism', *Textual Practice* (18 July 2019): https://www.tandfonline.com/doi/full/10.1080/0950236X.2019.1639914?needAccess=true&instName=University+of+Cambridge [accessed 3 October 2019].

more ideologically ambitious moments, this privatised lyric 'I' aligns itself with the possibility that it articulates as yet unacknowledged legislations that would radically reconfigure the values of the world. The fiction that there is a *subject* of lyric often turns, then, on the orientation of a lyric 'I' to a 'you' that stands in for the 'we' of the poem's potential audience. The fiction of the 'I' / 'you' relation is, however, quickly revealed to be historically superficial. Eve Kosofsky Sedgwick's analysis of the triangular exchanges of homosocial desire in Shakespeare's sonnets, for example, suggests gendered asymmetries in the drama of lyric pronouns, asymmetries bound up with the inter-pellation of readers in the socialised conversation of an implicit 'we' that remains ideologically indeterminate.[19] Comparing Thomas Wyatt and Frank O'Hara, Jeff Dolven notes that: 'O'Hara's *you* is a flexible instrument: it is usually intimate, sometimes named, sometimes not; ambiguously available to the reader to guess at or inhabit'.[20] The longer history of the flexible instrument of the lyric 'you' remains to be written. Even sketched abruptly, however, the fiction of the spoken lyric self in English poetry reveals a grammatical play of pronouns that is both flexible and overdetermined by asymmetries of power and projection. The grammar of 'I', whether in soliloquy, confession, prayer, reverie, or jeremiad, implies both structures of address to a *you* that can be singular and plural – the addressed lover, or the imagined republic of readers, or even God – and audiences who can read the drama of voices as spectators of the ideological scene imagined. The apparent authority of the ideologically sovereign, white male first-person voice is complicit with so many different and potentially supervening second and third persons. These second- and third-person addresses are often grammatically unmarked but constitutive of the ideological structure of address, whether figured as the objec-tified lover, the rival, the patron, or God. The *you* of John Donne's remarkable sonnet 'Batter my heart, three person'd God' exemplifies the complexity of ideological address in lyric form: 'I, like an usurpt towne, to'another due, / Labour to'admit you, but Oh, to no end'.[21] The

[19] Eve Kosofsky Sedgwick, 'Swan in Love: The Example of Shakespeare's Sonnets', in *Between Men: English Literature and Male Homosocial Desire* (New York: Columbia University Press, 1985), pp. 28–48.

[20] Jeff Dolven, *Senses of Style: Poetry Before Interpretation* (Chicago and London: University of Chicago Press, 2017), p. 19.

[21] John Donne, 'Batter my heart, three person'd God', in *Complete English Poems*, ed. C. A. Patrides (London: Everyman, 1994), p. 347.

flexible instrument of the lyric *you* stages grammars of complicity with which lyric is persistently intimate but which have also been persistently displaced into fictions of first-person lyric subjectivity and sovereignty.

Modern lyric inherits the profound difficulty that the artifice and authority of the lyric 'I' is suffused with aristocratic social powers, humanist wits, and religious spirits that have claimed authority over language and experience in earlier social formations. It has never been made fully explicit that the subject of modern lyric is not, after all, just a grammatical or legal 'subject', not yet quite a *citizen*, a citizen of the republic of letters that speaks, writes, and sings of the democratic 'we'. Walt Whitman's democratic 'barbaric yawp' in 'Song of Myself' (1855) exemplifies the grammatical and ideological pivots necessary for American lyric to share representations across 'we' / 'you' relations addressed to 'the people':

> I CELEBRATE MYSELF,
> And what I assume you shall assume,
> For every atom belonging to me as good belongs to you.[22]

Such democratic redistributions of the sensible mark out a new kind of modern, sociality.[23] This new American 'we' of a public, democratic speech is perhaps most explicitly inaugurated in the 1776 US Declaration of Independence: *we hold these truths*.[24] Such declarations were nevertheless tragically incomplete in their inability to recognise or articulate the reality of slavery and the limits of citizenship in US democracy. Seen from the perspective of Anthropocene disaster capitalism, moreover, the question of 'human rights' points inexorably to human wrongs and to the tragic absence of respect accorded to the rights of nature, the biosphere, and the environment. The histories of slavery, commodification, and carbon capitalism are, as yet, unacknowledged conditions of possibility for modern American citizenship. The rewilding of the subject of lyric poetry as the poetry of citizenship nevertheless remains a radical promise implicit in the conflicts of bourgeois representation.

[22] Walt Whitman, 'Song of Myself', in *Leaves of Grass: The First (1855) Edition*, ed. Malcolm Cowley (New York: Penguin, 1986), p. 25.
[23] Cf. Jacques Rancière, *The Politics of Aesthetics: The Distribution of the Sensible*, ed. and trans. Gabriel Rockhill (London: Bloomsbury, 2013).
[24] 'Declaration of Independence: A Transcription' (4 July 1776): https://www. archives.gov/founding-docs/declaration-transcript [accessed 3 October 2019].

These various fault lines and deficits of lyric citizenship are figured as substantive questions in Rankine's *Citizen*, not least the shifting address to 'you', poetry in the second person, singular and plural, addressed to an ideologically indeterminate 'we'. *Citizen* has been widely read as a powerful indictment of contemporary interpellations of race in America, but the book also exemplifies the emerging crisis of Anthropocene intersectionality: the underlying crisis of the book's ecology is implied rather than explicit, inviting readers to shift into new models of environmental citizenship, models that are only represented negatively. How might radical citizenship articulate solidarity with the environment? The burden of Anthropocene intersectionality falls on the articulation of human rights and human wrongs through the poetics of the citizen. This citizen nevertheless depends on an ecology of ideology it can scarcely recognise and name. At the heart of *Citizen* is Rankine's moving representation of the disastrous aftermaths of Hurricane Katrina in New Orleans. As extreme weather conditions become part of the deepening crisis of climate meltdown, Hurricane Katrina becomes prophetic for the prospects of environmental catastrophe, and the decisively unjust, if not explicitly racist, distribution of resources amid environmental disasters. Amidst the aftermaths of the 2019 Hurricane Dorian in the Bahamas, and only two years after the devastating impacts of Hurricanes Irma and Maria, Hurricane Katrina prefigures an intensification of climate injustice that, along with rising sea levels, threatens human society in the Caribbean and the south-eastern United States. Climate injustice is implicit in *Citizen*'s response to Hurricane Katrina, but the speed of environmental change brings the historical materiality of *Citizen* into a new conjunction with Anthropocene intersectionality.

The turn to Anthropocene intersectionality reveals that such questions are conditioned by historically unacknowledged ecologies. This unacknowledged ecology of citizenship becomes the dark matter of Anthropocene lyric. Rankine's *Citizen* puts pressure on the lived experience of American ecology, but reading *Citizen* as a book that speaks to Anthropocene intersectionality displaces the book's more explicit politics. How, then, is the representation of citizenship's racist deficits complicit with climate breakdown and climate justice?

Consider the role of what was once known, ideologically, as 'natural disaster', in the making of Rankine's *Citizen*:

I worked on *Citizen* on and off for almost ten years. I wrote the first piece in response to Hurricane Katrina. I was profoundly moved by the events in New Orleans as they unfolded. John and I taped the CNN coverage of the storm without any real sense of what we intended to do with the material. I didn't think, obviously, that I was working on *Citizen*.[25]

What emerges as the lyric texture of *Citizen* implicates a new sense of the scales and deficits of citizenship. The generative piece alluded to by Rankine takes the form of a script entitled 'August 29, 2005 / Hurricane Katrina' over pages 82–86 of *Citizen*. This short video script quotes from CNN coverage of Hurricane Katrina's aftermaths, and outlines a fluid chorus of found voices. The question of what news coverage makes visible and what remains ideologically invisible is embodied in the repeated line: 'Have you seen their faces?' The Situations video Rankine made with John Lucas, who is also credited with the book design and composition of *Citizen*, does not offer a documentary representation of events, but dramatises a voicing of lyric fragments apparently made of quoted responses from journalists and victims to unfolding news, mixed in with responses to the mediation of these voices by television images.

The script leaves open whose voices are sampled, interrupting statements with *détournements* of what initially seem like lyric apostrophes that quickly fall into place as reported speeches variously ascribed: 'climbing over bodies, one said'; 'Faith, not fear, she said'; 'This is a goddamn emergency, he said'; 'The missing limbs, he said'.[26] Tragic fragments are cut with intimations of associated arguments: 'The fiction of the facts assumes innocence, ignorance, lack of intention, misdirection ...'.[27] For anyone who remembers the television coverage of the events, the script offers powerful reminders of the heartbreaking scenes of suffering that went on for days, mixed with disbelief that a country with the resources of the United States could do so little to organise emergency support services. Television coverage of human suffering in the aftermath of extreme weather events across the world has become a familiar feature of global news, but the peculiar extremity of the aftermath of Hurricane Katrina was perhaps the slow realisation that climate disasters could devastate

---

[25] Claudia Rankine, 'The Art of Poetry No. 102' [interviewed by David L. Ulin], *The Paris Review*, 219 (2016): https://www.theparisreview.org/interviews/6905/claudia-rankine-the-art-of-poetry-no-102-claudia-rankine [accessed 3 October 2019].

[26] Rankine, *Citizen*, pp. 83–84.

[27] Ibid., p. 83.

a major US city, with more than a suspicion that more would have been done if the victims had not been so predominantly African-American. Rankine's script bears lyric witness to the unfolding climate disaster without explicating the structure of feeling, the sense of human helplessness combined with deep political injustice, and without naming the events as a prophetic sign of climate change or global warming. The script nevertheless reads as a mourning for the victims of Anthropocene violence, and as a prophetic warning for the new structure of feeling associated with climate injustice. Read retrospectively, Hurricane Katrina can be understood as an early warning of the climate disasters to come, but insofar as *Citizen* does not call out this ecology, focusing more on the symptoms of white liberal collusion with deep historical injustices, the questions posed by Anthropocene intersectionality remain implicit, not quite yet acknowledged. Set against the need to integrate awareness of climate disaster politics into new political formations capable of negotiating Anthropocene intersectionality, there are also resistances to the tendency of Anthropocene arguments to ignore or naturalise the politics and historical legacies of race.[28]

Rankine's vocal performance of the script for the Situations video is remarkable for keeping open a quality of blankness and transparency. Her mode of vocalisation sustains the video as a structure of mourning, disbelief, and anger that remains open-ended, a structure of ideological questions, rather than a performance of emotional responses. Her reading of the script remains 'in the difficulty' of it all.[29] This helps to illustrate the way Rankine's project is not to offer a realist or affective critique of contemporary American ideology, nor to represent the culture of white supremacist violence. Also characteristic of the book's approach to complicity and implication is the reproduction of an altered image of the notorious *Public Lynching* photo, often associated with Abel Meeropol's poem and song 'Strange Fruit', as performed by Billie Holiday.[30] Rather than reproducing the images of the lynched bodies hanging from the trees, the photograph has been doctored so that all that can be seen is the white lynch

---

[28]   See, for example, Nancy Tuana, 'Climate Apartheid: The Forgetting of Race in the Anthropocene', *Critical Philosophy of Race*, 7.1 (2019), 1–31; Axelle Karera, 'Blackness and the Pitfalls of Anthropocene Ethics', *Critical Philosophy of Race*, 7.1 (2019), 32–56.
[29]   Rankine, *Citizen*, p. 83.
[30]   Ibid., p. 91.

mob. Rather than reproducing images of black suffering for aesthetic consumption or outrage, the structure of address works to engage more awkward, thoughtful questions of complicity and implicature.

Rankine's constructions of representation work, then, more by inviting reflection on what it means to be hailed by ideology, and by finding forms and rhythms of attention that interrupt the rapid recycling of wounds and damage. Her representations of structures of cultural and institutional racism are nevertheless evidently critical and political, but sustained by mobilising a more lyrical politics of affect. There are novels written in the second person, but the decisive and collective voicing in *Citizen* is to imagine 'you' as a structure of lyric address across existing structures of ideological interpellation. Rather than offering a new realism, then, or representations that risk merely reproducing the ideology of racism as such, the question of collusion is constituted through the book's structure of address. This structure implicates not just a grammatical structure of pronouns awkwardly aligned, but what, after Raymond Williams, can be understood as a structure of feeling, an ideological conversation. Set, so to speak, largely in the second person, the interpellation of the second person, 'you', is such that this 'you' is both the subject and object of the book. In part, the reader can substitute this lyric 'you' with a more conventional lyric 'I' and read the books as Rankine's songs of herself, as if Rankine were addressing herself through the persona of the lyric 'you':

> You cannot say—
> A body translates its you—
> you there, hey you
> even as it loses the location of its mouth.
>
> When you lay your body in the body
> entered as if skin and bone were public places,
> when you lay your body in the body
> entered as if you're the ground you walk on,
> you know no memory should live
> in these memories
> becoming the body of you.[31]

The difference between skin and bones and the structures of address in language marks out the 'you' as a public place, the body in language

---

[31] Ibid., pp. 143–44.

figured as a space of potential citizenship haunted by its embodiments and memories. What does it mean to relay 'the' body as your body, to inhabit the ideological skin of this body, not as that body of yours, the body you might somehow come to recognise as your own, but as a body of you. Rankine's work often suggests scepticism around the idea of 'the' body as such, its apparent social abstraction and universality, registering rather the effect of estrangements from ideological embodiment. Resistance to ideological identification forms so much of the narrative content, it becomes evident, palpable even, that it is as much 'you' as an ideological subject that is in play as any concrete individual: *you*, the reader; *you*, the more or less critically implicated agent of imaginative identification and recognition. As Rankine puts it elsewhere: 'the second person for me disallowed the reader from knowing immediately how to position themselves'.[32] Readers experience both the collusion of recognising themselves in the 'you' of the book, but also the estrangements of the you as the other, even, as Rankine wittily suggests, the you of 'blackness as the second person'.[33] Put differently, Rankine's collective mode of lyric investigates the interpellation of the reader by the ideology of America across various hinges between sociopolitical collusion, critical reflection, and conversational implicature. Rather than offering a science or sociology of ideological interpellation, *Citizen* offers a poetics of collective representation, solidarity, and resistance that pivots not on the lyrical 'I' or privileged subject of lyric experience, but on ideological implicature and radical citizenship.

Here is another fragment from *Citizen* that implicates this 'you' in a structure of theoretical address, as if to say, directly, but what do you think?

> Not long ago you are in a room where someone asks the philosopher Judith Butler what makes language hurtful. You can feel everyone lean in. Our very being exposes us to the address of another, she answers. We suffer from the condition of being addressable. Our emotional openness, she adds, is carried by our addressability. Language navigates this.
>
> For so long you thought the ambition of racist language was to denigrate and erase you as a person. After considering Butler's remarks, you begin to understand yourself as rendered

[32] Rankine and Meara Sharma, 'Claudia Rankine on Blackness as the Second Person', *Guernica* (17 November 2014): https://www.guernicamag.com/blackness-as-the-second-person/ [accessed 3 October 2019].

[33] Ibid.

hypervisible in the face of such language acts. Language that feels hurtful is intended to exploit all the ways that you are present. Your alertness, your openness, and your desire to engage actually demand your presence, your looking up, your talking back, and, as insane as it is, saying please.[34]

That room is a room, not quite explicitly a classroom but nevertheless, by implication, a seminar room, a space that can be imagined as a public space open to political reflection. Reported speech opens a space not just for theoretical reflection but for emotional reflection on this sense of conversational implicature. Perhaps you agree, or perhaps you realise that you have not long considered the ambition of racist hurt speech in quite this way, and would prefer to defer critical judgement on this formulation. Where, indeed, are 'you' in the critical, academic, and sociopolitical deconstruction of hate speech? How other to you is this address of, and to, another? Can we be freed, even if only poetically, of the condition of being addressable?

Such moments in the texture of Rankine's American lyric interpellate a structure of feeling as a lyrical address to conversational implication and theories of experience and affect. This structure includes the awareness and repurposing of the work of Judith Butler, not so much as philosophy or theory, but as part of a mapping of ideologically salient voices and discourses which extends beyond common sense, probing the grounds of contemporary feeling and argument. In *Don't Let Me Be Lonely: An American Lyric*, written in part as a response to the aftermaths of 9/11, there are comparable moments of theoretical reflection:

> In college, when I studied Hegel, I was struck by his explanation of the use of death by the state. Hegel argued that death is used as a threat to keep citizens in line. The minute you stop fearing death you are no longer controlled by governments and councils. In a sense you are no longer accountable to life. The relationships embedded between the 'I' and the 'we' unhinge and lose all sense of responsibility. That 'you,' functioning as other, now exists beyond our notions of civil and social space.[35]

This reflection on terrorism and state terrorism across the hinge of grammatical and ideological responsibility is part of the willingness to address directly stated forms of theory and argument that is

---

[34] Rankine, *Citizen*, p. 49.
[35] Rankine, *Don't Let Me Be Lonely*, p. 84.

relatively unusual within lyric. The interpellation of the 'you' by the question of state terrorism includes glimpses of explicit philosophical and political theory that unhinge the location of structures of address in private experience, opening up questions about the social being of the privated 'you'.

Contrast the relation of openness to being as navigated through Judith Butler's reflections on racist language and hate speech, with the invitation to imagine a new 'we', the 'we' of the Biotariat:

> This is the reason to propose a **biotariat**: the enclosure and exploitation of life, in all its manifold aspects (from boreal forests to sea turtles to Bangladeshi garment workers to the homeless of the world's major cities to sex trade workers to the coral reefs and so forth and so on), has reached a stage in which 'we' – all of life – are in the same desperate and drunken boat – constrained there by a system of total and planetary accumulation that even the term 'capitalism' perhaps cannot adequately capture anymore.[36]

The fragile 'I' of human-centred subjectivity opens out on to an invitation to join 'we' the Biotariat. The Anthropocene is one name for this new condition in which 'we' are called on to recognise our collective, human collusion in the globalised capitalist system that threatens *life as such*. The invitation to recognise that the human class composition of *life as such* has become complicit with life's extinction – all of life – quickly poses a set of questions as to how to identify the collective agency of this new, imagined subject of biopolitical history. Even if it is possible to begin to imagine how the Biotariat might emerge out of the ruins of the historical Proletariat, how might the Biotariat intersect with white liberal collusion in white supremacist violence? The problem of political hierarchies and priorities across collective forms of intersectional solidarity is now evidently part of the environment of contemporary crises, but it is also an unacknowledged parameter in the as yet unwritten history of what Kathryn Yusoff imagines as a billion black anthropocenes:

> Noticing the meshwork of anti-Blackness and colonial structures of the Anthropocene, which constitute the distinct

---

[36] Stephen Collis, 'Notes Towards a Manifesto of the Biotariat', *Beating the Bounds* (2014): https://beatingthebounds.com/2014/07/25/notes-towards-a-manifesto-of-the-biotariat/ [accessed 3 October 2019].

underbelly to its origin stories, gives visibility to the material and bodily work that coercively carries the Anthropocene into being and challenges the narrative accounts of agency there within.[37]

How might environmental activism begin to intersect with Rankine's poetics of radical citizenship, and with the politics of Black Lives Matter, but without becoming another form of liberal collusion in racism?

One response would be to suggest that the history of racism and the ecology of climate breakdown are bound up with capitalist forces and relations of production that constitute a shared, global ecology. Even if this ecology is shared, it is nevertheless striated by a history of uneven conflicts of struggle and oppression, unshared histories and burdens that undermine the possibilities of concrete political solidarity. Worse still, giving environmental priority to preserving the conditions for the sustainability of *life as such* risks preserving, perhaps even reinforcing, existing ecological injustices, existing global north-south divides that are the historical consequence of racism and imperialism. The ecology of sustainability risks sustaining injustice.

What, then, is the ecology of ideology that might be understood as the shared ground or damaged world of such intersectionality? Is it possible to think the ecology *of* ideology as a double genitive? Various intersecting arguments motivate the double genitive: the dominant relation is that according to which ideology sustains the ecology of ecocidal capitalism: the ideology of existing capitalism. But there is also a sense in which ideology is sustained by a more specific ecology, that of news and the digital economy of social media. This is the ecology of media and mediation sustaining the production of ideology. One of the effects of the ideological displacements emerging under the impact of climate breakdown and ecological politics is the recognition that, long before digital media, ideology was sustained by the ecology of news and data management. The ecology that sustained ideology was scarcely acknowledged or addressed, nor was it widely understood that ideology was produced not just as ideas, as a theology of legitimation, but as an array of practices that were implicated in the ecology of forces and relations of economic production. It has long been evident, for example, that the technology of printing

[37] Kathryn Yusoff, *A Billion Black Anthropocenes or None* (Minneapolis: University of Minnesota Press, 2018), p. 104.

is constitutive of the ecology of ideology in early modern culture, but less evident that this ecology is also implicated in the ecology of metal, wood, and paper.

By extension, it has not been evident in understandings of lyric, even understandings that have emphasised the environmental politics of lyric, that the performance, circulation, and printing of lyric is implicated in the ecology of metal, wood, and paper. The ecology of life, of the biosphere, is as yet a largely unacknowledged condition of the possibility of lyric. The digital economy, aside from its role in the production of information as ideology, is far from being integrated into our understanding of the ecology of contemporary capitalism. To the extent to which digital consumption is pervasive, this constitutes a rather literal state of ideological misrecognition. Amid the terrain of existing ideological conflicts, the extent of social collusion in the ecology of the digital economy is scarcely understood, far less felt, as a significant environmental cost.

There is, then, a constitutive illusion in which we imagine ideology as a relatively autonomous sphere or ecosystem, an ecology that somehow produces itself, rather than one whose conditions of possibility are also biological. Recognition of this constitutive illusion – the illusion that human labour produces itself – has a history within the illusions of socialism:

> 'Labour is the source of all wealth and all culture.' Labour is *not the source* of all wealth. *Nature* is just as much the source of use values (and it is surely of such that material wealth consists!) as labour, which itself is only the manifestation of a force of nature, human labour power.[38]

There is also a constitutive illusion in imagining that recognition of environmental precarity – what might be called the environmental turn in sociopolitical argument, poetics, and activism – can become its own ideological orientation, tendency, or social movement.

All of which motivates a concluding review of Louis Althusser's account of ideology and ideological interpellation:

> the category of the subject is constitutive of all ideology [...] all ideology hails or interpellates concrete individuals as

---

[38] Karl Marx, *Critique of the Gotha Program* (1875), Marxists Internet Archive: https://www.marxists.org/archive/marx/works/1875/gotha/ [accessed 3 October 2019].

concrete subjects, by the functioning of the category of the subject [...] ideology 'acts' or 'functions' in such a way that it 'recruits' subjects among the individuals (it recruits them all), or 'transforms' the individuals into subjects (it transforms them all) by that very precise operation which I have called interpellation or hailing, and which can be imagined along the lines of the most commonplace everyday police (or other) hailing: 'Hey, you there!' Assuming that the theoretical scene I have imagined takes place in the street, the hailed individual will turn round. By this mere one-hundred-and-eighty-degree physical conversion, he becomes a subject. Why? Because he has recognized that the hail was 'really' addressed to him, and that 'it was really him who was hailed' (and not someone else).[39]

Just as arguments around lyric have wrongly fixated on the category of the subject rather than foregrounding and recognising lyric's structures of address, so critical theories of ideology have wrongly fixated on the category of the subject. The ecology of theory, the ecology of its imaginary street scene, cannot constitute itself, any more than the lyric 'I' can create its own world: both are structures of address that remain blind to their complicity with their environments, their conditions of possibility, whether as theory, streets, language, or lyric. Put crudely, without the street, no scene, no public environment in which to be hailed, even if only in theory. Lyric, like ideology, might appear to be constituted in and through language, as if out of the thin air of imaginary recruitments. But lyric's structures of address are mediated not just by the ecology of print, music, paper, strings, and so on, but also by digital social media, and indeed by the historical materiality of social relations, not least the historic injustices and social hierarchies of class, gender, and race. It is not that lyric is constituted out of itself, or is capable of creating its own imaginary environment, but that the imaginative structures of lyric address – whether as book, song, video, or performed reading – are constituted as social and biotarian interpellations. Such interpellations remain ideological insofar as human complicity with the destruction of the biosphere is not yet acknowledged, far less recognised and repurposed for the politics and poetics of Anthropocene intersectionality. Put differently, Claudia

---

[39] Louis Althusser, 'Ideology and Ideological State Apparatus (Notes Towards an Investigation)', in *Lenin and Philosophy and Other Essays*, trans. Ben Brewster and intro. Fredric Jameson (New York: Monthly Review Press, 2001), pp. 118–19.

Rankine recruits the theoretical scene of ideological interpellation in such a way as to suggest resistances to the constitutive ideology of the subject imagined by Althusser. Rankine's *Citizen* hails its readers in such a way that they cannot be fully recruited or transformed into subjects of her book, even if they recognise themselves as being hailed to reflect on the deficits of citizenship so as to imagine new modes of political affect and activism. Even if only by implication, it is nevertheless possible to imagine that Rankine's lyric structure of address reimagines the interpellation of ideological subjects, the 'you' of her book, as citizens newly attuned to their complicity with the prevailing climate of injustice, and, by extension, with the politics of Anthropocene intersectionality.

CHAPTER SIX

Ode

Veronica Forrest-Thomson and the Artifice of Resuscitation

Gareth Farmer

Transpontine Ovid made his ovoid obsequies.
                                    – Veronica Forrest-Thomson

'This next poem is an Ode', the poet explains to the audience whose heads immediately bow. 'It is written', he clears his throat, 'for my favourite cat who drowned in a tub of golden fishes'. The poet maintains a sombre countenance throughout his introduction, but some of the audience smirk; many look around trying to judge the right mood with which to compose their faces; most fidget, not quite sure how to comport themselves. It is an ode, they think, but it is dedicated to a cat who seems to have died in absurdly ironic circumstances. Is it a joke? As Thomas Gray starts to read about his 'pensive Selima, reclin'd' tenuously above the fish tub, the audience relax.[1] The conceit is that Gray inhabits the stately robes of the ode, adorning its accessories of mythical allusion, writing accomplished verse, and investing Selima's death with a pomp which is deliberately bathetic. While the audience may wonder why the poet stood by as poor Selima 'Eight times emerg[ed] from the flood' mewing 'to ev'ry wat'ry god' (help her out, Gray!), they will know that they are invited to take part, as secondary addressees, in the artificial performance space of the ode. The ode-zone – if I may call it that – is licensed to sell all manner of poetic draughts to its readers and audiences and

[1] Thomas Gray, 'Ode on the Death of a Favourite Cat, Drowned in a Tub of gold Fishes', in *Gray's Poems, Letters and Essays*, ed. John Drinkwater and Lewis Gibbs (London: Dent, 1970 [1912]), pp. 2–3.

to bring to its stage an array of poetic performances. Odes can offer complicated and often contradictory address and lyric witness, they can shift tone, register, and style, and they can serve up morsel-like moral epithets. 'Not all that tempts your wandering eyes / And heedless hearts, is lawful prize', Gray addresses his unfortunate cat, before concluding, sadly: 'Nor all that glisters gold'. Poor Selima's plight has taught us all a lesson in the perils of the thoughtless pursuit of self-gratification.

The ode-zone is created by the illustrious and elevated history of the mode, but it is also evoked by the sonorous word itself: *Ode*. To recite an ode necessitates the slight raise of the chin, the lofty elevation of the eyes towards heaven, the extension of the arm in a theatrical poise; to say the word itself is to extend the *o* sound out of normal usage into the realm of the histrionic and hyperbolic. Indeed, according to Jonathan Culler's recent *Theory of the Lyric* (2015), the hyperbole and apostrophe of many odes comprise one of the defining characteristics of the lyric in general.[2] In the history of Pindaric ode practice, at least, opening lines will contain a high sounding address; as Gray's more serious Pindaric ode, 'The Progress of Poesy', demands: 'Awake, Æolian lyre, awake, / And give to rapture all thy trembling strings'.[3] Such sonorous ode posturing is parodied in the opening of Veronica Forrest-Thomson's 'In Memoriam Ezra Pound', which gives the epigraph to this chapter. The poem was written on the occasion of Pound's death on 1 November 1972 and its opening offers a whole range of gestures characteristic of the ode: 'Transpontine Ovid made his ovoid obsequies'.[4] We are transported

---

[2] Jonathan Culler, *Theory of the Lyric* (Cambridge, MA: Harvard University Press, 2015), pp. 37–38. In his *Theory of the Lyric*, Culler surveys lyric poems throughout history and offers four 'parameters of a vital generic [lyric] tradition' (p. 32). These are: 1) complexity of enunciated apparatus and address which 'pose [..] question[s] of the lyric's relation to voice and voicing' (p. 34); 2) lyric as a present-tense event in itself rather than a representation or mimesis of events; 3) lyric as ritualistic rather than fictional. Culler argues that lyrics are comprised of patterns of rhythm and rhyme and other formal repetitions which he calls 'ritualistic'; these patterns have different functions than simply operating as fictional representations of states. As he writes: 'Insofar as lyrics offer not representations of speeches by fictional characters but memorable writing to be received, reactivated, and repeated by readers, they partake of what I have broadly called the ritualistic' (p. 37). Lastly, 4) lyric's hyperbolic qualities (pp. 33–38).

[3] Gray, *Poems*, p. 8.

[4] Veronica Forrest-Thomson, 'In Memoriam Ezra Pound', in *Collected Poems* (Exeter: Shearsman, 2008), p. 132.

to the transpontine (over the other side of the bridge or water) realm of the ode, with the assonant 'o' the fuel for our boat and the rhythm of the line our rolling waves. The reference or address to Ovid signals the epic mode and register of the poem, while the physical acrobatics required of our mouth and breath to pronounce 'Transpontine' and 'obsequies', as well as the obscurity of the words themselves, offer the theatrical prologue to this dense ode. Sonorous seriousness jostles with witty linguistic play to set up this peculiarly complicated ode-zone.

The ode is a conflicted mode, having been adopted and adapted for both highly public as well as acutely private memorialisation and rumination, and being comprised of a range of formal conventions. The fantasy reverence of the audience for Gray's ode imagined above is produced by its lofty history as that mode which, as Stephen Fogle and Paul Fry outline, has become associated with highly formal and ceremonious events, and which is 'frequently used as the vehicle for public utterance and state occasions'.[5] As the most 'complexly organized form of lyric poetry, usually of considerable length', the audience also braces itself for a long haul. The traces of the ode's origin from ᾠδή (*ōidē*), meaning song or chant, also confers a dimension of performance that other lyric poetry does not possess to such extremes. But the ode is also a mode in permanent crisis; while the poise may be public, the sentiments can be highly introverted. The ode's 'dual inheritance', as Fogle and Fry outline, contributes to its shifting and elusively compelling qualities. Poets writing odes inherit both 'the measured, recurrent stanza of the Horatian Ode, with its attendant balance of tone and sentiment [...] and the irregular stanzaic triad of Pindar, with its elevated, vertiginously changeable tone'.[6] Hence, the history of the ode offers us Alexander Pope's gentle and formally regular Horatian 'Ode on Solitude' – 'Happy the man, whose wish and care / A few paternal acres bound' – as well as Keats's intensely introspective and formally erratic Pindaric Odes – 'Thou still unravish'd bride of quietness / Thou foster-child of silence and slow time'.[7] Forrest-Thomson is not

[5] Stephen F. Fogle and Paul H. Fry, 'Ode', in *The New Princeton Encyclopedia of Poetry & Poetics*, ed. Alex Preminger and T. V. F. Brogan (Princeton: Princeton University Press, 1993), p. 855.

[6] Ibid.

[7] Alexander Pope, 'Ode on Solitude', in *Complete Poetical Works*, ed. Herbert Davies (Oxford: Oxford University Press, 1978), p. 59; John Keats, 'Ode on a Grecian Urn', in *Poetical Works*, ed. H. W. Garrod (Oxford: Oxford University Press, 1973), p. 209.

unusual in writing both Horatian and Pindaric odes – 'The Lady
of Shalott: Ode', for example, is Horatian, 'Le Pont Traversé: Ode'
is Pindaric – as well as ones somewhere in between, such as 'In
Memoriam Ezra Pound', which has the external look of the Horatian
and the internal chaos of the Pindaric. While the ode may offer diverse
forms and subject matters, its histrionic qualities mark it out for special
attention by poets and readers alike. As Fogle and Fry observe: 'The
serious tone of the ode calls for the use of a heightened diction and
enrichment by poetic device, but this lays it open, more readily than
any other poetic form, to burlesque'.[8] The ode's seriousness demands
concentration, but it also draws attention to its emphatic tensions of
address, tone, sincerity, and form. Such conflicted characteristics have
made it a particularly rich mode for the hyper self-reflexivity of much
contemporary verse. The formal conventions of a twin ode tradition
have also led to a type of productive, formal *agōn* suiting contemporary
articulations of conflicted aesthetics and politics.

Forrest-Thomson died at the young age of 27 in 1975, but her
posthumously published collection, *On the Periphery* (1976), exhibits
a late flourishing of Pindaric and Horatian ode writing.[9] Always
prone to idolise and imitate a range of poets in order to produce a
resonant tone of memorialisation, many of Forrest-Thomson's later
poems renovate or, to use Ezra Pound's word from *Hugh Selwyn
Mauberley* (1920), 'resuscitate' the elevated art of the ode.[10] These odes
exhibit formal battles between the loose and erratic Pindaric and the
contained and constrained Horatian; these formal battles, I argue, are
not only the occasion for Forrest-Thomson to honour, parody, and
playfully battle with her poetic predecessors, but are also her chance
to display the power and operation of poetic Artifice, her catch-all
term for 'all the rhythmic, phonetic, verbal and logical devices which
make poetry different from prose', as she puts it in her preface to *Poetic
Artifice*.[11] *On the Periphery* contains several odes, including an elaborate
reflection on death, pain, and memorialisation, 'The Ear of Dionysios',
and a Dadaist-inspired poem to Max Jacob, 'Le Pont Traversé: Ode'.
After a brief excursus on two of Forrest-Thomson's early poems, my

---

[8]   Fogle and Fry, 'Ode', p. 855.

[9]   Forrest-Thomson, *On the Periphery* (Cambridge: Street Editions, 1976).

[10]   Ezra Pound, 'E. P. Ode pour l'Election de Son Sepulchre', from *Hugh
Selwyn Mauberley*, in *Selected Poems*, intro. by T. S. Eliot (London: Faber, 1948),
pp. 173–76 (p. 173).

[11]   Forrest-Thomson, *Poetic Artifice: A Theory of Twentieth-Century Poetry*, ed.
Gareth Farmer (Bristol: Shearsman, 2016), p. 33.

discussion will primarily focus on these two later poems. In Forrest-Thomson's odes we get a complex and competitive echo of voices and forms in an ironised present tense. As I suggest towards the end of this chapter, Forrest-Thomson's odes also illustrate, in microcosm, a number of the theoretical and poetic struggles of much contemporary poetry. Her odes, for example, are dramatisations of the complexities and complicities of lyric address; their manic patterning – rhythms, repetitions, structural echoes, and reformulations – offer condensed and intense expressions of a fragile lyric voice struggling to articulate itself through the clamour of poetic voices as well as the hypostatised versions of theoretical issues and lyric formulae. Forrest-Thomson's inhabitation of the ode-zone enables her to offer a theatre for the battle of poetic voices and forms. The ode offers the artifices for resuscitation, but it is also the scene of the resuscitation of Artifice.

Strophe

The ode is a versatile and particularly self-conscious species of the lyric. It is as if its complicated and contorted modes of address create an echo chamber of self-reflection where a poet can argue with their own as well as others' craft, all the while working out ever more refined modes and registers of being in the world. The mode is hyperbolic and histrionic, and one which suited Forrest-Thomson's ironically argumentative poetic persona developed and played out in her poetry from a young age. In this, the initial 'strophe' of my chapter, I will introduce two of Forrest-Thomson's quite different early poems to illustrate twin aspects of her poetic style which then unite in her later odes. 'Contours – Homage to Cézanne' displays the competitive aspects of memorialisation while also celebrating poetic craft. 'Epicurus' is not an ode, but contains early expressions of the pleasures, pains, and complicities of craft which reappear in Forrest-Thomson's later odes.

'Contours – Homage to Cézanne' is arguably Forrest-Thomson's first ode and one which affirms the values of formal restraint and the order of Artifice. From her first collection, *Identi-kit* (1967), the poem is (as the title indicates) an homage to Paul Cézanne, specifically the undulating contours of his landscape paintings. It celebrates how, through long labour and 'complication', an artist has learned 'to simplify'.[12] 'Contours' registers her admiration for Cézanne's ability to arrange shapes together in formal tensions:

[12]   Forrest-Thomson, *Collected Poems*, p. 27. All quotations are from this page.

> Pattern, like a magnetic field,
> is passionate in restraint; limits compress
> significance; framed energy is sealed.
> Objects, having nothing to express
>
> except themselves, attain intensity
> in assumed balance [..].

The poem is indicative of Forrest-Thomson's complicated and conflicted modes of attention. The formal properties of Cézanne's work are described as consisting of patterns within a 'magnetic field'. This field creates 'limits', which 'compress' and frame 'significance' and 'energy', which in turn comprise what she describes as 'intensity / in assumed balance'. But Forrest-Thomson also uses line endings, rhymes, abrupt shifts of grammar, punctuation, and stanza breaks to emulate Cézanne's arranged landscapes. Hence, the mid-line semicolons, the inelegant enjambments ('compress / significance'; 'express // except') represent the structural arrangements of Cézanne's work, and these are set in tension with the poetic 'frame' or 'field' which tries to restrain the energy of fragments with end rhymes: 'field', 'sealed'; 'compress', 'express'. Forrest-Thomson's poetic form attempts to enact Cézanne's artistic style.

But 'Contours' also represents and reflects on the artist's struggles as inscribed in their artworks, as well as the role of a viewer or reader in creating an homage or ode to the artist. Hence, she writes that 'these tight contours owe / shape and definition to the eye / of inessential man', which might be an argument for a viewer's role in continuing to activate and give definition to the paintings. But, this 'inessential man' is, at the same time, the artist who is codified in their formal creations and who, as she puts it, 'from complication learns to simplify', to 'fuse form with what alone form can show' (they give over to pure form, perhaps). And, as she ends the poem, it is in creating such works that 'this act becomes as sure as they', where 'this act' is both the artist's in producing their paintings and the poet's in creating an ode to an artist, to their work, to craft in general, and to their own (the poet's) craft in particular. With 'Contours', then, we witness Forrest-Thomson turning to the ode to organise, arrange, and articulate complex modes of attention – towards an artist's work, towards poetic craft, towards the histories of artistic conventions – all of which are vying for the foreground, but none of which wins out.

'Contours' is an homage as well as an ode to craft. It at once describes and celebrates Cézanne's work, but also tests poetic craft against his painterly achievements. Odes usually contain celebration of achievements alongside lamentations of passing time or the fact that the poet's art has fallen short of fully capturing the subject and their work. The ode offers the space for a complex self-reflection on the acts of writing and memorialisation. In his excellent *Agonistic Poetry* (1987), William Fitzgerald outlines the paradoxes of the ode's positioning in relation to its subject: the ode implies deference, but it can also be the place of adversarial competition.[13] The tension between homage and hostility is produced as the ode becomes a site for the measurement or assessment of value. As such, it is also the place where a poet measures their own work and worth against the value of the person for whom they write, whether that person is a writer or a wrestler. Of poems by Pindar in which he celebrates an Olympian's prowess and success (*Olympian* 10, *Nemean* 5), Fitzgerald argues that Pindar figures his act of writing as a type of debt to be paid to the athlete, the same debt that society owes them for their success. But presenting the poem this way produces an evaluative mindset as the poet's words are brought into the market of relative duty and obligation. In order to assert his independence from such a market, the poet must, as Fitzgerald puts it, establish 'himself as one whose secondariness is his independence, his freedom to re-cognize'.[14] The poet's freedom is asserted as one who can stand slightly away from the common economy of praise; their poem is the space of 're-cognizing' aspects of their subject in poetic form. But, the poet is still in an awkward situation of having a dependence which may consume them. As Fitzgerald continues: 'Paradoxically, then, the poet as receiver of what he celebrates may appear as its adversary, insofar as its potentially absolute nature would relegate him to a radically secondary position'.[15] Pindar's awareness of his situation as secondary is expressed in what Fitzgerald calls a 'playful aggression'. Forrest-Thomson's own thinking about the knotty dependencies and competition of the ode mode manifests itself, in later poems at least, in what might be called an aggressive play.

While 'Contours' is rather sedate in its treatment of Cézanne's work and its display of poetic craft, an early, uncollected and unpublished poem, 'Epicurus', features Forrest-Thomson's aggressive play

---

[13] William Fitzgerald, *Agonistic Poetry: The Pindaric Mode in Pindar, Horace, Hölderlin, and the English Ode* (Berkeley: University of California Press, 1987), pp. 29–31.

[14] Ibid., p. 31.

[15] Ibid.

with classical figures and tropes, and wittily dramatises the pleasures and attendant pains of overindulgence in order to draw out broader conclusions about the discipline and responsibility of poetic craft and memorialisation. 'Dare I eat some cheese', the poem opens, even though it 'might cause dyspepsia or even appendicitis'; 'Dare I risk some wine', the speaker tentatively enquires a little later, before adding: 'a half-glass hung me over / last time'.[16] In order for pleasure to be pleasurable, the poem contends, one must approach it as one does an art, for 'Pleasure is such an exacting discipline', and one must know 'the score / in the trials of an empirical connoisseur'.

Forrest-Thomson here feeds a notion of rationalised consumption or carefully controlled pleasure into a vision of appropriate aesthetic comportment. Indulging in the pleasures of writing poetry, as in life, one must be exactingly disciplined so as not to cause aesthetic dyspepsia. In 'Epicurus', Forrest-Thomson outlines a vision of poetic craft which is already thinking through the complex issues raised by the ode. She uses the pitfalls of excessive consumption to occasion an outline of what might be called an ethics of poetic poise. A poet and their poem must tread the fine line between pleasurable play and perverting pain, where to pervert is to falsely represent a subject or nature. 'To stay dégagé / and yet to play', Forrest-Thomson writes, 'that I could dream of'. To be objective and disengaged, and yet to play, that is the poise for which a poet should aim. A poet should be in tune with their inner sensations as well as with the world in order to 'Give one's eyes to nature / for a mirror'. In such circumstances, as Forrest-Thomson writes, 'subject and object' are 'the same', while

> aesthesis path at prolepsis,
> focused by the security of doubt
> tuned lyre-like
> for the key to each sensation.[17]

Sense perceptions ('aesthesis') respond to or follow the direction of ('path at') learned anticipation ('prolepsis'); in other words, Forrest-Thomson describes a state of being highly attuned to, and thereby potentially in control of, the environment and poetic production. If this state implies a form of 'security' it is one that is at the same time radically sceptical of false projections of certainty. In other words, a poet should anticipate false representations and keep tuning

---

[16]   Forrest-Thomson, *Collected Poems*, p. 45.
[17]   Ibid., p. 46.

themselves to the particularity of sensation and natural states they seek to represent. As such, they will be 'tuned lyre-like' and finely poised to write with clarity, precision, and veracity. But the stakes of such lyric witness and representation are constantly intruding on a poet's craft, reminding them to check their hubris. As Forrest-Thomson writes, in creating this finely tuned poise,

> Have I changed desire, anxiety's death
> for fear of life
> its shifting-toned complexity
> in which a self is found and lost [?].[18]

The responsibility and ethics of the poet are maintained in the finely tuned poise between pleasure and pain, between fear and doubt and certainty. Such poise is created by and produces a formal and semantic 'shifting-toned complexity' in which 'self' – as both subject and object – can be 'found or lost'. As Mutlu Konuk Blasing has recently argued, lyric poetry is the site of an acknowledged loss of control but also a simultaneous working towards reconciliation or knowledge. 'Poetry', Blasing writes, 'is the discourse of the constitutive alienation of the subject in language – the alienation that constitutes the genesis of the "human"'.[19] The poem is the site of the reconciliation of the lyric subject into being, or into a shape resembling a form of unity, and poetic form and materials constitute this shaped 'I'. Poetry, for Blasing, is the medium which most accurately provides the forum for the drama of a subject coming into being in language. As she puts it: poetry 'speaks a kind of "second language" which must [..] be acquired, to graph the vernacular of communication into the grid of a cultural discourse called "poetry" – a set of conventions, forms, devices, and schemes that foreground the linguistic code, which must then be re-turned into sense'.[20] 'Epicurus' expresses Forrest-Thomson's troubled acknowledgement of the hardships of acquiring this 'second language' of the lyric, of achieving the right register, tone, style, and formal practices to 'graph' or trace a subject as well as the poet's own ongoing perceptions; 'Epicurus' maps a poet's acknowledgement of responsibilities of the lyric craft in making new forms of sense. Presciently and with prolepsis, in both 'Contours' and 'Epicurus',

---

[18] Ibid.
[19] Mutlu Konuk Blasing, *Lyric Poetry: The Pain and the Pleasure of Words* (Princeton: Princeton University Press, 2007), p. 13.
[20] Ibid., p. 13.

Forrest-Thomson anticipates her representations of the complex poise and contradictory conditions of the lyric of her later odes.

Antistrophe

While a number of Forrest-Thomson's poems offer veiled, vague, and variegated memorialisations – to people, styles, and theories – her Great Odes, if I can call them this, are all clustered at the end of *On the Periphery*. In 1973–74 – an *annus mirabilis* of the kind Keats experienced – she produced all of the poems for *On the Periphery*, as well as the odes 'The Ear of Dionysios: Ode', 'Le Pont Traversé: Ode', 'In Memoriam Ezra Pound', 'Strike', 'The Lady of Shalott: Ode', 'The Garden of Proserpine', and 'Sonnet'.[21] Of all the lyric species, the ode is the one which, by virtue of its modes of address, lends itself most readily to what might be called lyric status anxiety; it is the species most cognisant of its own lineage and most anxious about its status within this lineage and, as such, it has offered a fertile terrain for the evolution of the grammar of lyric in general. The hand-wringing histrionics of the Pindaric, Horatian, and Petrarchan odes have charted as well as produced poetic sensibilities and lyric personas, and have contributed to the evolution of what Culler describes as 'the modern mind, as poets came to know themselves as individuals with an inner life'.[22] In this 'antistrophe' section of my chapter, I will examine excerpts from 'Le Pont Traversé: Ode' and 'The Ear of Dionysios: Ode' to illustrate how Forrest-Thomson's memorialisation of poets, poetic traditions, and lineages led her to develop her own anxieties about writing odes in particular and lyric in general. These odes are formally complex: 'Le Pont Traversé: Ode' is written in a densely allusive and macaronic prose, while 'The Ear of Dionysios: Ode' is an example of what Simon Jarvis has called a 'hyper-Pindaric', featuring an array of formal patterns and styles.[23]

These two odes are influenced by Dadaist poetic practices. Forrest-Thomson outlined her interest in Dada poetry in a long section of *Poetic Artifice*, as well as in a 1974 article, 'Dada, Unrealism

[21] Forrest-Thomson, *Collected Poems*, pp. 127–41.

[22] Culler, *Theory of the Lyric*, p. 54.

[23] Simon Jarvis, 'The Hyper-Pindaric: The Greater Irregular Lyric from Cowley to Keston Sutherland', in *Active Romanticism: The Radical Impulse in Nineteenth-Century and Contemporary Poetic Practice*, ed. Julie Carr and Jeffrey C. Robinson (Tuscaloosa: University of Alabama Press, 2015), pp. 127–44.

and Contemporary Poetry'. For her, poetry by Tristan Tzara and André Breton contained the necessary stress on what she describes as the 'formal patterns of language, irrelevant to the communication of meaning'.[24] As such, a number of her poems attempt the 'formal patterns' of the Dadaist poets as an evasion of regular and regulated patterns of communication. Both 'Le Pont Traversé: Ode' and 'The Ear of Dionysios: Ode' feature a number of styles, modes, allusions, vigorous wordplay, and complex formal patterns resembling, in the Dada poet and philosopher Julius Evola's phrase, a 'Dada Landscape' ('Dada paesaggio', the poem's original, Italian title).[25]

The ode, Culler reminds us, is epideictic; that is, it is characterised by the display of rhetorical skill in the performance of praise, lament, grief, and joy. As Culler writes, the ode 'highlights the performative quality of public lyric, which accomplishes the act of praise that it spends time describing'.[26] Both 'Le Pont Traversé: Ode' and 'The Ear of Dionysios: Ode' offer elaborate and excessive excursuses on death, loss, and memory. Both poems also explore the role and function of poetic craft in keeping what Forrest-Thomson describes as the 'permanent tympanum' of past voices alive.[27] As Culler notes, the ode – the lyric mode most associated with public song – is a mode which declares its own status as much as it addresses its subject; an ode is always already an ode to itself.[28] 'The epideictic element of lyric', Culler writes, 'includes not just praise or blame but the many statements of value, statements about the world that suffuse lyric of the past and the

---

[24] See 'Dada and Its Avatars', in *Poetic Artifice*, pp. 183–98, and 'Dada, Unrealism and Contemporary Poetry', *20th Century Studies*, 12 (December 1974), 77–93 (p. 78).

[25] Julius Evola, 'Dada paesaggio', in *The Dada Market: An Anthology of Poetry*, ed. Willard Bohn (Carbondale and Edwardsville: Southern Illinois University Press, 1993), pp. 82–83.

[26] Culler, *Theory of the Lyric*, p. 55.

[27] Forrest-Thomson, 'The Ear of Dionysios: Ode', in *Collected Poems*, p. 127.

[28] For Hegel, Culler informs us, the ode is the mode 'where the subjectivity of the poet becomes "the most important thing of all"' (*Theory of the Lyric*, p. 95). Culler quotes from *Hegel's Aesthetics*, trans. T. M. Knox (Oxford: Oxford University Press, 1975), p. 1141. For Hegel, the lyric was the literary mode most capable of expressing the unity of subjectivity as well as enabling a 'subject to realize itself as itself' (Culler, *Theory of the Lyric*, p. 95). In Hegel's schema, whereas hymns and songs look outwards, the ode is the mode which foregrounds the subjectivity of the poet and in which the psychology of the poet is explored.

present'.[29] As such, one of its first characteristics is the identification
– often very elaborate – of value in the life, craft, or lessons of its
addressee.[30] Forrest-Thomson's elegiac poem 'Le Pont Traversé: Ode'
is designed to be both a 'Memorial to the deportation' of Jews under
Hitler, but also an homage to the value of the work of a poet, Max
Jacob, who was abducted and interned by the Gestapo at Drancy, that
horrendous halfway house to the concentration camps, where he died
in 1944. As Forrest-Thomson puts it: 'This is in memory of Max Jacob,
paysan de Paris à paraître'.

'Le Pont Traversé: Ode' is difficult to characterise, précis, or
extract from, but its primary form – as illustrated in the line just
quoted – is one of elaborate translingual punning, as well as phonic
and semantic free association. The poem is what might be described
as an oblique ode, where elegiac fragments are caught, captured, and
echo in the thick memorial of the poem. Forrest-Thomson builds a
variety of internal sound and image patterns, uses a clash of idioms
and perspectives, and incorporates a range of languages, punning
between each. The hyper-referentiality and internal patterning of the
poem signal an excessive search for meaning and significance against
the brute horrors of mass extermination. The poem is a desperate
scrabble for value amidst literary quotations and a range of voices,
as well as a rumination on loss. An excerpt from early in the poem
moves from a representation of a prison to a phenomenological riff on
translation and value:

White blocks　　black lines stone by　　steel grille　　by grille　　line by
line across the white and black block of the page.
There has been a new edition true to the new edition. (No God but
confusion and Pound is its prophet; it floats on the sterling market.
I smell a rat; I see it floating through the air; but I shall nip it in the
bud. Ring-a-ring-a-roses, all fall down.) There has been a new edition
of *L'Histoire de la folie* which costs too much; and in order to change
your traveller's cheques you must return whence you came
(a bench in the Luxembourg gardens) and know the place for the
first time. Deconstruction
costs too much [...].[31]

---

[29]　Culler, *Theory of the Lyric*, p. 128.
[30]　Ibid., p. 54.
[31]　Forrest-Thomson, *Collected Poems*, p. 130.

The lines describe some form of prison as well as the brute banality of 'steel grille   by grille' of a death camp's walls and bars. Such description and iconic representation are immediately followed by a reflection of what has just been described: 'grille   by grille' receives its analogy in 'line by / line'. A self-consciousness about the way the blocks and steel of the death camp are transmuted into the poem precipitates a series of observations on translation, reminding us of Pound's concerted attempts to 'make new' historical and neglected poetics. Words and images associated with translation, markets, exchange, and profit all evoke a sense of what might have been lost. Like the practices of translation, 'deconstructive' practices reflect on lost meanings, slippage of signification, and the gaps and losses between literal meaning and transliteration. In other words, Forrest-Thomson travels over the bridge (le pont traversé) from mass human loss to reflections on language and loss.

The driving force of these bridge crossings is the excessively playful and somehow poignantly desperate language play. Shadows, ghosts, traces, and memories – all are symptoms of what language holds off, of the differential, rational, and restrained calculus operating to enable communication and interpretation. Language is rich with echoes, which a poet can try to capture and constrain, to provide memorials to the necessarily deported meaning, or to allow full rein, drawing ever new patterns from the free play. Forrest-Thomson's poems of this period are odes to *significance*; they are memorials of the possibility of endlessly proliferating meaning. In 'Le Pont Traversé: Ode', meaning traces, echoes and slippages of rational meaning occupy the same realm as voices and memories of those who died. Forrest-Thomson collapses the physical and verbal pasts together; there is 'an integr-/ation between image and reality' in a text in which 'de-/constructed presences of speech and sense so run' as 'traces through our history like scarlet woven in / a sailor's rope'.[32] But Forrest-Thomson is aware of the ethical vacuity of the linguistic game of collapsing all significance into differential play. That is to say, she is troubled by the consequences of actual, simple, and pure representations of real pain, real life, real deportations, and real deaths when directed through a language that knows itself to be inadequate, compromised, and inaccurate. In the face of the deportation and elimination of Jews, 'Deconstruction / costs too much'; its

[32] Forrest-Thomson, 'Leaving the Library', in *Collected Poems*, p. 121; 'On Reading Mr. Melville's Tales', in *Collected Poems*, p. 119.

linguistic and poetic lessons take us further from memorialisation and closer to the descent into babel-babble.

In an excellent reading of Forrest-Thomson's 'irrational play of phonetic linkage', Simon Perril reminds us that she translated some of the essays and poetry of Denis Roche.[33] Roche's creative work explored the ramifications of a totally unconstrained poetics comprised of what he called, in a piece entitled 'Towards a New Scansion' in his preface to *Éros Énergumène*, 'pulsational mingling'.[34] Perril quotes from Forrest-Thomson's translation of another section in Roche's preface ('Eroticism of the struggle with the whole') in which he writes of poetic and 'erotic' writing yearning for wholeness, all the while destroying the possibility of such. To Roche, poetry exhibits a 'nervous tension' and '*de-figuration*' and one which simultaneously yearns to contain everything while 'annihilating' the vision entirely. In such writing, Roche claims, '[t]here is the terrifying idea [...] of an inveterate search for loss, for a reality of which one is aware *as a loss*. And this continuous awareness is communicated to writing by elaborate pulsations'.[35] 'Le Pont Traversé: Ode' offers Forrest-Thomson's own version of this 'inveterate search for loss', with its main formal device the 'elaborate pulsations' learned from Roche and others. As Perril notes, '[o]bviously, as a translator of this passage, Forrest-Thomson was profoundly aware of this abyss', adding, '*On the Periphery* articulates this search for a reality of which one is aware only as a loss'. Forrest-Thomson's poem performs what Denise Riley has called the 'linguistic unease' of never fully being in control of one's language or, to put it another way, of experiencing the intense loss of the real with every articulation.[36]

In the line, 'change / your traveller's cheques', in 'Le Pont Traversé: Ode', Forrest-Thomson draws attention to the exchange of meaning or transactions of sense as well as affect that occur in the ode. Such transactions operate between the reader and the poet but also across sight and sound patterns in the poem. But, in the

[33] Simon Perril, 'Contemporary British Poetry and Modernist Innovation' (unpublished PhD thesis, University of Cambridge, 1996).

[34] Forrest-Thomson, 'Excerpts from Denis Roche's Preface to *Éros Énergumène*: Lessons in Poetic Vacuity', in *Collected Poems and Translations*, ed. Anthony Barnett (London: Allardyce, Barnett, 1990), p. 150.

[35] Forrest-Thomson, *Collected Poems and Translations*, pp. 150–51.

[36] Denise Riley, 'Linguistic Unease', in *The Words of Selves: Identification, Solidarity, Irony* (Stanford: Stanford University Press, 2000), pp. 56–92.

broader context of the Holocaust, of the deportations of Jewish and many other peoples, physical and emotional transactions, translations, slippages from one state (State) and context to another, are all the more urgent and tragic. This poem dramatises a lyric collapse between the mania of words and the world. The maudlin wit which veins these poems is a register of this melancholic overlap as well as of the poor work that puns and irony do in memorialising and in producing wit from such horrors. The poem performs a kind of gallows humour whereby the descent into babel madness is offered as the only way to cope. Forrest-Thomson is at once writing and trying to do something – to memorialise – but she also accepts her complicity in revelling in such puns. But, perhaps this agonising contradiction is in keeping with Jacob's and the Dadaists' work, which was often designed to confront conventions, to upset, to challenge, and to disgust. Forrest-Thomson inhabits the lyric complicities and acknowledges the ambivalences and risks, violence and exploitations, of commemoration.

'Le Pont Traversé: Ode' is Forrest-Thomson's own commentary on poetry after Auschwitz. But, given the choice between silence and verbal excess, Forrest-Thomson plumps for the latter, despite its hysterical inadequacies. And there is a sense in this poem that she proposes an ethics of memorialising through failure. It is as if she states:

> I am trying to confront this overwhelming reality and provide a memorial to these people in the only way I can, through poetry, but I know – through reading and thinking about language, and through engaging with Derrida – that my only hope is perhaps to glimpse truths and clarity through spectres and in between languages and words. The costs are high with such excessive experiment, but it's worth it to memorialise you along with meaning. And aren't I showing that, while it was language that got you deported, it is also language that can offer your liberation and memorialisation, particularly as an homage to your own revolutionary style?

It might be an endlessly deferred revolution but, as Forrest-Thomson writes, 'even / Breton refrained from firing the revolutionary revolver'; we must continue to fight and to wrestle with language.[37]

---

[37] Forrest-Thomson, *Collected Poems*, p. 130.

In *Agonistic Poetry*, Fitzgerald notes that 'in a typical ending of a Pindaric ode, a swift paratactic succession of gnomic statements creates an oscillating rhythm in which human intention seems to have no place'.[38] Poetic conventions produce a no-person zone where the human is evacuated from the realm of pure language. As if deliberately evoking such conditions, 'Le Pont Traversé: Ode' concludes:

> in deportation in memory of Max Jacob. Rest in peace with
> the priest of revolution. Quos nunc abibis in locos? Les billets
> ne sont plus valables au Luxembourg. If I think of a king at
> star-fall Ἀστὴρ πρὶν μὲν ἔλαμπες ἐνὶ ζωοῖσιν Ἐῷος.[39]

Jacob is put to rest and gnomic statements in Latin, French, and ancient Greek follow. The Latin is from Hadrian's last poem, dictated on his death bed ('where are you going now?'); the French is a call-back quotation from earlier in the poem, but also evokes the famous literary hang-out spot of the Luxembourg Gardens in Paris; the ancient Greek is Plato's epigram to the stargazing Aster – famously used by Shelley as the epigraph to his ode to Keats, 'Adonais' ('Thou wert a morning star among the living') – and which has become a literary trope for death and aspiration to immortality.[40]

---

[38]   Fitzgerald, *Agonistic Poetry*, p. 183.

[39]   Forrest-Thomson, *Collected Poems*, p. 131.

[40]   The Latin line is taken from Hadrian's *Ad animam*, a poem which he apparently recited on his death bed. The whole poem, which has been translated a number of times in wildly different ways, reads: *Animula, vagula, blandula / Hospes comesque corporis! / Quæ nunc abibis in loca, / Pallidula, frigida nudula / Nec ut soles dabis joca?* Northrop Frye translates the lines as 'O fleeing should of mine / My body's friend and guest! / Whither goest thou, / Pale, fearful and pensive one? / Why not laugh as old?' (*Collected Works of Northrop Frye*, ed. Robert D. Denham et al., 30 vols (Toronto: University of Toronto Press, 1996–2012), XIII, p. 670 n.). Ἀστηρ πριν μεν ελαμπες ενι ζωοισιν Ἐῶος is Plato's epigram on Aster and was adopted by Shelley as the epigraph to 'Adonais: An Elegy on the Death of John Keats, author of Endymion, Hyperion, etc.' (*Poetical Works*, ed. Thomas Hutchinson (London: Oxford University Press, 1967), pp. 432–44). In his *Life of Shelley* (1847), Thomas Medwin wrote of a conversation with Shelley: 'Plato's epigram on Aster, which Shelley had applied to Keats, happened to be mentioned, – Αστηρ τριν μεν ελαμτις, ενι ζωοισιν Εωος, / Νυν δε θανων λαμπεις, Εσπιρος εν θιμεροις, and I asked Shelley if he could render it. He took up the pen and improvised: "Thou wert a morning star among the living, / Ere thy fair light was fled; / Now, having died, thou art as Hesperus, giving / New splendour to the dead." I said, the version was too paraphrastic, and suggested the following:– "Thou wert a morning star to us, / And dying

'Le Pont Traversé: Ode' has descended into the gnomic, but Forrest-Thomson is aware of her inhabitation of the ode-zone and pays fealty to these conventions.

Writing of 'Le Pont Traversé: Ode' and 'The Ear of Dionysios: Ode', Perril notes that both odes codify a type of formal anguish which phenomenologically evokes the loss of life and love, and which creates a strained, elegiac tone.[41] The connection between the formal dynamics of the ode form and its ability to evoke the experience of loss is part of the self-reflective history of the form itself. There is something in the Pindaric irregularity, its repetitions, and its formal structures which lends itself to resonant memorialisation, for example. As the closing lines of 'Le Pont Traversé: Ode' illustrate, Forrest-Thomson was conscious of these conventions and exploited them. 'The Ear of Dionysios: Ode' is more obviously Pindaric in that it features three distinct types of poetic arrangements used sporadically: a conventional, centralised stanza form with end rhymes; prose-like arrangement, as in 'Le Pont Traversé'; and a type of 'step-down' form, scattered across the page. The poem also contains a long epigraph explaining the story of the Ear of Dionysios.[42] As Denise Riley has written of her own long, meditative ode, 'Affections of the Ear': '[t]he poem wonders [... whether] Echo may be a figure or a trope for the troubled nature of lyric poetry, driven by rhyme, condemned to repetition of the cadences and sound-associations of others' utterances'.[43] Echoing the theme of echo and its melancholic

---

art our Hesperus'" (Thomas Medwin, *The Life of Percy Bysshe Shelley* (London: Thomas Cautley Newby, 1847), p. 176).

[41]   Simon Perril, 'Contemporary British Poetry'.

[42]   'Below the Greek amphitheatre / on the left of the Roman stadium / beyond the cord-maker's grotto, the monument thus named is found / to be one of the greatest engineering feats / of the ancient world. It was designed / for Dionysios, tyrant of Syracuse, / as a dungeon whence his prisoner's voices / would reach 1,000 ft to his own less / permanent tympanum. If the tourist / will try the experiment he may hear / his own words echo throughout the / vast moist aperture. But Dionysios doesn't / listen any more. Je suis la victime et le bureau' (Forrest-Thomson, *Collected Poems*, p. 127).

[43]   Denise Riley, *Selected Poems* (London: Reality Street Editions, 2000), p. 110. In 'Affections of the Ear', Riley writes: '"Ears are the only orifices that can't be closed" though force may get some others to succumb' (p. 96). Of the origins of her curious title, Riley explains: 'Robert Graves' first volume of *The Greek Myths* claims that narcissus oil was used as a cure for "affections of the ears". Here the word "affection" is an archaism for "disease" (an example from the *OED* – "an affection of the heart" was, in 1853, a heart disease)' (p. 110).

repetitions of others' words, the dominant organising device of 'The
Ear of Dionysios: Ode' is rhyme in many forms – pun, assonance,
consonance, and eye rhymes – each section has a distinct role.

The prose-like sections are chatty, gossipy, and witty:

> You are not like me; you are Giselle, Odette in the world of
> similar asparagus (and no crummy puns on corps de ballet
> from the audience; take your filthy words off her) or a waitress
> with a Cockney accent. You are not like me; you are me; you
> are me in any of these roles and your hair is not golden but
> brown if I want it to be, and your body, mine in the bath.[44]

Forrest-Thomson evokes the cacophonous and bawdy world of the
theatre and ballet, drawing on camp and innuendo-full registers.
The poem has two such sections. The 'step-down' form heightens the
phonic and visual organisation:

> Still white heliotrope
> topic of still waters which run deep
> when you are rowing
> towing a growing sense of fear of
> tropes in the boat.[45]

Forrest-Thomson's self-conscious reflection on poetic practices –
'tropes' (and figurative language), rhyming, internally generated
associations – are expressed in a playful poetic form. As she writes
later in the same form: 'from shore to shore, I can give you /
metaphor for metaphor'.[46] Lastly, the tight stanza forms are used to provide
reflections on the sexual politics of literary conventions. Hence:

> In places the mask slips, the man shows clear
> with his bigotry hatred and fear;
> and in others his passionate tender heart?
> No, I fear art's a hard thing, my dear,
> there one sees just the greatness of art.[47]

Forrest-Thomson lambasts the confusing and contradictory
copresence of 'bigotry, hatred and fear' and 'passionate tender hearts'
in male poets' work (Swinburne, Dowson, and Symons are named

---

[44] Forrest-Thomson, *Collected Poems*, p. 127.
[45] Ibid., p. 128.
[46] Ibid.
[47] Ibid.

earlier) in (quite) neatly metrical and end-rhymed verse, as if to mock the injunction that 'art's a hard thing' and out of the reach of a woman. The three types of poetic arrangement in the poem provide a form of three-way dialogue – as in the Pindaric – through which Forrest-Thomson reflects on the various ways in which odes offer memorialisation of people and events and about how art ensures the elevation but also the contortion of real life (like the 'bleeding toes in satin shoes' of ballet dancers attaining perfect form at the cost of real feet).[48] All of these reflections are overseen by a hyper self-awareness of the poetic forms, conventions, and tricks used to accomplish these themes and effects.

Rhyme and echoes are forms of memorialisation, and the poem encourages us to reflect on how long a person, their work, and their name resonate and reverberate in the present; how long their traces stay to chime and rhyme with our ongoing present. As 'The Ear of Dionysios: Ode' and 'Le Pont Traversé: Ode' show, odes can be cacophonous chambers of resonating memories, containing phonic riffs on forms and themes inaugurated by contemplation of the memorialised. The dense patterning of the sounds means that readers and performers must bring to the poems a high degree of concentration to try to catch all the cross-rhyming, multiple puns, and phonetic and semantic overlaps. In other words, readers, like the poet, must concentrate to mark and remark on the interlaying and overlapping of ideas. Rhyme is an important constituent in this process. As Simon Jarvis has argued of rhyme, the question that excessive rhyming poses is 'how long a rhyme stays a rhyme before it decays'?[49] In contemplating rhyme, we are also considering the life span of certain formal effects. '[T]he question', Jarvis writes of line-terminal rhymes, 'is not primarily one of time or space but of affective charge, of memory'.[50] In designating when a rhyme is a rhyme, we are attributing significance and function to certain effects, and this practice relies on memory as well as attention to make them function. 'English Pindarics', Jarvis writes, 'become studies in rhyme decay. How long', he asks, 'does is take a rhyme to go out, to stop burning?'[51] If sound patterns carry affective charges and rely on memory, the multiple rhymes, resonances, and echoes in 'Le Pont

---

[48] Ibid., p. 129.
[49] Simon Jarvis, 'The Hyper-Pindaric', p. 133.
[50] Ibid., p. 134.
[51] Ibid.

Traversé: Ode' and 'The Ear of Dionysios: Ode' are performances of memorialisation through sound pattern which, at the same time, are trials of memorialisation to a reader and to the poet: how much concentration is required (and how much are we willing to give) in order that the requisite attention is given to the poem to perform this memorialisation? How far will the memorialised burn in our memories, and are we willing and able to keep the flame alight? As Forrest-Thomson implores at the end of 'Le Pont Traversé: Ode', perhaps evoking a reader or performer of her ode: 'you can teach its candles to burn bright'.[52]

Forrest-Thomson's 'The Ear of Dionysios: Ode' is an example of what Jarvis has described as an irregular Pindaric. Such odes force a reader to confront the ordinary problematic subjects of the ode in intensified ways, as the form refuses the consolations of regularity from which we can momentarily switch off. Regular rhyme operates like a click track – a reliable base from which we can veer away, and to which we can comfortably return. The irregular Pindaric disables this level of complacency and forces a reader to attend to the frequent pattern shifts; in this way, rhymes are doubly operative – they are there, but might not be there for long, so we had better keep on our toes in order to discern their significance. Choosing what is and is not a significant rhyme in an irregular Pindaric, as well as which words resonate, produces what Jarvis describes as a 'difficulty [which] emerges as an aporia in the [...] schema' of regular rhyme.[53] In other words, the doubts that irregularities cause provide an apt space for poems which worry about the process of memorialisation as well as how such figures and the poems themselves will fit into the conventional or traditional literary schemas.

Forrest-Thomson exploits such irregularity in order to create a space for doubt and uncertainty to become part of the anxious memorialisation of persons and ideas. 'The pleasures of the Pindaric', Jarvis writes a little later, 'are in part masochistic, like those of an arcade racing-car game in which the challenge is to avoid crashing into the barrier'.[54] There is a form of masochism in subjecting oneself to memorialisation (the poet) and to the performance and interpretation of this poem (the reader). For Jarvis, '[t]he finest late-twentieth-century English hyper-Pindarics [he lists J. H. Prynne's

---

[52]   Forrest-Thomson, *Collected Poems*, p. 131.
[53]   Jarvis, 'The Hyper-Pindaric', p 134.
[54]   Ibid.

'Of Sanguine Fire', John Wilkinson's 'Harmolodics', and Keston Sutherland's *Hot White Andy*] deploy, mutilate, and grow traditions which are by no means constructs or simulacra but modes of largely inexplicit practical expertise and virtuosity in the particular handlings of given metrico-rhythmic repertoires'.[55] In doing so, he argues, they 'push at the necessary entanglement between archaism and innovation in contemporary verse'.[56] The contemporary ode often resembles a discordant, dysfunctional but manically productive choir, and one which makes explicit the dialectical, competitive, and agonistic struggle with voices of the past. Forrest-Thomson's odes reveal and revel in the discordant battles with the choir of voices from the past, vying for attention with the present. Sometimes a Dadaist happening, other times a kind of philosophical recitative, occasionally a beautiful multipart harmony, Forrest-Thomson's odes offer an elaborate sing-off, a babel of cacophonous competition, all overseen by a conductor-poet who marks time with an oversized baton of ironic self-reflection.

Epode

As one of the key features of the Ode is an attempted but failed strategic avoidance of the memorialisation of the self, the poetic genre offers a rich medium for contemporary poets to explore the complicities of lyric practice. In other words – as I put it earlier – an ode is always already an ode to itself. The history of the ode is freighted with the irresolvable struggle between the object, the topic, and the subject of the writer; it is both a celebration and lament of an object, but also of the poet themselves who are the covert subject. The sketching of the object is also the relief etching of the poet's psyche and their literary, cultural, and political struggles with the acts of writing. As I have shown with Forrest-Thomson's Great Odes, such struggles are manifest in the burlesque parody of the themes and forms of those people she laments, as well as in the historical forms and themes of the ode itself. The ode offers the space for poets to explore an *extended and tortuously ironised presence*, a phrase that could be said to characterise a good deal of contemporary poetry. Such poetry takes pride in its formal and semantic excesses, its outflanking or out-thinking charges of directness, complicity, fetishisation, commodification; but it also

[55] Ibid., p. 142.
[56] Ibid.

builds into its structures, into its very tone and style, an ironisation of the privileges of such gestures. Not only is the poet alive and able to continue to write, but 'all this fiddle' – as Marianne Moore memorably put it – seems trifling and excessively indulgent.[57] The lyric gestures comprising the ode already offer a literary-historical space which is accommodating to such anxiety-driven contortions. A new form of ode, both grand and excessive in its artifices as well as domesticated and used to critique commodity capitalism, is exemplified in Forrest-Thomson's Great Odes, and these anticipate, for example, Keston Sutherland's *The Odes to TL61P* (2013).[58] In Sutherland's hands, the ode is a complex critique of poetry's and poets' complicity in contemporary culture and politics, but it is also very aware of its contribution to an ancient lineage of ode writing. While much less consciously political than Sutherland's, Forrest-Thomson's odes articulate the complicated complicities of lyric writing, as the gnomic phrase from 'The Ear of Dionysios: Ode' testifies: 'Je suis la victime et le bureau'. The contemporary ode writer may adopt their office [bureau] or calling with control, they may construct this temporary office or headquarters from which to conduct their memorialisation, but they cannot help but fall victim to the genre. To follow a pun embedded in the French, the ode writer becomes their own *bourreau* (executioner). In following the path of the ode writer, they are prone to become a victim of the mode's formal traps, its leaden and heavy echoes, and its tendency towards manic self-analysis. But, as Forrest-Thomson proves, poets will continue to resuscitate the ode, if only to receive resuscitation in the 'antagonistic cooperation' of its warring embrace.[59]

---

[57] Marianne Moore, 'Poetry', in *New Collected Poems*, ed. Heather Cass White (London: Faber, 2017), p. 27.

[58] Keston Sutherland, *The Odes to TL61P* (London: Enitharmon, 2013).

[59] While I am using the phrases for slightly different ends here, I am quoting Simon Jarvis from a short piece called 'For a Poetics of Verse', *PMLA*, 125.4 (2010), 931–35. Jarvis writes of the '"war embrace" between poetry and philosophy', describing it as 'an antagonistic cooperation' (p. 935), quoting from S. T. Coleridge, *Biographia Literaria*, ed. Nigel Leask (London: Everyman, 1997), p. 191.

CHAPTER SEVEN

Souvenir

Lucie Brock-Broido's True Kitsch

Esther Osorio Whewell

'Father, in Drawer' comes across as both stoic and emotional, a really exquisite balance for an elegy to achieve. From your perspective, which particular elements of the poem help it to walk this line?
     I don't have a stoic bone in my body. Would that I could conjure even a feigned indifference to – anything. To the contrary, I am *different* to everything. In real life, emotion is easy; holding back is tough. On the page though, it's the opposite: that's what I strive for – the chill (of course), the stupor (a necessity), but never quite the letting go.[1]

In interviews, Lucie Brock-Broido still speaks in poems. From a height but not at odds and not aloof, she gently riddles with critical suggestions of what it is she meant, speaking never not half-askance, in codes and quotations. Twining, in the last line here, Emily Dickinson's stiff, ceremonious Nerves between her brackets, she bends their wooden way towards her and melts their freezing heart, rubs smooth and dull their hard, bright Quartz, like sea glass made softer and familiar by years of thumbing pages. Her formal feelings come dressed for dinner. Brock-Broido's poetry is close in, and it likes the touch of things – and if holding back, she says, is tough, she can hold very still, and very tight. Though not straightforward, her writing is strongly recognisable, and if she cannot conjure even a feigned indifference to – anything, she is still a conjuror. Her books are wreathed in Dickinson,

[1] Lucie Brock-Broido, 'Extreme Wisteria', *The Q&A Issue, Poetry*, 201.3 (2012), 312–19 (p. 314).

in Thomas Wyatt, Shakespeare, Hans Christian Andersen, classical Hollywood, blues, Rilke, the Brothers Grimm; they think constantly about grief and remembering, how to keep a hold of and about you the memories of things that have died and things that cannot be kept the way they are, or kept at all, and what the sounds of words have to do with it. She isn't feigning; and she's not messing about.

A souvenir is not an elegy (although sentiment and nostalgia live close by both). It is rather, I'd like to argue in this chapter, a particularly fraught subgenre of the remembering lyric, with a particularly fraught relationship to materialism and materialist poetics; to the authority of stories told through the properties of things, and who should speak them how. Literary craft and carefulness here will be found deeply oriented by owned (lent, stolen, coveted) objects and their wrappings, and self-styling discovered as potent paratextual accoutrement. This chapter will make the case for visible aesthetic – passions and preoccupations exquisitely brazen and undisguised – as a mechanism for the poietic and poetic organisation of complicated lyric thinking. Brock-Broido died in 2018, leaving four books of poetry – beginning in 1988 – with often almost a decade between one and the next. Her slender collections speak the determined amassing of lifetimes of small things sod with sentimental value – 'Victorian slippers that walked the bogs to moor', 'my toy / Pram filled with slippery mice', 'the tin sink light enough for travelling', 'endless strings of small whortleberry lights, ablaze', 'a tiny iron matador (he wore a hat)', 'the note pinned in the seersuckered / Left breast pocket of the Surrealist's suit, on his way to Cincinnati, then, by rail'.[2] This is the musty, tattling bureau of someone who cannot throw anything away, or leave anything behind. 'And here, in the red room / Of my Beaux Arts and my irony', she writes,

> all the fetishes will be safe
>
> And in their places like the hummingbird who lives here
>
> With me, just out of
> Reach. Pray then to leave here in my own sweet bed with
>
> All my charges safe from harm.[3]

    [2] Lucie Brock-Broido, *Stay, Illusion* (New York: Alfred A. Knopf, 2018), pp. 72, 73, 49, 57, 68, 74.
    [3] Brock-Broido, 'Fata Morgana', in *Trouble in Mind* (New York: Alfred A. Knopf, 2018), p. 31.

Brock-Broido's 'Gaudy Infinitesimal' is Beaux Arts with a sharp tongue – while thinking hard about keeping little things safe, it is keen enough to cut yourself on deeply. 'Flowers don't tend to be dangerous', she says, '[p]oems, in my opinion, always are'.[4]

In one of the first reviews of Brock-Broido's poetry, appearing in the *Washington Post* on Christmas Day in 1988, the critic who loves to call himself the most hated man in American poetry – William Logan's own dustjackets often relate delightedly how Pulitzer prize winners have offered to run him over with a truck – crowned *A Hunger*'s debutante author the 'poet laureate of *People* magazine and the evening news', 'with a taste for sensational stories, usually relegated to the headlines'.[5] Lucie Brock-Broido's poems, when Logan reads them, 'are rarely able to concentrate for a stanza on the show at hand'; her images, related with a 'preening mannerism', are 'all ajumble', and her voices, 'when she indulges in personae, are strained and tainted by a self-conscious artlessness – or worse, artiness'. Bad, incoherence; worse – artiness. Logan thinks Brock-Broido is kitschy.

And so she is. Though most of the objects in the bureau above might be listed more comfortably under what scholarship sometimes defines as 'mementos', a type distinct from the 'souvenir' as 'the very epitome of tourism's cultural *kitsch*',[6] there would be little use (and in fact, I will argue, little gain) in countering Logan's characterisation of Brock-Broido's overarching style. Sixteen years after *A Hunger*, by the evidence of her third book, *Trouble in Mind* (2004) – 'having done / All the proper and romantic things [...] lying still / In lemon light, the dried red Liar- / Roses strewn all around my Renaissance Revival bed' – this poetry still keeps kitsch like the Sabbath.[7] If such writing has a school of art, and it does, it is pre-Raphaelite: 'Liar-roses' strewn across a Renaissance bed are a kind of Edward Burne-Jones painting to a Tammy Wynette soundtrack.[8] The scene

---

[4] Brock-Broido, 'Extreme Wisteria', *The Q&A Issue*, p. 315.

[5] William Logan, 'Tough Guys Don't Rhyme', *Washington Post Book World* (25 December 1988): https://www.washingtonpost.com/archive/entertainment/books/1988/12/25/tough-guys-dont-rhyme/85e09ab6-3b9e-48b0-8308-74d64 6355ab0/?noredirect=on&utm_term=.1a0d5655194e [accessed 3 October 2019].

[6] Michael Haldrup, 'Souvenirs: Magical Objects in Everyday Life', *Emotion, Space and Society*, 22 (2017), 52–60 (p. 52).

[7] Brock-Broido, 'Fata Morgana', in *Trouble in Mind*, p. 31.

[8] The refrain of the Tammy Wynette song, 'Liar's Roses' is, 'Oh, I'm sleepin' in a bed of liar's roses / While he dreams of somebody else'; Edward Burne-Jones's

is Brock-Broido to the quick, and her poetry over a quarter of a century never abates its preoccupations with littleness and loveliness, heavy decoration, talking creatures, taxidermy, the rich furnishings of domestic interiors. Brock-Broido wouldn't think for a moment, moreover, to disagree with Logan's diagnosis herself: she read, it turned out, the daily broadsheets too, and not just the headlines; her second book, *The Master Letters* (1995) (after Dickinson's), contains an epistolary prose poem addressed '*To Recipient Unknown*' and entitled 'Haute Couture Vulgarity', explicitly citing the *Washington Post* review in the endnotes. In this prose poem, 'Imperial wizards roam the south of things, white Trash Arcana, cleaning this pale earth with their long rayon robes [...] In the pageantries of mystics'.[9] 'Be pristine in excess Rhetoric', it ends,

> vary the baroque of the High Romantic Tongue, regard the Nun starving for idea. There will be ruin in a new world worldliness.
> *All are very naughty, & I am naughtiest of all,*
> *Ever –*
>> *His,*
>> *Penitent Friend.*

Brock-Broido's High Romantic Tongue – she must be, Roger Gilbert thinks, 'among the last contemporary poets to persist in capitalizing every line of her poems',[10] as goes too for every word of her titles – can speak in many varied baroque timbres. Out of, as Beverly Gordon puts it, a 'Western culture [which] tends to define reality as "that which you can put your hands on"',[11] her poetry complicates the work of remembering by forms which, far from merely 'tacky' or 'corny',[12] might also be 'active, engaged, fraught with possibilities'.[13]

---

cycle of Sleeping Beauty paintings is called *The Legend of Briar Rose*. Half a glance or half a bar will reveal each individually as exquisitely Brock-Broidan territory, and both at once – almost too much so.

[9]   Brock-Broido, *The Master Letters* (New York: Alfred A. Knopf, 2014), p. 44.

[10]   Roger Gilbert, 'About Poems About', *Michigan Quarterly Review*, 46.3 (2005): http://hdl.handle.net/2027/spo.act2080.0044.319 [accessed 3 October 2019].

[11]   Beverly Gordon, 'The Souvenir: Messenger of the Extraordinary', *Journal of Popular Culture*, 20.3 (1986), 135–46 (p. 136).

[12]   Ibid., 138.

[13]   Lisa Love and Nathaniel Kohn, 'This, That and the Other: Fraught Possibilities of the Souvenir', *Text and Performance Quarterly*, 21.1 (2001), 47–63 (p. 50).

'If you find this fun –': Souvenir, Kitsch, and Truth

Susan Stewart's 1993 meditations on objects of desire (tiny, giant, amassed) in *On Longing* remains the definitive critical treatment of the 'souvenir'. Souvenirs for Stewart are metonymic objects, 'saturated with meanings', which come to exemplify 'the capacity of objects to serve as traces of authentic experience' in a world where (*pace* Gordon) 'the lived relation of the body to the phenomenological world is replaced by the nostalgic myth of contact and presence'.[14] The souvenir, Stewart writes, 'speaks to a context of origin through a language of longing, for it is not an object arising out of need or use value; it is an object arising out of the necessarily insatiable demands of nostalgia'.[15] And as Stewart's account evidences (she ends her 'Souvenir' chapter with a disquisition on *kitsch* and *camp*), 'kitsch' and 'souvenirs' go clammily hand in hand. Since you really can't do Lucie Brock-Broido without kitsch either, a short digression on the scholarly history of kitsch seems apposite.

'With your permission I shall begin with a warning', Hermann Broch begins his 1950 lecture 'Notes on the Problem of Kitsch': 'do not expect any rigid and neat definitions'.[16] Indeed, scholarly dealings with kitsch continue for much of the twentieth century to constitute transactions with 'a particularly evasive aesthetic phenomenon'.[17] In the introduction to his 1969 *Kitsch: An Anthology of Bad Taste*, Gillo Dorfles passes the buck rather platzhaltingly – in a footnote – to Ludwig Giesz's already diffident sense that 'the word *kitsch* could approximately be said to mean "artistic rubbish"'.[18] (Stewart says it comes 'from the German *kitschen*, "to put together sloppily"'.)[19] Matei Calinescu in *Five Faces of Modernity* is sterner, more helpful, outlining a concept of kitsch which 'clearly centers around such questions as imitation, forgery, counterfeit, and what we may call the aesthetics

---

[14]   Susan Stewart, *On Longing: Narratives of the Miniature, the Gigantic, the Souvenir, the Collection* (Durham, NC: Duke University Press, 1993), pp. 133, 135.

[15]   Ibid., p. 135.

[16]   Hermann Broch, 'Notes on the Problem of Kitsch' in *Kitsch: An Anthology of Bad Taste* [translated from the Italian], ed. Gillo Dorfles (London: Studio Vista, 1969), pp. 49–77 (p. 76).

[17]   Ulrich Schneider, 'Kitsch as Joyce Can: Zurich 1989', *James Joyce Quarterly*, 27.3 (1990), 639–42 (p. 639).

[18]   Gillo Dorfles, 'Introduction', in *Kitsch: An Anthology*, p. 10. Ludwig Giesz is the writer of *Phänomenologie des Kitsches* (Munich: Wilhelm Fink, 1971).

[19]   Stewart, *On Longing*, p. 168.

of deception and self-deception', where '[k]itsch may be conveniently defined as a specifically aesthetic form of lying'.[20] In a brilliant essay on Walter Benjamin's kitsch thinking in *The Arcades Project*, Winfried Menninghaus begins by collecting up '[o]ther monosyllabic German words that end in "tsch" – *Quatsch* (nonsense, rubbish), *Klatsch* (splash; smack; gossip), *Matsch* (mush; slush; sludge), *pitsch, patsch* (pitter-patter), *ritsch, ratsch* (rip!), *futsch* (bust)'.[21] Brock-Broido's kitsch does not answer to many of these accusations.

It is Clement Greenberg's 'Avant-Garde and Kitsch', published in the *Partisan Review* in 1939, which is usually credited as the first (English) gambit of a serious art-critical interest in the cohabiting of early twentieth-century modernity with kitsch-as-consumerism. Greenberg's 'kitsch' is synthetic artistic effect as 'simulacra of genuine culture' – 'vicarious experience and faked sensations' which constitute 'the epitome of all that is spurious in the life of our times'. 'For some reason', he wrote then, 'this gigantic apparition has always been taken for granted. It is time we looked into its whys and wherefores'.[22] (The opportunity to mention here that Brock-Broido deals partly, perhaps predominantly, in gigantic apparitions is impossible to pass up.) Broch's 'Notes' lecture (sometimes claimed, in its first incarnation in a 1933 essay entitled 'Kitsch and Art-with-a-Message', to have been an uncredited source for Greenberg's) tangles the production of kitsch by the 'radical aesthete' – '[t]he person who works for love of effect, who looks for nothing else except the emotional satisfaction that makes the moment he sighs with relief seem "beautiful"' – more explicitly with the wrong side of ethics:

> The producer of kitsch does not produce 'bad' art, he is not an artist endowed with inferior creative faculties or no creative faculties at all. It is quite impossible to assess him according to aesthetic criteria; rather he should be judged as an ethically base being, a malefactor who profoundly desires evil.[23]

---

[20]   Matei Calinescu, *Five Faces of Modernity: Modernism, Avant-Garde, Decadence, Kitsch, Postmodernism* (Durham, NC: Duke University Press, 1987), p. 229.

[21]   Winfried Menninghaus, 'On the "Vital Significance" of Kitsch: Walter Benjamin's Politics of "Bad Taste"', in *Walter Benjamin and the Architecture of Modernity*, ed. Andrew Benjamin and Charles Rice (Melbourne: re.press, 2009), pp. 39–59 (p. 39).

[22]   Cited in Clement Greenberg, 'Avant-Garde and Kitsch', in *Art and Culture: Critical Essays* (Boston, MA: Beacon, 1965), pp. 3–21 (pp. 9–10).

[23]   Broch, 'Notes', p. 76.

The next significant intervention, Saul Friedlander's *Reflections of Nazism: An Essay on Kitsch and Death* (1982), becomes still graver, and more explicitly political, setting out 'a debased form of myth, nevertheless draw[ing] on mythic substance', which represents a 'Kitsch of the Apocalypse'.[24] It is Friedlander's drawing of myth into the kitsch conversation which at this point, Daniel Tiffany argues, 'lays the groundwork [...] for a theory of high kitsch, of esoteric kitsch'.[25]

In 1990, a gaudily eminent line-up of 30 cultural critics and commentators – including Friedlander, who introduced the Symposium, and Susan Sontag and Irving Howe, among others – locked themselves in 'for two days in the living room of the Skidmore College conference center' to discuss the problem of kitsch, producing 15 hours of sound-tape later transcribed by Peg and Robert Boyers, almost in full, for a special issue of *Salmagundi*.[26] At the end of it all, Irving Howe has the last word:

> IH: My point is that we have not been able to, and probably no one else could, bound a territory for cultural use. I don't yet accept most of the correlations we've been trying out [S]ince now you people have put this damn word in my head for awhile – I will [often] think of kitsch, But I will also say to myself, since I am so vague, since it is so hard for me to know what this word is, a more responsible way of writing will be not to use the word, but to describe the effects which some people think the word has ...
>
> SG: I'm sure we could have sat down and agreed on a small group of art objects that deserve to be called kitsch. And we could have all said in a very constricted sense why these objects struck us as kitsch. But what's the fun of anything that would elicit that much consensus?
>
> IH: If you find this fun – and there I'm with you – then no one should take that away from you; there is so little fun these days in literary discussion that whatever you can get is desirable.[27]

[24] Saul Friedlander, *Reflections of Nazism: An Essay on Kitsch and Death*, trans. Thomas Weyr (Bloomington: Indiana University Press, 1993), p. 49.

[25] Daniel Tiffany, 'Kitsching *The Cantos*', *Modernism/modernity*, 12.2 (2005), 329–37 (p. 334).

[26] Peg and Robert Boyers, 'KITSCH: An Introduction', *Salmagundi*, 85.6 (1990), 197–200 (p. 199).

[27] Irving Howe and Sarah Goodwin in conversation, '[Discussion in Four Parts]', *Salmagundi*, 85.6 (1990), 208–312 (pp. 311–12).

End tape. We do know kitsch when we see it – we're not sure what it is, but we know we don't like it. As Tiffany has written in a recent counternarrative, 'the qualities associated with poetic kitsch – triviality, generality, reproducibility, fraudulence – appear to contradict (as its detractors emphatically contend) the ideology of modernism'.[28]

Within the academy, first Helen Vendler, and later Stephanie Burt, have been Brock-Broido's main champions.[29] In *Soul Says: On Recent Poetry* (1995), in which – alongside Rita Dove, Jorie Graham, and Louise Glück – Vendler first wrote about Brock-Broido's debut, the word 'kitsch' (though she doesn't use it of *A Hunger*) is definitely a part of her critical vocabulary. On the qualitative difference between Adrienne Rich and Jorie Graham (she prefers Graham), she writes in brackets that

> (In fact, the presence of undeniable truth is one of the usual criteria for separating true art from kitsch. True art, even of the most 'beautiful' Spenserian or Keatsian sort, doesn't shrink from the difficult, the ungraceful, the ugly, and the evil, whereas kitsch chooses to represent only the pliant, the pathetic, the lissom, the acceptable, and the inoffensive.)[30]

This is pretty cleanly along Greenberg's original lines, where kitsch – 'conveniently defined as an aesthetic form of lying' – constitutes 'synthetic', as against 'true' art,[31] and 'fraudulence', as Tiffany notes, is its '(essential feature)'.[32] 'True' and 'Kitsch' in Brock-Broido's poetry,

---

[28] Daniel Tiffany, *My Silver Planet: A Secret History of Poetry and Kitsch* (Baltimore: Johns Hopkins University Press, 2014), p. 16.

[29] See Stephanie Burt, *Close Calls with Nonsense: Reading New Poetry* (Saint Paul, MN: Graywolf, 2009), pp. 6, 126, 130; Stephanie Burt, '16. Lucie Brock-Broido, Domestic Mysticism (1988)', in *The Poem Is You: 60 Contemporary American Poems and How to Read Them* (Cambridge, MA: Belknap Press of Harvard University Press, 2016); *The Art of the Sonnet*, ed. Stephanie Burt and David Mikics (Cambridge, MA: Belknap Press of Harvard University Press, 2010), pp. 400–04; Helen Vendler, 'Drawn to Figments and Occasion: Lucie Brock-Broido's *A Hunger*', in *Soul Says: On Recent Poetry* (Cambridge, MA: Belknap Press of Harvard University Press, 1995), pp. 167–77. See also M. Wynn Thomas, '"The Grammar of the Night": Ekphrasis and Loss in Lucie Brock-Broido's *Trouble in Mind*', in *In the Frame: Women's Ekphrastic Poetry from Marianne Moore to Susan Wheeler*, ed. Jane Hedley, Nick Halpern, and Willard Spiegelman (Newark: University of Delaware Press, 2010), pp. 245–62.

[30] Vendler, *Soul Says*, p. 219.

[31] Greenberg, 'Avant-Garde and Kitsch', p. 15.

[32] Tiffany, *My Silver Planet*, p. 7.

though, are bedfellows more complicatedly entwined. By her own repeated declaration – in her poems, as we will see, as well as in her interviews – Brock-Broido is luridly entranced by and in thrall to truthfulness, 'wildly interested in the truth of content' (and thinking about truth often seems to bring with it a thought about her own wildness – she says in another interview that, '[t]hough I am wildly capable of certain linguistic fabrications, I am in it for the truth').[33] 'The impossible post- // Raphaelite world in which I live', she insists in *Trouble in Mind*, ' – is true'.

What seems really interesting about this distinctive investment in the truth of poetic content is that, rather than acting as a counter-poise to her lissom and pathetic attitudes, it falls down on the same side of cases against Brock-Broido as her kitschiness. If 'kitsch artiness' is defined in opposition to 'true art', there remains still something about 'true' which sticks in the craw of scholarly poetry readers; and it is partly this poetry's unabashed fealty to truth and sincerity, I think, which sometimes seems to make its writer suspect as a serious contender. A heart too beating on a sleeve seems to share with synthetic art that 'blindness to irony that is characteristic of kitsch', both making taste too evident in a way which puts the poet on an exposed back foot in relation to the critic.[34] Alignment with kitsch aesthetic – often described in terms of a critically stultifying 'addiction', which 'unfits people from having certain kinds of attention spans and an appetite for complexity'[35] – and with earnestness both speak the same unselfconscious unsophistication for which Vendler lightly chastised Brock-Broido in 1995, revealed in her 'persistent use of a few obsessive words, among them the adjectives "small," "little," "tiny," "frail," "fragile"; the nouns "child" and "girl"; the verb "curl"', and her frequent inhabiting of frail and vulnerable personae

[33] Wayne Koestenbaum and Lucie Brock-Broido, 'A Conversation between Wayne Koestenbaum and Lucie Brock-Broido', *Parnassus: Poetry in Review*, 23 (1998), 143–65 (p. 160).

[34] Barry Goldensohn, '[Discussion in Four Parts]', p. 274. Nonetheless, here's Brock-Broido at interview: 'Are extreme flowers like extreme sports? What I know of extreme sports: my favorite is called "Extreme Ironing." You think I'm making this up. Participants take baskets of heavily wrinkled clothes, their boards, their irons (electricity, not portable, seems to get there once you do). The sport is played in radical settings; at the edges of cliffs, or hanging from high bridges. The athletes are called "Ironists." I am one of those' ('Extreme Wisteria', *The Q&A Issue*, p. 316).

[35] Susan Sontag, '[Discussion in Four Parts]', p. 222.

who 'master their author' by the 'apparently unconscious repetition [which] suggests an as yet incomplete control over psychic material'.[36]

Souvenirs are fundamentally exposing, too, often approached in scholarship via micro personal case studies and 'autoethnographies', where their 'use value [...] rests on their ability to establish who we are[, as] objects we use to "design ourselves" [...] materially and emotionally'.[37] Of *Trouble in Mind*, dedicated to the poet Lucy Grealy, M. Wynn Thomas writes – albeit very admiringly – that in these poems grief for a mother and for a close friend 'has so usurped Brock-Broido's consciousness that in places it seeps through the pores of her writing'.[38] In this book Thomas finds that 'language and image double-cross the user', and '[i]ronized self-pity unintentionally reverses itself into a desolating vista of authentic pathos'.[39] *Trouble in Mind*, in particular, as well as those other poems by Brock-Broido which seem explicitly to address the death of her father, or her own anorexia, are often dissected predominantly by way of autobiography – and though there is nothing necessarily iniquitous about this version of critique (indeed, as we will see, Brock-Broido often seems to encourage it), unlocking this writing as though a *roman-à-clef*, or a kind of poetry-as-coping-mechanism, an unselfconscious 'autoethnography', seems often to mean stopping short of what Brock-Broido is really locking up with it – and what she is using her truth-telling to say about lyric memory. 'In [her] self-portraits', as Burt observes acutely, Brock-Broido 'is risking embarrassment, presenting her soul, by sharing her tastes, rather than telling the story of her life'. Like real grief, only much less excusably or commendably, real penchant gives too much away for taking seriously; 'it courts accusations of self-indulgence'.[40] This, I think, in Brock-Broido's hands is the souvenir poem's bravery, and also its magic.

---

[36]   Vendler, *Soul Says*, p. 170.

[37]   Haldrup, 'Souvenirs: Magical Objects', pp. 56–57; see also Daniel Miller, 'Designing Ourselves', in *Design Anthropology: Object Culture in the 21st Century*, ed. Alison J. Clarke (Vienna: Springer), pp. 88–99.

[38]   Thomas, 'The Grammar of the Night', p. 246.

[39]   Ibid., p. 253.

[40]   Burt, *The Poem Is You*, p. 97.

Little, Tat, Rag, Thread: Lyric Kitsch and Remembering

'Jessica, from the Well' is the longest poem in *A Hunger* and probably the one worst-placed to counter Logan's barbs, or Vendler's constructive criticisms. It is a poem whose impetus is in negotiating and interrogating the remnants of collective and individual labours of remembering, which posits the possibility (and problematics) of a human souvenir with a memory of its own. The poem is grown from the story of Jessica McClure – 'Baby Jessica' – who in 1987 fell down a well in her aunt's back garden in Texas and lay there for 58 hours before being rescued by a team of firemen, paramedics, and drillers, while the nation watched live on CNN. It has all of Brock-Broido's tiny, fragile 'talismanic words' in abundance – and 30 years on in 2017, its subject was still the front-page stuff of *People* magazine:[41]

> 'I had God on my side that day,' Jessica says in the upcoming issue of PEOPLE, on newsstands Friday. 'My life is a miracle.'[42]

'Jessica, from the Well' also offers, nonetheless, another compelling version of Mutlu Konuk Blasing's model of the lyric poem as born out of the 'properly, traumatic history' which produces human subjects before being 'consigned to oblivion by infantile amnesia', and of poetry's power – drawn out by Fiona Green in the first chapter of this collection – to synthesise a 'threshold condition' of language perception more richly alive and capricious than the everyday, which 'reminds us how to read unreasonably'.[43] The real Jessica McClure claims, now, no recollection whatever of falling down the well; and Brock-Broido remarks in her endnotes that 'psychiatrists assured the American public through the media that Jessica, though physically battered from her ordeal, would have no psychological scarring, no memory of the event'.[44]

Blasing argues that it is the severing of mind and body which delivers us into language, rendering 'an otherness [of] one's most intimate self'.[45] Brock-Broido's Jessica has a child's body and many

[41] Vendler, *Soul Says*, p. 170.

[42] Darla Higgins, 'Baby Jessica 30 Years Later', *People* (31 May 2017): https://people.com/human-interest/baby-jessica-30-years-later-my-life-is-a-miracle/ [accessed 3 October 2019].

[43] See this volume, Fiona Green, 'Aubade: Jorie Graham and "the pitch of the dawn"', pp. 13–36 (p. 14). Mutlu Konuk Blasing, *Lyric Poetry: The Pain and Pleasure of Words* (Princeton: Princeton University Press, 2007), pp. 16, 10.

[44] Brock-Broido, *A Hunger* (New York: Alfred A. Knopf, 2018), p. 59.

[45] Blasing, *Lyric Poetry*, p. 61.

different grown-up voices. 'I've never spoken aloud yet to anyone alive', she says, 'but I know all the words'. One of her voices, it would be foolish to deny, is quite plainly Brock-Broido's own:

> When I learn a word
> sometimes, I am compelled to use it.
> Given my disposition, I will always be
> circuitous, precocious, an Embellisher.[46]

Like the real Jessica, for whom rescuers listened out, for hours, above ground – '[a]s long as she was singing, she was still alive'[47] – this one can be heard by those 'somewhere above', 'humming along with myself & myself. / A choir of me's', 'in that throaty liquid lewd bowlegged / voice like kittens make'. It is Marilyn's fuzzy, knowing cloy at the surface of the singing in this poem, but here and elsewhere, Marlene's heavier-lidded cadence often underlies Brock-Broido's beguiling too.[48]

From the bottom of the well, then, Jessica has a voice. But when 'from the well, I am born',

> The heart is left   *in situ*, I am lifted
> from the oubliette
> divine by water, blinking by air.[49]

Heart and voice left behind, she doesn't have the gills for speaking, yet, by air – and becomes, now, above all a body – a little curled-up shape, fished out from a long, tall one. These are two of Brock-Broido's favourite forms. '*In the oubliette she will begin to sing*':[50] wells are already sites for spells and storytelling, and Brock-Broido's Jessica's ('[o]ubliette *n.* a secret dungeon with access only through a trapdoor in its ceiling':[51] when I learn a word sometimes, I am compelled to use it) is a well mythified, its tiny occupant a tissue of fable and fairy tale, waking to find herself an upside-down Rapunzel, 'with my own hair wound / into my fist'.[52]

---

[46]   Brock-Broido, *A Hunger*, p. 23.

[47]   Higgins, 'Baby Jessica 30 Years On', n. pag.

[48]   'I Wish You Love' is *A Hunger*'s most candid Marlene poem.

[49]   Brock-Broido, *A Hunger*, pp. 26–27.

[50]   Brock-Broido, 'Jessica, from the well', *The Virginia Quarterly Review*, 64.3 (1988), 443–48. The version in *A Hunger* does not have this first line, though the word 'oubliette' does appear later on, in the lines of the poem quoted above.

[51]   'oubliette, *n.*', *OED*.

[52]   Brock-Broido, *A Hunger*, p. 26.

The diminutive, feminised '[o]ubliette' (cf., it's hard not to posit, 'Lucie')[53] suggests deceitfully the furnishings of a nonsense boudoir in which also belongs the 'rose / caliche' (pink for a baby girl) against which Jessica presses her forehead to pray. A 'calash' is a silk hood with a whalebone frame, or the folding hood of a perambulator; but 'caliche' is a raw nitrate deposit. Flirting with sounds with the ears of an infant and then conjuring the consequences as home-improvements is a game of poetry magic with high stakes and risky forfeits. The word speaks etymologically as well as phonologically to Blasing's infantile amnesia, and to Brock-Broido's particular form of reconstructed remembering. With 'no memory of the event', Baby Jessica through the media is condemned to lose ownership of her own history, while simultaneously collected and commodified as historical artefact by the world whose archaeological enterprise lifted her from the earth; she much more of a *souvenir*, in her *oubliette* and out of it, than she ever was an 'oubliée'.

Roger Gilbert ends his review of *Trouble in Mind* with a note: '[f]inally a word must be said about the poet's hair'. 'This may seem', he writes, 'a purely extraneous matter, but in fact Brock-Broido has gone out of her way both to display and trope upon it, much as Whitman did his beard'.[54] This is right: Brock-Broido's second book has a poem called 'Rampion', and her third two 'Self-Portrait' poems (of seven in this collection) which are named for hair – ' – with Her Hair on Fire' and ' – with Her Hair Cut Off'. Many poems in *Stay, Illusion*, her fourth and final book, are concerned with what hair, whether by accident or design – 'the burrs of newly dying things were in my hair' – might catch and hold;[55] and in all her author photos, for books and interviews, Brock-Broido's own waist-length, everblonde hair preponderates the frame, held back from her face by a black velvet Alice band, and spread across her shoulders. Hair – John Donne's 'bracelet of bright haire about the bone' in 'The Relique' seems irresistibly an ancestor of Jessica's 'my own hair wound / into my fist' – has a strange relationship with material vitality, somewhere on the way to death and still attached to life.[56]

---

[53] 'Critics of Brock-Broido', Roger Gilbert is also shrewd about noting, 'find it difficult to resist the puns embedded in her name – baroque, brocade, embroidery, all of them terms that might be used to describe her intricately woven art' ('About Poems About', n. pag.).

[54] Gilbert, 'About Poems About', n. pag.

[55] Brock-Broido, *Stay, Illusion*, p. 16.

[56] John Donne, 'The Relique', in *The Complete English Poems*, ed. C. A. Patrides (London: Everyman, 1994), pp. 59–60 (p. 59).

It is always, of course, possible that Brock-Broido is just writing poetry about herself; but it seems more interesting to wonder in this case if the self she offers as a paratext is rather of – indeed, about – her poetry, ravelling up networks of memories refracted by associative materialities, what Lisa Love and Nathaniel Kohn seek to unravel as the 'dynamic interplay between humans and their souvenirs' here interplaying between poems, their readers, their writers, the separate memories of each and their shared objects.[57] Of 'Portrait of Lucy with Fine Nile Jar' in *Trouble in Mind*, Wynn Thomas writes that 'notional ekphrasis is being used as an attempt to fashion an icon for the soul, as if Brock-Broido were refashioning the Victorian practice of producing a miniature to commemorate the departed';[58] and the Victorian fashion for 'hair memento' jewellery, described by Deborah Lutz as 'a kind of metonymic tool of imagination' seems, too, not far off.[59] Wrapped in bandages and captured in a photograph frame, the real Baby Jessica won photojournalist Scott Shaw the 1988 Pulitzer Prize. In the two-dimensional 'oval / of the well', her tiny body viewed from above is already fixed in a circular frame, precisely a warped portrait miniature.[60]

'We need and desire souvenirs of events that are reportable, events whose materiality has escaped us', Stewart writes.[61] The souvenir

> represents not the lived experience of its maker but the 'secondhand' experience of its possessor/owner. Like the collection, it always displays the romance of contraband, for its scandal is its removal from its 'natural' location. Yet it is only by means of its material relation to that location that it acquires its value.[62]

In the Baby Jessica story, it is the reportability of the story, rather than its narrative, which evades us; with the chief witness nullified by a narrative which insists on her oblivion, there is no legible account of the 58 hours down the well except the one etched into, by, her bruised and broken body. Denied the agency and self-awareness of

---

[57]   Love and Kohn, 'This, That, and the Other', p. 48.

[58]   Thomas, 'The Grammar of the Night', pp. 256–57.

[59]   Deborah Lutz, *Relics of Death in Victorian Literature and Culture* (Cambridge: Cambridge University Press, 2015), esp. pp. 128–54 (p. 130).

[60]   Brock-Broido, *A Hunger*, p. 25.

[61]   Stewart, *On Longing*, p. 130.

[62]   Ibid., p. 135.

the reflexive 'se souvient', it is other people who read, onto her, the story out – 'secondhand'; 'vicarious'. If souvenirs generally 'function' – voicelessly – 'to generate narratives' of others, though, lyric souvenirs might be able sometimes to voice not just their own stories, but their own poetics. Thus Jessica's infantile eyes let us look as well as listen differently – unreasonably – at arrangements of alphabets and punctuation marks on the page. Brock-Broido is a virtuosic and inveterate devotee of the ampersand (on the rare occasions when she doesn't use them, all the Ands often come along at anaphoric once, at the start of successive lines, & are, I think, biblical). Gilbert suggests that this typographic tendency 'owes more to Blake than Berryman or the beats';[63] I think it does something, too, entirely Brock-Broido's own. In this early poem in particular, the ampersand – especially if we look with eyes for pictures, not words – becomes an icon for the twisted body, and hence a marker for the contorted child's transformation into art object, the words engraved on her forehead and the wall of the well making face indistinguishable from typeface, well from font:

> My forehead has opened now
> quite by happenstance, the etching on a wall
> of an undiscovered cave, unlucky hieroglyph.
> Take, for instance, my right leg
> which, by midnight, I have accidentally wedged
> in a notorious & irredeemable position.
> I hate to be unnatural, especially in personal geometry
> & by now, the leg has lodged irrevocably up
> against my face, unbound, unfortunate.[64]

The sculptor and typeface designer Eric Gill is credited with providing Britain – by way of the sans serif used on the covers of pre-war Penguins – with 'its first indigenous Modernist type design'.[65] 'Letters', Gill writes in his *Essay on Typography* (1931), 'are signs for sounds, not pictures of representations'.[66] But here, 'wedged / in a notorious & irredeemable position', Jessica's personal geometry is hard-pressed (and hard pressed) to become '& by now'. 'Notorious' not only apprehends – in an ironic kind of proleptic anteremembering – that 'Soon I will be

[63] Gilbert, 'About Poems About', n. pag.

[64] Brock-Broido, *A Hunger*, p. 24.

[65] *Modernism: Designing a New World, 1914–1939*, ed. Christopher Wilk (London: V&A, 2006), p. 398.

[66] Eric Gill, *Essay on Typography* (Boston: David R. Godine, 1988), p. 23.

famous' ('Someday, I will be buried above ground / like Monroe'), but also announces the appropriation of the wrought figure of the child into the poetic page's rubric of adult semiotic legibility: 'notory, *adj.* [..] after *notorious* [..] Dealing with or concerned with symbols or signs. Cf. notary'.[67] Also in *A Hunger*, the voice named 'Birdie Africa' (also based on a real child from a real news story) speaks of

> a new race springing
> from the dark continent of America.
> God keeps me pure & savage here
> before Moses
> before the gift
> before TV & toothbrushes
> before the alphabet.[68]

In the poem on the next page, 'extinct creatures', if they were still alive with us today,

> might have been confused,
> the cello playing solo,
> these brief black strokes –
> the Chinese character for rain.

while

> In the Vatican library, the letters
> to Anne Boleyn are pinned down to keep
> from coiling.[69]

'I want to know', says Brock-Broido in this poem, 'what the letters say & go on / saying, what her face looked like in sleep'. The brief black strokes of the alphabet, to those before TV & toothbrushes, have a capricious visual 'microrhetoric' (Blasing's term), which must be pinned to keep from coiling. Brock-Broido is the writer to harness this, partly, I think, because she finds visual decoration on the surfaces of things so hard to resist – and knows it. 'Sphinx, small print, you are inscrutable'.[70]

Gill argues of an ideal modernist architecture that, '[t]hose things are pleasing when seen which are as nearly perfect as may be in their

---

[67]   'notory, *adj.* 3', *OED*.
[68]   Brock-Broido, *A Hunger*, p. 6.
[69]   Ibid., p. 8.
[70]   Brock-Broido, *Stay, Illusion*, p. 3.

adaptation to function'. 'Such is the beauty', he says, 'of bones, beetles, of well-built railway arches'.[71] Souvenirs – 'not [...] arising out of need or use value' – are complicated objects with respect to function and utility.[72] It is worth noting too that Stewart remarks particularly that 'the original use value of kitsch objects is an elusive one'.[73] Although Stewart's souvenir 'still bears a trace of use value in its instrumentality', Jessica's tiny frame on Brock-Broido's pages misses the beauty of bones; her limbs, more like those objects belonging in Stewart's 'Collections', represent 'the total aestheticization of use value'.[74] After all, what is the body of a very small child good for?

> By dusk I am running out
> of ways to warm myself.[75]

The line break animates Jessica's capacity for escape, only to disappoint it: her legs are useless, they cannot run anywhere. Form fixes her jealously in place to keep a hold of her. 'Sometimes', she says, 'my imagination gets to running wild'. (And 'Running Wild' is also the title of a song sung by Marilyn Monroe in Billy Wilder's *Some Like It Hot*, several scenes after her first appearance in the film, from behind, swinging valise and ukulele in the smoke on the train platform out of Chicago. Jack Lemmon's Jerry, in leopard collar and cuffs: *Who are we kidding? Look at that – look how she moves – it's like jello on springs – they must have some sort of built-in motor.* Of legs with built-in motors, Baby Jessica – '*Move your foot for me, Juicy.* / And I wiggle it back for the man.' – can only dream.)[76]

Notwithstanding (or notwithrunning), Brock-Broido is also interested in forms which can't be fixed. Notional children are right for her thinking, as they are for Blasing's, because they are spongey and excitable learners and imitators, information-absorbent in a way that sometimes proves hazardous. They like liking and trying to be like; they are enthusiastic and passionate, evangelical, obsessive. But they also embody (indeed, inhabit) forms which – constantly, unstoppably changing shape – are fundamentally uncollectable. Children's bodies

---

[71] Gill, *Essay on Typography*, p. 25.
[72] Stewart, *On Longing*, p. 135.
[73] Ibid., p. 167.
[74] Ibid., p. 151.
[75] Brock-Broido, *A Hunger*, p. 24.
[76] *Some Like It Hot*, dir. Billy Wilder (MGM Home Entertainment, 1959) [DVD], 31:02–31:17.

make bad souvenirs. Lewis Carroll and John Tenniel's Alice, with long blonde hair and black velvet band, also fell down a rabbit hole and then grew, by turns, far too large and far too small to fit into the right spaces. 'On the descent', says Jessica, like Charles Kingsley's water baby Tom, 'I was magically compact / boneless, as agile as water'; but now, at the bottom, she lies listening in horror to

> The noise of my own form against the loosening
> walls as I am born into the dark
> rococo teratogenic rooms of the underground.

'Teratogenesis', even the rococo sort, is both mythical and biological: the formation of poisonous – marvellous – monsters and prodigies, and also processes of abnormal physiological development, causing birth defects or malformations in a developing embryo or foetus. In the penultimate section of the poem, Jessica's growing body is finally lifted from the well:

> Surrounded by jelly, an accoutrement of eros for ascent
> from the well I am born.
> Wide-eyed & swaddled in white linens, I emerge
> pristine and preserved, like some Egyptian form
> accompanied & gifted
> with all the Nilotic charms
> necessary for the long quicksilver moments
> of the Afterlife.[77]

The Nile winds through quite a lot of Brock-Broido's poetry. Often, it bears Cleopatra (and with her what is perhaps the ancestral paradigm of all high literary kitsch which ever tried to follow it):

> I will tell you.
> The barge she sat in, like a burnished throne
> Burned on the water. The poop was beaten gold;
> Purple the sails, and so perfumed that
> The winds were love-sick with them. The oars were silver,
> Which to the tune of flutes kept stroke, and made
> The water which they beat to follow faster,
> As amorous of their strokes. For her own person,
> It beggared all description. She did lie
> In her pavilion – cloth-of-gold tissue –

---

[77]   Brock-Broido, *A Hunger*, p. 26.

O'erpicturing that Venus where we see
The fancy outwork nature. On each side her
Stood pretty dimpled boys, like smiling Cupids,
With divers-coloured fans whose wind did seem
To glow the delicate cheeks which they did cool,
And what they undid did.[78]

Jessica has no mermaids or gentlewomen to tend her, but Brock-Broido certainly makes all her bends adornings and her fancy outwork nature. 'It is I', said the real Brock-Broido in an interview, in the half-attached third-first person which means she is always still partly in dramatic monologue, and that her dramatic monologues are always still partly herself, 'who fancied myself Cleopatra for a spell at the age of five, especially at Halloween. It was those gold sandals I longed for, the one-shouldered white drape of a sheet'.[79] Here's that '[e]arly childhood', in *Stay, Illusion*'s 'Extreme Wisteria':

Cleopatra for most masquerades, gold sandals, broken home;
Convinced Gould's last late recording of the Goldberg Variations
was for her.[80]

Gold, Gould, Goldberg. Jessica's 'long quicksilver moments', too, speak back to *Antony and Cleopatra*'s elemental state changes, and its flashing mercurial queen. In *The Master Letters*, the Cleopatra whom age cannot wither nor stale seems poised wonderfully to overpicture 'In the Attitude Desired for Exhibition', a poem 'about the art of taxidermy':

See – how she is
Poised – the right

Front paw aloft, it
Hovers in mid-air,

No gravity
Will interrupt her stance.

Age will
Not treat her kindly.[81]

---

[78] William Shakespeare, *Antony and Cleopatra*, II.ii.190–204.
[79] Brock-Broido, 'Extreme Wisteria', *The Q&A Issue*, p. 318.
[80] Brock-Broido, *Stay, Illusion*, pp. 29–30.
[81] Brock-Broido, *The Master Letters*, p. 51.

Many of the souvenirs Brock-Broido wants to keep which aren't children are flowers: like 'the red she / Fox in habitat', sooner rather than later, they will wither.

As the subject of the very first epic simile in Edmund Spenser's *The Faerie Queene*, the sixteenth-century poetic Nile was also thought to breed strange monsters:

> As when old father *Nilus* gins to swell
> With timely pride aboue the *Aegyptian* vale,
> His fattie waues doe fertile slime outwell,
> And ouerflow each plaine and lowly dale:
> But when his later spring gins to auale,
> Huge heapes of mudd he leaues, wherin there breed
> Ten thousand kindes of creatures partly male
> And partly femall of his fruitful seed;
> Such vgly monstrous shapes elswher may no man reed.[82]

Jessica, monstrous shape dredged from the riverbed, preferred it when she could fold herself up. Once 'small & aboriginal', as time passes in the well she notices, like Alice, that –

> Even without food, I am growing
> & I find this frightful that my body
> will become too large to live here comfortably.[83]

If changes in form frighten her, though, efforts to hold onto aboriginal smallness also risk making even that dimension grotesque. 'Like Oskar', she says, 'I can make a world / change with my voice, can shatter the diamond / tipped bits of drill can make the wells' walls glitter / back at me' – and 'Oskar', here, is Oskar Matzerath of Günter Grass's 1959 novel *The Tin Drum*, the terrible drummer boy who stops growing (though he keeps growing up) aged three, remaining child-sized by force of sheer hideous determination. Though 'many souvenirs', as Gordon writes, 'are childish or child-like', real children will not, should not, keep.[84]

But size and scale are the ways that Brock-Broido's poetry (like Stewart's criticism) thinks most deeply about form, and in her worlds, the fear of changing shape might sometimes be made safe by curling

---

[82]   Edmund Spenser, *The Faerie Queene*, I.i.21, ed. A. C. Hamilton in *Spenser: The Faerie Queene* (Harlow: Longman, 2001), p. 36.

[83]   Brock-Broido, *A Hunger*, p. 23.

[84]   Gordon, 'The Souvenir', p. 138.

back to fairy tales. 'Then shut these big ole eyes', croons Jessica to the weepy gamey men who pull her out of the ground: 'Ole Shut-Eye' is a Hans Christian Andersen figure, a dream god who sends the sleeping child, Hjalmar, on new adventures every night of the week. On the story's fourth night, in an episode which meddles Grass's Oskar with Carroll's Alice with Brock-Broido's Jessica, Hjalmar is invited to a mouse wedding:

> 'But how can I get through the little mouse-hole in the floor?' asked Hjalmar.
> 'Let me manage that,' said Ole Shut-Eye. 'I will make you small.'
> And he touched Hjalmar with his magic syringe, and the boy began to shrink and shrink, until he was not so long as a finger.
> 'Now you may borrow the uniform of a tin-soldier: I think it would fit you, and it looks well to wear a uniform when one is in society.'[85]

The tiny boy travels magnificently to the wedding in a thimble carriage drawn by mice. Oskar also 'borrows the uniform of a tin-soldier', and Jessica, too, is inside a thimble: 'My own voice travels sideways', she says, '& curls back up to me / like a seamstress' needle against her thimble', just as the & does, too. Having largely lost their use value and become estranged from their function, commemorative thimbles have become paradigmatic objects of the modern kitsch collection. Alice awards herself one as a Caucus-race prize. They are also packed dense with fairy-tale matter; much the smallest household vessel, and a scale marker explicitly standardised in relation to human dimensions, they are rendered extraordinary by processions of miniature characters – Tom Thumb, the Valiant Little Tailor, Thumbelina – whose littleness, as Stewart observes, 'has the capacity to make [their] context remarkable'.[86] A woman's pitiful fragment of armour to match her darning-needle sword, this mending-box weaponry makes a domestic slave of its female knight even while it vows to defend her from the tiny pricks of her own inadvertent self-wounding.

---

[85] 'Ole Shut-Eye', *Wonder Stories Told for Children*, at *The Baldwin Online Children's Literature Project*: http://www.gatewaytotheclassics.com/browse/display.php?author=andersen&book=wonder&story=shut [accessed 3 October 2019].

[86] Stewart, *On Longing*, p. 46.

And yet, such warlike armaments are right for Brock-Broido's textile dreaming. Whether divined by the rich damask of October sunlight (October is Brock-Broido's favourite month) or fixing on 'the hemp clothesline' or 'last week's laundered sheets, triangled / like sails', swaddled in white linens, the thread of Jessica's song is twined through the eye of a needle, silked from 'corn yellow husks', and wound round 'a spool of me'. 'Jessica, from the Well' is not Brock-Broido at her most 'poet laureate of *People* magazine', her most passionate for the beautiful, or most mastered by her preoccupations. It is just Brock-Broido, writing. Her strange remembering souvenirs – hard to grasp, with withering, dying, transmogrification built into the way they keep – formed fast and set hard.

Stay, Allusion: Lyric Kitsch, Beauty Is Truth

'Brock-Broido has a penchant for taking over carapaces left behind by other poets', picking up hard shells and trying living and listening from inside them.[87] She has, she says, 'been in *Widerruf* with Dickinson for decades'. 'Widerruf', she explains, is the refutation of one poem by another: 'we're all in conversation on the page with that which came before us, or even during us. We inherit whatever canon we're in the midst of, a great collective influenza'.[88] Emily Dickinson's poems in our imagining are little, written things – folded in drawers, onto the backs of envelopes, held together fragilely by dashes, often dashing off, hard to hold or capture. Captivated by the three 'Master Letters' found in a locked box among Dickinson's papers after her death, Brock-Broido went on in her second book to write 'fifty-two poems, a series of latter-day Master Letters, echo[ing] formal & rhetorical devices from Dickinson's work'.[89] The ninth poem in the series, 'And Wylde for to Hold', is also in *Widerruf* with Thomas Wyatt's 'Whoso list to hunt', a sonnet – many sonnets are – about following after something beautiful and failing to catch it up. Here's Wyatt's closing sestet:

> Who list her hunt, I put him out of doubt,
> As well as I may spend his time in vain.
> And graven with diamonds in letters plain

---

[87]   Gilbert, 'About Poems About', n. pag.
[88]   Brock-Broido, 'Extreme Wisteria', *The Q&A Issue*, p. 313.
[89]   Brock-Broido, *The Master Letters*, p. vii.

There is written, her fair neck round about:
'*Noli me tangere*, for Caesar's I am,
And wild for to hold, though I seem tame.'[90]

In an essay on reading Wyatt's poetry 'for the style', Jeff Dolven begins by quoting from a nineteenth-century reviewer: '[t]he mystery of Wyatt is simply whether he knew what he was doing or whether he did not'.[91] Brock-Broido, said Logan in that first review, 'seems to know what she is doing even when it's not worth doing well'. Well might a girl want something graven with diamonds for her best friend, but – *hélas* – if we can't touch it, we can't hold it: 'I leave off, therefore', says Wyatt's speaker, 'Sithens in a net I seek to hold the wind'. Can letters and warnings graven with diamonds still speak plain? Brock-Broido, writer of poems about death and execution entitled 'Extreme Wisteria' and 'A Cage Goes in Search of a Bird', knows well that things seeming tame are sometimes wild.

Brock-Broido has described the work of *The Master Letters* as a gradual process of channelling the 'blathering, indulgent, bubbling, frothing, mess of a prose poem' into tight couplets and sonnet 'cages'.[92] Wyatt is also a famous plunderer of Italianate forms, training his voice by 'translating' Petrarch. Wyatt, too, is a poet famously preoccupied by truthfulness. The word 'truth' appears in more than half his poems, and his first letter out of Spain to his young son, 'then xv yeres old' (letters and postcards, says Gordon, are 'artifacts saved as reminders of a particular heightened reality', which 'come[...] back to the ordinary realm almost as a living messenger of the extraordinary'), is often quoted on the matter of Tudor poetic honesty:

> In as mitch as now ye ar come to sume yeres of vnderstanding, and that you should gather within your self sume frame of honestye, I thought that I should not lese my labour holy if now I did something advertise you to take the suer fondations and stablisht opinions that leadith to honestye. And here I call not honestye that men comenly cal honestye, as reputatid for

---

[90]   Thomas Wyatt, 'XI' ('Whoso list to hunt'), in *Sir Thomas Wyatt: The Complete Poems*, ed. R. A. Rebholz (London: Yale University Press, 1981), p. 77.
[91]   Jeff Dolven, 'Reading Wyatt for the Style', *Modern Philology*, 105.1 (2007), 65–86 (p. 65).
[92]   Brock-Broido, 'Lucie Brock-Broido by Carole Maso', *Bomb*, 53 (1995): https:// bombmagazine.org/articles/lucie-brock-broido/ [accessed 3 October 2019].

riches, for authorite, or some like thing, but that honestye that I dare well say your grandfather (whos soule God pardon) had rather left to me then all the land he did leaue me, that was wisdome, gentlenes, sobrenes, desier to do good, frendlines to get the love of manye, and trovgth aboue all the rest.[93]

'In the art of words, in the domain of poetry', wrote Wyatt's editor A. K. Foxwell in 1913, 'Wiat is by no means the least among those who, in the sixteenth century, sought to express the Beauty of life through Truth. The upholding of Truth in life, and the continual war waged against falseness, are the two dominant notes in Wiat's poetry'.[94] 'When one wants to disparage the souvenir', says Stewart, 'one says that it is not authentic' – and, what is more, 'in all their uses, both *kitsch* and *camp* imply the imitation, the inauthentic, the impersonation'.[95]

And yet, Wyatt, upholder of Truth, speaks, still, of and into a court where most 'Use wiles for wit, and make deceit a pleasure / And call craft counsel, for profit still to paint',[96] his poetry of the very kind to necessitate and problematise Sir Philip Sidney's 1580 gift of provocation to generations of theorists: '[n]ow, for the poet, he nothing affirms, and therefore he never lieth'.[97] If it is true, as Irving Howe posits in *Salmagundi*, that sometimes '[h]ibernation may lead to de-kitschifying', 'Whoso list' is among the least prudently hibernated poems in the sonnet canon, its pivoting final transformation of object into subject almost (right with a click like a closing box) a cliché – almost a kitsch – of modern lyric theory.[98] Brock-Broido's 'And Wylde' is not a sonnet but ('[d]on't', says one of the little wounded speakers of *Stay, Illusion*, 'be coy with me') it seems no coincidence that it is on

---

[93]   Thomas Wyatt, 'Letter 1: Wyatt's First Letter to His Son Thomas', in *The Complete Works of Sir Thomas Wyatt the Elder: Volume 1: Prose*, ed. Jason Powell (Oxford: Oxford University Press, 2016), pp. 61–65 (pp. 61–62).

[94]   Agnes Kate Foxwell, 'Introduction', in *The Poems of Sir Thomas Wiat*, ed. A. K. Foxwell (London: University of London Press, 1913), II, xii–xxii, quoted in *Thomas Wyatt: The Critical Heritage*, ed. Patricia Thomson (London: Routledge, 1995), p. 111.

[95]   Stewart, *On Longing*, pp. 159, 168.

[96]   Wyatt, 'CXLIX' ('Mine own John Poyntz'), in *The Complete Poems*, p. 187.

[97]   Philip Sidney, 'The Defence of Poesy', in *Sidney's 'The Defence of Poesy' and Selected Renaissance Literary Criticism*, ed. Gavin Alexander (London: Penguin, 2004), pp. 1–55 (p. 34).

[98]   Howe, '[Discussion in Four Parts]', p. 211.

page 14.[99] The *Master Letters* project was originally intended to be 56 poems: four sets of 14, including 14 prose poems and 14 sonnets. Just as Gilbert wants to mention her hair, and Vendler and Thomas – '[j]acket illustration is not usually integral to the meaning of a volume, but it may be so in this case' – want to talk about the pictures, it's hard not to start counting the fonts and the page numbers into the confection of her mythomania too.[100] All the paraphernalia of Brock-Broido's pages – the front covers, the author photos, the endnotes, the carefully curated typefaces – seem as speaking paratexts for gathering together the kleptomaniac scrapbook life of her poetry, as formally expressive, and equally as never above a joke, as her stanza shapes, or her answers in interviews.

Burt thinks that Anne Boleyn, in this poem, may be 'the best of Brock-Broido's many personae'.[101] Certainly, Hampton Court Palace and its lavish memories are home ground for Brock-Broido – and the clothes fit. 'Form is mortal & habitual', she writes of the Tower of London ravens in 'And Wylde', proposing a shape of selfhood not only earthly, temporal, grounded in customs and behaviour, but also woven into 'habits' ('*n*. Bodily apparel or attire; clothing, raiment, dress'). 'I will listen for its habit', says this speaker, 'Especially about the throat like an Elizabethan cuff'. As an emblem of the unknowable and generally hostile female world, sewing kits in Wyatt's poetry are usually disobliging. The intractable seamstress-heroine in 'She sat and sewed' threatens to make her lover's 'heart the sampler', and is punished (for lack of a thimble) with a bleeding finger.[102]

But the characters in 'And Wylde' – clipping, scissoring, lining the nests of their mouths with hair, and shredded sycamore – are Brock-Broidan découpage master tailors. The Ravenmaster, lord of the fabric landscape Wyatt couldn't hold in a net, 'wraps his limbs in combs of wind': as Dan Chiasson has noted, breezes and squalls through Brock-Broido's writing often whistle and whisper memories of other poets;[103] and 'limbs in combs of wind' here murmurs distinctly of Gerard Manley Hopkins, whose letters Brock-Broido quotes in the

[99] Brock-Broido, 'Dove, Abiding', in *Stay, Illusion*, p. 69.
[100] Thomas, 'The Grammar of the Night', p. 257.
[101] Burt, *Close Calls with Nonsense*, p. 348.
[102] Wyatt, 'XLI', in *The Complete Poems*, p. 92.
[103] Dan Chiasson, 'The Ghost Writer: Lucie Brock-Broido's "Stay, Illusion"', *The New Yorker* (28 October 2013): https://www.newyorker.com/magazine/2013/10/28/the-ghost-writer-3 [accessed 3 October 2019].

Master Letters' 'To A Strange Fashion of Forsaking' (this title taken
from Wyatt's 'They flee from me') and 'Work', and whose 'Carrion
Comfort', she says, is in 'In the Attitude Desired for Exhibition', by
way of 'homage & refract'.[104] As Gilbert has noted, if Hopkins is
Brock-Broido's 'most audible influence', he is a late Victorian master
well-aligned with Swinburnes and Rossettis.[105] And, in fact, it is
writing the wind which seems most often apt to half-hurl her into
Hopkins hurricanes. In the opening poem from *Trouble in Mind*, 'The
Halo That Would Not Light', 'the wind is hover- / Hunting'; where
Hopkins's words 'Fall, gall themselves, and gash gold-vermilion',
Brock-Broido's poem has a raptor who has 'dropped your tiny body',
with corresponding iridescent colour compounds, 'in the scarab-
colored hollow':[106]

> As certain and invisible as
> red scarves silking endlessly
> From a magician's hollow hat
> And the spectacular catastrophe
> Of your endless childhood
> Is done.[107]

As if Brock-Broido, who can never resist winding and wounding,
winds and wounds, could resist gold-vermillion gashes. 'The rims of
wounds have wounds as well'.[108]

'*Ruin is formal*' in 'And Wylde' is Dickinson's take on the ageing
stories which kept souvenirs – markers of 'intimate distance' – cannot
help show and tell over time:[109]

> Crumbling is not an instant's Act
> A fundamental pause
> Dilapidation's processes
> Are organized Decays.
> 'Tis first a Cobweb on the Soul
> A Cuticle of Dust

---

[104] Brock-Broido, *The Master Letters*, p. 81.
[105] Gilbert, 'About Poems About', n. pag.
[106] Gerard Manley Hopkins, 'The Windhover', in *The Major Works*, ed. Catherine
Phillips (Oxford: Oxford University Press, 2002), p. 132; Brock-Broido, *Trouble in
Mind*, p. 3.
[107] Brock-Broido, *Trouble in Mind*, p. 3.
[108] Brock-Broido, *Stay, Illusion*, p. 3.
[109] Stewart, *On Longing*, p. 147.

> A Borer in the Axis
> An Elemental Rust –
> Ruin is formal – Devil's work
> Consecutive and slow –
> Fail in an instant, no man did
> Slipping – is Crash's law.[110]

Dickinson's fragments of slow, fearful decay, and her occasion, her locked box of letters, Wyatt's title and his deer and diamonds, Hopkins's soundscapes, his hybrid colourways, his birds of prey: these are Brock-Broido's souvenirs from reading, the ways she does active poetic remembering by different kinds of surfaces. 'The Halo That Would Not Light' is one of the orphan titles that Brock-Broido adopts in *Trouble in Mind* from Wallace Stevens:

> In a small notebook called 'Pieces of Paper,' Wallace Stevens transcribed several hundred titles for poems which he never wrote. From this journal, I've adapted the following: 'The Halo That Would Not Light', 'still Life with Aspirin' [..] 'Morgue Near Heaven', 'Brochure on Eden' [..].[111]

If Wyatt, in all the finery of the Tudor court, is a wordsmith for whom all can 'cloak the truth for praise, without desert', then Stevens by contrast has been dubbed 'the poet of nakedness'.[112] Unable to relinquish faith in either truth or mantles, Brock-Broido's intertextual poiesis hovers, torn, between the two. Though her mania for textiles nothing abates, she is also increasingly beguiled by Stevensian simplicity, by 'The woman in the field dressed only in the sun'.[113] With the poised red she-fox in mind, it's striking that garments made from animals in this poetry do not always keep their wearers safe or warm. In 'And Wylde',

> Virgin wool still with the body's
> Oils keeps the cold, an augury.[114]

---

[110] Emily Dickinson, 997, in *The Complete Poems of Emily Dickinson*, ed. Thomas H. Johnson (London: Faber, 1970), p. 463.

[111] Brock-Broido, *Trouble in Mind*, p. 71.

[112] Wyatt, 'Mine own John Poyntz', p. 186; Michel Benamou, 'Wallace Stevens and the Symbolist Imagination', *English Literary History*, 31.1 (1964), 35–63 (p. 53).

[113] Brock-Broido, *Stay, Illusion*, p. 7.

[114] Brock-Broido, *The Master Letters*, p. 14.

where 'Lady with an Ermine' in *Trouble in Mind* describes,

> In the keep at Castlestrange, an ermine pelt in the shape
> Of an ermine animal, but empty, slung over the carved
> Oak chair, carelessly & keeping no
> One warm.[115]

Leonardo da Vinci's lady of *Lady with an Ermine*, from whom this poem takes its name, grips long-fingeredly a live, even wriggling one, with animated eyes and pricked-up ears, tensed leg, lifted paw – far from a slung pelt. Brock-Broido shows 'keeping' often going wrong, or going off: that which was once alive and is no longer cannot forever recall its warmth, and you can't force it to by wrapping a fur or a skin around yourself; such remembering becomes surreal, distorted. Good taxidermy, as Brock-Broido knows, is a precise art.

Hence, taking care of his charges at the top of the Tower, the 'man who lives in a circular / Stair' (towers are upside-down wells, as wells are upside-down towers) 'keeps watch', but not in touch. In the midst of a reality defined as '"that which you can put your hands on"' – where '[w]hen one puts his hands on a souvenir, he is not only remembering he was there but "proving" it' – speakers in this book, sometimes with 'prosthetic wrists',[116] often have trouble with their hands. His vantage point, from a height, of a topography, is not a holding or a feeling, and although this poem grasps over and over for ways to preserve and possess – ringing, tethering, salting, hewing – these actions of trying not to let go cannot help destroying in every instance the qualities of what they try to hold tame. The Ravenmaster 'breeds the bird to clip its wings'; behind the birds, the voice of Anne Boleyn with stabbing resignation grieves longed-for unborn children: 'Eggs, incubating, after being held Round / So long. None will fly'. 'I have this theory', Brock-Broido told the writer Carole Maso,

> that there are two kinds of poems: the first kind is the Seamus Heaney ilk – the inclusive, universal, political, religious poem full of humanity, where his finger is curled: come here, come hither: *this is what it was like* [And then] the other kind – a Frank Bidart poem, which is also a come hither: *listen, you have never felt like this*, as opposed to Heaney's: *you have felt this way*.[117]

---

[115]   Brock-Broido, *Trouble in Mind*, p. 37.
[116]   Brock-Broido, *The Master Letters*, p. 9.
[117]   Brock-Broido, 'Lucie Brock-Broido by Carole Maso', n. pag.

Distance and detachment are matters of poetic interest to Brock-Broido, but they aren't always the right platform for speaking, and it is partly her poems' particular overwhelming by being (or, solemnly, wanting to be) wrapped up in things they care about that can make a critic or a reader feel uncomfortable. Really, it seems, if there are two sorts of poems, Brock-Broido's enchantments are both the ilk and the other kind: *listen, you have never felt like this: come hither, feel it now.*

The opening of her *Widerruf,* in 'Brochure on Eden', with Stevens's one-line title, is torn between a blissful prelapsarian unity of words and things, and the tantalising touch and gorgeous decoration of the fabrics which mark humanity's expulsion from such a paradise:

> I want to call things as they are: *madness* –
> Callous, eventual mutants assuming our place in the sun,
> Shiny, longing, dying young.
> Here, waistcoat would stand for – *waistcoat,*
> Your hunter paisley one, your green adulterated sackcloth
> Of a once great-cloak.[118]

In Stevensian synaesthetics, 'green' stands for actuality and innocence (making *'green adulterated* sackcloth' a good oxymoron for poetic-colour-scheme initiates). The yearning to 'call things as they are' – although ': *madness*' complicates the problem – strongly echoes 'The Man with the Blue Guitar', and 'waistcoat would stand for – *waistcoat'* recalls the opening of the 'Study of Two Pears':

> Opusculum paedagogum.
> The pears are not viols,
> Nudes or bottles.
> They resemble nothing else.[119]

Stop thinking about viols, nudes, and bottles. Don't mention the pear. As in Stevens's writing, the separations of words and things from the words and the things they resemble is difficult: the semblances and connotations of lyric reading are too seductive, and too remarkable. Every figure and voice in Brock-Broido's poetry is, not callously, an eventual mutant of sound, or image, or gradual, organised decay, consecutive and slow – mutable and muteable still, like Baby Jessica;

[118]   Brock-Broido, *Trouble in Mind,* p. 30.
[119]   Wallace Stevens, *Collected Prose and Poetry* (New York: Library of America, 1997), p. 180.

showing up both the difficulties of holding and keeping, and the wonder of it. *Come here, come hither, rub this great-cloak between your fingers: you have never felt this.*

Mantle, Mantel, Altar: Lyric Cloak and Knick-Knack

Brock-Broido's favourite colour is yellow – into ochre, into gold. The white hart set marvellously on the golden jacket of her final book is borrowed or stolen out of a court before Wyatt, from the Wilton Diptych, painted for Richard II, 1394–96.[120] Like her page numbers, her author photos, and her interviews, Brock-Broido's covers are part of the illusion, and deer (or what look like them, and not only Wyatt's) flash fleetly through this book, as they do through her whole oeuvre. Whatever there is in Brock-Broido's poetry, there is a lot of; 'Pronouns are not to be trifled with, possessive ones or otherwise. // (Mine is a gazelle, of course.)'.[121]

Of all painted objects, the diptych is that which is most like a book. It can be closed to protect the inner panels, but the paintings on the outer wings must fend for themselves. Not only like a book, the diptych's physical nature is also 'essentially that of a portable altarpiece':[122] it might have been set up, on a chapel altar, the real king kneeling before the pictured one, to pray. You could put it on a mantelpiece. The white hart on the front of the Wilton Diptych is a densely symbolic microcosm writ, grown, large first: as Richard's emblem, it wears his crown about its neck, and its bed of rosemary (and that – *Stay, Illusion!* – is for remembrance) is the symbol of his wife, Anne of Bohemia. The gown of the kneeling Richard in the central picture is also decorated with white harts and rosemary – and he also wears a gold collar (ringed at neck, where the Ravenmaster's birds were ringed at ankle), the hart as a livery badge, with the same badge also pinned on all the angels on the right-hand side. This is a serious religious object which is also uncommonly gorgeous, in which the beautiful, intricate animal ornament miniature (trinket, jewel) is made the main event by becoming the front-page headline.

---

[120] For useful poetic context around the Wilton Diptych, see John M. Bowers, *The Politics of Pearl: Court Poetry in the Age of Richard II* (Cambridge: D. S. Brewer, 2001).

[121] Brock-Broido, *Stay, Illusion*, p. 15.

[122] Dillian Gordon, *The Wilton Diptych* (London: National Gallery, 2003), p. 21.

Figures 7.1 and 7.2.
Richard II presented to the Virgin and Child by his Patron Saint
John the Baptist and Saints Edward and Edmund ('The Wilton
Diptych', c. 1395–99), by permission of The National Gallery.

'Pax Arcana' in this book is the short poem-story of the Amish
housemaid who 'lived in one small room inside the lemon cookie jar',
whose 'only jewels were bobby pins', and who each night,

> folded her floury hands beneath her head
> And went to her knees by the doll-sized bed.[123]

Inside the diptych, it is the drapes and shadows of textiles that
mostly fill the painting's frames and command the viewer's eye,
and on which are lavished the most care and attention. If the silks
and velvets, satin shoes, pinkened laundry, linsey-woolsey pinafores,
seal and cashmere, chintz, chenille, flannel, Iron Curtains, coppery
leather limbs, Ten-thousand-count Egyptian cotton sheets, dirndl
skirts, poplin nightgowns, mallow-colour shoes of *Stay, Illusion*'s
poems ask just what manner of fabric it is a Rumpelstiltskin poet
spins from words, and what pleasure we ought to derive from reading
them, this is a question we might also put to the diptych, where the
angels' robes are stitched of lapis lazuli, Richard's of gold leaf and
red vermillion.

'Kitsch', Greenberg warned in 1939, 'is deceptive. It has many
different levels, and some of them are high enough to be dangerous
to the naïve seeker of true light'.[124] For Stewart, kitsch souvenirs
'destroy the last frontier of intrinsicality'.[125] Both speak a reflected
artistic effect without the capacity for self-reflection – a flat vapidity,
too-easy aesthetic pleasure with nothing beneath its surfaces. But
when, as Burt puts it right, Brock-Broido gambles embarrassment
on 'presenting her soul, by sharing her tastes', the risk is coura-
geous, and intensely deliberate. Without a stoic bone in her body and
different to everything, her undeceptive – and *undeceived* – lavish and
ostentatious high kitsch never functions as standing in for something
realer or truer; it is its own poetic. Her forms – long, thin, or little,
tight-curled fists – ring through shot silk and high-pile carpet
with her own voice and other poets', her lyric practice a meticulous
omnivorousness, collage as cabinet choreography, gorgeous clutter
in endless drawers.

This chapter began with an interview about 'Father, in Drawer',
an elegy which starts with,

[123]   Brock-Broido, *Stay, Illusion*, p. 21.
[124]   Greenberg, 'Avant-Garde and Kitsch', p. 11.
[125]   Stewart, *On Longing*, p. 167.

Mouthful of earth, hair half a century silvering, who buried him.
With what. Make a fist for heart. That is the size of it.
                                        Also directives from our DNA.
The nature of his wound was the clock-cicada winding down.
                                        He wound down.

and ends at,

Living may have been still at supper while he died.
That same July, his daughters' scales came off in every brittle
                                        Tinsel color, washing
To the next slow-yellowed river and the next, toward west,
                                        Ohio-bound.
                    This is the extent of that. I still have plenty heart.[126]

In between are angels 'stillbound in / The very drawer of salt and
ache and rendering', with wings bound up by shimmering pearl satin
slip. This poem speaks, Brock-Broido has said, to one of Dickinson's,
in whose second stanza,

The General Rose – decay –
But this – in Lady's Drawer
Make Summer – When the Lady lie
In Ceaseless Rosemary –.[127]

In the very drawer of salt and ache and rendering, we are spell- as
much as stillbound, and 'brittle / Tinsel color', in a poem threaded
through with Dickinson, calls out to Dickinson too –

Glass was the Street – in tinsel Peril
Tree and Traveller stood –
Filled was the Air with merry venture
Hearty with Boys the Road –

Shot the lithe Sleds like shod vibrations
Emphasized and gone
It is the Past's supreme italic
Makes this Present mean –.[128]

'To make glittering with gold or silver (or imitations thereof) inter-
woven, brocaded, or laid on', and also '[t]o subject to loss; to

---

[126] Brock-Broido, 'Father, in Drawer', *The Q&A Issue, Poetry*, 201.3 (2012), 311.
[127] Dickinson, 675, in *Complete Poems*, p. 335.
[128] Dickinson, 1498, ibid., p. 630.

impoverish, to endamage; to punish by a fine'. 'Tinsel', *v.*, *adj.*, passing
into *n.* − '[o]f satin, etc.: Made to sparkle [..] by the interweaving
of gold or silver thread, by brocading', and '[t]he condition of being
"lost" spiritually; perdition, damnation', '[t]he losing of something, or
the sustaining of harm, damage, or detriment; loss'.[129] 'Tinsel Peril'
might be Brock-Broido's calling card, with all the fear of loss and
distance, and the magpie and *People* magazine delight in the scandal
of contraband that shimmers.

'I wake with my own hair wound / Into my fist', said Brock-
Broido's Baby Jessica. Now read the opening of 'Father, in Drawer'
again. 'Will the child leave the rocking basket?' asked Vendler of her
protégée in 1995,

> Will she leave the restless, sheltering automobiles that are
> her grownup version of the basket? Will she loosen the tight
> stanzas that are the metrical equivalent of the basket? Will she
> become someone other than little-small child-girl?[130]

She didn't need to. Twenty-five years later, Brock-Broido was still
thinking about buried bodies, their reliquary hair, their strange
dimensions, about Cleopatra, pearl satin, rings, things wrapped and
wound uncomfortably. Like the objects they do their remembering
by, Brock-Broido's poems are rarely 'insignificant trinkets',[131] but
rather 'catalysts, facilitators, fetishes, things with minds of their own'.[132]
Stewart says that the kitsch souvenir

> Offers a saturation of materiality, a saturation that takes
> place to such a degree that materiality is ironic, split into
> contrasting voices: past and present, mass production and
> individual subject, oblivion and reification [..] The inside
> bursts its bounds and presents a pure surface of outside.[133]

The way Brock-Broido's materialities present pure irresistible surface
to speak past to present by the look and touch of things is − in the
many gathered voices always recognisable as her own − both sincere
and ironic, incontrovertibly kitschy and deeply, wantingly truthful.
The fine, spiny, leeway ley lines of this fastidiously conscious poetry

---

[129] 'tinsel', *OED*.
[130] Vendler, *Soul Says*, p. 175.
[131] Love and Kohn, 'This, That, and the Other', p. 51.
[132] Ibid., p. 48.
[133] Stewart, *On Longing*, pp. 167–68.

were not something she ought to have thought better or grown out of. Hers are songs and whispers sometimes in too close at ear, too rich and real and stifling, for comfort or critique. Her poetry clutches tight and thinks hard about what it means to try to and when and whether we can; it will hold.

CHAPTER EIGHT

Song

Denise Riley in Parts

Ruth Abbott

Denise Riley has been incorporating parts of songs into her poetry for as long as she has been publishing it. A poet, philosopher, and theorist who began her career with small press pamphlets in the 1970s, her recent work has won and been shortlisted for Forward Prizes. To read across all this verse is to be continually surprised by echoes of 1950s and '60s pop, old ballads, and the odd bit of Bowie – often in altered form, and always introducing counterpoint rhythms that make her description of composition as 'an inrush of others' voices' an apt account of what it feels like to read her too.[1] For just as long, however, she has also been writing poems that occasionally sound like songs in their own right, poems that shift into and out of the four- or three-beat lines by which song as a metrical form has generally been characterised, evoking choruses and hymns prosodically as well as through citation.

The fragments of popular songs that surface in Riley's poetry have been a frequent subject of recent criticism, particularly in relation to her philosophical work on the ways in which language destabilises any sense I might have that my identity is my own, formed from the inside out ('the "inner voice" is something largely fetched home from the outside', she has suggested).[2] Yet Riley's longest work on this subject, *The Words*

---

[1] Denise Riley, *The Words of Selves: Identification, Solidarity, Irony* (Stanford: Stanford University Press, 2000), p. 65.

[2] Denise Riley, *Impersonal Passion: Language as Affect* (Durham, NC: Duke University Press, 2005), p. 44. And see, for example, Susan M. Schultz, '"Unlock a Marvell Karaoke": Quotation as Adoption in the Work of Denise Riley', *How2*, 3.1 (2007): http://www.asu.edu/pipercwcenter/how2journal/vol_3_no_1/ cambridge/pdfs/schultz.pdf [accessed 3 October 2019]; Tom Jones, *Poetic Language: Theory and Practice from the Renaissance to the Present* (Edinburgh:

of Selves, is as preoccupied by rhyme as it is by personhood – so preoccupied, in fact, that it includes a whole chapter that not only reflects
on rhyme but is also often written in it.[3] Earlier in the book, Riley
laments the fact that reviewers of contemporary poetry rarely 'attempt
technical commentaries', preferring to 'imagine character profiles' or
to offer 'textual interpretations' by tracing sources.[4] In this chapter, I
would like to try to do what she feels is missing, tracing echoes, not
of particular songs, but of the form – *song* – through her oeuvre, with
a view to reflecting on the changing part that it plays in her practice.

'Denise has your sense of what constitutes song changed over time,
from the earlier poems to the more recent', asked Kelvin Corcoran in
an interview in 2014; 'The only constant is a commitment to the thing
that is song', Riley replied, which has 'always been there, altering
only in shape as it goes along'.[5] Yet her first few collections can
seem more preoccupied by language than music. Linda A. Kinnahan
has outlined how significantly Riley's early work reflected on what
expression means for women, and women poets in particular.[6] Such
questions surface throughout her first collection, *Marxism for Infants*
(1977), which contemplates the kinds of social and political relations
that '"articulacy" articulates'.[7] But there are also moments when the
collection seems to lift beyond speech into something different.

Edinburgh University Press, 2012), pp. 148–60; Zoë Skoulding, 'Misremembered
Lyric and Orphaned Music', in *The Oxford Handbook of Contemporary British
and Irish Poetry*, ed. Peter Robinson (Oxford: Oxford University Press, 2013),
pp. 266–85.

[3]   Riley, *Words of Selves*, pp. 93–112.

[4]   Ibid., p. 74. Lacy Rumsey provides a counterexample in 'Formal Innovation
in Non-Mainstream British Poetry Since 1985: Notes Towards Analysis', *Études
Anglaises*, 60.3 (2007), 330–45.

[5]   Kelvin Corcoran and Denise Riley, 'Interview with Denise Riley', 15 March
2014: http://www.shearsman.com/ws-blog/post/365-an-interview-with-denise-
riley [accessed 3 October 2019].

[6]   Linda A. Kinnahan, 'Experimental Poetics and the Lyric in British Women's
Poetry: Geraldine Monk, Wendy Mulford, and Denise Riley', *Contemporary
Literature*, 37.4 (Winter 1996), 620–70; Linda A. Kinnahan, *Lyric Interventions:
Feminism, Experimental Poetry, and Contemporary Discourse* (Iowa City: University
of Iowa Press, 2004), pp. 180–221.

[7]   Denise Riley, *Marxism for Infants* (Cambridge: Street Editions, 1977), f.7 (n.
pag.). This poem, beginning 'the speaking,   the desire to be heard', was not
reprinted when Riley and Wendy Mulford collected work of the 1970s in *Some
Poems, 1968–1978* (Cambridge: C. M. R. Press, 1982), or when Riley reprinted
work from *Marxism for Infants* in *Dry Air* (London: Virago, 1985).

'[W]hile I am overcome by some grief and wholly / given over to my distress', begins one poem, only to jump abruptly from these variable, longer lines onto the following closing couplet, separated by blank space:[8]

> the clearness that it must be you.
> who cannot ever be arrived at

Not even the apparent finality of the full stop after 'you' can prevent this from sounding like an iambic tetrameter couplet, softened only by the lack of rhyme and the hypercatalectic 'at' that spills over the end of what I want to call the last foot of the poem. The lines seem suddenly to have pitched up in *Hymns, Ancient and Modern*, that eclectic Anglican hymnal that Riley invoked in her most recent collection, *Say Something Back* (2016). 'Hymns ancient / & modern, buoy us up', she pleads, in a poem whose title, '"When we cry to Thee"', summons the similarly stark tetrameter of 'Eternal Father, strong to save': 'O hear us when we cry to Thee / For those in peril on the sea'.[9]

Something even stronger emerges later in *Marxism for Infants*, in a poem beginning 'such face bones honeycombed sockets', which ends:[10]

> it is the "spirit" burns in & far
> through   "sex"   which we know about
>
> saying It's true, I won't place or
> describe it   It <u>is</u> & refuses the law

The first two lines here resemble those that precede them: short, variable, typographically playful. The concluding two lines could be described the same way, were it not for the fact that another, older form seems to cut across them, its alternative shape reinforced by capital letters, blank space, and underlining. Its three-beat, triple metre cadence could hardly have been more prominent had Riley lineated like this:

[8]   Ibid., f.13. This poem was not reprinted in *Some Poems* or *Dry Air* either.
[9]   Denise Riley, *Say Something Back* (London: Picador, 2016), p. 26; *Hymns, Ancient and Modern*, ed. William Henry Monk (London: J. Alfred Novello, 1861), Hymn 222 (n. pag.).
[10]   Riley, *Marxism for Infants*, f.20. This poem was not included in *Some Poems*, but was reprinted in *Dry Air* (p. 19), with speech marks replaced by quotation marks, and underlining by italicisation.

⌐It's true, I won't place or describe it
It is & refuses the law⌐

It is as if, just as it is ending, the poem and Riley's choices about
lineation have been overcome by the sweeping cadences of a folk song
(compare *My bonnie lies over the ocean* / *My bonnie lies over the sea*).
   'I hear all sounds within my ear', Riley wrote in *No Fee* (1979),
her next collection; 'all words return to bright / heavy echoes run
in me'.[11] In *No Fee*, it is Riley's collaborator Wendy Mulford who
seems most attracted to song forms, in poems such as 'back-street
rhymes' ('dont rule dont guess dont buy dont lay / anything on
my voice', Mulford chants).[12] But song was evidently never far from
Riley's mind in this period, even in theoretical work such as *War in
the Nursery: Theories of the Child and Mother* (1983), which investigates
the relationship between child psychology, childcare policy, and the
ways in which women were understood and understood themselves
in the aftermath of the Second World War. Two of its six chapters
open with epigraphs that evoke song forms, taken from William
Butler Yeats's 'Those Images' and William Blake's 'Infant Sorrow';
the book's publisher, Virago, even used the Blake on the back cover.[13]
When Riley described her childhood in 1985, for another Virago
publication, it was through song forms that she recollected Francis
Turner Palgrave's verse anthology, in a flurry of misremembered,
barely distinguished fragments that swarm across her prose ('⌐t⌐he
long brilliant, shocking lines hidden under your mattress to read in
the endless summer nights: a copy of Palgrave's *Golden Treasury*. Poor
Ruth, thou hast been worse than dead. Or let my Lamp at midnight
hour Be seen in some high lonely Tower Where I may oft outwatch
the Bear', she wrote, following these unattributed snatches of William
Wordsworth's 'Ruth' and John Milton's 'Il Penseroso' with fragments
of 'Lycidas' and Andrew Marvell's 'Bermudas').[14]

[11] Denise Riley and Wendy Mulford, *No Fee: A Line or Two for Free*, second
edition (Cambridge: Street Editions, 1979), f.8, f.9 (n. pag.). Riley and Mulford
note on f.20 that the first edition was produced 'in more disposable form' for a
reading at the ICA in 1978.
[12] Ibid., f.16. None of the poems is attributed here, but details are given at the
back of *Some Poems*.
[13] Denise Riley, *War in the Nursery: Theories of the Child and Mother* (London:
Virago, 1983), pp. 1, 42, back cover.
[14] Denise Riley, 'Waiting', in *Truth, Dare or Promise: Girls Growing Up in the
Fifties*, ed. Liz Heron (London: Virago, 1985), pp. 237–48 (p. 243).

The new poems published in Riley's next collection evoke song forms more extensively. *Dry Air* (1985) reprints several poems from *Marxism for Infants* and *No Fee*, and its investigations of sexed expression extend the work of *War in the Nursery* (*Dry Air* was published by Virago too). But in the second half of the collection something new starts to echo, beginning with the sequence titled 'Versions of Six Poems by Friedrich Hölderlin (1770–1843)'. Riley gives details of the provenance of all six, and for the most part evokes their formal features, too, albeit imprecisely. In 'Each Day I Take …', however, Riley's version of 'Wohl geh' ich täglich', Hölderlin's Alcaic ode, is turned into what sound like 15 near-perfect iambic tetrameters.

The last two lines of each of Hölderlin's stanzas hint at tetrameter, too, and the words that he leaves hanging at line endings occasionally summon the ghosts of rhyming patterns, like flashes of *kunstballaden*. Consider his final stanza:

> Leb immer wohl! es scheidet und kehrt zu dir
> Die Seele jeden Tag, und es weint um dich
> Das Auge, daß es helle wieder
> Dort wo du säumest, hinüberblicke.[15]

In 'Each Day I Take …', Riley seems to allow the ballad cadences that fleetingly haunt such moments to get settled and strike up a chorus. Her condensed version of Hölderlin's last three stanzas is therefore not only an exquisite rendition of his lamentation for lost songs ('wo seid ihr / Zaubergesänge'), but also, paradoxically, the very sound of song's renovation:[16]

> Yes, you are far away; your face
> and clear sounds of your life are lost.
> Where are the songs that brought me peace?
> This man's grown old; the earth lacks grace.
>
> Go well. Each day my restless mind
> goes out to you, is turned away.

[15] Friedrich Hölderlin, 'Wohl geh' ich täglich', in *Poems and Fragments*, trans. Michael Hamburger, third edition (London: Anvil Press Poetry, 1994), pp. 98–99. Hamburger translates this stanza as follows: 'Farewell, then, always. Daily the soul takes leave / Of you, returns to you, and the eye will weep / For you each day, to look more keenly / Into the distance where you are staying'.
[16] Ibid., pp. 98–99 (Hamburger translates these words as 'where are you, / Magical songs'); Riley, *Dry Air*, p. 40.

> My eyes strain after you to see
> lightly straight through to where you stay.

Riley's lifelong commitment to song, she told Corcoran, 'is in some
way linked to the persistence of hope', and in her versions of Hölderlin,
song acts as both echo and beautiful bowdlerisation, a joyous, oxymo-
ronic renewal of what his poem laments.[17]

From here on, the sensation of iambic tetrameter starts to pervade
Dry Air. Take the following couplets from 'The Man of Grass' and
'History': 'it is not right when posing moons / elaborate the heart's
desire'; 'can we revolt to con the man / the idiot taurus won't let
be'.[18] In the fourth line of 'History', 'hermaphrodité's silvery ways',
the acute accent insists upon a rhythm as well as a pun: it is just
as important for maintaining a metrical pattern as for making you
think simultaneously of Aphrodite's passion and the androgyny of
her intersex son. 'No' shifts into the cadences of formal elegy in
its second stanza, as the variable lengths of its opening give way
to this:

> This one you lose you could not love.
> You were deceived, your flat blood knew
> to open its bright factual eye.
> This that you leak you never grew.[19]

Riley then lets the sensation of a four-beat pulse fade away briefly –
'The officer is at the scarlet door. / Here is his evidence. Some body
lied.' – only to snap shut upon it again, with repetitions that tighten
the ABCB rhyming pattern to identicality ('lied'/'lied'), and insist,
brutally, upon a beat:

> That body's mine but I am it.
> And I am it and I have lied.

A few pages later, the first poem that Riley titles 'Song' describes
'A pale strain / under the matted sounds'.[20] Something like this
strain rustles into and out of earshot throughout *Dry Air*, like the
phenomenon evoked as the collection closes, in the last line of 'In
Granada, 1936': 'A music, waiting'.[21]

---

[17] Corcoran and Riley, 'Interview'.
[18] Riley, *Dry Air*, p. 43.
[19] Ibid., p. 51.
[20] Ibid., p. 59.
[21] Ibid., p. 63.

To say this is to court confusion, however, for it suggests that song form is something determinate, when in fact it is barely understood. Like the category 'women', which Riley investigated during the same period, song form is not just historically constituted but also historically unstable; there are no agreed limits to the metrical patterns, rhyme schemes, or line lengths that might constitute it, as the range of forms in *Hymns, Ancient and Modern* itself attests.[22] In *'Am I That Name?' Feminism and the Category of 'Women' in History* (1988), Riley proposes that 'any attention to the life of a woman, if traced out carefully, must admit the degree to which the effects of lived gender are at least sometimes unpredictable, and fleeting', not just because '"women" is indeed an unstable category', but also because 'this instability has a historical foundation'.[23] There are comparably complex (different) histories behind the fact that it is difficult to be sure that any poem really *is* a song, or *is in* song form – let alone to say what song form is. Should its lines have four beats or three, or perhaps two, or a mix, and if the latter, does it matter how the mix is arranged? Should there be one relatively weaker syllable between each beat, or two, or is such counting unimportant? Should it sound like it starts with an upbeat, or come in strong and then fall away, or does it not matter, and can these arrangements properly be called iambic and trochaic or would other terms be more appropriate? And what about rhyme? Song form comes and goes in Riley's poetry of the 1970s and '80s: it is not what her poems unequivocally are or have, but something that they move into and out of, something that blossoms into prominence and then fades away or is roundly rejected. But that something is also unstable in its own right; indeed, it is categorically imprecise.

In this, it can be contrasted to the specific songs that break into Riley's next collection, *Stair Spirit* (1992): songs that are not just identifiable, but also identified with care in extensive endnotes. The notes detail, for example, the fact that 'A shortened set' 'repeats one

---

[22] For further discussion of the form's indeterminacy, see e.g. Mark W. Booth, *The Experience of Songs* (New Haven: Yale University Press, 1981); Steve Newman, *Ballad Collection, Lyric, and the Canon: The Call of the Popular from the Restoration to the New Criticism* (Philadelphia: University of Pennsylvania Press, 2007); Robert von Hallberg, *Lyric Powers* (Chicago: Chicago University Press, 2008).

[23] Denise Riley, *'Am I That Name?': Feminism and the Category of 'Women' in History* (Basingstoke: Macmillan, 1988), pp. 5–6. The final chapter was reprinted in *The Language, Discourse, Society Reader*, ed. Stephen Heath, Colin MacCabe, and Denise Riley (Basingstoke: Palgrave Macmillan, 2004), pp. 138–56.

Steve Winwood phrase and a Lesley Gore line from "It's my Party" written by W. Gold, J. Gluck Jnr. and H. Wiener', giving me everything that I need to work out what is being invoked in lines such as 'And I / can't find my way home' and 'It was my party and I wept not wanting to'.[24] There is no note to identify 'Let's Dance', mentioned in the previous line, but the Bowie track is probably famous enough to identify itself, and since Riley describes it as 'hammered out again on the radio', she makes it clear in any case what kind of thing is at stake: not song as a formal category, but this particular song.

The endnote for 'Lure, 1963' is comparably precise: it invokes 'a painting by Gillian Ayres', Riley indicates, and again 'quotes or rephrases song lyrics: "The Great Pretender" written by Buck Ram, recorded by The Platters; "The Wanderer" written by Ernest Maresca, sung by Dion; "It's In His Kiss" by Rudy Clark, sung by Betty Everett; and the title of "When Will I Be Loved" written by Phil Everly, recorded by The Everly Brothers'.[25] In the poem, the songs' strong rhythms swim into and out of prominence amidst swathes of colour, blurring into each other like the paints with which they are interspersed: 'Navy near-black cut in with lemon, fruity bright lime green. / I roam around around around around acidic yellows'; 'When / will I be loved? Flood, drag to papery long brushes / of deep violet, that's where it is, indigo, oh no, it's in / his kiss'; 'Oh yes I'm the great pretender. Red lays a stripe of darkest / green on dark. My need is such I pretend too much, I'm / wearing. And you're not listening to a word I say'.[26] But the songs themselves are both specific and carefully specified: I can look them up, listen to them, and work out where they end and Riley begins.

In conversation with Romana Huk in 1995, Riley insisted that song quotations of this kind did not stand in her poems 'as historical markers'; the endnotes recording their provenance, she explained, simply responded to 'a feeling that the original authors of those lyrics never get any public acknowledgement outside the specialist music press'.[27] But she also acknowledged that 'some of them might

---

[24] Denise Riley, *Stair Spirit* (Cambridge: Equipage, 1992), f.13r, f.3v, f.4v (n. pag.).

[25] Ibid., f.13r. Riley quotes the same song by The Platters in *Words of Selves*, p. 59.

[26] Ibid., f.6v.

[27] Romana Huk and Denise Riley, 'In Conversation with Denise Riley', *PN Review 103*, 21.5 (May–June 1995): http://www.pnreview.co.uk/cgi-bin/scribe?item_id=1912 [accessed 3 October 2019].

work better' when recognised, 'for example, where there are jokes that only come clear if you can complete a half-line of quotation for yourself'. This is surely the case with 'A misremembered lyric', which actually misremembers two or three. As its endnote details, it draws on '"Rhythm of the Rain" written by Gummoe, sung by The Cascades, and "Something's Gotta Hold of My Heart" by R. Cook and R. Greenway, recorded by Gene Pitney', and as the borrowed phrases surface, they joke with what they alter: '"Something's gotta hold of my heart / tearing my" soul and my conscience apart'; 'you get no consolation anyway until your memory's / dead: or something never had gotten hold of / your heart in the first place'; 'and once the falling rain starts on the upturned / leaves, and I listen to the rhythm of unhappy pleasure / what I hear is bossy death telling me which way / to go'.[28] To recognise the songs is to see where their edges are, and how Riley is playing with them, and her endnotes ensure that everyone can do just this. They openly advertise the fact that, as Andrea Brady points out, the phrases to which Riley alludes are 'commodity sentiments, drawn from popular discourse': however much they 'seem like personal confessions', the collection wears their separateness on its sleeve.[29]

Riley was equally overt when appealing to particular songs in her prose of this period; introducing her anthology, *Poets on Writing: Britain, 1970–1991* (1992), she cited Gerry and the Pacemakers to characterise the desire of a reader or writer to know how a poem has been achieved: 'as Gerry sang, "How do you do what you do to me? I wish I knew. If I knew how you did it to me, I'd do it to you"'.[30] But song quotations feel different when they emerge in her verse, for the verse thrums with other kinds of song, too, kinds that are harder to attribute and therefore harder to manage. *Stair Spirit* is often troubled by the question that Riley asks by quoting Gerry, but it also recognises that it is, as it were, actually doing it as well as asking how it gets done ('I'd thought to ask around, what's lyric poetry? / Its bee noise starts before I can', Riley acknowledges in 'A shortened set').[31] At times, this recognition intensifies into what sounds like panic at a felt loss

---

[28] Riley, *Stair Spirit*, f.13r, f.7r.

[29] Andrea Brady, 'Echo, Irony, and Repetition in the Writings of Denise Riley', *Contemporary Women's Writing*, 7.2 (July 2013), pp. 138–56 (p. 141).

[30] Denise Riley, 'Introduction', *Poets on Writing: Britain, 1970–1991*, ed. Denise Riley (Basingstoke: Macmillan, 1992), pp. 1–5 (p. 4).

[31] Riley, *Stair Spirit*, f.5r.

of control. 'Grabbed by remote music / I'm frightening myself', Riley admits in 'Poem beginning with a line from Proverbs': 'Stammering it fights to get / held and to never get held' is how she describes lyric in the poem of that title; 'I take on its rage at the cost / of sleep'.[32] Writing a song seems to feel nothing like citing one, at such moments; it sounds more like being spoken through than like quoting someone's speech.

There is a difference between allusion and composition, then, where song is concerned, for a quoted song has rhythms that are fixed and someone else's, but the origins and nature of song forms are indeterminate, and they therefore seem to come from inside as well as out. To Huk, Riley spoke of deliberation: '[i]f I entitle things "Lyric" it's because the main property that I've aimed at in those poems is some musical brightness', she explained; 'what I think in retrospect I've done is to put a shadowy or painful content into a short, musical form'.[33] But *Stair Spirit* evokes a more ambivalent, less clear-cut relationship with what Riley describes in 'When it's time to go' as the 'great classic cadences of English poetry'.[34] The poem witnesses those cadences infiltrating their own description with the help of another song from *Hymns, Ancient and Modern*, 'O Little Town of Bethlehem':[35]

> O great classic cadences of English poetry
> We blush to hear thee lie
> Above thy deep and dreamless.

This is not an allusion so much as an invasion, perpetrated not so much by the particular song as by the shapes of song more generally. Riley wriggles away from the words of her source text, presses a pun out of 'lie', and dodges internal rhyme by skipping the word 'sleep'. But in doing so, she falls into something older and less quotable, generating a new three-beat rhythm in her altered line, 'Above thy deep and dreamless', which she articulates distinctly in performance, and which echoes and reinforces that of the line before.[36] This at once

---

[32] Ibid., f.11r, f.11v.

[33] Huk and Riley, 'In Conversation'.

[34] Riley, *Stair Spirit*, f.9r.

[35] *Hymns, Ancient and Modern*, Hymn 642, added in 1916 (see the Oremus Hymnal Index to the Standard Edition): http://www.oremus.org/hymnal/amstd. html [accessed 3 October 2019]).

[36] Listen, for example, to the recording that Riley made for the Brown University Contemporary Writers Reading Series, 22 October 2009 ('When it's time to

turns the poem away from the specific song that it plays with, and turns it into a song in its own right, a song that really is deep and dreamless, because its history is not so easily delineated.

'I don't have the choice to "abandon" it', Riley told Huk, when asked why she has persisted with lyric: '[y]ou get formed in a certain way. You get formed with attachments to, for instance, Blake'.[37] As 'for instance' suggests, the earworm of a beat can be hard to locate. Is it Blake's iambic trimeter that takes over at the end of 'When it's time to go' ('I love the jocund dance'), or Emily Dickinson's ('The only news I know'), or perhaps A. E. Housman's ('When I was one-and-twenty'), or was Riley remembering all those three-beat hymns that are sung at evening ('The sun is sinking fast'; 'The day is past and over'; 'Our day of praise is done')?[38] The point is that it is not possible to say. 'Who sang / "you don't have to die before you live" – well who', Riley asks at the end of 'Well all right' – and there is an answer: 'Sylvester Stewart, recording as Sly Stone', as she notes at the back of the book.[39] The provenance of a song form is not so easily identified. What endnote could capture where the rhythm that rises up in the last stanza of 'Lyric' comes from, beyond another vague gesture at triple metre, trimeter, and 'My bonnie lies over the ocean'?

> It is my burden and subject
> to listen for sweetness in hope
> to hold it in weeping ears though
> each hurt each never so much.[40]

Authorless and unfixed as they are, song forms are at once every-one's, no one's, and uniquely mine ('Take up a pleat in this awful / process and then fold me flat / inside it so that I don't see / where I was already knotted in', Riley asks in 'Lyric'). In *Stair Spirit*, such forms therefore seem to generate a frightening intimacy, something

go' is found 19.20 minutes in): https://www.brown.edu/academics/literary-arts/writers-online/authors/riley-102209-full-reading [accessed 3 October 2019].

[37] Huk and Riley, 'In Conversation'.

[38] William Blake, *The Complete Poetry and Prose of William Blake*, ed. David V. Erdman, revised edition (Berkeley: University of California Press, 1982), p. 414; Emily Dickinson, 827, *The Complete Poems*, ed. Thomas H. Johnson (London: Faber, 1970), p. 401; A. E. Housman, *The Poems of A. E. Housman*, ed. Archie Burnett (Oxford: Oxford University Press, 1997), pp. 16–17; Hymns 17, 21, and 30 of *Hymns, Ancient and Modern* (see the Oremus Hymnal Index).

[39] Riley, *Stair Spirit*, f.8r, f.13r.

[40] Ibid., f.11v.

that sounds more like possession by an unknown force than like the appreciative, distinct relationships established between the collection and the specific singers and songwriters that it cites. As Riley puts it in her next pamphlet, *Four Falling* (1993), 'this hot scowl on songs marks rage for / closeness just not found in a true human love'.[41]

When Riley published *Mop Mop Georgette: New and Selected Poems, 1986–1993* (1993), she reprinted poems from *Stair Spirit* and *Four Falling* alongside newer work, much of which plays in similar ways with the differences between citing a song and finding oneself writing one. Her debts to particular songs are again dutifully noted: 'Marvin Gaye is quoted in "Shantung"', her endnotes record; '"Rayon" ends with a line sung by Neil Sedaka', '"Lucille's Tune" draws on the refrain in the Penniman/Collins song "Lucille", covered by The Everly Brothers', and 'Phrases from the American ballad "Frankie and Johnny" and from lyrics as sung by Jimi Hendrix and by Howlin' Wolf are in "Stair Spirit"'.[42] The notes do not detail everything: in 'Shantung', Riley's line 'Come on everybody. Especially you girls' echoes with Eddie Cochran's 'C'mon Everybody' as well as with Marvin Gaye's 'Can I Get a Witness' ('Listen everybody, especially you girls'), while Howlin' Wolf is quoted in 'Oleanna' too (Riley's phrase *'hurt me so bad to see my baby get / away'* invokes his song 'I've Got a Woman').[43] But they indicate her ongoing interest in detailing the provenance of the specific songs to which she alludes.

This interest is shared by the editor of one of the collection's most significant sources: the 1893 edition of Alexander Gardner's *Ballad Minstrelsy of Scotland*. Pressed by Huk on the question of lyric, Riley explained that she associated it, not with 'Swinburnian' or 'Tennysonian refrain-based lyrics', but with 'the intense and very harsh musicality of border ballads of the thirteenth to fifteenth centuries, transcribed in the seventeenth-century [*sic*]'.[44] Her phrasing is as attentive to the complex history of these songs' transmission and collection as the note at the back of *Mop Mop Georgette* in which she explains that 'Wherever you are, be somewhere else' draws among other sources upon 'the ballads "Fair Annie of Lochryan" and "Sweet

---

[41]   Denise Riley, 'Cruelty without beauty', *Four Falling: Poetical Histories No 26* (Cambridge: Peter Riley, 1993), f.2r (n. pag.).

[42]   Denise Riley, *Mop Mop Georgette: New and Selected Poems, 1986–1993* (Saxmundham: Reality Street Editions, 1993), p. 72.

[43]   Ibid., pp. 32, 58.

[44]   Huk and Riley, 'In Conversation'.

Willie and Fair Annie" in Alexander Gardner's *The Ballad Minstrelsy of Scotland*, 1893 – also a source of the lines italicised in "Knowing in the Real World" and "Spring, 1993".[45] Rather than claiming to quote the ballads themselves, Riley is precise here about her use of a particular edition. This is interesting, because that edition is preoccupied by provenance too. Gardner's introduction, which immediately precedes his text of 'Fair Annie of Lochryan', offers a thoroughly referenced history of ballads, their collection, and their editorial treatment, and his headnotes and footnotes detail the complex oral and textual histories of each that he includes, recording variants from other editions in manuscript and print.[46]

In some ways, Riley participates in these editorial practices – with her endnotes, for example, and by italicising what she lifts so that her own variants can be identified, as in 'Wherever you are, be somewhere else':

where did you get that rosewater to make your skin so white?

I did get that rosewater before I came to the light grass
shakes in a wind running wild over tassels of barley
the sails were of the light green silk sewn of both gold

*and white money take down take down the sails of silk set up
the sails of skin* and something dark and blurred upon the ground[47]

But where Gardner, citing William Motherwell, is bitter about those who 'under no authority of written or recited copy [...] recklessly and injudiciously cut and carve as they list', Riley participates in the acts of recomposition that he merely records, testing the difference between particular songs and anonymous, unstable song forms as she does so.[48]

Riley's phrase *'sewn of both gold / and white money'*, for example, which so elegantly chimes with the other quotations that precede it, is actually an interpolation, linking two widely spaced couplets in Gardner's reading text of 'Fair Annie of Lochryan' ('The sails were of the light green silk, / The tows of taffetie'; 'Take down, take down the

---

[45] Riley, *Mop Mop Georgette*, p. 72.

[46] See the 'General Introduction' and textual notes of *The Ballad Minstrelsy of Scotland. Romantic and Historical. Collated and Annotated. New and Revised Edition*, ed. Alexander Gardner (London: Paisley and Paternoster Square, 1893), pp. ix–xxxiv and passim.

[47] Riley, *Mop Mop Georgette*, p. 29.

[48] Gardner, *Ballad Minstrelsy*, p. iii.

sails of silk, / Set up the sails of skin').[49] Similarly, the tight call and response that characterises her couplet about the rosewater is stitched together from two different stanzas of 'Sweet Willie and Fair Annie', with word order altered to make a new rhyming pair. In Gardner's text, it is the nut-brown bride's 'spite' that rhymes with her pointed question, "'And where got ye that rose-water, / Makes ye sae fair and white?'", to which Annie replies:

> "Oh, I did get that rose-water
>   Where ye'll ne'er get the same;
> For I did get that rose-water
>   Ere to the light I came.⌜"⌟[50]

Riley therefore acts as both editor and poet at once: she simultaneously venerates textual history and cuts it to pieces, for even in recording her debts to Gardner she allows her readers to see that she has made new songs of her own.

As in *Stair Spirit*, this does not often sound like an easy process. Gardner's practice is confident and unifying: his reading texts are the result of collation according to aesthetic criteria, a practice that he likens to 'repairing gradually the weather-worn face of an ancient cathedral by the insertion here and there of a freshly-hewn stone, as need may require'.[51] Riley is at once more hands off and hands on. She certainly sounds less sure of herself, surrounding what she takes from Gardner with reflections on a sense of inadequacy: 'I've only earned a modern, what, a flatness', she suggests in 'Wherever you are, be somewhere else'; 'I can't talk like any of this'.[52] In 'Knowing in the real world', she does not identify her quotations from Gardner's edition – they are from 'Jellon Grame' ('The red sun's on the rain') and 'Cospatrick' ('And wash my son in the morning milk') – but she does distinguish them with italics, and wrap them in acknowledgements of their otherness:[53]

> Another kind of thought,
> liquid behind speech, bleeds away from it altogether.
> *I washed my son in the morning milk.*

> Sliced into the shine of now, a hand on a blade.

[49]   Ibid., pp. 3, 6.
[50]   Ibid., p. 266.
[51]   Ibid., p. iv.
[52]   Riley, *Mop Mop Georgette*, p. 29.
[53]   Gardner, *Ballad Minstrelsy*, pp. 336, 226; Riley, *Mop Mop Georgette*, pp. 33–34.

In 'Spring, 1993', Riley is self-deprecating about her capacity to sing what she quotes, which is similarly set apart, although again not identified in the endnotes (it draws on Gardner's text of 'The Twa Brothers'):

> don't you see that it's all that I *can* do
> don't you see that it's terribly ordinary
>
> if a full clean voice sings blankly
> *When will you come home again?*
> *When sun and moon leap on the hill.*[54]

But it is Riley's very capacity to sing, blankly or otherwise, which sets her apart from Gardner and his like, and takes her beyond quotation into the less traceable places from which all these songs come.

A glance at Gardner's text of 'The Twa Brothers' reveals how much Riley has altered; it also reveals her participation in a history of alteration that Gardner's footnote merely records:

> "Oh, when will ye come hame again?
>   Dear Willie, tell to me."
> "When sun and mune leap on yon hill;*
>   And that will never be."
>
>   * "When the sun and moon dance on the green." – Jamieson[55]

Most remarkable, I think, is the way in which Riley's excisions from this stanza when she incorporates it in 'Spring, 1993' generate a new rhythm distinct from that of her source. In 'Summer', she invokes the variable dactylic cadences of Robert Herrick's 'The Night-piece, to Julia': first implicitly, in the rhythm of her line 'but biscuit rock stare over water', and then explicitly, splicing a version of one of his lines over two of hers: 'What though / the dark thee cumber'.[56] A similar three-beat falling rhythm invades her quotation from 'The Twa Brothers' in 'Spring, 1993'. '[I]f a full clean voice sings blankly', she begins, and the sensation of trimeter spills on into what follows: *'When will you come home again? / When sun and moon leap on the hill'.* In Gardner's text, these last two lines sound like iambic tetrameter;

[54] Ibid., p. 11.
[55] Gardner, *Ballad Minstrelsy*, p. 293.
[56] Riley, *Mop Mop Georgette*, p. 25; Robert Herrick, *The Complete Poetry of Robert Herrick*, ed. Tom Cain and Ruth Connolly, 2 vols (Oxford: Oxford University Press, 2013), I, pp. 199–201.

Riley makes them feel dactylic. She is not just quoting, and not just editing, here; she is also making new songs herself. '*A greenish patina / may roughen these spent shells / for future curious songs*', she hopes in 'Laibach Lyrik: Slovenia, 1991', after three stanzas of what often sounds like iambic tetrameter, which she always performs with an intensely sing-song cadence and a long mid-line caesura ('*The settling scar agrees to voice / what seems to speak its earliest cut*', they begin).[57] 'You hear me not do it', is how Riley concludes 'Wherever you are, be somewhere else', but in all these poems, you hear her do it, too.[58]

'Now of course "you hear me not do it" is, in the cadence of that short line, almost self-negating', Riley admitted to Huk.[59] Self-negation is a preoccupation of her next theoretical work, *The Words of Selves: Identification, Solidarity, Irony* (2000), which extends the work on identity and language begun in '*Am I That Name?*' Here, too, Riley thinks as often about sound as about language, and much of the book proceeds through reflections on the experience of poetic composition, which she describes as being 'dethroned authorially by being spoken across by words' and their 'anarchic sound associations' ('[t]here seems to be little which *isn't* driven by sound-association, maybe in the form of puns, maybe in the form of cadence, maybe in the form of half-realised borrowings', she suggests).[60] This leads her to disclaim for herself her 'status as originator' in writing, for 'it wasn't my self at work. It was my ear that had a field day, and the accidents of rhyme in time raced through their pathways in my passive skull'.[61] Moreover, rhyme plays a particularly important part in such discussions, for although Riley acknowledges that 'the guise of form' creates a 'simulacrum of control', she is powerfully aware of the ways in which *it* controls *her* ('[t]he aural laws of rhyme both precede and dictate its incarnation', she notes).[62]

---

[57] Riley, *Mop Mop Georgette*, p. 9. Compare Riley's performances of this part of the poem at the Royal Albert Hall in 1993 and Brown University in 2009, starting 6:20 and 11:34 minutes in, respectively: https://www.youtube.com/watch?v=tlyyttEhQ08; https://www.brown.edu/academics/literary-arts/writers-online/authors/riley-102209-full-reading [both accessed 3 October 2019].

[58] Riley, *Mop Mop Georgette*, p. 29.

[59] Huk and Riley, 'In Conversation'.

[60] Riley, *Words of Selves*, pp. 2, 76.

[61] Ibid., p. 91.

[62] Ibid., p. 66.

Riley's explorations of the interplay between passivity and choice in identity and composition alike are at once performed and undermined in chapter 3, in which, she explains, '[s]ome speculations which run throughout these chapters are put directly as prosaic verse'.[63] Riley quotes her own poetry often in *The Words of Selves*, and as she pointed out to Corcoran, 'lurching between verse and prose' as she explores an idea is a common practice for her – so common, in fact, that she was able to show him a verse note on this very subject, thereby describing and exemplifying it at once.[64] But what happens in chapter 3 is more extraordinary. In volume 10 of the *Penguin Modern Poets* series (1996), among several poems from *Mop Mop Georgette*, Riley had published a poem titled 'The Castalian Spring'; here she reprinted it with a punning new subtitle ('a first draught'), inserting her own prose commentary after each stanza.[65] Much of this commentary extends the book's exploration of identity by elucidating the implicit argument of the poem's narrative. But that narrative is explicitly compositional – briefly, the speaker drinks from the Castalian spring, turns into a toad, tests various poetic modes in turn, then becomes human again – and its arguments are articulated compositionally, too.

In the tenth stanza, for example, the poet-toad wonders, 'Did I need to account for myself as noise-maker', then speculatively mocks up a 'conclusive autobiography' that slips, virtuosically, into that anapaestic jingle of self-description in four beats used with similar irony by Dr. Seuss, which Riley renders with music-hall lilt in performance:

> Should I wind up my own time,
> Chant, 'I was dropped on the Borders, a poor scraplet of
> Langholm, illegit. and state's burden, lone mother of three'?[66]

The abbreviation 'illegit.' embeds many forms of brutality, not least of which is the brutality of abbreviating a whole personal history just to maintain the self-assertive gallop more familiar from the Grinch

---

[63] Ibid., p. 93.

[64] Corcoran and Riley, 'Interview'.

[65] Douglas Oliver, Denise Riley, and Iain Sinclair, *Penguin Modern Poets 10* (Harmondsworth: Penguin, 1996), pp. 82–85.

[66] Riley, *Words of Selves*, pp. 101–02. The stanza can be heard 38:55 minutes into Riley's 2009 Brown University recording: https://www.brown.edu/academics/literary-arts/writers-online/authors/riley-102209-full-reading [accessed 3 October 2019].

or Yertle the Turtle (compare 'I'm Yertle the Turtle! Oh, marvelous me! / For I am the ruler of all that I see!').[67] Riley summarises the stanza as follows: '[t]he pretender to lyric worries with reason, then, about espousing self-presentation within the conventional categories'.[68] In the stanza itself, this is said metrically, too, and the conventional categories are evidently formal as well as sociological.

The effect is so self-conscious and so smart, however, that it speaks against as well as for the argument that it illustrates. Reflecting on an allusion in her third stanza to Shakespeare's *As You Like It*, Riley describes herself as uncomfortably aware of being 'a sounding chamber in poetry', and not only metaphorically, 'since more than the content of the poem is derived. Its style is also a set of mechanical effects which spring up, felicitously or miserably, as that inescapable unconscious of language'.[69] When she makes her toad shift into an anapaestic song form, she exemplifies this splendidly, but in so designed a way that the poem feels like an exemplification rather than a living example: a dramatisation of the sounding chamber, rather than its more uneven result. The same could be said of the similar jingle that cuts across the next poem that Riley includes in chapter 3, 'Affections of the Ear', at the moment when its narrator, Echo, castigates Narcissus's self-regarding. 'He lay dumb in the daze of himself by the glaze of the lake with his face set like stone', Echo wails, until the maze of internal rhymes seems to kindle an outburst in the anapaestic ballad form that Edgar Allan Poe also used to evoke obsessive fidelity: 'If your mother was blue and your father was water, then mightn't you try to be true?' (compare 'For the moon never beams, without bringing me dreams / Of the beautiful Annabel Lee').[70] '[P]oems of ideas are easy to spot in my work, and they're anomalous – they've got a kind of attempted control, which in my own case I'm dubious about', Riley told Huk, and these feel to me something like that: poems that extend the book's exploration of that experience of being possessed by song forms to which Riley's earlier collections testified, by virtuosically dramatising it in the utterance of these poet-avatars.[71]

---

[67]   Dr. Seuss, *Yertle the Turtle and Other Stories* (New York: Random House, 1958), p. 8.

[68]   Riley, *Words of Selves*, p. 103.

[69]   Ibid., p. 96.

[70]   Ibid., p. 108; Edgar Allan Poe, *Complete Poems*, ed. Thomas Ollive Mabbott, revised edition (Urbana: University of Illinois Press, 2000), p. 478.

[71]   Huk and Riley, 'In Conversation'.

In the commentary that follows 'Affections of the Ear', Riley notes that 'Echo might be taken as a figure or a trope for the troubled nature of lyric poetry, driven on by rhyme, and condemned to hapless repetition of the cadences and sound associations in others' utterances'.[72] She also points out that those cadences can be hard to catch, noting that '[t]his piece also deploys such a long line itself that any listening ears will not catch its structure of rhymed alternating couplets'. The exception is the poem's moment of most intense self-reference, which is also its moment of most intense formal play – the moment when Echo makes this very argument about herself:

> His beauty drove me deeper into repetition as a sounding-board,
>   a ringing rock, a mere eardrum.
> A rhyme rears up before me to insist on how I should repeat a
>   stanza's formal utterance – other
> Than this I cannot do, unless my hearers find a way of speaking
>   to me so I don't stay semi-dumb
> Or pirouette, a languid Sugarplum. Echo's a trope for lyric
>   poetry's endemic barely hidden bother:
> As I am made to parrot others' words so I am forced to form
>   ideas by rhymes, the most humdrum.[73]

'A rhyme rears up before me', Echo remarks, and suddenly it rears up before me, as well, as Riley swiftly follows 'semi-dumb' with 'Sugarplum', and I finally realise what 'eardrum' and 'humdrum' are doing here, too. 'Sugarplum' lands with all the force, at once bathetic and brilliant, of a punchline, not because the allusion to Tchaikovsky's *The Nutcracker* is particularly apposite, but precisely because it is not, and, then again, really is: like the Sugar Plum Fairy herself, the word at once brings everything around it to life and shows up its artifice, simultaneously illuminating how much rhyme there really is here and how oddly ideas have been forced to form it. 'There seems to be a "natural" length for the heard line, beyond which the ear cannot stretch, so that here an elaborate structure has turned out to be a workup for nothing', Riley remarks of the poem, but at moments like this she gives the ear a workout, giving what in her earlier collections can feel like a fight to the death with song's cadences the shape of a complex, brilliant joke.[74]

---

[72] Riley, *Words of Selves*, p. 111.

[73] Ibid., p. 109.

[74] Ibid., p. 111.

Later the same year, Riley published a *Selected Poems* (2000), which reprinted six pieces from *Marxism for Infants*, *No Fee*, and *Dry Air*, and everything from *Mop Mop Georgette* except 'Spring, 1993', 'Metallica', and 'Stair Spirit', followed by 'The Castalian Spring', 'Affections of the Ear', and seven more previously uncollected poems. Formal dramas are evident in this newer work, too: in 'Goethe On His Holidays', for example, Riley has her Goethe flirt with a blank verse line, then comments ruefully on the habit – 'But my neat wooden song does yodel so' – before winding up in what sound like tetrameter couplets ('Natural history, do me proud / As cover from the self out loud', he chants).[75] But the wit with which Riley imitated song forms around the turn of the century marked the beginning of a decade in which she seems to have found them less compelling, as if mocking them up so brilliantly somehow took away their charm ('Getting the hang of itself would undo it', she warns of awkward lyric in *Say Something Back*).[76] In *The Force of Language* (2004), Riley's next theoretical work, she argues that 'ventriloquy is not only a passing and banal companion to any inner voice, but is its incisive constituent', including 'archaic injunctions from hymns, and the pastel snatches of old song lyrics' alongside 'reiterated quotation' among her examples of what makes it up; reflecting on the force of 'bad words' later in the book, she notes, similarly, that 'not only imperious accusation is apt to indwell. So can lyric, gorgeous fragments, psalms and hymns'.[77] But her focus throughout the first decade of the twenty-first century, here and in *Impersonal Passion: Language as Affect* (2005), was primarily linguistic, and at such moments she seems to have been thinking of specific songs rather than of song forms more generally. What she describes as 'the internal strumming of metrical quotation', which is resonant precisely because it has no words and is therefore less traceable, is rarely discussed.[78]

By 2012, Riley seemed to be questioning song's very purpose. 'A Part Song', a 20-part poem published in the *London Review of Books* that responded to the death of her adult son, opens with bewildered incomprehension at what had seemed so important for so long: 'You principle of song, what are you *for* now'.[79] Much of this sense of

---

[75] Riley, *Selected Poems* (Hastings: Reality Street Editions, 2000), pp. 105–07.
[76] Riley, *Say Something Back*, p. 53.
[77] Jean-Jacques Lecercle and Denise Riley, *The Force of Language* (Basingstoke: Palgrave Macmillan, 2004), pp. 20–21, 49. Part I is by Riley, Part II by Lecercle.
[78] Ibid., p. 50.
[79] Riley, 'A Part Song', *London Review of Books*, 34.3 (9 February 2012), 14.

purposelessness is attributed to the experience that Riley describes in
the short prose work published the same year, *Time Lived, Without Its
Flow* (2012): an 'acute sensation of being cut off from any temporal flow
that can grip you after the sudden death of your child'.[80] Composition,
Riley suggests, feels impossible in such circumstances, for '[a]ny
written or spoken sentence would naturally lean forward towards its
development and conclusion, unlike my own paralyzed time'.[81] She
reflects upon an account of this condition by Emily Dickinson:

> The thought behind I strove to join
> Unto the thought before,
> But sequence raveled out of sound
> Like balls upon a floor.

'Sequence out of sound' indeed. One note no longer implies
another's coming.[82]

Riley hears 'sound' musically rather than as a form of structural
integrity or alignment, and suggests that Dickinson 'implies that sound
is the natural ally or shelter of the sequential': '[s]ound is sustained on
the ear by its repetition, and by the expectation that another sound
will follow on', she notes, so '[i]f sequence were truly to fall apart from
sound, then the hearer could no longer expect any future unrolling'.[83]

Yet Dickinson is not only writing about what Riley calls 'sounding
rhythm' here, but also making it – making exactly what the condition
that she describes seems to render impossible. 'But sequence raveled
out of sound', recounts Dickinson, and so it must have done, for these
lines to be written, because ravelling intimates connection as well as
coming apart, spinning yarns as well as dropping threads ('Must I
rauell out / My weaud vp Folly', asks Shakespeare's Richard II).[84] The
sequence of the poem really is 'raveled out of sound' – in the sense of:
unwound from it, drawn out of it – for the poem is a ballad, or a hymn,
or in common measure, or common metre, or whatever you want to call
that form that oscillates between four- and three-beat lines and is so
intimately associated with song – and Riley's, once again, often is too.

Any lines that so gesture towards song form – any lines of any
verse, I would hazard – necessarily count time, even if they lament

[80]   Riley, *Time Lived, Without Its Flow* (London: Capsule Editions, 2012), p. 7.
[81]   Ibid., p. 10.
[82]   Ibid., p. 34.
[83]   Ibid., pp. 64–66.
[84]   See 'ravel', v. 1, *OED*.

its suspension. 'A Part Song' is startlingly full of such lines, and they generate moments of remarkable pace when Riley performs them.[85] Sometimes they sound ironic or deflating, like the tetrameter couplets that make up part (vi), which conclude their fussy sartorial advice with a weary snap: 'Your dead don't want you lying flat. / There'll soon be time enough for that'. But they can also lift the poem beyond wilful understatement to something older, more reminiscent of the border ballads in which Riley is so interested, as in part (xv):

> The flaws in suicide are clear
> Apart from causing bother
> To those alive who hold us dear
> We could miss one another
> We might be trapped eternally
> Oblivious to each other
> One crying *Where are you, my child*
> The other calling *Mother.*

There are also the unrhymed lines of part (xvii), whose four-beat gorgeousness starts to falter as Riley describes the experience of halted time that characterises her grief:

> Suspended in unsparing light
> The sloping gull arrests its curl
> The glassy sea is hardened waves
> Its waters lean through shining air
> Yet never crash but hold their arc
> Hung rigidly in glaucous ropes
> Muscled and gleaming. All that
> Should flow is sealed, is poised
> In implacable stillness. Joined in
> Non-time and halted in free fall.

Despite themselves, these lines testify to something that beats on: in performance, Riley gives them the same intensely sing-song cadence and long mid-line caesura with which she rendered the final four-beat section of 'Laibach Lyrik', all those years before.[86] As Peter Riley

---

[85] Listen, for example, to parts (vi) and (xv) in the podcast that Riley recorded for the *LRB*, 4:20 and 10:40 minutes in: http://www.lrb.co.uk/v34/n03/denise-riley/a-part-song [accessed 3 October 2019].

[86] This can be heard 11:15 minutes in: http://www.lrb.co.uk/v34/n03/denise-riley/a-part-song [accessed 3 October 2019].

points out, '[a] part song is a song for voices as well as a song of apartness or part of a song', and in 'A Part Song', many of those voices come from the past – not just Riley's past, but the long, less knowable past of poetry itself.[87]

'It's all a resurrection song', Riley admits in part (xviii), with something of a nod to Bob Marley. What it resurrects is not a loved one, but song itself, and, through song, a paradoxical sense of time's continuation. In part (xix), Riley asks with desperate self-deprecation and no hope of a response: 'Won't you be summoned up once more / By my prancing and writhing in a dozen / Mawkish modes of reedy piping to you / – Still no?' But there is an answer, and it comes as a song, as the poem closes with part (xx):

> *My sisters and my mother*
> *Weep dark tears for me*
> *I drift as lightest ashes*
> *Under a southern sea*
>
> *O let me be, my mother*
> *In no unquiet grave*
> *My bone-dust is faint coral*
> *Under the fretful wave.*

The most explicit reference here is probably to the ballad of long mourning collected by Francis James Child as number 78, 'The Unquiet Grave', but there are also echoes of Ariel in *The Tempest* ('Of his bones are coral made'), and 'unquiet' is sufficiently unusual a word to summon Tennyson's *In Memoriam A. H. H.*, too, specifically its reflections on the efficacy of verse: 'But, for the unquiet heart and brain, / A use in measured language lies'.[88] It feels right to hear these last two songs, both of which lament lost loved ones whose bodies have passed over the sea, just as Riley lets her own loved one speak out of the water into which his ashes were scattered. But it also feels right that she does not invoke their tunes. Neither 'The strain of strutting chanticleer' nor 'The sad mechanic exercise' is at work metrically here; rather than echoing Shakespeare's or Tennyson's four-beat elegies, or Child's alternating ballad stanza,

[87]   Peter Riley, 'Denise Riley and the force of bereavement', in *The Fortnightly Review* (New Series, 21 March 2012): http://fortnightlyreview.co.uk/2012/03/denise-riley-force-bereavement/ [accessed 3 October 2019].

[88]   Shakespeare, *The Tempest*, I.ii.400; Alfred Tennyson, *Tennyson: A Selected Edition*, ed. Christopher Ricks, revised edition (London: Longman, 2007), p. 349.

Riley generates a different kind of song, with a shorter, three-beat line, ravelling a new sequence out of sound just as everything seems to have unravelled.

Riley opened her most recent collection, *Say Something Back* (2016), with the lines by W. S. Graham from which her title is taken: 'Do not think you have to say / Anything back. But you do / Say something back which I / Hear by the way I speak to you'.[89] The way in which Riley speaks in the collection, which includes 'A Part Song' and like that work often addresses itself to her dead son, is remarkably metrical. It plays across a range of established forms, including blank verse and the sonnet, and is often arranged in what look like stanzas, although they do not always sound like them. Even when Riley seems to be rejecting the consolation of music, as in 'Let no air now be sung', its rhythms throb regardless through her plea for their absence: 'Let no air now be sung, let no kind air – / sorrow alone reveals a constant pulse', Riley asks, contrarily filling the air with the pulse of iambic pentameter.[90] But it is song form that is most significant to the collection, I think, and its resonance comes precisely from rather than in spite of its historical and formal indeterminacy.

For the song forms that run wild in *Say Something Back* are legion. Even in a small, shifty piece like 'With Child in mind', there is, as Peter Riley points out, a recognisable ballad narrative, a hint of a pun on the ballad collector's name, and 'a few lines of a cross-line ballad rhythm' (he is surely thinking of the sense of a trochaic tetrameter couplet that suddenly cuts in on 'somewhere / on the rainy wind, far / along the sobbing wind', a sense that also pervades 'Oh go away for now', and erupts in the middle of 'I admit the briar': 'Full of wist, I needn't be. / The fuller world's not "cruel" to me').[91] The first two lines of 'After "Nous n'irons plus au bois"' echo with the three-beat nursery music of the French folksong (compare 'We've had it with the woods. / The underbrush got felled' and *Nous n'irons plus au bois / Les lauriers sont coupés*).[92] Sequences such as 'Four blindfolded songs'

[89] Riley, *Say Something Back*, p. v. The quotation is no. 33 of W. S. Graham's 'Implements in Their Places', in *New Collected Poems*, ed. Matthew Francis (London: Faber, 2004), p. 247.

[90] Riley, *Say Something Back*, p. 59.

[91] Ibid., pp. 30, 48, 60; Peter Riley, 'Denise Riley and the "awkward lyric"', in *The Fortnightly Review* (New Series, 3 October 2016): http://fortnightlyreview. co.uk/2016/10/denise-riley/ [accessed 3 October 2019].

[92] Riley, *Say Something Back*, p. 33.

have strongly dactylic sections, which evoke even darker children's rhymes, and which Riley gives a swift lilt in performance (compare 'Bright brown the water / And bright brown the fur / Near drowned the barking / Through coffee liqueur' and *Here comes a candle to light you to bed / Here comes a chopper to chop off your head*).[93] In '"A gramophone on the subject"', a sequence commemorating the First World War, Riley's verse replays the rhythms of the period's songs as well as the written historical records from which she draws several of her phrases. There is the variable iambic tetrameter of part 2 ('Those of a tender conscience swear / Their vows that they will fail to keep'), the classic ballad beat of parts 3 and 5 ('We do not draw our curtains closed. / We're told we should not mind'; 'Death's tidied up in rows and lists. / The scratched are "Known to God"'), and the loose dactylic trimeter of parts 1 and 4, which rises up again suddenly in the closing couplet of the whole sequence, at the end of the freer part 7 ('Exhumation squads dug to unearth them / In bits that got dropped in cloth bags'; '"Tucked in" is not quite how we'd put it. / We weren't plumped up neatly in bed'; 'What to do now is clear, and wordless. / You will bear what can not be borne').[94]

What is song, then, if it embraces such variety? It is all of these forms, and none of them. It is like a form without a form. 'The shadow of ballad or hymn meter haunts Riley's fragmented parts', notes Ange Mlinko in her review of the collection.[95] Yes, but as Mlinko's 'or' tacitly admits, it is difficult to say exactly what it is that is doing the haunting. Writing of *Say Something Back*, Peter Riley describes lyric as 'a poetical technique' for creating 'an illusion of song', and suggests that poets attempt it because '[s]ong (actual, sung song) is collective. It is sent out into the world in search of auditors and to form or confirm a body of felt mutuality. It is this whether it is social song or art song or graveside lament or "Ta-ra-ra Boom-dee-ay" or whatever'.[96] What I am interested in is how mutuality is elicited by something so dizzyingly protean and imprecise ('social song or art

[93]   Ibid., p. 16. Riley recorded this sequence for the University of East Anglia Poetics Project Reading Series, 14 January 2014; this part is found 2:46 minutes into what were then 'Nine Blindfolded Songs': http://www.newwriting.net/ writing/poetry/say-something-back/ [accessed 3 October 2019].

[94]   Riley, *Say Something Back*, pp. 63–71.

[95]   Ange Mlinko, 'A Part of Denise Riley's Song', *The Nation* (20 September 2016): https://www.thenation.com/article/a-part-of-denise-rileys-song/   [accessed 3 October 2019].

[96]   Peter Riley, 'Denise Riley and the "awkward lyric"'.

song or graveside lament or "Ta-ra-ra Boom-dee-ay" or whatever', itself an openly incomplete list). Riley closes 'You men who go in living flesh' with a hymnal evocation of imagined afterlife:

> Hope is an inconsistent joy
> Yet blazes to renew
> Its lambent resurrections of
> Those gone ahead of you.[97]

The verse of the collection is full of renewal, too – it is both a resurrection song and a resurrector of songs – but like hope, it is inconsistent. 'Little Eva', Riley notes beneath that poem, 'contains brief excerpts from the lyrics to "The Loco-Motion", words and music by Gerry Goffin and Carole King, originally performed by Eva Boyd as Little Eva'.[98] The movements that characterise poems such as 'You men who go in living flesh' cannot be so precisely attributed.

In conversation with Corcoran, Riley made an attempt, explaining that she wrote it and its companion poem, 'Death makes dead metaphor revive', 'with an eye to the kind of affect that rises up from Isaac Watts' boxy hymn quatrains'.[99] But when she identified what was probably meant to be the same source for her audience at the University of East Anglia – 'the next two pieces are really in a sort of Isaac Newton hymn metric' – her verbal slip fortuitously captured the difficulty of saying where any such song form originates: its real impersonality, and therefore its real communality, too.[100] 'Death makes dead metaphor revive', Riley told Corcoran, is a poem that speculates about 'rhyme's own relation to temporality'; in contrast to 'that feeling of "time stopped" that you might inhabit after someone's unexpected death', 'rhyme, both anticipated and recurring, acts as a guarantor of continuing and perceived time, and of human listening, attuned to that faithfulness of sounding language'.[101] But for all its timeliness, rhyme does not summon a particular history: it hearkens back to what has come before it, in the poem in which it is found and

---

[97] Riley, *Say Something Back*, p. 61.
[98] Ibid., p. 57.
[99] Corcoran and Riley, 'Interview'.
[100] This can be heard at the beginning of Riley's recording of 'You men who go in living flesh' for the University of East Anglia: http://www.newwriting.net/writing/poetry/say-something-back/ [accessed 3 October 2019]. Riley discusses such slips in *Words of Selves*, pp. 71–73.
[101] Corcoran and Riley, 'Interview'.

in all the rhyming poems in the world that precede it, but it is also rootless, and must therefore be endlessly remade.

For who can say where it comes from, or whose it was or is? 'Disjointed anthems dip and bob / Down time's defrosted spate', Riley recounts in 'Death makes dead metaphor revive', then concludes:

> Over its pools of greeny melt
> The rearing ice will tilt.
> To make *rhyme* chime again with *time*
> I sound a curious lilt.[102]

'I sound': both *I take soundings of* and *I sing*. Riley plays with song form here, flooding what already sounds like a ballad stanza with further felicitously rhyming song terms ('tilt'/'lilt'; 'rhyme'/'chime'/'time').[103] But she also makes song form herself; she also really sings. 'There's an impersonality in rhyme that's, in the same breath, deeply personal', Riley continued to Corcoran; song form could be described the same way.[104] At once richly historied and definitively ahistorical, instantly recognisable and categorically unfixed, song has no fixed parts, and can therefore take the part of everyone and no-one. It is hers for she has to remake it, and ours for it comes from the past, but like 'this whole business of "song"', as Riley described it to Corcoran, that past is 'a plain bright mystery', so it is also no-one's, nothing, something apart.[105]

---

[102] Riley, *Say Something Back*, p. 62.
[103] 'Felicitous' is Riley's term in *The Words of Selves* (p. 71), when she discusses the 'strange *time* of rhyme' and notes the 'felicitous rhyming' of these words.
[104] Corcoran and Riley, 'Interview'.
[105] Ibid.

CHAPTER NINE

Dramatic Monologue

R. F. Langley and the Poem of 'Anyone in Particular'

Jeremy Noel-Tod

We speak
from out there and we keep things
alive.
– R. F. Langley, 'Still Life with Wineglass'

Critical discussion of the work of R. F. Langley (1938–2011) has focused on its preoccupation with questions of perception: 'not things, / but seeing things'.[1] The prose and verse collected in *Journals* (2006) and *Complete Poems* (2015) returns to a cluster of subjects known through the eye – birds and insects, rural landscape, church architecture, Renaissance sculpture and painting – with an attention to detail that alternates exactingly between subjective and objective modes of knowledge. For Conor Carville, Langley investigates 'the extent to which an object [...] can be attended to in all its sensuous specificity without having a human subjectivity foisted on it', resulting in poetry that continues the modernist 'torque between propositional knowledge and direct perception' made by Ezra Pound's Imagist dictum: 'direct treatment of the thing, whether subjective or objective'.[2] Stephen Benson, meanwhile, locates Langley's *Journals* in a history of minutely observant English prose that includes Dorothy Wordsworth, John

[1] R. F. Langley, *Complete Poems*, ed. Jeremy Noel-Tod (Manchester: Carcanet, 2015), p. 81.

[2] Conor Carville, '"The Degree of Power Exercised": Recent Ekphrasis', in *The Oxford Handbook of Contemporary British and Irish Poetry*, ed. Peter Robinson (Oxford: Oxford University Press, 2013), pp. 286–302 (p. 287); Mark Byers, 'R. F. Langley: "Seeing Things"', *English*, 66 (2017), 331–50 (p. 331).

Ruskin, and Adrian Stokes, noting in particular how Langley habitually sets up his first-person descriptions as 'a matter first of framing
[..] in performative and self-summoning injunctions to gather what
is to hand'.[3]

In what follows, I want to propose that the intense looking which
is so often the occasion of Langley's *Journals* is differently framed
in his poems by another modernist fascination: the dramatic nature
of lyric voice. Langley spent his working life as an English teacher
in secondary schools, and observed that reading 'the same small
number' of Shakespeare plays on a regular basis profoundly influenced
his writing.[4] His final collection, *The Face of It* (2007), for example,
is peppered with allusions to *A Midsummer Night's Dream* and the
play-within-a-play staged by the Mechanicals.[5] But if the playfulness
of many Langley poems vibrates with Shakespearean meta-comedy,
their formal staging of lyric speech recasts a more solemn staple of
schoolroom English: the dramatic monologue.

Ina Beth Sessions's 1947 essay on dramatic monologue as a
generic category helped to establish Robert Browning's 'My Last
Duchess' (1842) as its *locus classicus*. Browning's full-dress depiction
of an Italian duke who insinuates to an envoy that he had his wife
murdered fulfils all seven of Sessions's essential criteria: 'speaker,
audience, occasion, revelation of character, interplay between speaker
and audience, dramatic action, and action which takes place in the
present'.[6] Later critics such as Alan Sinfield loosened their definition
so as to account for the liberties taken with the realist verities of
'occasion' and 'character' by modernist works of monologue such as
T. S. Eliot's *Prufrock and Other Observations* (1917) and Pound's *Hugh
Selwyn Mauberley* (1920).[7] After the fragmented monologues of high
modernism, notes Glennis Byron, histories of the form 'tend to slide to
an uneasy halt', concluding that such anti-realist experiments mark a
limit to dramatic monologue as a medium for the creation of character.[8]
Philip Hobsbaum, for example, considering Eliot's 'Gerontion' (1920)

[3]   Stephen Benson, 'Description's Repertoire: The *Journals* of R. F. Langley',
English, 67 (2018), 43–63 (pp. 43–45).

[4]   Langley, *Complete Poems*, p. 158.

[5]   For three poems in which *A Midsummer Night's Dream* is a prominent allusive
backdrop, see 'Sixpence a Day', 'Blues for Titania', and 'Cash Point'.

[6]   Ina Beth Sessions, 'The Dramatic Monologue', *PMLA*, 62.2 (1947), 503–16
(p. 508).

[7]   Alan Sinfield, *Dramatic Monologue* (London: Methuen, 1977), pp. 65–72.

[8]   Glennis Byron, *Dramatic Monologue* (London: Routledge, 2003), p. 117.

in 1975, complained that 'at the end of the poem we know less about Gerontion than at the beginning. Any attempt to develop this particular technique would make for incoherence'.[9]

R. F. Langley's development from the late 1970s of what he called 'dramatic monologue-like' techniques, however, does exactly this, by exploring the formal and philosophical implications of what Carol T. Christ calls 'the project of imagining oneself as a character' – even if that project involves imagining oneself to be incoherent.[10] One convention of dramatic monologue established by Browning is that it is spoken by a persona evidently and often egregiously distinct from the poet. As Isobel Armstrong writes, this 'double' form of poetic speech enabled the Victorian poet to see 'utterance as both subject and object [..] to explore expressive psychological forms simultaneously as psychological conditions *and* as constructs, the phenomenology of a culture'.[11] Langley retains this psychological doubleness of structure, along with the relativism implied by a phenomenological approach to culture. But he largely dispenses with the nineteenth-century costume of a named character, so that there is no clear chalking on the stage of subjective and objective positions: Langley's anonymous lyric speakers are both 'the poet' and other people. As dramatis personae in thought experiments, these lyric half-masks open up the epistemological distinction implied by Oscar Wilde's remark about Browning: 'it was not thought that fascinated him, but rather the processes by which thought moves'.[12] Langley was fascinated not by habits of character but by habits of mind: reflecting on 'The Love Song of J. Alfred Prufrock' he wondered, 'what of the style where brackets intrude other ways of ordering things into the overall attempt to do so?'[13] In his own poetics, which was influenced by the art criticism of Richard Wollheim, formal organisation is foregrounded as the physical frame of the thinking mind, equivalent to the implied body of a focalising

[9] Philip Hobsbaum, 'The Rise of the Dramatic Monologue', *Hudson Review*, 28.2 (1975), 227–45 (pp. 243–44).

[10] 'R. F. Langley Interviewed by R. F. Walker', in *Don't Start Me Talking*, ed. Tim Allen and Andrew Duncan (Cambridge: Salt, 2006), pp. 237–57 (p. 247); Carol T. Christ, *Victorian and Modern Poetics* (Chicago: University of Chicago Press, 1984), p. 44.

[11] Isobel Armstrong, *Victorian Poetry: Poetry, Poetics and Politics* (London: Routledge, 1993), p. 13.

[12] Oscar Wilde, 'The Critic as Artist' (1891), in *Plays, Prose Writings and Poems* (London: David Campbell, 1991), pp. 3–67 (p. 7).

[13] R. F. Langley, *Journals* (Exeter: Shearsman Books, 2006), p. 55.

speaker. Through this conceit, Langley continued the displacement of a speaking persona by the performative 'mask' of lyric voice that George T. Wright saw as characteristic of the modernism of Pound, Eliot, and Yeats: 'it is the poem, not the speaker, through which the poet speaks, and which therefore serves as his persona'.[14]

The idea that *all* lyric poems can to some extent be read as the monologue of a persona created by the poet, observes Jonathan Culler, 'has come to dominate lyric pedagogy and much literary criticism in the Anglo-American world'. Culler suggests that this consensus derives from a culture that reads poetry alongside realist fiction. Readers are trained to 'novelize' poetry as the speech of a fictional characters, and to undervalue the non-narrative aspects of poetic voice, such as 'presentness of lyric utterance, the materiality of lyric language [...] and the rich texture of intertextual relations'.[15] An influential book in the evolution of this consensus was Robert Langbaum's *The Poetry of Experience: The Dramatic Monologue in Modern Literary Tradition* (1957). Langbaum's thesis projected the paradigm of Browning across the long nineteenth century, finding its origins in the 'conversational' lyric poetry of the Romantics, and its furthest development in the early poetry of T. S. Eliot. In 'Prufrock', Langbaum contends, Eliot makes 'explicit what is implicit in all dramatic monologues': that they are 'addressed ultimately [...] to some projection of the speaker [...] the speaker speaks to understand something about himself [...] directing his address outward in order that it may return with a meaning he was not aware of'. Prufrock *'comes to see* the pattern of his life' by revealing it to the 'other self' whom he addresses in the first line ('Let us go then, you and I'), and it is this impression of a process of discovery that keeps Eliot's poem within Langbaum's definition of dramatic monologue:

> Take away at least the implication of the present-tense situation, and the poem [...] becomes a traditional lyric, the logically reworked recollection of an idea rather than the dramatic presentation of how through a particular dialectical situation the idea comes to be perceived.[16]

[14]   George T. Wright, *The Poet in the Poem: The Personae of Eliot, Yeats, and Pound* (Berkeley: University of California Press, 1962), p. 59.

[15]   Jonathan Culler, *Theory of Lyric* (Cambridge, MA: Harvard University Press, 2015), pp. 115, 119.

[16]   Robert Langbaum, *The Poetry of Experience: The Dramatic Monologue in Modern Literary Tradition*, revised edition (Harmondsworth: Penguin, 1974), p. 187.

Prufrock's 'Let us go then, you and I, / When the evening is spread out against the sky', in other words, is as important to framing what follows as the opening lines of Browning's 'My Last Duchess', which raises the curtain on a speaker in a furnished room with a companion ('That's my last Duchess painted on the wall, / [..] / Will't please you sit and look at her?').[17]

R. F. Langley owned two copies of *The Poetry of Experience*: a first edition with a note indicating that it was purchased in 1964, during his first teaching job, and a revised paperback edition from 1974. He used the book in class, and a former pupil recalled how, in the mid-1980s, he would habitually lend 'precious copies' to promising students.[18] Every phase of his poetry can be read in dialogue with Langbaum's theory of dramatic monologue as a form of lyric self-discovery, from early sequences on historical subjects ('Matthew Glover', 'The Ecstasy Inventories') to poems which narrate projected, perceiving selves ('Mariana', 'Man Jack'), and finally ekphrastic pieces on depicted figures ('The Bellini in San Giovanni Crisostomo', 'The Best Piece of Sculpture in Perugia'). Langbaum characterises dramatic monologue's 'special effect' as 'the tension between sympathy and judgment', arguing that it tends (as in Browning's verse novel, *The Ring and the Book* (1868–69)) to a relativist attitude towards '*knowable reality*'.[19] In Langley's late modernist poetics of perception, relativism is a philosophical given, and his 'dramatic presentation of [..] a particular dialectical situation' is less concerned with moral judgement than with the tension between sympathy (defined by Langbaum as 'a way of knowing [..] a romantic projectiveness') and epistemological doubt: to what extent can we know a perspective on the world that is not our own – and so, by triangulation, the world itself?[20]

---

[17]   T. S. Eliot, 'The Love Song of J. Alfred Prufrock', in *The Poems of T. S. Eliot*, ed. Christopher Ricks and Jim McCue, 2 vols (London: Faber, 2015), I, p. 5; Robert Browning, 'My Last Duchess', in *Poetical Works: 1833–1864*, ed. Ian Jack (London: Oxford University Press, 1970), p. 367.

[18]   Charles Mundye, 'Roger Langley – An Appreciation', *PN Review 199*, 37.5 (May–June 2011), 17.

[19]   Langbaum, *The Poetry of Experience*, pp. vii–ix.

[20]   Ibid., p. vii.

'Filled with Particulars': History as Monologue

Browning was drawn to dramatic monologue as a form that could give a living voice to historical subjects, and so by implication a historical perspective on the present. As Christ observes in her study of Victorian and modernist poetics, however, 'the stuff of history – facts, documents, personalities, situations – often seems to reveal only a contextual relativism that denies any teleological pattern', giving rise to the anxiety that there may be no 'cosmic point of view [..] which assigns ultimate meaning'.[21] In his working notebooks Langley quoted with approval Thomas Nagel's essay 'Subjective and Objective' (1979) on the 'incredulity that one should be anyone in particular, a specific individual of a particular species existing at a particular time and place in the universe'.[22] This sense of existential vertigo frequently informs Langley's writing. Take, for example, the opening passage of a journal entry dated 15 November 2002:

> It is probably 404 years since Hamlet first said, 'The rest is silence.' I woke up in the small hours thinking this, without doing the sum but feeling the length of time, and, most vividly, how every moment since had been, has been, filled with particulars. For instance, the nose of an aardvark [..] Other notions poured in after this, also particular.[23]

The associative leap between Hamlet's dying words, as first spoken by an actor on the Elizabethan stage, and the nose of an aardvark, is striking not only for its spontaneous surrealism but also for the way in which it places two contrasting historical phenomena – dramatic and natural – on the same plane of 'particular' reality, without hierarchy. Recollecting the associative joy of 'all these specifics devoid of any consequences', Langley remarks that 'to fit them into any scheme instantly seemed to melt them into a phoney glamour, make them part of a poor sort of drama, the sort that an audience at a reading of an autobiography would enjoy'. Instead, he continues:

> I had a notion of giving a reading where, to begin it, I stunned an audience with the full sense of this before I began [..] And

[21] Christ, *Victorian and Modern Poetics*, pp. 101–02.
[22] Thomas Nagel, 'Subjective and Objective', in *Mortal Questions* (Cambridge: Cambridge University Press, 1979), pp. 196–213 (p. 206); Langley, *Complete Poems*, p. xii.
[23] Langley, *Journals*, p. 100.

the poems themselves would not be, as it were, 'treatment' to give one a sense of having dealt with anything by writing about it, smoothing it down. No soothing the aardvark, or the rest of all the rest since 1598, or 1601, whenever a mouth first opened on those words.[24]

This resistance to the 'phoney glamour' of using poetry to 'smooth' the randomness of experience into the easily consumable narrative of a life ('the reading of an autobiography') is a characteristic concern of Langley's poetry from the first. All four poems in his first small-press pamphlet, *Hem* (1978), are interested in recovering the historical traces of other lives by lyric rather than narrative means. In 1996, Langley gave an account of the sources of each, drawing attention to their permeation by historical voices. 'Blithing' is 'full of different fragments', including 'bits of Darwin reporting from The Voyage of the Beagle'; 'Saxon Landings' was inspired by the Romano-British Great Dish buried at Mildenhall in Suffolk, and a radio play about the end of Roman Britain; 'The Ecstasy Inventories' was a response to a detailed inventory for the seventeenth-century English household of Arthur and Elizabeth Coke, as well as to their memorial sculpture in St Andrew's church, Bramfield, Suffolk; and 'Matthew Glover' is concerned with an obscure historical figure who was uncertain whether to vote for the enclosure of common land in 1800, while also incorporating reflections by John Clare on the same subject.[25]

'Matthew Glover' was the earliest of Langley's poems that he preserved for publication, and it establishes the characteristic flickering of his verse between objective and subjective voice. 'To start with throve heavy forest', runs the first line, initiating a sketch of human settlement informed by chapter 1 of Mircea Eliade's anthropological study, *The Sacred and the Profane* (1959). The poem then switches to a present-tense description of a certain 'edge of the parish', where small birds are observed flitting in a bush, and then to an overview of how one English village was affected by enclosure. From this point to the end of the poem, the feelings of the present-day speaker who watches the 'warblers' in the bush seem partly to merge with the thought of 'Matthew Glover // resident, who would not / speak for or against'. Following the (unidentified) quotations on enclosure from Clare ('saw

---

[24] Langley, *Journals*, p. 101.
[25] 'R. F. Langley Interviewed', pp. 250–52. Further bibliographic notes on the sources of individual poems are given in the *Complete Poems*.

an old wood stile / taken away') – which could also be the words of either the poet or his subject – Matthew Glover appears to speak directly:

> Owning very little land
> rated at eightpence
> very little soil
>
> maybe I did wish
> to oppose the Bill
>
> but I dared not do it
> for fear I had missed ...
>
> > A long time
> > I imagined
> >
> > each square
> > five acres
> >
> > I turned it
> > over
> >
> > in my mind
>
> no distractions.[26]

The reticent Glover is brought to life here in a minimalist monologue adapted from a historical source, James T. Gould's *Men of Aldridge* (1957):

> [One person] whose property was rated at eightpence who would not declare for or against the Bill [...] The man who would not declare for or against the Bill must have been Matthew Glover, a resident, but owning very little land. His attitude is hard to understand unless he wished to oppose the Bill but was frightened of the possible results of downright opposition to his more influential neighbours.[27]

The further indented passage that follows 'for fear I had missed ...' may similarly be heard as the thoughts of Glover, or it may signal a reversion to the present-day observer, who at the end of the poem muses on Glover in the third person, comparing the man's vanishingly

---

[26] Langley, *Complete Poems*, pp. 25–30.
[27] James T. Gould, *Men of Aldridge* (Bloxwich: G. J. Clark, 1957), pp. 59–60.

slight historical trace with the small movements of the birds in the bush: 'he is / a bird for this moment / and the next // but no more'.[28]

'Matthew Glover', Langley said, was 'a fairly naive attempt to do a minuscule [Charles] Olson in an English setting'.[29] The poem's composition in (free, indented) 'projective verse' is one indication of Olson's influence; another is the overlapping movement between the voices signalled by these alignments – in particular, the blending of the present-day poet with a historical persona. Olson's use of this technique in *The Maximus Poems* (1960–75), like Ezra Pound's *The Cantos* (1930–69), continued the quixotic ambition of Browning's historical monologues, whereby the poet 'at once represents man's consciousness as determined by history and implies a point outside of history from which that consciousness can be judged and the structure of history comprehended'.[30] Pound strove and failed in *The Cantos* to arrive at the latter ('I am not a demigod, / I cannot make it cohere').[31] Olson, by assuming the quizzical half-mask of the second-century Neoplatonist philosopher Maximus of Tyre, acknowledged from the start the difficulties faced by his own project to comprehend human history through the epic of a particular place (Gloucester, Massachusetts). As the opening poem, 'Maximus, to himself', muses

> ... we grow up many
> And the single
> is not easily
> known.[32]

Olson later commented that 'the purpose of Maximus, the person who addresses himself to the City, is to measure: *the advantage of a single human figure*'.[33] The conscious modesty of Langley's ambition in making 'Matthew Glover' a 'minuscule Olson' involves shrinking the poem's 'measure' further, to a figure 'too slight, almost / for one word'; the poet steps in and out of the consciousness of Matthew Glover only to coincide, in its last line, with his ambivalence: 'not enough to

[28] Langley, *Complete Poems*, pp. 25–32.

[29] 'R. F. Langley Interviewed', p. 239.

[30] Christ, *Victorian and Modern Poetics*, p. 114.

[31] Ezra Pound, 'CXVI', in *The Cantos* (London: Faber, 1981), p. 796.

[32] Charles Olson, *The Maximus Poems* (1960–75), ed. George F. Butterick (Berkeley: University of California Press, 1983), I.52, p. 56.

[33] Quoted in George F. Butterick, *A Guide to 'The Maximus Poems' of Charles Olson* (Berkeley: University of California Press, 1980), p. 8.

decide'.[34] The quiet decisiveness of this final identification between poet and subject underlines how Langley's poetics of perception is not concerned, as Browning was, with inviting judgement of a rhetorical performance, but with sympathetically knowing the irreducible particularity of an individual life.[35]

Another poem in *Hem*, 'The Ecstasy Inventories', confronts the impossibility of knowing another existence through its material record: namely, the household inventory and memorial sculpture of Elizabeth Coke of Suffolk. Langley remarks that this poem was an attempt to '[come] to terms with her, not by writing a dramatic monologue, but in a dramatic monologue-like sort of way, which was a major notion'.[36] With its disorienting dance of pronouns, from 'we' to 'I' to 'she', 'The Ecstasy Inventories' is not obviously a monologue of any kind. What Langley meant by working with his material in 'a dramatic monologue-like sort of way', however, is also suggested by this inconsistency of address. If the point of view of Elizabeth Coke is not coherently articulated in the poem, neither is that of the present-day speaker: the poem begins in between times and places, in an abstract space of becoming where

> We slow out and curve
> then the deep lawlike
> structures loom and bob
> through.[37]

Coming into focus on a particular landscape, the second stanza opens with a description of a stony beach and ends among 'the great presse' of clothes listed in the 1629 inventory of the Coke household:

> The beach is stocked with one cobble
> and another until you have to be
> particular
> [..]
> I've been noticing
> how they needed low light and stale eyes
> to catch such humble cajolery, all along,

[34] Langley, *Complete Poems*, p. 32.

[35] Discussing 'Matthew Glover', Langley noted that he was attracted to collecting historical material about 'pretty obscure people' ('R. F. Langley Interviewed', p. 247).

[36] 'R. F. Langley Interviewed', p. 247.

[37] Langley, *Complete Poems*, p. 15.

> hatching with soft pops into articulate
> habits or costumes or clothes in a great
> press: the broad, the heavy, the paragon,
> her most scarlet gowns.[38]

It is a dreamlike moment, as the archetypal solid – stone – is observed 'hatching' into animate evidence of another life, 'the articulate / habits' of a women's wardrobe' (where 'habits' quibbles on habitual actions and 'costumes or clothes', and 'articulate' suggests the paradoxical eloquence of the mute inventory). As Langley commented: '[o]bjects in a way take you close to people, I suppose, and yet they don't as well, of course'.[39] The desire for a more intimate knowledge of another life across time and space results in bewildering jump-cuts of perspective. 'Take now and make a then', commands the next stanza, which is followed by a section evoking the sensory overload induced by elaborate lace garments:

> The lace can be
> mentioned as strips with discs
> or wheels, as sunbursts
> of logical straps, rays, pips,
> split pods or crooked stars, as
> much as counting and nice
> as a pocketbook with every
> species, in flight, at rest,
> in colour. These inroads let
> me understand, and mark
> sharply
> [...]
> In the trees I can't see the tiny
> passerines all about in the
> sparkling confusion. Or
> her cheeks. Or her chin.[40]

Once again, the speaker negotiates profusion by being 'particular', enumerating the details of the garments as if they were birds to be spotted ('a pocketbook with every / species'), just as earlier they were compared to stones on a beach.

---

[38] Ibid. See Francis W. Steer, 'The Inventory of Arthur Coke of Bramfield, 1629', *Proceedings of the Suffolk Institute of Archaeology*, 25 (1951), 264–87.

[39] 'R. F. Langley Interviewed', p. 250.

[40] Langley, *Complete Poems*, p. 16.

Both stanzas quoted above end their 'sparkling confusion' with a brief sighting of a female figure: 'her most scarlet garments'; 'her cheeks. Or her chin'. Much of the description here derives from a journal entry Langley made in August 1975 about Coke's memorial sculpture:

> Suddenly, all the strips of lace about her catch my attention. Thick lace, cut with bold packed patterns [..] Something that the mind can cope with on its own terms, like numbers stamped over the carved clothes, over the drapery which was cut while nobody counted anything, by hands and skill, straight from the eyes and touch and the grain of the stone and the temper of Caroline England, impossible to explain or even describe.[41]

Langley's prose expands on the theme later condensed in his verse: a dazzling variety of pattern resolving itself into quasi-scientific order. He also expresses the desire to know this world imaginatively; not through Coke herself, but through the 'temper' of the craftsman who rendered her image. This suggests a possible dramatic reading of the related passage in the poem (similar to the merging of identities in 'Matthew Glover') whereby the speaking 'I' briefly becomes the mason in the act of carving. Considering the patterning of the sculpted bedspread, Langley writes in his journal: '[t]hese inroads open up the stone like grill[e]s. They let shadow into the surface as they let mathematics into the sculpture'.[42] This reflection becomes, in the poem, 'These inroads / let me understand, and mark / sharply' – a more immediate and active thought, whereby it is the observer who is 'let' into the sculpture, temporarily becoming a sculptor also ('mark / sharply').

The figure of a well-dressed woman returns towards the end of the poem. 'White hedonism cut on blue / intelligence and laced / with silver anxiety' embroiders abstract nouns into the verbs of dressmaking to ply between inner and outer life. The lines that follow then seem to describe the historical passage of Elizabeth Coke from the vulnerable life of body and mind to dispersion in the natural world:

---

[41]　Langley, *Journals*, p. 17.

[42]　Ibid. Langley's journal entries are not always accurate on small points of spelling. Here, the image of carved lacework as a reticulated pattern that 'open[s] up the stone' suggests 'grilles' as the intended meaning rather than 'grills' (as printed).

> It braces milady's cortical
> layer to take what could
> have been trauma but now snugs
> a bee in a comfort.[43]

As in the journal entry on Hamlet and the aardvark, at this point history pours in to the poem as an abstract mass of restless particulars, filling the gap between now and then ('men press on [..] Folds pack away'). But the conceit of the inventory returns in the final stanza, which reads in full:

> In heaven, where they don't
> refurnish often, there will
> still be an old white bodice
> cut on blue and two lost
> roses. Sure, in Walpolelane
> there is a whirlwind of old
> clothes. You would have thought.
> Until a closer look saw each
> was not vexed but folded
> in unexpected readiness
> in the press of the storm.[44]

The effect is one of diminuendo, folding the poem's range of reference back to its origins in a seventeenth-century lady's wardrobe, from the complex hybrid of garment-as-mind ('White hedonism cut on blue / intelligence') to the simple itemisation of 'an old white bodice / cut on blue'. The brief approach to an impossible intimacy of minds ('milady's cortical / layer') fades into a historical tableau of 'old clothes' preserved 'in expected readiness' for the resurrection that the poem has attempted.

What is left are the traces of the approach to intimacy, which in the context of the dramatic monologue tradition recalls the voyeuristic sensuality of many of Browning's speakers; an imaginative quality that, as Robert Langbaum argues, works to engage our sympathy even as it disturbs us morally.[45] Such speakers often reveal themselves in relation to a silent, idealised female figure: 'Porphyria's Lover' (1836), for example, the earliest of Browning's 'dramatic lyrics', describes Porphyria's body in aesthetic terms even during the brutal process of

---

[43] Langley, *Complete Poems*, p. 18.
[44] Ibid.
[45] Langbaum, *The Poetry of Experience*, pp. 76–81.

murdering her ('all her hair / In one long yellow string I wound').[46] By creating such misogynist monsters, U. C. Knoepflmacher suggests, Browning ironises the poetic 'act of projection by which a devouring male ego reduces [a] Female Other into nothingness'. The effect is to make the reader 'the suppressed Other's chief ally', tasked – like the envoy listening silently to the Duke in 'My Last Duchess' – with her imaginative recovery.[47] Langley's tentative approach to recovering Elizabeth Coke leaves us aligned instead with the poet who stands quietly on the edge of the 'storm' of his vision in the final stanza, observing the woman's folded clothes. His title, meanwhile, alerts us, via the Greek etymology of 'ecstasy' ('withdrawal of the soul from the body'), to the poem's 'out-of-body' perspective on history. The result is an Eliotic decentring of monologue, in which a free-floating 'zone of consciousness' partially inhabits – as in 'Prufrock' and 'Gerontion' – the 'deep lawlike / structures' of a particular existence.[48]

Persona Poems: 'Mariana' and 'Man Jack'

In 'The Three Voices of Poetry' (1953), T. S. Eliot criticised what he saw as the incomplete artifice of Browning's monologues, characterising them as a 'fancy dress' version of the non-dramatic 'second voice' ('the poet addressing an audience, whether large or small'), and noting with approval Ezra Pound's adoption of 'persona' as a technical term 'to indicate the several historical characters through whom he spoke', without claiming for them full dramatic life.[49] Eliot's own early practice, culminating in *The Waste Land* (1922), had taken this insight to a more radical conclusion: once the 'voice' of a lyric poem is split between poet and persona, there is potentially no end to the number of multiplications by division that it might undergo. W. S. Graham had Eliot's example in mind when he wrote about his long poem *The Nightfishing* (1955):

[46] Browning, *Poetical Works*, pp. 399–400 (p. 400).

[47] U. C. Knoepflmacher, 'Projection and the Female Other: Romanticism, Browning, and the Victorian Dramatic Monologue', *Victorian Poetry*, 22.2 (1984), 139–59 (pp. 142–43).

[48] The term 'zone of consciousness' was first used by Hugh Kenner to describe 'The Love Song of J. Alfred Prufrock' (*T. S. Eliot: The Invisible Poet* (London: W. H. Allen, 1950), p. 35), and later by Carol T. Christ to describe Eliot's practice in 'Gerontion' and *The Waste Land* (*Victorian and Modern Poetics*, p. 47); Langley, *Complete Poems*, p. 15.

[49] T. S. Eliot, 'The Three Voices of Poetry' (1953), in *On Poetry and Poets* (London: Faber, 1957), pp. 89–102 (pp. 95–96).

> I needed the dimension in which I could be to a certain extent
> DRAMATIC, and I mean 'dramatic' not so much in the sense
> of creating other spokesmen to speak for me but dramatic in the
> sudden shocking bringing together of different and seeming
> incompatible textures of narrative and gestures of language
> [..] Where, in a short poem, the poetic shock usually has to
> occur in an immediate way, in the very texture of the verse,
> the long poem can also create the massive montage of one such
> theme upon another, one age upon another as in T. S. Eliot's
> *The Waste Land*.[50]

Langley's early lyric sequences, in which different voices overlap
disruptively, can similarly be seen as an attempt to create poetic
drama through 'seeming incompatible textures'. His work underwent
a distinctive stylistic shift in the 1980s, however, which saw him
turning back towards the possibilities of 'creating other spokesmen'.
Speaking in 1996, Langley explained how his later work aspired to
make a 'body' of each poem, following Richard Wollheim's proposal
in *Painting as an Art* that 'painting metaphorizes the body':[51]

> It just occurred to me that [..] my poems weren't very
> body-like. And I might find ... the things that would make
> the poem body would obviously be the small formal elements,
> wouldn't they? [..] those little things that Wollheim talks
> about that make a picture into a body and pull it together as a
> structure and give it a head and a tail and make it exist.[52]

In a note on his own practice following the appearance of *Twelve
Poems* in 1994, Langley reflected on how, after *Hem*, he experimented
with new compositional strategies, such as finding out 'what would
happen if rhyme came back in to do a lot of the running. So, six years
later, "Mariana"'.[53] In this poem, first published in 1984, an irregular
but continual thread of rhyme does indeed do a lot of the 'running',
joining the dots of a laterally moving argument conducted in verse
that adopts a strict syllabic template (here, a line of six syllables), like
the fixed dimensions of a canvas. This 'body-like' effect of formal

---

[50] W. S. Graham, *The Nightfisherman: Selected Letters*, ed. Margaret and Michael
Snow (Manchester: Carcanet, 1999), p. 144.
[51] Richard Wollheim, *Painting as an Art* (Princeton: Princeton University Press,
1987), p. 305.
[52] 'R. F. Langley Interviewed', pp. 241–42.
[53] Langley, *Complete Poems*, p. xvii.

coherence reflects Langley's new framing of his lyric speech within a naturalistic space experienced by a focalising figure: a framing much closer, that is, to the realism of Victorian dramatic monologue.

The choice of the figure of Mariana as a proxy consciousness is loaded with intertextual implication. Tennyson's 'Mariana' (1830) gives a voice to Angelo's mistreated lover in *Measure for Measure*, who is first mentioned in Act III scene 1 ('There, at the moated grange, resides the dejected Mariana').[54] Told in the third person, it is not technically a dramatic monologue, but the dominance of Mariana's depressive state of mind through the poem's eidetic detail ('With blackest moss the flower-plots / Were thickly crusted') make it a precursor to the claustrophobic psychology of Tennyson's later 'monodrama', *Maud* (1855). Langley's 'Mariana' is also presented in the third person, by a speaker who seems to intend a riposte to the ennui of Tennyson's poem ('She only said, "My life is dreary, / He cometh not," she said; / She said, "I am aweary, aweary, / I would that I were dead!"'):[55]

> And, looking out, she might
> have said, 'We could have all
> of this,' and would have meant
> the serious ivy
> on the thirteen trunks, the
> ochre field behind, soothed
> passage of the cars, slight
> pressure of the sparrow's
> chirps – just what the old glass
> gently tested, bending,
> she would have meant, and not
> a dream ascending.[56]

Speaking on behalf of the figure fixed in melancholy by Tennyson's rhyming 12-line stanza, Langley's freer equivalent opens Mariana's confinement up to 'looking out', and to the happier possibility of a gently sensuous world of perception: the optical 'bending' that the

---

[54]   For a response which notes Mariana's various Victorian afterlives, see John Hall, 'A Title in a Constellation of Texts: R. F. Langley's "Mariana"', in *Writings Towards Writing and Reading* (Bristol: Shearsman, 2013), pp. 28–30.

[55]   Alfred Tennyson, *Tennyson: A Selected Edition*, ed. Christopher Ricks, revised edition (London: Longman, 2007), p. 4.

[56]   Langley, *Complete Poems*, p. 8.

glass effects upon the outside world as opposed to the 'ascending' dream of escape.

'Mariana''s tacit rejection of Tennyson's mood music is in the modernist tradition of Eliot ('he had nothing to which to hold fast except his unique and unerring feeling for the sounds of words') and Langley's friend and contemporary, J. H. Prynne.[57] In 'The Elegiac World of Victorian Poetry' (1963), Prynne attacked 'the traditional Tennysonian narcotics' of a post-Romantic lyricism in which lulling melancholy had become the dominant mode:

> Meditative poetry [...] abandoned the ambition to present the reflecting mind as part of an experiential context and withdrew into a self-generating ambience of regret. With this went an amazing degree of control over incantatory techniques, designed to preserve the cocoon of dream-like involvement and to present a kind of constant threshold movement – the apparent movement of a gravely thoughtful mind.[58]

Rather than tolling the 'dream-like' inevitability of Mariana's fate, Langley's free rhyme in 'Mariana' sounds a note of lively invention, weaving in and out of the syllabic verse as it makes connections and extends the poem's thinking about reality and artifice across a stanza – here, with three sentences that converge on a final rhyme-sound ('key' / 'tree' / 'be'):

> It was the old glass cooled
> the colours and transposed
> them in a different key. It
> chastened most of what the
> sparrow said, and made an
> affilatura of
> the tree. She would have known
> the consolation that
> it gave, and smiled to see
> the unthought-of tricks she
> needed, and the sort of
> liar she was, or might soon be.[59]

[57] T. S. Eliot, '*In Memoriam*', in *Selected Essays* (London: Faber, 1951), p. 337.

[58] J. H. Prynne, 'The Elegaic World of Victorian Poetry', *The Listener* (14 February 1963), 290–91.

[59] Langley, *Complete Poems*, p. 9.

The busy technique and subjunctive mood of speculation ('the speaking voice is the making voice', comments John Hall on this poem) is set in deliberate counterpoint to the passive figure of Mariana: Langley's argument is her transposition to 'a different key'.[60]

The major dramatic figure of Langley's later poems is also the spirit of the prosodic tricks that produce him: 'Jack'. Rhyme, Langley said, 'came back in to do a lot of the running' in 'Mariana', and later, so did the sprite-like Jack: '[y]ou know who Jack is don't you? He's that little figure you see running alongside beside the train jumping over hedges and swinging from the telegraph poles'.[61] Jack, in other words, is a projection of rapid perception, an idea partly suggested to Langley by Marion Milner's book *A Life of One's Own* (1934), in which she described how she learned to improve her attention span while listening to a concert performance by 'send[ing] something which was myself out into the hall'.[62] 'Man Jack' (1993), as he is called by the title of the first poem to feature him, is figured as both servant and master, an obedient spirit who leads the speaker on:

> So Jack's your man, Jack is your man in things.
> And he must come along, and he must stay
> close, be quick and right, your little cousin
> Jack, a step ahead, deep in the hedge, on
> edge.[63]

The five poems collected as *Jack* (1998) – 'Man Jack', 'Jack's Pigeon', 'Poor Moth', 'The Barber's Beard', and 'Tom Thumb' – are dramatic monologues which create the voice of Jack's unnamed interlocutor: seemingly autobiographical in the diaristic experiences recounted, but also full of arcane verbal life, much of it drawn from Shakespeare. The passage in 'Man Jack' that momentarily addresses him as a servant figure called 'Tom', for example, echoes the song of winter from *Love's Labour's Lost* ('When icicles hang by the wall [...] / And Tom bears logs into the hall'): 'For all the world Tom poke, Tom / tickle and Tom joke! Go back and carry / logs into the hall'.[64] Echoing the exuberant archaisms of Browning and Pound in their

---

[60]   Hall, 'A Title in a Constellation of Texts', pp. 29–30.

[61]   'R. F. Langley Interviewed', p. 248.

[62]   Marion Milner ('Joanna Field'), *A Life of One's Own* (1934), revised edition (Harmondsworth: Penguin, 1952).

[63]   Langley, *Complete Poems*, p. 5.

[64]   Shakespeare, *Love's Labour's Lost*, V.ii.912–14; Langley, *Complete Poems*, p. 6.

historical monologues, Langley mixes colloquial and Shakespearean English to create a speaker distinct from the reader by idiosyncrasy of speech, yet sympathetic in linguistic vitality.[65]

The lyric drama of *Jack* restages the speculative debate of 'Mariana': some division between the world and the mind must be overcome through the activities of Jack as an intermediary. Langley recorded his own thoughts on the relationship between the Jack poems and the dramatic monologue in the notebooks that he kept as a record of the source materials of his poems.[66] Under an entry titled 'The Pensive Traveller & Jack', Langley copied out a discussion by Neil Hertz of Wordsworth's 1798 blank-verse lyric 'A Night-Piece'. Hertz describes how the poem 'traces the movement of a mind imaginatively engaged with the external world', which at the same time involves 'the transformation of the voice we hear telling the story'. The speaker of 'A Night-Piece' begins by 'calmly and rather distantly observing' a moonlit landscape until, in the ninth line, another figure appears in it: 'the pensive traveller'. Hertz comments how the poem then grows in excitement until its climactic lines, in which 'the speaker's response is indistinguishable from the traveller's'. The emotional movement of the poem, Hertz argues, is not towards 'a more highly individualised subject but a more impersonal and generalised one', so that Wordsworth's last lines ('the mind / [..] Is left to muse upon the solemn scene') encompass poet, pensive traveller, and reader in one reflective 'mind'.[67]

Langley followed the excerpt from Hertz with a reflection on its significance, which begins:

> Here seems to be, then, the disjunction of Jack from RFL at its start, the dialogue that becomes dramatic monologues, and the coalescence in ecstasy in which all such disjunctions hope to end, inside or between poems, at the end of each Jack poem anyway.[68]

---

[65] Pound paid parodic homage to the rococo obscurities of Browning's quasi-Shakespearean diction in 'Mesmerism': 'Aye you're a man that! ye old mesmerizer / Tyin' your meanin' in seventy swadelin's' (*Personae* (New York: New Directions, 1990), p. 13).

[66] See Langley, 'Notes', in *Complete Poems*, pp. 157–74.

[67] Neil H. Hertz, 'Wordsworth and the Tears of Adam', in *The End of the Line: Essays on Psychoanalysis and the Sublime* (New York: Columbia University Press, 1985), pp. 21–39.

[68] R. F. Langley, 'The Pensive Traveller & Jack', unpublished notebook.

The phrase 'the dialogue that becomes dramatic monologues' indicates Langley's familiarity with Langbaum's argument that dramatic monologue continued 'the imaginative apprehension gained through primary experience' of Romantic poetry.[69] Central to this thesis is the characterisation of Romantic lyricism as 'one side of a dialogue, with the other side understood by its effect', in which 'the poet speaks through the observer [...] the way a playwright speaks through his characters', and thereby dramatises a thought process.[70] This 'dialogue' form is nascently present in 'A Night-Piece', which divides and then unites its point of view between unnamed speaker and 'pensive traveller', and is more fully developed in Wordsworth's and Coleridge's 'conversation' poems from the same period – such as 'Tintern Abbey' and 'Frost at Midnight' – in which the speaker explicitly addresses a silent listener.[71]

Langley's comment on 'the coalescence in ecstasy in which all such disjunctions hope to end, inside or between poems, at the end of each Jack poem anyway', suggests (as in 'The Ecstasy Inventories') the possibility that a poem might arrive at a perspective where subjective and objective merge. The Jack poem that affirms this experience most explicitly is 'The Barber's Beard', which concludes:

> This is the moment when,
> flummoxed to know what else to do,
> Jack and the poet and the pronouns shrug,
> take a breath each, and melt into the blue.[72]

Here, the words that created the illusion of different viewpoints within the poem – Jack, 'the poet', and the various other figures identified in the poem as 'it', 'he', or 'they' – are transformed into a flock of fieldfares as they ready themselves for flight ('They are / about to go'). The poem figures the dissolution of its own body in the winter landscape it has been exploring: to use another term from Langbaum (who borrowed it from James Joyce), it is a moment of 'epiphany'.[73]

---

[69]   Langbaum, *The Poetry of Experience*, p. 28.

[70]   Ibid., p. 47.

[71]   Langley: 'I would guess my deepest feelings have always been for Coleridge's Conversation Poems' (*Complete Poems*, p. xii).

[72]   Langley, *Complete Poems*, p. 69.

[73]   Joyce's fictional alter ego, Stephen Dedalus, defines epiphany in *Stephen Hero*, the draft version of *A Portrait of the Artist as a Young Man*: 'by an epiphany he meant a sudden spiritual manifestation' (*Stephen Hero*, revised edition (London: Jonathan Cape, 1956), p. 216).

In *The Poetry of Experience*, Langbaum claimed that the subjective revelation was 'the essential innovation' of Wordsworth and Coleridge:

> Epiphany, in the literary sense, is a way of apprehending value when value is no longer objective [...] The epiphany grounds the statement of value in perception; it gives the idea with its genesis, establishing its validity not as conforming to a public order of values but as the genuine experience of an identifiable person.[74]

Epiphany becomes Langbaum's name for 'the climax of a dramatic action' which 'lasts a moment only' and is a 'victory over [...] an original dissociation of thought and feeling'. The 'poetry of experience' is the lyrical drama that arises from this moment.[75] In a letter from 2004, Langley used 'epiphany' to describe his own inspiration in the post-Jack poem 'Touchstone' (2005), contrasting this with the avant-garde poetic doctrine – advanced by Eliot's theory of impersonality in 'Tradition and the Individual Talent' (1919) – that requires 'the removal of the poet's self as source system'. 'This is where I come from', he commented, 'but also where I have never been, in as much as I write epiphanies. [In "Touchstone"] I face the issue squarely, and even allow that other evil, the unmediated philosophical opinion, direct access, without a persona'.[76]

Yet 'Touchstone' is also concerned with the idea that even the 'personal poem' can be a naturalised form of dramatic monologue. It proposes one of the classic scenarios of Romantic poetry, the lyric poet who listens to a bird singing, which prompts a series of aphoristic reflections on the instantaneous nature ('the idea with its genesis') of such an epiphany:

> Augustine was right.
> There was no 'before'. The world
> set off with time, not into it.
> Accompanied by dusk the
> further phrases sing out
>
> off the line-post, melodic,
> desultory, sweet snatches at

---

[74] Langbaum, *The Poetry of Experience*, p. 40.

[75] Ibid., p. 40.

[76] Personal correspondence, 7 September 2004.

> masks, small personal cheers,
> most of your education for
> these years.[77]

Commenting on these lines, Langley observed:

> 'Personal', so it has been surmised, comes from 'per son' [...]
> through sound, and resulted from the use of dramatic masks
> in Greece, with their sound amplification tendencies. Which
> makes the person find himself in a stage projection, a role.
> This took me to 'snatches at masks' [...] grabs for masks, or
> little songs written for masques, and, keeping 'personal', 'small
> personal cheers', where 'cheers' are the applause, the little
> self-discoveries, or the faces, masks [...] what cheer my love?
> [...] to be found, by the listener, in the clusters of articulations
> in the Robin's song [...] It felt like a little run of discoveries
> rather than the poet's self![78]

Although the experience was 'personal', that is, the experience
of writing the poem was not: it involves the 'self-discoveries' of
artifice, expression that finds form via borrowed thoughts, voices,
and masks. This is also the implication of the poem's title, which
alludes to Touchstone the clown in *As You Like It*, who in Act III
scene 3 famously avers the paradox that 'the truest poetry is the most
feigning'.[79] The Shakespearean allusion is underlined in the final
stanza, which begins: 'It has to be a material fool. / His warranty
tempts me back'.[80] This echoes Jaques' description of Touchstone in
the same scene as a 'material fool' – a fool, that is, with serious matter
to impart – shortly after the clown has affirmed that to be 'poetical'
is not to be honest. In 'Touchstone', however, Langley sets epiphany
against scepticism. The memory of the live song of the robin is his
'material fool', a symbol of the poetic which may yet be a genuine
'touchstone' of reality ('His warranty tempts me back').

---

[77] Langley, *Complete Poems*, p. 109.
[78] Personal correspondence, 7 September 2004.
[79] Shakespeare, *As You Like It*, III.iii.16–17.
[80] Langley, *Complete Poems*, p. 111.

The Speaker in the Picture: Ekphrasis and Presence

Langley's notion of the person as a 'stage projection' is something readers have often commented on. Peter Riley suggests that 'the invitation offered is to a fictive or dramatic process', which in later poems 'focused on the difference of an actor'.[81] Similarly, Adam Piette observes that Langley's development of embodied speakers reflects Richard Wollheim's notion of 'central imagining', which

> entails a temporary act of role-play that cedes agency to the fictional avatar who becomes, fleetingly, the 'protagonist of my project' [...] But that act of identification is only possible because the act of dramatization [...] is dependent on a threefold structure of dramatist, actor, audience, all of whom are necessary corollaries to any imaginative project. In Langley's poems, more often than not, we have creepy triangles [...] which parallel the trifold theatrical points of view in these internalized dramatic monologues.[82]

Piette's conceit of 'creepy triangles' neatly identifies the way in which Langley's poetic voice restlessly switches between subjective and objective: an 'internalized' dramatic structure which informs poems that otherwise appear to have no dramatis personae other than poet and contemplated object. The effect can be called, broadly, ekphrastic, in the double sense proposed by Stephen Benson's discussion of the poetics of description in Langley's *Journals*: 'the restricted modern usage as a verbal description of a visual artwork, and [...] the original sense of the bringing to presence of a scene in the imagination of an auditor, through force of language'.[83]

In 'The Bellini in San Giovanni Crisostomo' (2006), for example, Langley explores one application of Wollheim's central imagining hypothesis: 'the spectator in the picture'. Over the course of this monologue the speaker *of* the poem becomes the speaker *in* the poem,

---

[81] Peter Riley, *A Poetry in Favour of the World* ([London]: Form Books, 1997), n. pag.

[82] Adam Piette, 'Review of R. F. Langley, *Complete Poems*, *Blackbox Manifold*, 16: http://www.manifold.group.shef.ac.uk/issue16/AdamPietteBM16.html [accessed 3 October 2019]. Piette summarises the discussion of 'central imagining' to be found in Wollheim's 'Iconicity, Imagination, and Desire', in *The Thread of Life* (1984), a book cited several times in Langley's notebooks.

[83] Benson, 'Description's Repertoire', p. 40.

absorbed into his own description of Bellini's painting of Saint Jerome (who is figured, by iconographical convention, reading a book). As the poem explores the picture, Jerome seems gradually to come alive:

> the old man's face becomes more than
> it was. His profile is on the
> sky above the mountains. Nor does
> he look at me, but only at
> his book. He veils his eye and sucks
> his lip, as he considers what
> is read. And so it starts to move.[84]

With the next sentence, the observation of the landscape of the painting migrates from the mind of the speaker into Jerome's own consciousness:

> The castles and the clouds and the
> asplenium which I still make
> out, splayed on the rock, are taking
> their places in his head.[85]

This reversal of perceptions then spreads beyond the frame of the picture to include the smallest particular from the life of the present-day speaker:

>   Each
> thing he brings is sharp as a stone
> which I discover as I shake
> my shoe.[86]

'The spectator in the picture', writes Wollheim,

> need not be a particular person [...] he may be any old person. But – and this is the point I am making – what he must be is a person. He must be a perceiving, thinking, feeling, acting, creature. What he cannot be is a merely disembodied eye [...] unless he can do more than perceive, as a person can, he cannot offer, through identification with himself, distinctive access to the content of the picture.[87]

---

[84]   Langley, *Complete Poems*, p. 120.
[85]   Ibid.
[86]   Ibid., p. 121.
[87]   Wollheim, *Painting as an Art*, p. 30.

Transposing this idea to a poem about a picture, Langley makes his speaker, with the stone in his shoe, just such an unparticular 'person'. As well as being the eye through which we look at a painting, he has a physical life of his own, which takes place within the frame of the church's nave, and makes him a part of all that is implied by the title's metonymic elision of artwork and artist; as he looks at 'the Bellini', he becomes another Bellini, absorbed by the painterly intensity of feeling with which Jerome has been imbued. The poem ends with the hope that

> the next words he reads will
> mention me, as someone waiting
> in the nave, at twilight, here in
> line fifty-seven, arrested
> by green and rose. By rose and brown.[88]

Counting its own lines, the poem has become self-conscious, a speech that contains its own speaker, who – by his present-tense participation – gives the reader 'distinctive access' not to the picture itself but to a person 'arrested' by an epiphany of colour. Bellini's painting does not speak, but by being spoken of, it comes alive; by being seen, it sees. To borrow a paradoxical term from Langbaum's discussion of Gerard Manley Hopkins's 'Harry Ploughman' (a sonnet that evokes the physical beauty of a rural labourer), the effect of Langley's ekphrasis here might be called 'mute dramatic monologue': it gives voice not to the verbal quirks of character, but to the particularity of physical presence.[89]

Langley's exacting yet tentative poetic manner, suggests Vidyan Ravinthiran, is 'a style of cultural enquiry, into how disparate minds could possibly meet'.[90] Such a lyric 'I' is the opposite of the classic monster of dramatic monologue, whose pungent subjectivity invites a diagnosis of narcissism. For Langbaum, 'My Last Duchess' is a quintessential dramatic monologue precisely because of the way that it creates 'tension between sympathy and moral judgement'.[91] But the notion of the dramatic monologue as a detective genre – in which the rhetorical performance of self reveals a 'real' self, between

---

[88] Langley, *Complete Poems*, p. 121.

[89] Langbaum, *The Poetry of Experience*, p. 65.

[90] Vidyan Ravinthiran, 'All the Animals in My Poems Go into the Ark', *Poetry*, 207.4 (2016), 409–25 (p. 418).

[91] Langbaum, *The Poetry of Experience*, p. 80.

the lines – has perhaps been too readily agreed as its defining essence.[92] Taking up Langbaum's emphasis on the impression made on the reader, Cornelia D. J. Pearsall has proposed instead that 'the genre might ultimately be defined [..] by the processes it initiates and unfolds'; specifically, the performative transformation of a self through speech:

> The form of the dramatic monologue itself represents speech seeking to be efficacious, to cause a variety of transforma-tions. The act of the dramatic monologue, its performance of thoughts, simultaneously creates a self and alters that self, and may perhaps ultimately destroy the self it held so dear.[93]

Pearsall cites Browning's 'The Bishop Orders His Tomb at Saint Praxed's Church', in which the dying speaker seems to transform his mortal body by imagining its memorial form ('And stretch my feet straight forth as stone can point').[94] And it is even possible to read 'My Last Duchess' as a performance concerned with such a metamor-phosis: the one thing that can be said for certain about Browning's poem is that it creates a vivid *impression* of a suave psychopath who had his young wife murdered rather than endure disobedience. But what if this is, in fact, a fictional self the widowed Duke *wants* to create, a rumour he has decided to spread for political purposes? The hypothesis cannot be disproved because the actor cannot be separated from the act: it is a condition of dramatic monologue's omniscient subjectivity that there is nothing beyond the moment of speech.

Another late ekphrastic Langley poem, 'The Best Piece of Sculpture in Perugia' (2007), seems to be in dialogue with Browning's evocation of Renaissance Italy as a place of high art and brutal politics, while exploring monologue as a form of lyrical self-realisation, grounded in the unfolding notation of the phenomenological reality of a speaker. It begins:

---

[92] See, for example, John Lennard, *The Poetry Handbook*, second edition (Oxford: Oxford University Press, 2006): '[t]he *dramatic monologue* [...] has a single speaker throughout, not the poet, whose mind and character are revealed by what s/he does/n't say' (p. 57).

[93] Cornelia D. J. Pearsall, 'The Dramatic Monologue', in *The Cambridge Companion to Victorian Poetry*, ed. Joseph Bristow (Cambridge: Cambridge University Press, 2000), pp. 67–88 (pp. 71, 84).

[94] Pearsall, 'The Dramatic Monologue', pp. 71–72.

> Old vendettas, and no
> details of them, or whose
>
> heads were on the spikes. I
> don't want to go down this
>
> sad, steep street.[95]

The melancholy tourist who speaks this is heading towards a transformative encounter with the marble relief on the façade of the
Oratorio San Bernardino known as 'The Obedience', by Agostino
di Duccio (1418–c. 1481), which depicts a robed woman pulling
the yoke of a plough. Like Browning's Duke, ventriloquising 'Frà
Pandolf', the painter of the Duchess's portrait, Langley's speaker
describes this representation of a female figure in sensuous and
attentive terms (Browning: 'perhaps Frà Pandolf chanced to say
"Her mantle laps / Over my lady's wrist too much [...] the faint
half-flush that dies along her throat"'; Langley: 'her right // hand
catches up her cloak. / Her body rouses to // the surface, luminous /
and streaming drapery').[96] In Browning, this animating tenderness
serves to heighten the murderous coldness with which the Duke cuts
off his story: 'I gave commands; / Then all smiles stopped together.
There she stands / As if alive'. But in Langley, the ekphrastic
moment transcends the horror of historical consciousness with
which the poem began:

> Now there is nothing on
>
> spikes to hurry by. No
> guilt in the voice or shame
>
> in the eye. It is her
> lovely marble, tawny
>
> white, one rim of it scrazed
> red, and many pearly
>
> passages bruised with
> dim mussel blue. She knows
>
> that it behaves for her.
> Her mouth is opening

---

[95] Langley, *Complete Poems*, p. 137.
[96] Browning, *Poetical Works*, p. 368; Langley, *Complete Poems*, p. 137.

but she is wondering
what I can find to say.

She is *Obedience.*
All of my audience.[97]

The final off-rhymed couplet lightly suggests both the theme and the form of Browning's monologue: the tightly rhyming Duke, having been unable to command obedience from his wife, now extracts it from his audience. As in the Bellini poem, however, Langley's Perugian epiphany – or ecstasy – involves the surprise inversion of subject and object: 'she is wondering / what I can find to say'. The speaker, it seems, has not spoken at all and the sculpture has not been an 'audience' in the usual sense of a silent witness; rather, like a duchess, she has granted an audience. In his notebook sources for this poem, Langley copied out a passage from *The Rough Guide to Italy* on Perugia's violent history; a paragraph from the art critic Adrian Stokes on how pleasure in the contemplation of natural things (and also, art objects) transforms them into 'powerful people with whom we miraculously entertain a rapport that eludes jealously';[98] and an extract from a book by the philosopher Drew Leader, which argues that Western thought has become trapped within a Cartesian dualism that undervalues body at the expense of mind – a thesis encapsulated in Leader's title, *The Absent Body* (1990). If reading the poems of R. F. Langley allows us to rethink the conventional definition of dramatic monologue as a lyric genre in which speakers 'present' themselves for judgement, the simplest way to do this may be to hear that verb as the opposite of 'absent'.

[97]   Langley, *Complete Poems*, p. 139.
[98]   Adrian Stokes, 'On Resignation', in *A Game That Must Be Lost: Collected Papers*, ed. Eric B. Rhodes (Cheshire: Carcanet, 1973), p. 77.

CHAPTER TEN

Nocturne

J. H. Prynne Among the Stars

Edward Allen

I.

Our closest celestial neighbour has been in the news a lot of late. NASA's ambition to get back to the Moon and engineer a Deep Space Habitat was renewed with a vengeance under the last US administration, and it is thought now that the Lunar Orbital Platform will be in place just in time for a crewed landing in 2024.[1] The name of that projected mission, Artemis, will seem to some a rather gauche reminder that lunar exploration has an ancient history; we need only look back to the fiction of Lucian to see that the Moon has long weathered the advances of imperialists and fanatics, even if more recent despots seem to have trumped their classical forebears in recognising the Moon for what it is, a satellite rather than an epigonic planet.[2] That the Moon continues in today's news cycle to make waves should come as no surprise to us, perhaps; that is what our Moon does, and has done, day in day out, for as long as anyone can remember. The writings of the geographer Pytheas of Massalia are now lost to us, and with them his record of daylight hours and tidal patterns along Britain's coastlines. But the Moon Pytheas is thought to have

I would like to thank Sophie Read, who oversaw an early draft of this work one cold fortnight in 2008. Thanks, too, to David Rowland, for his encouragement and advice, and to the many students with whom I've discussed Prynne and night songs in the last few years, particularly Jerome Lim and Charlotte Howson.

[1] Paul Rincon, 'Nasa Moon Lander Vison Takes Shape', *BBC News* (23 July 2019): https://www.bbc.co.uk/news/science-environment-49084696 [accessed 3 October 2019].

[2] See Lucian, *Verae Historiae*, ed. and trans. A. M. Harmon (Cambridge, MA: Harvard University Press, 1913), [section 11].

been tracking at the end of the fourth century BC – 'the fulness of the moon gives the flow, the wane the ebb' – that selfsame Moon exerts a pull still on the itinerant imagination, and on the kind that would have us see the poetry as well the politics, as Charles Olson once did, in 'Pytheus' sludge [*sic*]'.[3]

I want in this chapter to pick up where Olson left off, and to dwell on the night writing of one of his last regular correspondents. It's 1966 – a crisp March evening – and Jeremy Prynne is keeping watch.

Moon Poem

The night is already quiet and I am
bound in the rise and fall: learning
to wish always for more. This is the
means, the extension to keep very steady
    so that the culmination
    will be silent too and flow
    with no trace of devoutness.

Since I must hold to the gradual in
this, as no revolution but a slow change
like the image of snow. The challenge is
not a moral excitement, but the expanse,
    the continuing patience
    dilating into forms so
    much more than compact.

I would probably not even choose to inhabit the
wish as delay: it really is dark and the knowledge
of the unseen is a warmth which spreads into
the level ceremony of diffusion. The quiet
    suggests that the act taken
    extends so much further [..].[4]

In its dissembling regard for the usual formalities, 'Moon Poem' is not the first of its kind to sense disquiet in the quietness of nightly ritual. Here, quietness is not so much broken by the line break as

---

[3] Pseudo-Plutarch, *Placita Philosophorum*, 3.17.3, trans. from the Greek by several hands, corrected and ed. William W. Goodwin (Boston: Little, Brown, & Co., 1874), p. 104; Charles Olson, *The Maximus Poems* (1960–75), ed. George F. Butterick (Berkeley: University of California Press, 1983), I.78, p. 82.

[4] J. H. Prynne, 'Moon Poem', in *The White Stones* (1969), repr. *Poems* (Hexham: Bloodaxe, 2015), pp. 53–54 (p. 53).

encouraged by it to distend – 'The quiet / suggests ...' – and among the things to arise by way of suggestion is the influence of another sentinel, Samuel Taylor Coleridge, whose enraptured predicament in 'Frost at Midnight' ("'Tis calm indeed! so calm, that it disturbs / And vexes meditation') sets the scene in Prynne's case for musings no less abstruse.[5] Unlike Coleridge, who spies in his soliloquy a 'companionable form' in the dying embers of the hearth (that 'sole unquiet thing'), Prynne's attention to the possibility of locating an interlocutor is rendered shapely by 'the knowledge / of the unseen'. This, too, appears to give off some metaphysical heat, 'a warmth which spreads into / the level ceremony of diffusion'; yet it may be that Prynne comes closest to sounding Coleridgean, not in his desire to fetishise the silence, or to do so 'with no trace of devoutness', but in the extent to which he knows, with Coleridge, that the search for a companionable form is not only an ontological concern when it comes to dreaming up a conversation poem, but a prosodic one too.

Although Prynne has recourse twice in 'Moon Poem' to the spectre of 'form' – once to its 'dilating', once to its 'insurgence' – his interest in that word as a *rhythmic* category is stealthily realised in the poem's very opening breath. Among the first things to gather about this breath-turned-voice is the extent to which its apparatus of feeling, the semblance of a waking subjectivity, is enfolded in the kinetic life of its subject. Having settled quickly into 'the rise and fall' of a predictably sleepy routine, the issuing body turns, 'learning / to wish always for more', as though taken by the pulse of an alternating current, first this way, then that. Fumbling for a foothold, our urge to scan these lines might be quite strong in its way, and so the experience of reading the poem – of feeling stirred to somatic procedure – might seem very close indeed to the experience of getting the measure of a memory like 'Frost at Midnight'. Coleridge's sly purchase on 'the numberless goings-on of life, / Inaudible as dreams!' was never meant to preclude the hum and fingerwork of metrical analysis, and no more should we assume that 'Moon Poem' isn't intended to spark a similar quality of attention to pulse or pacing, or to play with our expectations of a patterning logic that may seem fitting precisely because it's fitful.

If, as one critic puts it, the blank verse of Coleridge's poem 'lets itself be mistaken for prose', then 'Moon Poem' conceivably counts upon our making a similar sort of mistake, or double take, in response

[5] Samuel Taylor Coleridge, 'Frost at Midnight' (1798), in *Samuel Taylor Coleridge*, ed. H. J. Jackson (Oxford: Oxford University Press, 1985), pp. 87–89.

to its modulations in and out of a phantom verse technique.[6] Eliot's thought about 'even the "freest" verse' has rarely sounded so apposite – that a mode like this seems 'to advance menacingly as we doze, and withdraw as we rouse' – though we might hesitate to conclude that what Prynne's trying to do amounts in any emulative fashion to Eliot's sense of 'mastery'.[7] On the contrary, such cute pockets of rhythm as we find in 'Moon Poem' are as likely to indicate the in-rush of a tender, child-like apprehension as the exhibition of a polished prosodic theory – something akin to the creak of a cradle song, perhaps, whose words have been half-forgotten but whose play of stress and cadence is still there, somewhere, bundled up in a kind of lyric muscle memory. I've often wondered what 'a toy of Thought' should look like, in Coleridge's teasing phrase. I'm still not quite sure – it remains a worry – but I wonder now whether Prynne's 'learning / to wish always for more' betrays a similar air of whimsy, born of the shadowy object life that structures a 'nursery consciousness'.[8] Soft toys, of course, play an important role when the lights go out on early infancy, but D. W. Winnicott himself was keen to stress that just about anything can provide the comfort of a comforter in those dark days of maturation: 'a bundle of wool or the corner of a blanket or eiderdown' – one of these will often do – but so might as slight a thing as 'a word or tune, or a mannerism'.[9] If such things can be termed 'transitional objects', it doesn't seem too much of a stretch to conclude that the essential components of lyric – a well-turned phrase, the hard-won image – should provide their own form of succour. Theirs is not a mnemonic integrity alone, we might feel, but a textured sort of materiality, which tickles even as it attenuates anxiety.

It is a truism that life's slightest things come back to haunt us at night; that's one of the reasons that old phrase, *the small hours*, can sound so belittling. The same may pertain to this order of lyric,

[6]   Ewan Jones, *Coleridge and the Philosophy of Poetic Form* (Cambridge: Cambridge University Press, 2014), pp. 35–39 (p. 36).

[7]   T. S. Eliot, 'Reflections on *Vers Libre*' (1917), in *To Criticize the Critic and Other Writings* (London: Faber, 1965), pp. 183–89 (p. 187).

[8]   Prynne, *Stars, Tigers and the Shape of Words: The William Matthews Lectures 1992 Delivered at Birkbeck College, London* (London: Birkbeck College, 1993), p. 10.

[9]   D. W. Winnicott, *Playing and Reality* (New York: Routledge, 2005 [1971]), pp. 2, 5. My thinking in this passage chimes with that of Charlotte Howson, whose work on lullaby and lyric theory is also inflected by Winnicott's theory: 'Lyric in the Wings: Reading Lullaby' (unpublished MPhil thesis, University of Cambridge, 2020).

in which the 'merest acoustic accident of a word' is wont to rise up, unannounced, suddenly bigger than you'd think in the clear light of day.[10] This is one way to make a sort of non-sense of the poem's recourse to what the *OED* calls 'nouns of condition or action': 'Moon Poem' is gently rippled with them – 'extension', 'culmination', 'revolution', 'diffusion', 'notion', 'condition', 'affliction', 'passion' – and it will probably seem a small thing that the thing holding each and all of them together is a variety of '-tion'.[11] To imagine that something is going on in and between these nouns at the level of sonic design might lead you to suspect, with Prynne, that 'some element of motivation has come into them by virtue of the history of their formation'.[12] It's not an easy thought to shun – motiva*tion* in forma*tion* – and in this case it might prompt a further thought, which is that there's something particular about the twilight, something terminal even, that promises to efface the arbitrary nature of the language we use to organise our last waking moments.[13] 'To take sounds and embedded part-words out of the phonetic or graphic shapes of words is to treat them like objects', Prynne admits, 'as a child might do and also an alert reader of poetry; we habitually call this activity "word-play", as if it were not quite real or not quite grown-up'.[14] 'Moon Poem' indulges this type of activity, surely, and indulges *in* it. Yet the end to which those endings set off a specific kind of reading must be considered something more than a midnight feast, for they intimate too, as object lessons do, the limits of a reading captivated by its own capacity for distraction. Here, again, we might sense a ticklish materiality, but it would be a mistake to assume the blinking white noise (*-tion -tion -tion*) signals an end in itself.

That way madness lies – or lunacy – and once you begin 'to recognise the signs', as this poem tempts you to, then it does get harder to say how playful 'playful over-reading' can be before it slips too firmly into the realm of wish fulfilment.[15] If you're minded to hear a teeny whimper in 'it really is dark', for instance, or to imagine

---

[10] Prynne, *Stars, Tigers and the Shape of Words*, p. 15.

[11] Cf. entries in the *OED* for compound suffixes *-ion* (*-s-ion*, *-t-ion*, *-x-ion*).

[12] Prynne, *Stars, Tigers and the Shape of Words*, p. 9.

[13] The *OED* helpfully confirms that the Latin suffix in question is 'equivalent to the native ending -ing' to which Fiona Green draws attention in this volume's first chapter: 'Aubade: Jorie Graham and "the pitch of the dawn"', pp. 13–36 (pp. 17–18).

[14] Prynne, *Stars, Tigers and the Shape of Words*, p. 16.

[15] Ibid., p. 10.

a breath and nose held wistfully to the window – 'I must hold to the gradual in / this, as no revolution but a slow change / like the image of snow' – then it would be as well to notice these projections for what they are, toysome but densely imbricated with the instincts of the worldly-wise. For 'Moon Poem' is certainly a lyric of and about desire, too, and the lengths we go to understand it, or fail to. That all-important word arrives later in the poem entwined with another – 'pastoral desire' – so that the mind preoccupied with moon-gazing appears at the height of its vision to contemplate its grounds for feeling settled. This is not to say that it is entirely down-to-earth about its conduct – 'ethical' or not – or that the sensation of 'dispers[ing] into the ether / as waves' doesn't have something of the extraterrestrial about it. Yet nor, even in this light, would it be easy to lose sight of 'the compact modern home', which stands in awkward relation to 'the steppe' of some uncharted territory. There is, as Sophie Read suggests, a 'constricted and crossed desire' running through this poetry, a desire whose possible sublimation recedes as each 'wish' suffers articulation – sounded and singly expressed at first, then shared, divvied up into so many 'wishes' – in service of collective ambition.[16] Was this the dream all along – 'learning / to wish always for more' – to wish away singularity?

Prynne's is a style of dialectical poetic thought that pulls you, by definition, in two directions. Just as the promise of 'wide personal vacancy' would have you think the grass beyond is greener, something happens to prompt a perspective shift, like the 'mere', say, in 'the mere wish to wander at large', which has the effect of sizing up and scaling down the thought that *Wanderlust* has made it big. There was a lot of that in the air in 1966 – moon walking was not such a distant prospect any more – such that Prynne might be said to have made a virtue of his occasion. Yet the telling thing about 'Moon Poem' – its obduracy, in fact, which results from 'the working encounter with contradiction' – is its quiet, unshakeable conviction that a new frontier will not satisfy 'this / pastoral desire', because the wish to wander, however 'mere' it seems, 'will never end'.[17] There is an arc to Prynne's

[16]   See above, Sophie Read, 'Pastoral: "Language-Landscape Linkage" in Michael Haslam's Verse', pp. 55–78 (p. 59).

[17]   Prynne, 'Poetic Thought', *Textual Practice*, 24.4 (2010), pp. 595–606 (p. 597). My discussion here is inflected by David Herd's piece, 'Prynne and Olson', in *For the Future: Poems & Essays in Honour of J. H. Prynne on the Occasion of His 80th Birthday*, ed. Ian Brinton (Bristol: Shearsman, 2016), pp. 196–215.

meditation, in keeping with this periodic logic, which might pass for a homecoming. This was not lost on the first reader of 'Moon Poem', but to suggest, as he did, that the 'we' alone appears to 'bring it home' feels a little off.[18] It doesn't sound to me like a 'we' in those closing lines, but an 'I', rather, re-embodied and re-enchanted, mindful of the hushed fiction that gave rise (and fall) to the night in question.[19]

*   *   *

It cannot be such an uncommon thing to lose sleep over Jeremy Prynne. In view of a poem calculated to rouse and provoke, one recent critic has logged a frank catalogue of woes – he claims to have felt 'unwell' on appraising Prynne's *Acrylic Tips* (2002) – and has done so knowing that his complaint has a history.[20] Few bodies of work have challenged readers so completely to reflect on the changing nature of their own embodiment as reading subjects, or to confront the possibility that a poem's not agreeing with them might be the very reason to hold their nerve. Prynne's poetry raises significant questions as to how cognition and affect actually happen for his readers, and what having a thought or a feeling about a thought can feel like in the heat of lyric happenstance. The 'bite and burn' of such encounters remains a vivid memory among his early converts, for whom the experience of sharing worksheets and small print runs – eyes open, lights dimmed – seemed an 'awakening' like no other.[21] And for once the cliché's apt. For the material in question, *without* question, was intended to scramble its readers' photoperiodic rhythms, and to give in that way a startling substance to the run of darkling metaphors – obscure,

[18]   Olson to Prynne, 11 March 1966, *The Collected Letters of Charles Olson and J. H. Prynne*, ed. Ryan Dobran (Albuquerque: University of New Mexico Press, 2017), p. 173.

[19]   Prynne himself attends to the possibilities of the plural pronoun – 'a code or screen for the singular' – in *They That Haue Powre to Hurt: A Specimen of a Commentary on Shake-speares Sonnets, 94* (Cambridge: [privately printed], 2001), p. 5.

[20]   Timothy Thornton, '*Acrylic Tips*', in *On the Late Poetry of J. H. Prynne*, ed. Joe Luna and Jo Lindsay Walton (Brighton: Hi Zero & Sad Press, 2015), pp. 77–86 (p. 77).

[21]   Iain Sinclair, 'Hearing Light', in *For the Future: Poems & Essays in Honour of J. H. Prynne on the Occasion of His 80th Birthday*, ed. Ian Brinton (Bristol: Shearsman, 2016), pp. 227–36 (p. 227).

opaque, shady, shrouded – in which a certain kind of modernist difficulty has often been thought to consist. It did so, I want to suggest, by providing a poet who claims to have never been 'much of a morning person' with a formal correlative for his nocturnal habits. 'My natural habitat seems to be the hours of darkness, *ad libitum*', so he's said. 'So I'll be pretty useless until about ten thirty or eleven a.m. at best: but at the other end of the day I never tire'.[22]

It is no secret that the hours of darkness gave rise to 'Moon Poem'.[23] That's part of the story, but not all of it. On the same day Prynne penned the poem, 2 March 1966, his daily paper ran a piece that might have passed for a valediction:

> After the Moon, Venus. Never again will the imperial votaress pass on in maiden meditation, fancy free; always she will have with her a nagging memory of the humiliation of that soft landing and that garrulous gadget Luna 9 ensconced on her breast. Now she has a sister in misfortune. Love's Harbinger, the Evening Star, victim of the same cold scientific invaders, bears the weight of a robot visitor from earth which, adding insult to injury, has on board a Soviet pennant and coat of arms. That is no way to treat a darling of the poets. At the news, if it reaches, as it is bound to do, the Elysian Fields, quires of the old sonneteers and balladmongers will be making quill pens splutter, as they wrathfully indite denunciatory verses.
>
> Alas, poetry cannot alter facts.[24]

The context for this editorial was a sequence of more-or-less successful attempts by the Soviet space programme to overtake its US counterpart in early 1966. Luna 9 had been the first probe to survive a moon landing on 3 February that year, and Venera 3 is thought to have reached the Venusian surface on 1 March; although its communications system had failed some weeks before, Venera 3's close encounter with Venus was celebrated all the same.[25] The *Daily*

[22] Prynne, 'The Art of Poetry No. 101' [interviewed by Jeff Dolven and Joshua Kotin], *The Paris Review*, 218 (2016): https://www.theparisreview.org/interviews/6807/j-h-prynne-the-art-of-poetry-no-101-j-h-prynne [accessed 3 October 2019].

[23] See Prynne to Olson on 3 March 1966, *The Collected Letters*, p. 170.

[24] 'Venus in Eclipse', *The Times* (2 March 1966), 13.

[25] See Asif A. Siddiqi, *Beyond Earth: A Chronicle of Deep Space Exploration, 1958–2016* (Washington, DC: NASA History Division, 2018), pp. 55–56, 51.

Express had been quick in the first instance to laugh at lyric's expense: the surface of the Moon 'is spongy', it had seemed to one reporter, 'and – alas for the poets – it is not silver or even cheese-green: it is CHOCOLATE'.[26] Four weeks on, *The Times* for its part could not bring itself to sugar-coat the latest development, and its message to the Jeremy Prynnes of the world was graver still. Having decreed that 'poetry cannot alter facts', the editorial reroutes its logic and suggests – with Racine 'put into reverse' – that the very syntax of the *ancien régime* is up for review: '"C'est Vénus toute entière à sa proie attachée" needs to be sadly twisted. For Venus herself has become the prey'.[27]

There would have been several reasons to deride this line of thinking at the time. As literal-minded as it is misty-eyed, *The Times* miscalculates the reach of the imagination even as it purports to be advocating poetry's cause, for who could seriously claim that poets have played no part in rendering celestial bodies objects of fancy or desire? The Moon is many things, but 'fancy free' it is not, and never has been. It is hard, too, looking back, not to wince at the clumsiness of the editorial's parting shot – 'Your fiery darts are missiles to be guided to the Kremlin' – which pits the muse of 'amatory poets', Eros, against all those 'cold scientific invaders'. Make no mistake, the reds were still in people's heads, if not under their beds, in '66.

But not, it would seem, in Prynne's. In its closing reference to 'the grace which is open to both east and west', 'Moon Poem' openly refuses, with some grace, to rehearse the political attitudes embedded in the newspaper editorial.[28] And yet there are things about the piece which must have seemed to Prynne on that day in March 1966 inadvertently perceptive. There was no immediate need to worry about 'old sonneteers and balladmongers', or new ones for that matter – formalists of one stripe or another would continue long after the '60s to squeeze these imperialist exploits for rhyme and reason – but the journalist was not wrong to imply that there were other kinds of writer for whom these events already had the look of a renaissance.

---

[26] 'From Luna 9 to Manchester: THE *EXPRESS* CATCHES THE MOON', *Daily Express* (5 February 1966), p. 1. The *Express* was particularly quick to publicise this scoop because a team of its journalists had found a way to intercept the Soviets' signal at Jodrell Bank Observatory.

[27] 'Venus in Eclipse', p. 13. The famous line – 'it is Venus herself who is fastened on her prey' – comes from Racine's *Phèdre* (1677), ed. Richard Parish (London: Bristol Classical Text, 1996), I.iii.306, p. 13.

[28] Prynne, 'Moon Poem', in *Poems*, p. 54.

One such kind was the social realist, whose purchase on 'the terrestrial space race' would hinge precisely on the fact of its mundanity: just think of John Updike's unlikely hero, Harry Angstrom, who remains to this day a crucial witness to the machinations of Apollo 11, not because he finds himself glued to the TV, but because he can't help feeling he's come unstuck ("'I know it's happened, but I don't feel anything yet'").[29] *The Times* could scarcely bring itself to contemplate such prosaic wonderings that spring. But nor was it quite ready to imagine the ways a different kind of writer might respond to its claim that the whole matter had been 'thrown over to prose', or to the unspoken caveat – a corollary of that claim – that lyric should suddenly find itself pervious or annexed to styles of discourse that appreciate the facticity of 'facts'.

In its sensitivity to 'this insurgence of form', I believe, 'Moon Poem' speaks to that dicey condition. Taken together, the poem and editorial might also be thought to amplify a broader set of questions that had begun to inform Prynne's practice as poet and teacher. His records reveal a special effort in the mid-'60s to steer students towards a scheme of work as rich in prose as poetry – 'a worthwhile experiment', he liked to think, though nothing more than 'a starting-point' – and indeed his own course of reading demonstrates a certain degree of fluidity in this regard.[30] His correspondence with Olson gives us some sense of that reading's scope, and of the extent to which it drew the men into a form of transatlantic alliance at just the moment Prynne longed to give the balladmongers of 'Betjeman's England' the slip.[31] His disaffection comes through loud and clear in the early letters – from the very first he talks of 'provincial squeamishness' – but the real interest of the correspondence has to do with a shared commitment, thickening with every missive, to 'the development of our modern cosmology'.[32] With access to extensive libraries, and to experts in relevant fields – astronomy, geophysics – Prynne was more than a source of information to Olson in the closing stages of *The Maximus Poems*; he was also a kind of shadow aspect, or second self, whose own writing from the period begins to show up not only the strength of

---

[29]   John Updike, *Rabbit Redux* (London: Penguin, 2006 [1971]), p. 86.

[30]   Prynne outlines his '"course" of readings' in a dispatch to Olson, 17 May 1965, *Collected Letters*, pp. 126–27.

[31]   Prynne to Olson, 26 November 1961, ibid., p. 16.

[32]   Prynne to Olson, 4 November 1961, ibid., p. 11; 28 December 1963, ibid., p. 77.

Olson's influence, but its limits too. When Prynne writes mooningly to his ageing valentine in February '66 – wanting to 'recognize with whatever twist to it that we are, post Pythias [*sic*], the starting-point for so much else outward from here' – it's just possible to tell that something's on the wane.[33]

It has become clear in recent years that Prynne's development as a cosmologist was not without its setbacks or second thoughts. 'For Charles', one redacted dedication reads, 'the shades of Manilius, Henry Howard, Earl of Surrey, & the Department of Geodesy and Geophysics in the University of Cambridge [England]'.[34] The accompanying poem, 'The Wound, Day and Night', has been known to readers since its appearance in *The English Intelligencer*, but there are others of this sort – poems shading into nocturnes – that have never seen the light of day. Following the publication of his first, suppressed volume, *Force of Circumstance and Other Poems* (1962), Prynne set his mind in '64 to a new collection, *Under the Fixed Stars*; when that idea came to nothing, he appears again to have drifted in focus, perhaps in keeping with the sense of one of his new poem's 'lovely tides' – later cast away – that his central concern should be 'an alternate gravity'.[35] The revised and expanded collection, slated for publication in '66, was to be called *In Sight of the World*.[36]

Quite apart from their serving to illuminate our sense of his re-formation as a poet, these aborted plans do help to clarify the particular ways in which the connection between cosmology and lyric practice took its time to crystallise for Prynne. They provide in that respect a suggestive prelude to the work I'm going to undertake in the third section of this chapter, though I intend there to steer a different course to the one undertaken by most Prynneans. In recent years, and for good reason, critics have come to see 'The Ideal Star-Fighter' (1971) as a pivotal lyric in his development, and an important moment for Anglo-American poetics in general.[37] The piece itself recalls a pivot of historic proportion – 'the backward / glance' performed by

---

[33] Prynne to Olson, 21 February 1966, ibid., p. 167.

[34] Prynne, 'The Wound, Day and Night', Folder 1501, MS Add.10144, J. H. Prynne Papers, University Library, Cambridge (hereafter, JHPP).

[35] Prynne, 'Love For & Granted', Folder 1597, MS Add.10144, JHPP. Folder 1516 contains a provisional contents page for *Under the Fixed Stars*.

[36] See Folder 1597, MS Add.10144, JHPP.

[37] See, for instance, Ed Luker, 'J. H. Prynne's Cosmology', *Textual Practice*, 33.7 (2019), 1131–53; and Stephen Ross, '"Nature is bad art": Bad Transnationalism from Earthrise to Deep Horizon', in *Navigating the Transnational in Modern*

Apollo 8 in December '68 – memorialised forever in William Anders's 'Earthrise' photograph.[38] Prynne's was not the first to do so, and in a way, that's the point. Where others had rejoiced right away to 'see the earth as it truly is', he pauses in 'The Ideal Star-Fighter' to see *through* the picture, not to salvage an event evacuated of its aura, but to articulate his own reaction to 'the reaction of sentiment' for which the snapshot has already become an icon.[39] The significance of Anders's vision, to a mind appalled by 'mawkish regard', consists in the nature of its mediation, the fact of its being 'shattered to a granulated pathos' as it passes 'daily' through the 'switchboard', 'the printed circuit', and the 'photochemical dispatch'. Prynne thinks of it as an 'image of suffered love'. Today, we'd call it a meme.

It is an important, absorbing poem, and one whose subject – 'the news image' – would aggravate Prynne for some time to come. Just a month or so after the poem's publication, he turned to it again, 'that unbelievably gross photograph', with a view to disabusing an audience in Vancouver of its cosy sentiments.[40] That this picture might in some way have captured what it feels like to look on the 'earth as home' – the very idea – seemed to Prynne a matter of 'stunning alienation', and a reason to wonder whether anything, even a lyric, can go the distance of an 'obscure epic' such as Olson's. Prynne wished to get the measure of his late correspondent, that much is clear, but I do not believe for an instant that he meant on this occasion to disavow his own 'lyric set-up'. His readings in subsequent days would suggest quite the opposite – he seemed glad to give in to 'popular request' – though listeners may have blinked a little incredulously to hear Prynne *not* reciting 'The Ideal Star-Fighter'.[41]

They should not have been surprised, I think. Not because that poem doesn't have things to tell us about the cosmos, or lyric, or the daily news cycle – it evidently does – but because its blending of

American Literature and Culture, ed. Tara Stubbs and Doug Haynes (New York: Routledge, 2017), pp. 33–51.

[38] Prynne, 'The Ideal Star-Fighter', in *Poems*, pp. 165–66.

[39] Archibald MacLeish, 'A Reflection: Riders on the Earth Together, Brothers in Eternal Cold', *The New York Times* (25 December 1968), 1.

[40] Prynne, 'Lecture on *Maximus IV, V, VI*', Simon Fraser University, 27 July 1971, transcribed by Tom McGauley, *Iron* (October 1971): http://charlesolson.org/Files/Prynnelecture1.htm [accessed 3 October 2019].

[41] Prynne's readings in Vancouver on 30 July and 1 August 1971 are archived online: http://www.archiveofthenow.org/authors/?i=77 [accessed 3 October 2019].

those things is realised, unswervingly and to a shameless degree, at the expense of a form Prynne had perfected well before the dawn of 'Earthrise'. On a number of counts – the 'tidal flux', a glint afforded by its Byronic shimmy ('We walk / in beauty down the street'), its objection to 'lethal cupidity' – it's true that 'The Ideal Star-Fighter' would not look out of place among the dark dreams Prynne began to articulate in March '66;[42] yet in one important respect – its prominent triadic structure – the poem appears also to make too much of a form we find more subtly achieved in the pieces of '66–'68. As it happens, these are exactly the pieces Prynne used to structure his reading tour of Vancouver in '71 – 'Moon Poem', 'In Cimmerian Darkness', 'Star Damage at Home', 'As It Were An Attendant' – and I want to return to some of them in this chapter, to think again about how and why they appeal to a returning soul.

My claim, simply put, is that these poems would seem to reward a musical mode of reading. I say *would seem* because I want to be clear that any notion that such poems could or should be treated as musical objects is a fiction. It is, however, an operative fiction, an irresistible one. In allowing myself to entertain it in Prynne's case – to see the sense in what must otherwise be considered one of the oldest category errors going in the history of poetics – I intend to stress-test a form that migrated long ago from the repertoire of musical composition into a mode of textual practice whose supposed formal properties (rhythm, tone) sound similar but are crucially not identical to those at stake in the proverbial song without words. Having come to terms with this migration, some might argue that almost any poem in *The White Stones* could be called a nocturne; most of them were written at night, after all. But my intention here is to narrow the definition somewhat in order to account for the kind of poem that would appear to summon music – as a point of reference or *idée fixe* – with a view to seducing a reader into fancying that some sort of analogical relation is at work. Giving in in this sense to the operative fiction is not merely to take the poetry at its word – 'Music is truly the / sound of our time' – but to make sense of the way Prynne completes the thought, since logic insists that music 'is how we most / deeply recognise the home we may not have'.[43] What might it mean, in the terms of that poem, to 'mimic the return', to feel

---

[42] Prynne is remembering Byron's nocturne 'She Walks in Beauty', in *The Major Works*, ed. Jerome McGann (Oxford: Oxford University Press, 2008), p. 258.

[43] Prynne, 'Thoughts on the Esterházy Court Uniform', p. 100.

'the pulse very / slightly quicken[ing]' at the touch of a 'warm hearth', to witness 'the profane sequence suddenly graced' – notice the turn – 'by / coming back'?[44] As we'll see, and hear, Prynne's commitment to homecoming is part and parcel of a broader cosmological project; but the argument I wish to prosecute here is that the local recursions of lyric are central to that epic-sounding project, that the fantasy of homecoming is, so to speak, never more at home than when it's unfolding within the parameters of a nocturne. First, to chapel.

II.

People have always found songs to sing at night. From the earliest stirrings of rite and liturgical process in the Christian church, variations on the 'nocturn' have been used to mark and structure a particular office in the canonical hours. At first this was known as the Office of the Vigils, in deference to the night watch recounted in the Gospels; in time, however – and certainly by the fourth century – it had dilated in such a way as to require formal divisions, hence the adjectival colouration to be found in the *Rule* of Saint Benedict (516 AD). There we hear a good deal about the timings and protocols of *nocturnae vigiliae*, though the word drifts occasionally into something that looks a bit like a noun in its own right, as in chapter 15, where Benedict explains the seasonal role of the Alleluia: *A Pentecosten autem usque caput Quadragesimae, omnibus noctibus cum sex posterioribus psalmis tantum ad nocturnos dicatur.*[45] The divisions in question – *nocturnos* – involved an uneven blend of prayer, psalmody, and plainchant, thick with the kind of antiphonal textures that still characterise a number of the divine offices, sung and spoken. And it's a blend, of course, to which Prynne himself gestures at the end of 'Moon Poem' in the twinkling of an eye. For his is no ordinary music but a music that finally suggests the flash of Revelation: 'These are psalms for the harp and the shining / stone: the negligence and still passion of night'.[46]

---

[44]　Ibid., pp. 99, 100.

[45]　*The Rule of Saint Benedict*, ed. and trans. Bruce L. Venarde (Cambridge, MA: Harvard University Press, 2011), pp. 60, 76. ['Every night from Pentecost until the beginning of Lent, [the Alleluia] should be said only with the last six psalms at Vigils'.]

[46]　Prynne, 'Moon Poem', *Poems*, p. 54. For an extended reading of Prynne's biblical debts – as well as his debts to Hölderlin and Heidegger – see James Keery, '"Schönheit Apocalyptica": An Approach to *The White Stones* by J. H. Prynne',

But for a poem like Prynne's, you would be hard-pressed to detect so much as a vestige of the early nocturne in the night writing of late modernism. If a post-war lyric thrums, it will have more to do with 'the private motor-car' cruising through it, or the 'Pepsi-Cola sign' that has come to occupy it – brightly, fizzingly – than the strain of a well-pointed psalm.[47] In one of the few recent attempts to anatomise the genre, Erik Martiny has drawn attention to the nocturnes of Auden and O'Hara precisely because they appear to him to be doing something different with the night, even if the 'tonight' in question has the look of 'umpteen other nights'.[48] Martiny is determined to make a virtue of the modern nocturne's quotidian nature, a form divested of its once numinous possibilities, and one wholly at odds therefore with the kind of 'nocturnals' to have appeared in the early decades of the seventeenth century.[49] This, in Chris Fitter's view, had been a more than usually intense period of experiment and definition, in which an essentially motivic style of witness had changed almost beyond recognition, from 'tradition' to 'cult', 'topos' to 'genre'.[50] Religious orthodoxies had played a part, as had the infiltration by a number of continental artistic practices; taken together, these had given rise both to a particular kind of devotional mode, such as we find in Donne's 'A nocturnall upon S. Lucies day', and to the revival of a supernatural one, born in many ways of the masque tradition, but now transposed to lyric proper. The 'Cavalier fairy-nocturne', in Fitter's memorable phrase, 'offered the reassurance of an enchanted conservatism, Catholic in dignity and wrought with courtly preciosity'.[51]

Jacket, 24 (November 2003): http://jacketmagazine.com/24/keery.html [accessed 3 October 2019].

[47] W. H. Auden, 'Nocturne' (1951), in *Collected Shorter Poems: 1927–1957* (London: Faber, 1969), pp. 283–84 (p. 284); Frank O'Hara, 'Nocturne' (1955), in *The Collected Poems of Frank O'Hara*, ed. Donald Allen (Berkeley: University of California Press, 1995), pp. 224–25 (p. 225); Erik Martiny, '*Nox Consilium* and the Dark Night of the Soul: The Nocturne', in *A Companion to Poetic Genre*, ed. Erik Martiny (Oxford: Wiley-Blackwell, 2012), pp. 390–403 (pp. 396–97).

[48] Auden, 'Nocturne', *Collected Shorter Poems*, p. 284.

[49] For more on the early modern night – its complexion and the strategies adopted to light it up – see A. Robert Ekirch, *At Day's Close: Night in Times Past* (New York: W. W. Norton, 2006).

[50] Chris Fitter, 'The Poetic Nocturne: From Ancient Motif to Renaissance Genre', *Early Modern Literary Studies*, 3.2 (September 1997), 2.1–61: http://purl.oclc.org/emls/03-2/fittnoct.html [accessed 3 October 2019].

[51] Fitter, 'The Poetic Nocturne', 2.48.

Skipping ahead to the graveyard shift of the Augustans, we begin
to see the emergence of a third way. Although he hesitates to say that
these were the years in which the nocturnal mode lost its magic – that
it did so, to a perceptible degree, was the result of industrialisation in
part, and of street lighting in particular – Martiny advocates strongly
for the effects of a Gothic turn. Robert Blair's and Edward Young's
studies in blank verse, *The Grave* (1743) and *Night-Thoughts* (1742–45),
were not so much a dead end for prosodic technique as a provocation
to other kinds. And it follows, according to this telling, that the
likes of 'Carrion Comfort' and 'Dover Beach' should be considered
signal cases, not because they indulge in the doom and gloom of a
Blair or Young, but because they signify flashpoints in a tradition
of meditative writing whose thematic singularity had threatened so
often to attenuate its capacity, structurally speaking, to look alive. In
their different ways – distressing the sonnet, pushing towards a *vers
libre* – Hopkins and Arnold perfectly demonstrate the extent to which
'done darkness' has become the medium, and not just a backdrop, for
an undreamt and tormented formalism.[52]

That both poets could be said to have raised 'confused alarms' in
doing so should give us pause.[53] For the issue at stake in these cases
evidently pertains – beyond their estrangements of voice, verse, and
sensibility – to the complex dynamic between definition and expectation that underwrites all such encounters with lyric. Would we feel
more or less astonished by 'Dover Beach' if it were actually called a
nocturne? And what of Arnold's first readers? One way to ascertain the
relative weight of such counterfactuals would be to assume a quanti-
tative approach, thereby generating a fine-grained view of the term's
fluctuating currency across period designations. Such a view might
confirm my own sense that the 'nocturne' enjoyed a curious revival
among the modernists, high and late: Langston Hughes, Federico
García Lorca, Thomas MacGreevy, Louis MacNeice, Gabriela
Mistral, Sylvia Plath – Auden and O'Hara too, of course – each of
these startlingly different poets returned to it in their own time with
a view to treating it as a thing as well as a concept.[54] But what the

[52]   Gerard Manley Hopkins, 'Carrion Comfort' (c. 1887), in *The Major Works*, ed.
Catherine Phillips (Oxford: Oxford University Press, 2002), p. 168.
[53]   Matthew Arnold, 'Dover Beach' (c. 1851), in *The Major Works*, ed. Miriam
Allott and Robert H. Super (Oxford: Oxford University Press, 1987), p. 146.
[54]   Langston Hughes, 'Nocturne for the Drums', in *The Collected Poems of
Langston Hughes*, ed. Arnold Rampersad (New York: Vintage, 1994), p. 108;

computer wouldn't allow me to do is work out whether any of those iterations demonstrate so much as a hint of fidelity – or learned resistance – to the term's historical freight. Nor would it afford me much insight into the paradox that some poems, though spared the name, may be closer to the real thing than 'nocturnes' apparently blessed with that entitlement. As it is, Martiny's impressionism won't do. 'Like the aubade', he claims, 'the nocturne harbors a rather limited set of expectations. When faced with a poem entitled "Nocturne," the only expectations most readers have will be that the poem is going to deal with a generally soothing or comforting contemplation of the beauties of a night scene'.[55] *Only? Most?* I wonder. What are 'most readers' really like? Genre-minded, for sure, and prone sometimes to a certain kind of essentialism; but are most readers so dozy as to imagine that a nocturne is only one thing, or that a piece by any other name doesn't count?

It should go without saying that a survey of this genre is bound to founder if it assumes too strict or loose an approach to naming nightly musings. No more is it likely to succeed if it imagines that readers only read. It is hard to think of a modernist better placed to appreciate that fact than Frank O'Hara, for whom the word 'nocturne' in 1955 will have conjured the spectre of a nineteenth-century form long since tailored to the operations of mixed media. In his own workspace, New York's Museum of Modern Art, O'Hara would have grown used to seeing cityscapes of the sort he himself depicts in 'Nocturne', such as Armin Landeck's dry point vision, *Manhattan Nocturne* (1938). But he'd have known too the heightened pedigree of an earlier, rival style championed by a man after his own European heart, James McNeill Whistler. Scotopic, rich in splash and blur effect, and softened to the point of abstraction – *Nocturne in Black and Gold: The Falling Rocket* (1875) is just one of four dozen oils to have taken nocturne for a name – Whistler's experiments in this vein were always intended to

Federico García Lorca, 'Nocturnos de la ventana', 'Ciudad sin sueño. Nocturno del Brooklyn Bridge', 'Nocturno del hueco', in *Poesía Completa*, ed. Miguel García-Posada (New York: Random House, 2012), pp. 135–37, 442, 457; Thomas MacGreevy, 'Nocturne', 'Nocturne of the Self-Evident Presence', 'Nocturne', 'Dream Nocturne', in *Collected Poems of Thomas MacGreevy*, ed. Susan Schreibman (Dublin: Anna Livia Press, 1991), pp. 1, 42–43, 51, 85; Gabriela Mistral, 'Nocturno de la consumación' and 'Nocturno de la derrota' (among others), in *Tala: Lagar* (Madrid: Cátedra, 2001), pp. 92–96; and Sylvia Plath, 'Aquatic Nocturne', in *Collected Poems*, ed. Ted Hughes (London: Faber, 1981), pp. 305–06.

[55] Martiny, '*Nox Consilium* and the Dark Night of the Soul', p. 396.

confound the horizon of expectation established by the Hudson River School.[56] 'By using the word "nocturne"', he once declared, 'I wished to indicate an artistic interest alone, divesting the picture of any outside anecdotal interest which might have been otherwise attached to it. A nocturne is an arrangement of line, form, and color first'.[57]

Or so he liked to claim. In fact, Whistler had to admit that the name he'd bestowed on his 'moonlights' had come down to him from Fryderyk Chopin: 'You have no idea what an irritation it proves to the critics [...] it is really so charming and does so poetically say all I want to say and no more than I wish!'[58] He would not be the last to feel stirred by Chopin. 'I was listening to a Chopin Nocturne when I woke up' – this is O'Hara again, in 1953 – 'and suddenly felt so unalterably great just by the contact with it that I swear that I must have thought I was Homer at the edge of the sea'.[59] Whatever else these roguish snapshots betray, it should be clear that 'comforting contemplation' accounts in no way for the projected affect of the form in question. It could be that Martiny's thinking of the most famous one of all – the Notturno for horn and orchestra by Felix Mendelssohn – when he nods in passing to 'the mellifluous musical composition'.[60] Yet even a cursory listening to that schmaltzy interlude will reveal something more complicated about its conditions of possibility than Puck would have us presume when he intoxicates the sylvan lovers ('Auf dem Grund schlaf' gesund ...').[61] What *is* it about the Romantic nocturne that has kept its listeners guessing?

When Mendelssohn came to write his Notturno in 1842 in the course of a royal commission, his decision to do so must have looked

[56]   See Hélène Valance, *Nocturne: Night in American Art, 1890–1917*, trans. Jane Marie Todd (New Haven and London: Yale University Press, 2018).
[57]   Minutes of the Whistler-Ruskin trial, repr. in Linda Merrill, *A Pot of Paint: Aesthetics on Trial in Whistler v. Ruskin* (Washington, DC: Smithsonian Institution Press, 1992), p. 144.
[58]   Whistler to Frederick Richards Leyland, 2–9 November 1872, in *The Correspondence of James McNeill Whistler, 1855–1903*, ed. Margaret F. MacDonald et al., http://www.whistler.arts.gla.ac.uk/correspondence [accessed 3 October 2019].
[59]   O'Hara to Larry Rivers, 27 June 1953, cit. in Olivia Cole, 'Frank O'Hara's "To the Harbormaster"', *The Paris Review* (15 December 2011): https://www.theparis-review.org/blog/2011/12/15/to-the-harbormaster/ [accessed 3 October 2019].
[60]   Martiny, '*Nox Consilium* and the Dark Night of the Soul', p. 396.
[61]   'On the ground / Sleep sound [...]'. Op. 61, No. 7 (*Ein Sommernachtstraum*, 'Con moto tranquillo (Notturno)') is prefaced by Puck's spell from Act III scene ii, in a mixed translation by Wilhelm Schlegel and Ludwig Tieck (*Musik zu Sommernachtstraum von Shakespeare* (Leipzig: Breitkopf & Härtel, 1874), p. 123).

doubly belated. He'd started work on *A Midsummer Night's Dream* in July 1826, after all; this he'd called a 'grenzenlose Kühnheit', and for 16 years all he'd had to show for that particular attack of 'boundless boldness' was a programmatic overture (Op. 21).[62] At the time of the overture's composition, the young Mendelssohn had already called something a *notturno* – the hendectet (Op. 24) from 1824 – but it was not until the 1830s that a composer's choosing to write such a thing could be considered a meaningful pursuit rather than a mere indicator as to what time of day a piece of this sort should be performed. Thanks to a variety of material coincidences – the growth of salon culture, a readier supply of sheet music, more sophisticated instruments, and changing attitudes to pedalling technique – the nocturne had begun to make a name for itself in the late 1810s as a regular feature of Romantic piano literature; by the early 1830s, it had developed in the hands of John Field into a self-supporting genre: a *romance sans paroles*, usually in a major key, and usually comprised of a repeating figure (in the left hand) and a simple melody, given to ever more elaborate levels of decoration, in the right.[63]

Where Field might be thought to have spied a gap in the market, Chopin appeared in the 1830s to tax the genre, performer, and listener in new and unsettling ways, thereby setting the nocturne apart from the lullaby and its continental relatives, the *berceuse* and *Wiegenlied*, which would continue to enjoy lives of their own. Chopin did so by embedding in his nocturnes precisely the type of dynamic, structural shift we later hear in Mendelssohn's Notturno in the form of an *agitato* (see Figures 10.1 and 10.2). Following the restatement of his first theme, Mendelssohn shifts to the relative minor (C# minor), and instigates a triplet figure that has the effect of building in volume and rhythmic intensity. It's a subtle and by no means radical shift in modality; the harmonic progression is tempered to some degree by chordal inversion, and you can sense where the melodic line is going in the top violin part because its impetus is drawn, rhythmically speaking, from the preceding horn motif. But you do feel something – a temporary escalation, a quickening of attention, a distortion of

[62] Felix Mendelssohn to Fanny Mendelssohn, 7 July 1826, Mendelssohn Family Correspondence (New York Public Library). For a detailed analysis of the work's genesis, see R. Larry Todd, *Mendelssohn: 'The Hebrides' and Other Overtures* (Cambridge: Cambridge University Press, 1993), pp. 11–20.

[63] See David Rowland, 'The Nocturne: Development of a New Style', in *The Cambridge Companion to Chopin*, ed. Jim Samson (Cambridge: Cambridge University Press, 1992), pp. 32–49.

Figures 10.1 and 10.2.
Felix Mendelssohn, *Ein Sommernachtstraum*,
'Con moto tranquillo (Notturno)', Op. 61, No. 7 (1844).

mood – and when the first theme returns some 40 bars later, back in the home key, it would be hard to maintain that nothing's changed.

Although the episode is typical of Mendelssohn's late orchestral writing, the shade of Chopin is palpable in those crucial transitional bars. Of the eight nocturnes Chopin composed in the period 1830–35 – the period of the composers' most intimate contact with one another, in Munich and Paris – four of them harbour just such an episode; he would go on to pen five more, evidently convinced by the pattern and its evolving possibilities.[64] In each of these, he fabricates an idiosyncratic structure, loosely modelled on a ternary form (A-B-A). He makes use of that form elsewhere, notably in the mazurkas, which often involve a literal return to thematic material by way of conclusion. The mature nocturnes, though given to recapitulation, are different. There is often a wonkiness about their triadic structure, owing to the abbreviation of repeated 'A' material, which can feel like a subtle kind of memory error. And that sense of confabulation is hard to see in the round because the interludinal section (the 'B' material) is never less than contrastive in character: it either mutes and softens – through plainchant, hymn, or reverie – or it scares the nocturne out of its wits. In the F major nocturne, Op. 15, No. 1, the nightmare episode could not come more abruptly (see Figure 10.3). Having returned to his opening subject, Chopin breaks off in bar 24 in the fashion of an aposiopesis – mid-phrase, mid-bar – before plunging into the tonic minor. A key change, a new rhythmic pattern, a leap in melodic ideation, and markings to match (dynamic, expressive, and metronomic): taken together, these agitations of mood and texture witness a rhetorical strategy that we hear time and again in the nocturnes. It is a strategy manifestly designed to reveal depth where you'd only suspected surface, a depth achieved in this case by the melodic line passing from the right hand into the left, and passing quickly through a two-octave compass, down and up, as it appears to shake off the composer's opening directive (*semplice e tranquillo*).

If, as Edward Said once claimed, canon makers have been wrong to assume that 'the word *salon* pretty much sums [Chopin] up', then it's also true to say that his being an 'astonishing revolutionary' doesn't

---

[64]   The nocturnes in question are Op. 9, No. 3 (B major); Op. 15, No. 1 (F major); Op. 15, No. 2 (F# major); Op. 27, No. 1 (C# minor); Op. 32, No. 2 (A♭ major); Op. 37, No. 1 (G minor); Op. 37, No. 2 (G major); Op. 48, No. 2 (F# minor); and Op. 62, No. 2 (E major). Many recordings are available, though Arthur Rubinstein's first interpretation, for EMI in 1936–37, is still hard to beat.

Figure 10.3.
Fryderyk Chopin, Nocturne in F major, Op. 15, No. 1 (1834).

quite account either for the fact that the nocturne came to possess
a surprisingly descriptive impetus on his watch: his are nocturnes
that can and do appeal to a programmatic sensibility, to that part of
a listening self which will not rest until it has determined the shape
of a drama at the heart of even the most simply structured lyric.[65] In
one way, then, Whistler's gilding of the genre in the 1870s might
indicate a significant departure, predicated as it seems to have been
on frustrating anecdote and projections of character. But that, I think,
is where Chopin's practice was heading all along. In the manner of
ersatz apparitions, his nocturnes merely *seem* to ghost the possibility of
drama – its semblance rather than a fully embodied representation of
it – and they do so, just as Whistler's are wont to, in order to wake us
up, to spotlight our most unthinking attachments to particular kinds
of scene and scenario, to spook us out of our readerly orthodoxies
even as they might appear to supply an alternative. Learning to expect
the unexpected would be one way to describe the experience of that
alternative. Having, as another nighthawk once put it, to 'earn [our]
insights' would be another.[66]

[65] Edward W. Said, *Musical Elaborations* (London: Chatto & Windus, 1991),
pp. 59–60.
[66] Prynne to Olson, 26 November 1961, *The Collected Letters*, p. 16.

III.

When *Kazoo Dreamboats; or, On What There Is* appeared some years ago, readers were excited. And not just by the kazoo. Here, it seemed, was belated proof of Prynne's listening habits, or an indicative list at any rate: Chinese rock, Greek lyric, Christian Wolff, *Wozzeck*. But what to do with these 'reference cues'?[67] That should remain an open question, for Prynne's attitude to song, and to the supposed musicality of lyric, has rarely suggested any degree of stability. Back in 1962, the poet's 'memory bank' was still filling up, and with its filling thoughts surfaced about a certain strain of music making, remarkable for its 'self-generating ambience of regret'. This will have struck an odd chord with some listeners in December '62 – Frank Ifield's chirpy cover of 'Lovesick Blues' had been top of the charts for five weeks – but Prynne's target that Christmas was in fact 'Dover Beach'. In its day, he claims in his BBC talk, this type of meditative lyric had been underwritten by a gamut of 'incantatory techniques' whose purpose had been 'to preserve the cocoon of dream-like involvement and to present a kind of threshold music'.[68] Given Prynne's eagerness at this time to recant his first collection ('[z]ip-fastener type of thing'), 'cocoon of dream-like involvement' must have sounded to those in the know like a personal stitch-up.[69] Yet to what ends precisely, it is still hard to say, for Prynne's 'threshold music' would not go quietly. Though he seems, looking back, to have recognised his predecessors' complicity in touching up 'the industrial north' – 'every / songbird [..] has carolled about / that beautiful black colour' – he also appears to have sensed the possibility that one or two ('the Nightingale come / down from the hills') would continue to pipe the usual lyric jargon.[70]

Strange things do come to light as day turns into night, and you could be forgiven for mistaking the coalface for a source of false lyric glitter:

---

[67] Prynne, 'Reference Cues', in *Kazoo Dreamboats; or, On What There Is* (2011), in *Poems*, p. 662. Prynne's prefatory remarks in the event of a reading in Cambridge (27 November 2011) can be heard here: https://www.archiveofthenow. org/authors/?i=77&f=1766#1766 [accessed 3 October 2019].

[68] Prynne, 'The World of Elegy', broadcast on the Third Programme, 15 December 1962; later published as 'The Elegiac World in Victorian Poetry', *The Listener* (14 February 1963), 290–91 (p. 290).

[69] Prynne to Olson, 28 September 1962, *Collected Letters*, p. 39.

[70] Prynne, 'Shadow Songs', in *Poems*, p. 81; 'Die A Millionaire', in *Poems*, p. 15.

Small flares skip
down the coal
    face   how can I
       refuse them
              the
warm indolence
    of fancy the
solace of wheels
   muffled in sheep-
skin
   then Bruckner
on the radio & how
  easily I am taken
    from the hearth &
returned
         changed
  & unnoticed   it
is the pulse of
birch tar &
   molten amber
           the
  estranged blood
in the vein.[71]

In wondering why it is he can't 'refuse' the spectacle of fireside rumination, Prynne quickly gets to the nub of what's fuelling this poem. Coal is nothing but refuse, after all – a carbon deposit, composed of impacted organic matter – and to think of refusing something is not only to show it the cold shoulder, but to ignite it once more.[72] Prynne is attentive to the buried seams of words, just as he is in this case to the integrity of coal itself, whose formation, layer upon layer, is recollected in the strata of the poem's lineation, right down to the 'birch tar & / molten amber'. It may be that the and-turned-ampersand is as significant as the matter it's connecting. For some, perhaps, it symbolises a showy kind of shorthand: a mini act

[71] Prynne, 'Sun Set 4·56', in *Poems*, p. 153.
[72] See *OED*, 're-fuse', *v*. 2. I'm minded to subject 'refuse' to particular scrutiny in this case because of Prynne's drafting process. A manuscript in the archive reveals that, at some point along the line, Prynne thought better of 'how can I not gaze', and opted instead for 'how can I / refuse' (Folder 1502, MS Add.10144, JHPP).

of rebellion, and a sure sign of 'swiftness'.[73] But it would be a mistake to think that Prynne has only typographic expedience in mind, or that the poet's work, as Allen Ginsberg once bragged, equates to 'a secretarial job'.[74] What might it mean to look on the ampersand here as a kind of trace fossil instead, not the preserved remains of a ruined organism, but the ghostly imprint of its last gasp or 'pulse', a grasping gesture suspended in time? For even as he presses his matter into place, compressing conjunctions and cracking open words to reveal unstudied complexions ('coal / face'), Prynne also prompts us to imagine that there's something metamorphic about this found sedimentary medium. His is a poem of and about transformation – alchemical, linguistic, fabular ('muffled in sheep- / skin') – but the most striking transformation of all is that of a voice warming to its vocation, a voice whose reluctance to refuse refuse in the dying moments of the day provides at once the scene & fuel for the rehearsal of a distinctly Romantic sensibility.

We have been here before, certainly, and it won't be the last time. Prynne would return some years after this poem to the subject of coal-fired lyric, and to the example of Blake's industrial-age nocturne in particular. 'The process of imaginative transformation is metamorphic and is done in the mind-furnace', he remarks of 'The Tiger'; '[t]he words are both agencies of expression and also a material substrate for smelting and re-working into new forms'.[75] As in Blake's case, so in Prynne's, there is something of the heat shimmer about 'Sun Set 4·56', and it is no easier to say in this instance whether such an effect is the figment of a lonesome but contented imagination – 'the / warm indolence / of fancy' – or the by-product of a more tangible sort of venture in historical materialism. Either way, it will be clear that these *are* poems 'to which music stands in an especially salient relation' – that's Christopher Ricks's formulation – but it should be equally clear that the quality of that relation is not continuous between the two.[76] If 'The Tiger' is crouched somewhere between nursery rhyme and hymn, then 'Sun Set 4·56' confounds the possibility of practicable rendition in favour of internalising the spectacle of reception.

---

[73]   Allen Ginsberg, 'The Craft Interview' (1970), repr. in *The Essential Ginsberg* (New York: Penguin, 2015), pp. 297–311 (p. 303).

[74]   Ibid.

[75]   Prynne, *Stars, Tigers and the Shape of Words*, p. 30.

[76]   Christopher Ricks, *T. S. Eliot and Prejudice* (London: Faber, 1988), p. 158.

It does so by dramatising the apprehension of suddenly feeling one's ear tugged. '[T]hen Bruckner / on the radio' signals a turn in this poem, a warping of attention that is of a piece with the distortion of mood for which the musical nocturne supplies the quintessential blueprint, as we have seen. Because what Prynne is saying at the centre of 'Sun Set 4·56' is that the interlude has worked its magic, not by collapsing the lyric's structure of feeling, nor by extinguishing the thing that sparked it, but by effecting a subtle and definite move in thought towards connecting deep time and domesticity. Only at this point, as one crackle gives way to another, radio for fire, might we recognise the world within that homely word – 'hearth' – which contains *earth*, and the *heat* long embedded within it, but also perhaps the aspirated whisper of something circling back into earshot. For as well as his being a forensic philologist, Prynne is a Kentish lad at heart – that too is at stake in this fireside rumination – so we can bank on his knowing that 'hearth' is a southern dialect word for 'hearing', nourished by a knotty string of Germanic verbs (*híeran, hôrjan, hôrren, hauzjan*). To tend a hearth, in local speak, or indeed to be 'widin hearth' – this, we might say, is what it once meant to domesticate an ear.[77]

It may be enough to say that Prynne has always kept his own to the ground, though we should hesitate to determine anything as precious-sounding in his case as the fealty or quality of 'Englishness' – 'a kind of piety towards their local origins' – to which Seamus Heaney once attributed the work of Hughes, Hill, and Larkin.[78] 'Sun Set 4·56' first found a home in *Brass* (1971), a collection characterised time and again by critics as a turning point in Prynne's praxis, and a turning away from the 'hoarders and shorers' of Heaney's digging expedition.[79] There *is* something more than usually testy about that collection – one reader characterises it memorably as a stark confrontation of 'anti-pathos' – yet it should be clear on looking back to *Brass*, and to the poems published but uncollected at the end of the '60s, that Prynne's seeming to take aim more forcefully at politicians and current affairs was not at all a bolt from the blue.[80] Nor was it

[77] 'hearth', n. 2: 'the sense of hearing; hearing-distance; (also) something which is heard'. The *OED* refers to Parish and Shaw's *Dictionary of the Kentish Dialect* (1887): 'I called out as loud's ever I could, but he warn't no wheres widin hearth'.
[78] Seamus Heaney, 'Englands of the Mind' (1976; 1980), repr. in *Finders Keepers: Selected Prose, 1971–2001* (London: Faber, 2002), pp. 77–95.
[79] Ibid., p. 77.
[80] David Trotter, *The Making of the Reader: Language and Subjectivity in Modern American, English and Irish Poetry* (Basingstoke: Macmillan, 1984), p. 197. Whilst

a shot in the dark. Feeling his way through 'the incessant *passage de nuit*', and ever-attuned for that reason to the pointed arrangements of sonic material – to aria shading into chorus, to 'flocks / of songsters' and 'credal echoes', to all the ways the most remote events assume a 'life in / the ear' – Prynne's recourse in *Brass* to song as a medium for critique is utterly consistent with the project first touted in *The White Stones*.[81]

There are readers of Prynne to whom the non-verbal arts have sometimes seemed, quite reasonably, the only option going. '[T]here are [...] many poems with which I never expect to make any headway', Robert Potts admits, 'however often I return to them, and which might as well be music. Or nonsense'.[82] The difficulty of *The White Stones* is of a different order. Rather than figuring music as the last word in epistemological enquiry – a sort of go-to no-go discourse when words look set to fail – Prynne moves in this collection to make a musical way of knowing a vital and efficacious part of his subject's homework. For that is what it is, a collection about home: the sights and sounds of it, the sickness of it, the double edge of missing it, of wanting it but falling short. You can feel these attitudes material-ising across the collection in small repeated gestures – love, passion, dreams, hearts, stars – almost as though they were (in the strict 'musical / sense') a kind of theme or *leitmotif*, susceptible to embel-lishment, diminution, shifts in key, and the like.[83] This is something more than mood music. For *The White Stones*, though more than the sum of its parts, is no less interested in the way those parts might put such thematic material to work, so that the form of any given poem might itself become a vehicle for nostalgia. If the end of the collection's opening number sounds like Prynne is stuck in the Eliot loop – 'the end of our exploring / Will be to arrive where we started' – then it would be as well to notice that his coming full circle with 'love', 'back / to where / we are', is about as close to an articulation

---

reiterating that *Brass* should be considered a 'fracture' in Prynne's corpus, Keston Sutherland observes that the thinking in that collection was already detectable in the second half of *The White Stones* ('XL Prynne', in *Complicities: British Poetry, 1945–2007*, ed. Robin Purves and Sam Ladkin (Prague: Litteraria Pragensia, 2007), pp. 43–73 (p. 54)).

[81]　Prynne, 'Lupin Seed', in *Poems*, p. 174; 'The Kirghiz Disasters', in *Poems*, p. 157; 'Wood Limit Refined', in *Poems*, p. 164.

[82]　Robert Potts, 'Smirk Host Panegyric', *LRB*, 38.11 (June 2016).

[83]　Prynne, 'Thoughts on the Esterházy Court Uniform', p. 99.

of ternary form as you could hope to find in a poetry perplexed by its own flightiness.[84]

'Airport Poem' sets the agenda in this way for a sequence of neo-Romantic nocturnes, all of them, I would say, exercised by the guilty pleasure of sleepwalking into a learned routine. 'Love', a mere slip of a lyric, knows 'the night is young' and makes a show – a mockery, even – of harnessing the tonal exuberance of dreamers who 'ride / the bel canto of our / time'; 'Night Song', likewise, takes shape 'in the fading daylight', but sounds less than full-throated as it dawdles over disambiguating the origins of 'our passing / sounds'.[85] This, too, shades into a loose kind of ternary form – 'Come back to the step I call as the house / turns and it is almost night' – and there is something feverish about the way such poems go about triangulating the fantasy of recursion. The 'I's and 'you's so often take care of themselves in Prynne's early poetry, or seem to; but what of the 'they's who come and go unnamed in 'Night Song', 'calling / for the sick ones', or of the 'we's to whom 'Moon Poem' gravitates?

Questions along these lines are not easy to resolve, in part because Prynne's pronouns provide cover for so many kinds of clandestine activity and activism. Even as that socialising 'we' appears to accrue a degree of integrity across the collection, flashes of resistance serve here and there to confuse and multiply its internal differences. Where, for instance, a diasporic 'we' reconciles itself in 'Song in Sight of the World' to wondering at a night 'beautiful / with stars', no such consolation is to be found in 'Star Damage at Home'; there, a watchful community elects instead to pick out 'some star / not included in the middle heavens', a community convinced that the threat posed by the music of one sphere in particular – 'its fierce & / unbearable song' – should disturb 'this / fertile calm'.[86] This is a poem possessed by its own modality and capacity to mean – 'we must make room for / the celestial victim [..] We live here / and must mean it' – and the challenge in the event of any reading is to take account of its choric impetus without seeking to naturalise the deep-seated contradictions for which that show of impetus is a front rather than a solution. These contradictions have been

---

[84] Eliot, 'Little Gidding', *Four Quartets*, in *The Poems of T. S. Eliot*, ed. Christopher Ricks and Jim McCue, 2 vols (London: Faber, 2015), I, p. 208; Prynne, 'Airport Poem: Ethics of Survival', p. 38.

[85] Prynne, 'Love', in *Poems*, p. 118; 'Night Song', in *Poems*, p. 119.

[86] Prynne, 'Song in Sight of the World', in *Poems*, p. 76; 'Star Damage at Home', in *Poems*, p. 108.

variously characterised over the years, no more suggestively perhaps than by Anthony Mellors, to whom the presiding spirit of *The White Stones* has the look of a nomad in search of a home, a figure 'stuck oscillating wildly between sceptical spleen and cosmic ideal'.[87] This captures something of Prynne's ebb and flow, but it hardly accounts for the overdetermined sense of urgency that is peculiar to 'Star Damage'. Surely this poem's 'must's and 'mean's must mean something, and must mean something more than a crash course in Heideggerian critique?

Whatever we now wish to make of its existential convolutions, inlaid in the sparkling texture of *The White Stones*, it would have been hard to mistake the target of 'Star Damage' at the end of the long, hot summer of 1967.[88] In its glancing reference to 'civil war / in the U.S.', the poem looks to 'fix the eye' on Lyndon Johnson's Great Society, and thus to scrutinise an administration for whom two long-standing but ostensibly unconnected policy commitments – space travel and civil rights – had escalated by that time to the point of crisis. The first had suffered a setback in January '67, following Apollo 1's disastrous rehearsal at Cape Kennedy; the second had discovered renewed expression in a series of violent race riots, unprecedented in scope, whose momentum had been attributed instantly at both ends of the political spectrum to the passage of the Civil Rights Act in July '64. Some witnesses to these events could see a connection, and were eager to expose the warped priorities of the legislative agenda. Gil Scott-Heron remains the celebrated example.[89] His response to the first successful moon landing still hits the mark, not because it portrays the imperialist endeavour as an expression of white supremacy, but because it seeks to do so – as though to anticipate the method of digital sampling – by transforming the prime location into a regular, pallid locution. What begins as a punchline verges on refrain ('Whitey's on the Moon'), gathering a force that feels deliberately forced rather than forceful through interpolation. What better way to satirise the prospects or complexion of lunar exploration than by suggesting NASA's besuited elite has become – in more than one sense – a burden to taxpayers of colour?

[87]   Anthony Mellors, *Late Modernist Poetics from Pound to Prynne* (Manchester: Manchester University Press, 2005), p. 125.

[88]   'Star Damage at Home' was first published in *The English Intelligencer*, second series, 10 (August 1967), 444–45.

[89]   Gil Scott-Heron, 'Whitey on the Moon', *Small Talk at 125th and Lennox* (Flying Dutchman Records/RCA, FD-10143, 1970).

The refrain and conga rhythm are not Prynne's style. In 'Star Damage', rather, he complicates the projections of a speaker who seems to be speaking for a starry-eyed chorus by intercalating them with hints that this mouthpiece has a mind and history of its own. Scott-Heron's does too, needless to say, but the vocal line of 'Star Damage' is rigged in such a way as to suggest that its trappings – its 'tinsel past', the jaunty sense of 'confidence' – should not be mistaken for a predisposition to candour or full-blown confession. At the heart of this nocturne, in fact, we find an almost parodic act of self-fashioning. By cutting a figure in the image of the classic conspirator – 'like Cassius I flaunt the path / of some cosmic disaster' – the tearaway gives voice to a kind of doublespeak which depends for its effect, here as in Shakespeare's telling, on a richly ironised attitude to reading the sky at night. In one way, doubtless, Prynne's tearaway means to say that he is like Caesar's very modern assassin because he pretends to have no truck with astrology ('The fault, dear Brutus, is not in our stars').[90] Yet to 'flaunt' something doesn't only mean to flout it, and to flaunt something in the style of Cassius after the fact – knowing, in other words, that the assassin's choosing to flout 'portentous things' in Act I did nothing in the end to preclude 'some monstrous state' – surely to 'flaunt' in this sense 'the path / of some cosmic disaster' also means to *parade* it, to proceed knowingly, publicly towards the fallout of a word whose meaning now might require a harder squint: 'disaster', < *dis-* + *astro* >. It is not that the speaker of 'Star Damage' doesn't know an omen when he sees one; it is precisely because he does, and that he knows that bad stars bring mixed blessings – regime change, political realignment, civil war – that his following the radical's lead in 1967 must have seemed something more than a fool's errand.

In the true spirit of apology, 'Star Damage' assumes a complex attitude to the 'shrill / havoc' that is its subject. And like so many nocturnes before it, the threat of a 'simple deflection' midstream is too much for it, or for its speaker, rather, whose wariness of 'this fecund hint' sends him off course. Prynne invokes Shakespeare's sceptic at that moment with a view to wondering all over again what it should mean to have 'misconstrued everything', and yet to have succeeded in exposing a structural problem in the ways the government of the day distributes its resources and attention.[91] Is the 'blaze of violent purpose' in this poem a memory of Apollo 1's devastating ignition, or

[90] Shakespeare, *Julius Caesar*, I.ii.141.
[91] Ibid., V.iii.84.

is it an attempt to document the spectacle of race rioting – the flares and arson attacks – at a time when politicians were as likely as they are today to weaponise the material effects of civil disobedience?[92] In the sense that it could be both, the poem does appear to convoke the politics of space and race. Yet it does so without attempting to conflate those spheres of experience, or to suggest that their rough orchestration here need render the 'we' more binding or transparent than the community imagined in any other poem.

Nor does its music seem likely to resolve any time soon into anthem or protest ballad. In 'Star Damage', as throughout *The White Stones*, Prynne is attentive to eruptions of song, to the ways 'we' look to contain it, and to the ends to which we do so; but his attentions in this regard are always already tempered by an anxiety as to what an individual's ontological status might be – in relation to the collective – if song is allowed to become an organising principle. And it is more than an incidental anxiety, as we learn in 'As It Were An Attendant'. In one barely parsed summation – 'shot towards venus, march / on the pentagon' – this poem captures the mood of one long weekend in October '67, which began with news of Mariner 5's navigation of Venus, and ended on the bank of the Potomac with the arrest of several hundred anti-war demonstrators at the Department of Defense.[93] In its responsiveness to 'face', 'facade', and 'frontage', it is a poem critically versed in the optics of an aggressive foreign policy – conducted on two fronts – to which the TV generation has been granted access. Yet Prynne is under no illusion as to what comforts the electronic hearth will provide a viewer torn between Venus and Vietnam. The promise of long-range transmission ('playback of the perfect') gives way to intimate conversation, to the habits of a group for whom the matter of 'stars, starlight & their twinkle' represents a subject as well as a setting.[94] It would seem the stuff of campfire banter but for the nagging thought that Prynne sets spinning once more, that the proper end of any night song is action, not inertia. True to form – for there *is* a form to Prynne's nocturnal practice – the middle of the poem suggests as much: 'we can begin with the warmup / about the politics of melody'.

---

[92] John Noble Wilford, 'Criticism Sharp: Faulty Wire Is Termed the Probable Cause of Blaze Fatal to 3', *The New York Times* (10 April 1967).

[93] Prynne, 'As It Were An Attendant', in *Poems*, p. 124.

[94] See Wilford, 'Mariner 5 Sending Venus Data; Full Playback Will End Today', *The New York Times* (21 October 1967), 12.

* * *

It would be gratifying to think the stars aligned for Prynne at the end of the 1960s. In some ways they did, quite spectacularly, for a poet who'd spent so much of that decade spellbound by the Star-Spangled Banner. 'I was also <u>homesick</u> for the United States of America', he complains in one letter to Olson, thinking back to a frosty day spent driving down to London in October '67.[95] That he wished on days like that to get closer to his allies, to 'cut away this strange 3000-mile domesticity', did not preclude his coming to see the land of opportunity as a capitalist formation no less compromised or estranging than his own.[96] From this point of view, *The White Stones* would appear to encompass peregrinations that may sound unusually close in sentiment to the kind of writing produced by émigrés proper. I can't help thinking 'Star Damage at Home' owes its thrust to 'The Stars Down to Earth', the essay Theodor Adorno penned in 1953, some ten years after his move to California.[97] Like Prynne's poem, whose 'we' claims to 'live in compulsion', the essay unpicks the 'compulsive behaviour' of a community beholden to a newspaper horoscope; and like 'Star Damage', crucially, it declines to trivialise 'the astrological fad'.[98] The practice of reading stars, it seems to Adorno, 'represents a threat and a remedy in one'; even as the horoscope pretends to comfort the soul who wants to 'fix his home', it needles at a low-level paranoia.[99] Far, then, from defusing the anxiety of readers, the horoscope ensures as best it can that the sources of paranoia – conflict with the Soviet Union, 'the racist slant' of a turf war in the US itself – remain just visible between the lines of its daily forecast.[100]

There are too many points of contact to dismiss the possibility that Prynne was thinking of Adorno when he penned 'Star Damage'. The affinities are compelling, and all the more damning for that: signs of progress were few and far between in 1967, depending on your perspective. What sets Prynne apart from Adorno, even so – a

---

[95] Prynne to Olson, 15 October 1967, *The Collected Letters*, p. 222.

[96] Ibid., p. 221.

[97] T. W. Adorno, 'The Stars Down to Earth: The *Los Angeles Times* Astrology Column. A Study in Secondary Superstition', *Jahrbuch für Amerikastudien*, 2 (1957), 19–88.

[98] Ibid., 55, 80.

[99] Ibid., 83, 70.

[100] Ibid., 29.

sign that he'd begun to make his own way in a world uncertain of lyric's staying power – is the shape of his critique, and the granularity that comes of a practised night vision. The politics of this writing, beyond its resistance to imperialism and power grabs of one kind and another, subsists in the challenge it poses to the phenomenology of a received reading practice, whose directives and assumptions – linearity is key – are disrupted at just about every turn. Putting it that way puts me in mind once again of Ian Patterson's brainwave, that Prynne's 'poems are, in a sense, photographs of processes of thought'.[101] This holds true for me every time I read him. Yet I've also come to apprehend the kinetic life of Prynne's early work in a qualitatively different light, which not only rewards but might be thought to require a mode of reading that has been adjusted to catch the qualia of a particular strain of lyric, whose sound forms, or 'cosmic vibrations', are not at all incidental to its homing impulse.[102]

So what, at the end of the day, does it feel like to read *The White Stones* in a 'musical / sense'? The answer will vary a little each time you return to it. For the volume is not only a 'series' of poems to be read one after another; it is a collection whose chronology is not identical to its history, which is of a subtly different order, as Eric Griffiths would put it, because a text's 'history' amounts to the sum of all those 'sequential meanings which arise in time but arch across temporal instants'.[103] Prynne's collection comes alive to this means of apprehension, which is really a kind of 'specialized audition', to borrow a phrase of his.[104] If as a consequence *The White Stones* seems to aspire to the condition of cantata or concept album – 'the whole order set in this, the / proper guise, of a song' – then it follows that the constitutive episodes of that grand design will add up to something greater, perhaps something as majestic and surprising as motivic coherence.[105] Which is to say, *The White Stones* is so much more than a succession of poems, for it is a collection that counts no less strongly than *The Cantos* or *The Maximus Poems* or *Briggflatts* do upon a reader's getting

[101]　Ian Patterson, '"the medium itself, rabbit by proxy": some thoughts about reading J. H. Prynne', in *Poets on Writing: Britain, 1970–1991*, ed. Denise Riley (Basingstoke: Macmillan, 1992), pp. 234–46 (p. 234).

[102]　Prynne, 'In Cimmerian Darkness', in *Poems*, p. 74.

[103]　Eric Griffiths, 'Timing', in *If Not Critical*, ed. Freya Johnston (Oxford: Oxford University Press, 2018), pp. 29–46 (p. 31).

[104]　Prynne, 'Mental Ears and Poetic Work', *Chicago Review*, 55.1 (2010), 126–57 (p. 128).

[105]　Prynne, 'The Wound, Day and Night', in *Poems*, p. 64.

to know how different kinds of historical formation – constellations, geological shifts, patterns of migration and pilgrimage – are prone to erupt and play out in the fluid time zone of lyric. None of this is to suggest anything that hasn't occurred to many readers before, I suspect. A more suggestive point of departure, as I've had cause to speculate here, would be to think of *The White Stones* as a sequence that bears comparison to the meaning-making of another medium entirely – Chopin's corpus of nocturnes – not on account of anything like a causal connection, but because of the reciprocal ways in which these very different modes of articulation help to illuminate principles of organisation that might otherwise go unnoticed. Give it a go. Listen to some of them (maybe start with Op. 37, No. 1 in G minor), and then turn to 'Smaller than the Radius of the Planet'. I can't say how many times I've read that poem and wondered at its embedded soundbite – '"The gradient of the decrease may be de– / termined by the spread in intrinsic lumin– / osities"' – perplexed in part by its obscurity, of course (a nice irony), but also by the simple fact of not knowing how to sound or assimilate it.[106] As though it were an intermission, perhaps, or a voiceover voiced *sotto voce*? The stab at a new frequency, or the residue of bedtime reading? No single analogy quite captures the textural effect of the poem's peculiar interlude, the drift of its attentions and intimations, or the mood of its closing, hopeful clinch; but as parallel cases go – with its brief discursive shift into E♭ major, from heartbreak to hymn and back again, and the tonal surprise of its final, rising cadence – that nocturne in G minor comes unusually close.

At the same time, a reading of any such sequence, and the search for any such notional correspondence, risks a sort of critical irresponsibility if its attention to 'sequential meanings' has the effect of smoothing over 'temporal instants'. This is as true of Chopin's writing as it is of Prynne's.[107] In the latter's case, a reader might treasure the NYRB's reissue of *The White Stones*, but would be right to feel frustrated by the editor's decision to elide the constituent lyrics' histories, each of which reveal a responsiveness to circumstance, and to sounding circumstantial.[108] Which is to say, Prynne's nocturnes

---

[106] Prynne, 'Smaller than the Radius of the Planet', in *Poems*, p. 115.

[107] See, for instance, Jeffrey Kallberg, 'The Rhetoric of Genre: Chopin's Nocturne in G Minor', *19th-Century Music*, 11.3 (1988), 238–61.

[108] Peter Gizzi alerts a reader to the circumstances of the poems' composition, but no precise bibliographic information is provided (*The White Stones*, intro. Peter Gizzi (New York: New York Review of Books, 2016)).

resonate on local terms as well, and in ways that their collection for the first time in '69 did something to obscure even as it revealed broader arcs of thought and feeling.

This point is unremarkable; it is what comes of negotiating wholes and parts. And yet it's a point worth making, by way of conclusion, because this essay collection has turned repeatedly, if implicitly, to the question of what it means to generate a thick description of any genre under the sign of late modernism. Such a project, which begins with a compulsion to theorise, must reckon constantly with this suspicion: that a full-fledged description is only likely to count in the end if it finds a way to coordinate a particular poem's historical specificities – which are not immaterial to the fact of that poem's being an aubade, or ode, or specimen of kitsch – in relation to the demands of synoptic work, which would have us take the more or less bumpy passage of that genre through time as evidence of its lasting value as one kind of articulation. Reading for the meaning of any form would appear to involve a two-track mind. For even as I find myself piecing together the dispersed proofs of a definite and sustained preoccupation – the 'still passion of night', the song that 'shines / with embittered passion', the prospect of being 'there & without passion' under a starry sky – I do sense a depth and fizz to those passions, which are not the same, though they speak to a condition that is typical of the nocturne's final moments.[109]

[109]　Prynne, 'Moon Poem', in *Poems*, p. 54; 'Star Damage at Home', in *Poems*, p. 109; 'As It Were An Attendant', in *Poems*, p. 125.

Index